Stedman's Surinam

Stedman's Surinam

Life in an Eighteenth-Century Slave Society

An Abridged, Modernized Edition of
*Narrative of a Five Years Expedition against
the Revolted Negroes of Surinam*
by John Gabriel Stedman

Edited by
RICHARD PRICE and SALLY PRICE

THE JOHNS HOPKINS UNIVERSITY PRESS

Baltimore and London

© 1992 The Johns Hopkins University Press
All rights reserved
Printed in the United States of America

The Johns Hopkins University Press
701 West 40th Street
Baltimore, Maryland 21211-2190
The Johns Hopkins Press Ltd., London

The paper used in this book meets the minimum requirements of
American National Standard for Information Sciences—Permanence of
Paper for Printed Library Materials, ANSI Z39.48-1984.

Library of Congress Cataloging-in-Publication Data

Stedman, John Gabriel, 1744–1797.
Stedman's Surinam : life in an eighteenth-century slave society /
edited by Richard Price and Sally Price.
p.   cm.
"An abridged, modernized edition of Narrative of a five years
expedition against the revolted Negroes of Surinam by John Gabriel
Stedman."
Includes bibliographical references.
ISBN 0-8018-4259-X. — ISBN 0-8018-4260-3 (pbk.)
1. Surinam—Description and travel.   2. Surinam—History—To
1814.   3. Slavery—Surinam—History—18th century.   4. Indians of
South America—Guiana.   5. Stedman, John Gabriel, 1744–1797—
Journeys—Surinam.   I. Price, Richard, 1941-   .   II. Price,
Sally.   III. Stedman, John Gabriel, 1744–1797. Narrative of a five
years expedition against the revolted Negroes of Surinam.
IV. Title.
F2410.S8152   1992
988.3'01—dc20
91-27470

The cover illustration for the softbound edition is reproduced from the
editors' copy of the large paper hand-colored 1796 first edition. All
other illustrations from the Narrative are reproduced from the plain
1796 first edition—the majority from the editors' copy but some from
the copy in the James Ford Bell Library, University of Minnesota.

This edition is dedicated
to Stedman's maroon adversaries
who staked their lives on the attainment of
freedom, justice, and peace.
And to their present-day descendants
who refuse to forget.

CONTENTS

PREFACE AND
ACKNOWLEDGMENTS

This abridged edition of John Gabriel Stedman's *Narrative* is intended to make widely available, at a price affordable by students, one of the richest contemporary accounts of a plantation society in the Americas. Like the complete critical edition of 1988, it is based on Stedman's own handwritten manuscript, finished in 1790; in this regard it differs—substantively, ideologically, and stylistically—from the heavily edited first edition of 1796 and all the many editions and translations that were based on it. The deletions we have made, in both text and plates, as well as the editorial adjustments we have effected (in punctuation, spelling, and phrasing), are discussed at the end of the Introduction.

The preparation of Stedman's 1790 manuscript for publication began in 1978, when we first confirmed its authenticity and significance at the James Ford Bell Library, University of Minnesota. Richard Price conducted the first years of research alone; Sally Price joined him as co-editor in 1982. A large number of people contributed to the preparation of this edition, and their generous assistance is acknowledged *in extenso* in the 1988 edition (ix–xii). Here, we simply reassert our gratitude to all of them, collectively, for sharing so generously their time, energy, and knowledge. At the same time, we once again take full and unambiguous responsibility for any errors, whether of fact or interpretation, that may still remain. We are especially grateful to the National Endowment for the Humanities, which supported this project for three years and which, along with the Menil Foundation, generously contributed to the publication of the complete critical edition.

INTRODUCTION

In 1759, when Voltaire needed a setting for his satirical discussion of New World slavery, he turned to Suriname.

> As they drew near the town they came upon a Negro lying on the ground wearing only half his clothes, that is to say, a pair of blue cotton drawers; this poor man had no left leg and no right hand. "Good heavens!" said Candide to him in Dutch, "what are you doing there, my friend, in that horrible state?"
>
> "I am waiting for my master, the famous merchant Monsieur Vanderdendur."
>
> "Was it Monsieur Vanderdendur," said Candide, "who treated you in this way?"
>
> "Yes, sir," said the Negro, "it is the custom. We are given a pair of cotton drawers twice a year as clothing. When we work in the sugar mills and the grindstone catches a finger, they cut off the hand; when we try to run away, they cut off a leg. Both these things happened to me. This is the price paid for the sugar you eat in Europe." (*Candide,* chap. 19)

By this time, Suriname had developed into a flourishing plantation colony and had earned a solid reputation, even among such rivals as Jamaica and Saint Domingue, for its heights of planter opulence and depths of slave misery. Stedman's "Narrative" makes clear on almost every page that Voltaire's choice of mid-eighteenth-century Suriname was chillingly on target.

The colony was founded in 1651 by the English but was ceded sixteen years later to the Dutch, who built it into "the envy of all the others in the Americas" (Nassy 1788, 1:56). By the mid-eighteenth century, it was said to be producing more revenue and consuming more imported manufactured goods, per capita, than any other Caribbean colony (ibid., 2:40). The local plantocracy was, to borrow Gordon K. Lewis's phrase about the Caribbean more generally, "crassly materialist and spiritually empty . . . the most crudely philistine of all dominant classes in the history of Western slavery" (1983, 109). As Stedman describes, planters were routinely served at table by nearly nude house slaves, who also fanned them during their naps (and sometimes all night long), put on and took off all of their clothes each morning and evening, bathed their children in imported wine, and performed other similar tasks; wealthy planters in the capital often had forty or fifty such hand-picked domestic slaves. The estates that generated this wealth were large by comparative standards: an average sugar estate had a slave force of 228, more than seventeen times as large as contemporary plantations in Virginia or Maryland (R. Price 1976, 16). Likewise, Suriname's slave population, which came from a variety of West and Central African societies, contained an unusually high ratio of Africans to Creoles, and of recently arrived Africans to seasoned slaves. The colony's ratio of Africans to Europeans was also extreme—more than 25:1, and as high as 65:1 in the plantation districts. (For comparison, Jamaica's ratio in 1780, "the highest in the British West Indies," was 10:1 [Craton 1975, 254].)

Marronage plagued the colony from its earliest years, as slaves escaped into the rain forest that grew up almost to the doorsteps of the plantations. By the mid-eighteenth century, "the colony had become the theater of a perpetual war" (Nassy 1788, 1:87), and organized bands of maroons kept planters living in constant fear for their lives and in constant risk of losing their investments. The 1760s witnessed a tremendous increase in the extension of credit by Amsterdam bankers, as Suriname planters mortgaged their estates and engaged in ever-increasing conspicuous consumption. By 1773, when Stedman arrived in what he called "this Blood Spilling Colony" to help quell the most recent maroon depredations, heavy speculation, planter absenteeism, and rapid changes in plantation ownership were posing a serious threat to the colony's viability. In short, this was a maximally polarized society—some three thousand European whites, who must have sensed that their world was coming unglued, living in grotesque luxury off the forced labor of some fifty thousand brutally exploited African slaves.

Stedman's *Narrative* has been much admired, and has gone through more than twenty-five editions in six languages; it has also been much misunderstood. Although some commentators have accepted the work uncritically, as a soldier's unproblematical eyewitness account of unvarnished truths, and others have regarded it as some sort of abolitionist tract, we feel that its real significance stems from its being neither. Comparison of Stedman's text with his unpublished Suriname diaries and with other contemporary Suriname sources permits us to analyze the complex ways in which he constructed his work while living in very changed personal and political circumstances, a decade after the events that it describes. The text consists of a half-dozen interwoven strands—the romance with Joanna and his efforts to gain her freedom; the military campaigns against the rebel slaves; his relations with other soldiers, particularly his commanding officer, Fourgeoud; the description and investigation of exotic flora and fauna; the description of Amerindian and African slave life; and, most important, the description and analysis of relations between planters and slaves—all structured by a chronological framework taken from his Suriname diaries. Stedman himself provides considerable assistance to the critical reader: a keen observer who, in his more than four years in the colony, moved comfortably through an unusual variety of contexts in this rigidly stratified society, he took pains, throughout his "Narrative," to distinguish his sources and to separate first- and second-hand accounts. Much of what he reports indeed derives from first-hand observation, but even his reports of hearsay represent key primary data, in that they disclose rich details about everyday plantation discourse.

Ironically, the power of Stedman's indictment of plantation slavery stems in part from his middle-of-the-road political position. Precisely because he was no abolitionist, Stedman's accounts of the behaviors and attitudes of Suriname's masters and slaves take on special authority. It is true that Stedman was caught in a paradox not easily seen at the time: "to the extent that cruelty was inherent in slavery, humanitarian amelioration [of the sort advocated in the text by Stedman] helped perpetuate cruelty" (Jordan 1968, 368). Yet Stedman's descriptive prose and illustrations, of both planter decadence and slave dignity, transcend his stated political views. It is as if he saw and understood and wrote and drew something more than he was prepared to admit to himself or to others. His original "Narrative," published for the first time in 1988, stands as one of the richest, most vivid accounts ever written of a flourishing slave society. Whatever his own mixed intentions in writing and publishing it (and we discuss these in detail, below), others began using versions of his work for the antislavery cause as soon as they appeared, and—in part because his own critical apparatus is relatively accessible to us today—we can find in these pages a unique vision of an often-terrible past world that allows us better to understand our own.

"STUDYING TO BE SINGULAR"

At the age of forty-two, having retired from military service in the Scots Brigade to a country house in Devonshire, John Gabriel Stedman wrote a rollicking account of the first twenty-eight years of his life (until his departure for Suriname), "principally . . . to amuse miself," but also for "my friends during my life[time]," and then afterwards, perhaps, "for all sorts of peaple to read" (*1786, 20 bis*).[1] Adopting the tone (if not quite matching the style) of *Tom Jones* or *Roderick Random*, Stedman envisioned his younger self as fearlessly iconoclastic and rebellious, jumping from one merry prank or drunken brawl to the next, and from one (often, married) woman's bed to another, all across the face of the Netherlands. The first child of a commissioned officer in the Scots Brigade and his Dutch wife, he described his boyhood (spent largely with his parents in Holland but partly with a paternal uncle in Scotland) as chock-full of misadventures and abrasive encounters of every description. The "premier mobile of all hurly-burly's, and street battles, which were my greatest delight" (*1786, 6*), he was "cald by some a good nut for the Devil to Crack, and By others a good fire stick to light his furnace" (*1786, 4*). Although his talent for drawing was "universally admired" (*1786, 5 bis*), he rejected his parents' attempts to arrange for him to study with painters in Holland "from merely a motive of pride—scorning to be instructed by block heads" (*1786, 5*).

Stedman depicted a childhood filled with the same kinds of experiences, attitudes, and personal relationships that were to characterize his years in Suriname. He dwelt, for example, on his early feelings of being tormented by authority figures, first in his interactions with the servant who accompanied him on a trip from Holland to Scotland (whom he consistently referred to as "my tyrant") and subsequently in his relationship with the cold, stern uncle who served as his guardian and tutor for two years; later, in Suriname, such feelings came to dominate his stormy relationship with his commanding officer, Colonel Fourgeoud. According to the autobiography, his volatile reaction to the personal injustices committed by these unsympathetic figures was also well developed long before the outbursts and impulsive acts of destructive rage that pepper his Suriname "Narrative." When, for example, his French instructor refused to honor a bet about how long it would take the ten-year-old Stedman to memorize a difficult passage, he claimed to have shattered instantly "in ten thousand pieces [the teacher's] beloved statue of Erasmus . . . although I knew I must be whipt for it the next moment" (*1786, 7*). And he reported that in Scotland he protested his uncle's harshness through a full range of rebellious acts—from milking cows into his hat to startling old women by firing pistols behind their backs (*1786, 3 bis*).

Stedman was proud of being unusually sensitive, even in an age of pervasive and modish sentimentality. He described the intensity of his empathy for all creatures from early childhood, which paralleled his troubled reactions to much of what he later witnessed in Suriname. For example, he wrote that when eight years old he cried "til I actually fell in convulsions" over seeing a fish broiled alive, and suffered "unspeacable mortification" at the slow torture of a cock by a group of boys (*1786, 6 bis*). These feelings were softened by neither age nor experience; in a 1787 letter of advice to his son, he urged him to "rejoice in good nature not only to man—but to the meanest insect—that is the whole Creation without exception[.] Scorn to hurt them but for thy food, or thy defence" (*14 January 1787*);[2] and a diary entry written just two years before his death noted, "a poor cow hamstrung by the infernal butchers. May God damn them" (*1795*).

Throughout his life, Stedman regularly interceded in order to alleviate the suffering of both people and animals. He described how, as a child, he went to great lengths to avoid drowning a mouse that had been discovered in the house; for this disobedience he was later whipped (*1786, 6 bis*). He recounted how, in the rain forest, after shooting but not killing a monkey, he was forced to put the animal out of its misery with his bare hands:

> my heart felt Seek on his account; here his dying little Eyes still Continued to follow me with seeming reproach till their light gradually forsook them and the wretched Creature expired. never Poor Devil felt more than I on this occasion, nor could I taste of him or his Companion when they were dress'd, who afforded to some others a delicious repast and which ended the Catastrophe [1790/1988, 141; cf. p. 71, below].

In describing one of his rare battlefield encounters with rebel warriors, Stedman admitted that "my Sensibility Got so much the Better of my Duty, And my Pity for these poor miserable, illtreated People Was such, that I Was rather induced to fire with Eyes Shut . . . than to take a Proper Aim, of Which I had Frequent Opportunities" (1790/1988, 405; cf. p. 212). And when a lone, elderly rebel appeared in his camp, Stedman gave orders that he should not be harmed and left him some biscuits, beef, and rum (p. 295). In planters' homes he quickly interceded to prevent punishment of slaves (e.g., by paying for five plates broken by a slave girl to "save her from horrid whipping" [*24 February 1773*]). And back in England, a diary entry mentioned "a mouse dead in the snap and cold, by care once more revived" (*16 May 1792*).

In his own writings, Stedman's concern for animals was explicitly related to the characteristic Enlightenment belief in the "wonderfull chain of Gradation, from Man to the most diminitive of the above Species [here referring to monkeys] . . . who if wisely viewed and desected, bear such general resemblance with /nay little difference from/ myself" (1790/ 1988, 144; cf. p. 72). From this perspective, Stedman saw Africans as the close kin of both nonhuman primates and himself: "does not the face, Shape, and Manner of the african Negroe /whom in every respect I look on as my brother/ I say does this not often put us in Mind of the Wild Man of the Woods or *Orangoutang?*" (1790/1988, 144; cf. p. 74).[3]

The passions that are so prominent in Stedman's account of his tragic romance with the mulatto slave Joanna appear also in his memories of childhood; for example, he describes himself at age eleven weeping bitterly over parting from a school companion named Alida Paris (*1786, 2 bis*). But he depicted most of his relationships with women as of an entirely different kind. Indeed, his self-image as a Lothario, and the sometimes unexpected advances this led to, developed long before the famous incidents in which Suriname slaves and planters' wives alike repeatedly forced themselves upon him. As he pictured himself in his youth,

> I was certainly much beloved amongst the girls, but particularly of a certain sort, not by the best of them . . . on account of my person which was without vanity allowd to be a lure for most of women species—I had a Je ne say qwoy about me, of the fasquinating kind, which attracted the girls as the eys of the Rattlesnake attrakts Squirls, and unaccountably persuades them to submission. (*1786, 18, 29*)

Stedman larded his autobiographical sketch with amorous adventures. He told in some detail how, at age seventeen, he was tricked into entering the bedroom of an elderly, foul-breathed woman, "half dres'd en negleegee," who gripped his hand and pulled him, struggling, into an unwanted embrace (*1786, 10 bis*). After various similar encounters during the subsequent months, his diary records that "one Gauseman's servant maid commits a rape on me," to which he appended the marginal note, "I acknowlege miself at this time one of the compleetest fleks and was verry careless of what was to become of me" (*1786, 15*). Nonetheless, he persisted in his adventures, having by then (he says) read "Joseph Andrews, tom Jones, and Roderick Random which heroes I resolved to take for my models" (*1786, 15*)—by which he seems to have meant models of the real-life (rather than merely literary) variety. "R. Random," he added, "I liked best and in imitation of he [I] emedately fell in Love at the Dancing assembly with a Miss diana Bennet whom I shall call narcissa [after the heroine of that book]" (ibid.). And accordingly, he followed that infatuation not only by falling "desperately in love" very soon after, but also by taking advantage of the frequent sexual opportunities that were coming his way. The wife of his landlord, for example, on the excuse that Stedman was ill, "pays me frequent visits in my bedroom[.] I treat her like Joseph did potiphars wife and prefer her maid Maria Bymans"—which preference ultimately ends this rather complex domestic farce when the landlady, "mad with jealousy . . . in consequence [causes] Maria Bymans and poor I [to be] turn'd out of the howse at the same time" (*1786, 16; see* also the scene in *Joseph Andrews* in which Joey begins to be called Joseph as Lady Booby unsuccessfully attempts to seduce him [Fielding 1742: bk. 1, chap. 5], as well as Genesis 39).

Stedman seems to have thoroughly enjoyed being (and depicting himself as) a merry prankster. During his childhood, after having had an argument with his brother, he first threatened to hang himself and then let his brother discover him hanging, apparently lifeless, by a rope from the rafters, "my Eys turnd up—my head on one shoulder—and my tung down over my chin . . . which [the truth having eventually been discovered] occationd a curious scene of mirth and consternation" (*1786, 14 bis*). Or again, believing that his mother was favoring his brother, he decided to interrupt her while she was "with a group of fine Ladies . . . sipping theyr limonade in the moonshine," by "quietly strip[ping] miself in the howse and running through the middle of them stark naked. . . . The allarum was to me exceedingly entertaining" (ibid.). During his later youth, his practical jokes and related exploits became more closely involved with drinking, brawling, and sex, as he sometimes visited three bawdy houses in a single night, shared various women with his friends, watched his "best mate . . . cohabit with [a girl they had just picked up] on a publick country road," and so on (*1786, 19 bis*). And right alongside his affectedly penitent asides to the effect that "I am ashamed almost of my scandalous life" (*1786, 20 bis*), or that "nothing could be more wild than I was at this present time" (*1786, 19 bis*), he always liked to remind his readers that, nevertheless, "none could have a better heart, however strange tis truth" (ibid.).

Stedman viewed himself, with a certain pride, as a perpetual misfit because of his principled refusal to pay homage to the conventions of his day. In 1785, during the period when he was writing the autobiographical account of his youth, he noted in his diary that

> in all places I have been beloved by the inhabitants when known but at first cald mad in Scotland, mased [confused] in England, fou [crazy] by the namurois [Belgians], gek or dol [crazy or mad] by the Duch, and law [Sranan for insane] by the negros in Surinam, owing intirely to my studying to be singular in as much as can be so. (*29 November 1785*)

Stedman's "studying to be singular" followed him to the grave.

> Before he died he expressed a wish to be interred, as our kings and queens
> were formerly, at midnight and by torchlight and, of all the odd things, he
> wanted to lie at Bickleigh, side by side with Bampfylde Moore Carew
> [known as the King of the Gypsies]. (Snell 1904, 138)[4]

In defense of his writings, Stedman consistently championed the cause
of artless candor, asserting, for example, that "some stuff to be sure may
lie hard in sour stomachs," but that "I neither wryte for profit nor applause—purely following the dictates of nature, & equally hating a made
up man and made up storry" (*1786, 5 bis*). This same dedication to reporting things exactly as he saw them, regardless of the consequences, is also
reiterated frequently in his Suriname "Narrative" and used there to justify
many of the very passages that were eventually excised by the publisher
in the version that finally went to press.[5]

Stedman's diaries make clear that eighteenth-century Europe was a
world in many ways extremely distant from the Europe of our own day.
Certainly, the way in which death had to be accepted as part of everyday
experience jumps out from his pages with startling regularity. The diaries
and autobiography record, for example, that

> when, but a boy at scool, my most loving scool companion . . . was
> snached away by the smallpox . . . When a cadet, my best friend . . . was
> run through the heart by an artillery man, in a duel . . . when ensign, my
> best companion . . . in a fitt of Frensy, poisoned himself [*1786, 8*]; my
> nephew, a Lieut in the 64th Ret. was kild by his horse [*February 1792*]; we
> saw a most dreadfull execution of 7 malefactors 2 of whom were hang'd,
> and 5 were broak upon the rack, without ever having done murder but
> once or twice in self defence [*1786, 18 bis*]; I saw a rascal for comitting mur-
> der, executed on the rack [*1786, 26 bis*]; in France a 14 headed guillottine
> [was] invented . . . [and] above 4200 prisoners . . . [were] all waiting to be
> put to death. (*31 December 1793*)

The sense of strangeness and distance that the modern reader may feel
reading Stedman on eighteenth-century Suriname, then, is not solely a
function of that colony's exotic history. Though his Suriname descriptions may seem, for example, to include a startling number of untimely
deaths (the death of sailors from drowning, of slaves from punitive tortures, of soldiers from lack of proper food in the rain forest, and of colonists from tropical diseases), they should be read in the broader context
of the contemporary European world, which Stedman and his intended
readers used as their point of reference. As Darnton has recently re-
minded us, perhaps with just a touch of hyperbole, plebeian eighteenth-
century Europe now seems "an almost inaccessible world . . . a world so

saturated with violence and death that we can barely imagine it" (1984, 34–36).

"A Five Years Expedition"

In 1771, friendless, in debt, and saddened by the recent death of his father, Stedman resigned himself to "the desperate ressourse of going as a common sailor to North America or the Mediterranean, or even up the Baltick incognito for a voyage not longer than 9 months" (*1786, 29 bis*) in order to accumulate enough cash to pay off his debts. For the previous eleven years, since the age of sixteen, he had been serving—first with the rank of ensign, then as lieutenant—in the Scots Brigade, in the pay of the Dutch Stadthouder, defending various Low Country outposts. In response to a call for volunteers to serve in the West Indies, he left Holland on 24 December 1772 on the frigate *Zeelust,* with the rank of captain (by brevet), and arrived in Suriname on 2 February 1773. His stay in the colony, which lasted just over four years (rather than the hyperbolic five proclaimed in the title of the "Narrative"), resulted in one of the most detailed "outsider's" descriptions ever written of life in an eighteenth-century slave plantation society. Stedman's ongoing and intimate dealings with members of all social classes, from the governor and the wealthiest planters to the most oppressed slaves, gave him special opportunities to observe and describe the full panorama of Suriname life.

Stedman was part of a corps of eight hundred European volunteers—professional soldiers trained for the battlefields of Europe—who were sent to Suriname by the Dutch States-General to assist the beleaguered local troops then fighting against marauding bands of escaped slaves in the eastern region of the colony. In 1760 and 1762, the two largest groups of maroons (the Ndjuka and the Saramaka, settled along the upper Marowijne and Suriname rivers, respectively) had won their independence by treaty, after a century-long guerrilla war against the colonists. But the succeeding decade witnessed unexpected and lively hostilities involving newer maroon groups that lived just beyond the borders of the flourishing Cottica and Commewijne River plantations, trapped between the slave society of the coast and the free Ndjukas and Saramakas (who, as part of their treaties, were pledged to turn over to the colonists any new maroons they encountered). Between 1768 and 1772, the frequency of raids on plantations by these small new groups, and of military expeditions sent after them, increased tremendously.

By 1772, the entire Cottica-Commewijne plantation economy was grinding to a halt as great numbers of slaves began "deserting" to these nearby maroons, who by then were not only destroying plantations almost at will (carrying off slave women, tools, weapons, and ammunition) but even successfully capturing outlying colonial military posts. Citing the "awful and sad circumstances of the colony" caused by the "audacity of the runaways" (and having decided as a matter of principle not to negotiate peace treaties with them), Governor Nepveu and his council requested, and received, professional troops from Europe, among whom was Stedman.

We now know that the maroons against whom Stedman and his comrades fought consisted of a number of very small bands—at the height of their strength a total of no more than several hundred men, women, and children.[6] Organized primarily according to the plantations on which they had served as slaves, these maroon groups periodically banded together, split apart, and rejoined, depending on the immediate military situation and on the shifting alignments of their leaders—the charismatic Boni and his "father," Aluku; their major allies Coromantyn Codjo and Suku; and other lesser-known chiefs such as Kwami (Quamy), Ariko, and Pudja van La Paix. Between 1769 and 1776/77 (when the surviving members of these groups crossed over the Marowijne River to settle in French Guiana), they lived in some twenty different villages or camps, never staying long enough for more than a single harvest of crops, sometimes forced to move even more quickly when discovered by a colonial commando sent out to burn their houses and fields.[7]

The most dramatic single battle of what has come to be known as "The First Boni War" (1765–77) actually unfolded several months before Stedman's arrival in Suriname. In April 1772, troops of the Suriname government had discovered Boni's palisaded village, Boucou, which was surrounded by a deep swamp fordable only by secret paths hidden just below the water level. For five months, as Boni somehow managed to continue sending out raiding parties that destroyed plantations and terrorized the colonists, government troops attempted unsuccessfully to conquer his besieged stronghold. In July, the government made the "desperate" but sage decision to create an elite corps of fighting men, the "Neeger Vrijcorps" (whom Stedman referred to as "Rangers")—116 slave volunteers, purchased specially from their planter-masters for the purpose, who were promised their freedom, a house and garden plot, and military pay in return for fighting the maroons.[8] Although in their first attempt to storm Boucou two Rangers drowned trying to cross the swamp and twelve others were captured (and then maimed or executed), these troops displayed "unexpected" courage and perseverance, and within a month the government had purchased and manumitted another 190 slaves to join the corps of Rangers.

In September 1772, a heavily armed force, including the enlarged

Figure 1. Boucou, during the final siege, with the attackers' camp in the foreground (1772). A, officers' barracks; B, storehouse; C, soldiers' barracks; D, Negroes' huts; E, kitchen; F, watch-house; G, path or trace to the gardens. Drawn by J. F. Friderici, commander of the Rangers. As Boni's people finally fled the village, they taunted their attackers, "shout[ing] out to us that their old village [Boucou] was [now] called 'Mi Sal Lossij' [I may be taken] but their new one was 'Jou no sal vindij' [You will not find it]" (de Beet 1984, 100; and see pp. 35–39, below). Algemeen Rijksarchief.

corps of Rangers, finally took Boucou, killing at least five men and capturing twenty-five women, four men, and nineteen children who were unable to escape with the rest of the population. Chief Boni had successfully resisted the siege for five long months, demonstrating impressive strategic acumen while relying on his gods to control the rains so that his adversaries could not cross the swamp. But the fall of Boucou—in which near-starvation seems to have played the decisive role—was a serious military and moral blow to Boni's people; within weeks, some one hundred to one hundred twenty additional maroons from the community were captured wandering in the forest (some even turning themselves in to the colonists) and another fifty to sixty were shot by patrols.[9]

Stedman's arrival in Suriname in February 1773 coincided with a rare moment of optimism on the part of the colonists. Boucou had just fallen; Chief Boni was on the run; the plantations, for the moment, seemed secure. Almost immediately, however, Colonel Fourgeoud (commander of the newly arrived troops) and Governor Nepveu began to argue about the further conduct of the war, and this conflict lasted until Fourgeoud's departure nearly five years later.[10] For example, Nepveu stood firmly behind an ambitious plan to construct a "protective cordon" ninety-four kilometers long, consisting of scores of manned posts along a road ten meters wide that would mark off the boundaries of the civilized plantation zone from the forest and its marauding maroons, while Fourgeoud disdained such "passive" defenses;[11] Nepveu wished to depend heavily on the recently formed corps of Rangers, while Fourgeoud was suspicious of its relative independence and mistrusted the Africans' "unorthodox" fighting tactics; Nepveu greatly feared renewed hostilities with the already "pacified" Saramaka and Ndjuka, while Fourgeoud believed he could count on their active support in fighting Boni and the other new "rebels." Amidst these ongoing disagreements about overall strategy—complicated by the existence of the corps of Rangers and the troops of the Society of Suriname, initially under a command structure distinct from Fourgeoud's forces—military activity of one kind or another nevertheless continued throughout the period of Stedman's stay in the colony.

Again and again, Boni or one of his allies would stage lightning-quick assaults on plantations, and one or another of the colony's forces would pursue them through the forests, destroying any fields and villages they were able to discover. Captured maroons were often forced to serve as guides for these expeditions, but it seems clear—both from Stedman's "Narrative" and from other contemporary documents—that most of the military expeditions against these maroons were fruitless. Stedman's own experience was typical in this respect: on seven campaigns in the forest, averaging three months each, he engaged in only one battle, the taking of

Figure 2. Colonel Louis Henry Fourgeoud. Engraving by Th. Koning, ca. 1778, apparently after a painting made by Stedman in 1775. The memorial poem by F. Lentfrinck reads (roughly): "This Warrior is FOURGEOUD, whose hero's fist and courage / Restored the security of Suriname, / Sweeping the forests clean of the plundering swarms, / Who, Year after year, tormented the industrious planter. / He Died, to the regret of all good men, having served so well, / But his memory lives forever in their hearts."

Gado Saby in 1774. (His moving descriptions of this encounter, graphically portrayed in the frontispiece [where the burning village appears in the distance], make clear that even this great "victory" served mainly to chase the courageous but miserable rebels farther into the forest [see pp. 200–217].) The war, then, was characterized by the colonial troops' crisscrossing, more or less blindly, vast expanses of treacherous forests and swamps, with the maroons—through an efficient system of spies and lookouts—almost always remaining at least a step ahead, and often setting fatal ambushes for their pursuers. In the end, however, Fourgeoud's general strategy of cruising the forests proved successful in driving out the maroon guerrillas, though at the cost of enormous loss of life among his troops; some eight hundred thirty additional men were sent from Holland in 1775 to supplement the original contingent of eight hundred, yet only a couple of hundred lived to return to Europe.[12] For Fourgeoud's men and the government troops did finally manage to make the eastern forests of Suriname so uncomfortable that Boni and his people (by this time only some two hundred to three hundred strong) chose to settle in French Guiana, crossing the Marowijne River by canoe in two groups, in 1776 and 1777, just before Fourgeoud's own departure for Holland.[13]

"My Little Wrytings"

In addition to the manuscript of the "Narrative," completed in 1790, Stedman left diverse notebooks and papers that have helped us piece together the history of the work from its beginnings in the form of a log kept in Suriname in the 1770s through the various stages of writing, editing, and negotiating with the publisher that led to the first edition of 1796.

Stedman's log of daily events during his years in Suriname recorded details of his personal life (from dinners with planters to nights spent wenching), military activities, and anecdotes about the natural and social worlds around him. Throughout his stay in the colony, Stedman divided his time between two settings that could not have stood in sharper contrast to each other. The homes of planters, where he was a frequent guest, were notable even in the context of New World plantation societies for both the opulence and the decadence of their daily life. The military campaigns in the rain forest were extended ordeals of frustration, danger, malnutrition, sickness, and death. Stedman's way of coping with these contrastive settings seems to have involved both his consciously chosen role as scientific observer (which encouraged him to distance himself from much of what he witnessed) and his incurable romanticism (which encouraged intimate personal involvements and a responsiveness to the natural beauty of the colony, even during the most trying moments of his stay). His easy movement between different social settings owed much to his linguistic facility; he spoke English, Dutch, French, and, most important, Sranan (the English-based creole that was the everyday language of slaves and many whites—see p. 261).

Faithfully, he kept on-the-spot notes—sometimes jotted down on cartridges or even on "a Bleached bone" when writing paper was not available (1790/1988, 578; cf. p. 299)—and then strung them together in a small green notebook that once lay briefly at the bottom of the Commewijne River before being recovered and dried out for later consultation (p. 189), as well as on ten folded sheets of foolscap, written on both sides.[14] From the outset, Stedman had the intention of some day expanding these notes into a book. On the final page of his "small green almanack," covering 29 October 1772 to 29 April 1774, he wrote, "This Small Journall is written with the greatest attention, founded on facts allone By Captt. John G. S——n, who Shall explain it more at large one day, if Providance Spares him in life."

In addition to his practice of keeping up a diary no matter what the circumstances, Stedman systematically studied and drew whatever caught his curious eye. He described, for example, how on a military campaign in the forest,

> while we were Unsuccessful in taking the Rebels I Availed myself of Taking a Draft of Every Animal, reptile, or shrub, that I thought Could Illustrate my Little Collection of Natural Curiosity, which I now began to form some Idea of Exhibiting one Day to the Publick if I was Spared to return to Europe. (1790/1988, 347; cf. p. 179)

Similarly, Stedman avidly collected both natural and ethnological "curiosities," some of which he presented to the Leverian Museum, others to the Prince of Orange upon his return to Europe (1796, May 1796, 1790/ 1988, 620), and some of which have been recently rediscovered at the Rijksmuseum voor Volkenkunde in Leiden. These latter include the oldest extant Afro-American banjo in the world, collected by Stedman from a slave in Suriname (see R. and S. Price 1979; Whitehead 1986).

After his return to Europe, Stedman composed the retrospective autobiographical sketch covering his life prior to the Suriname expedition and continued to keep a diary, recording personal matters, noting financial dealings, listing his correspondence, and summarizing the major political events that occurred in Europe each month. Some of these diaries were kept in a bound *dagwyser* [datebook], others in a thin, marbled-paper notebook, still others on fifty-one loose folded sheets of foolscap and two other loose sheets; the entries vary significantly in their length and inclu-

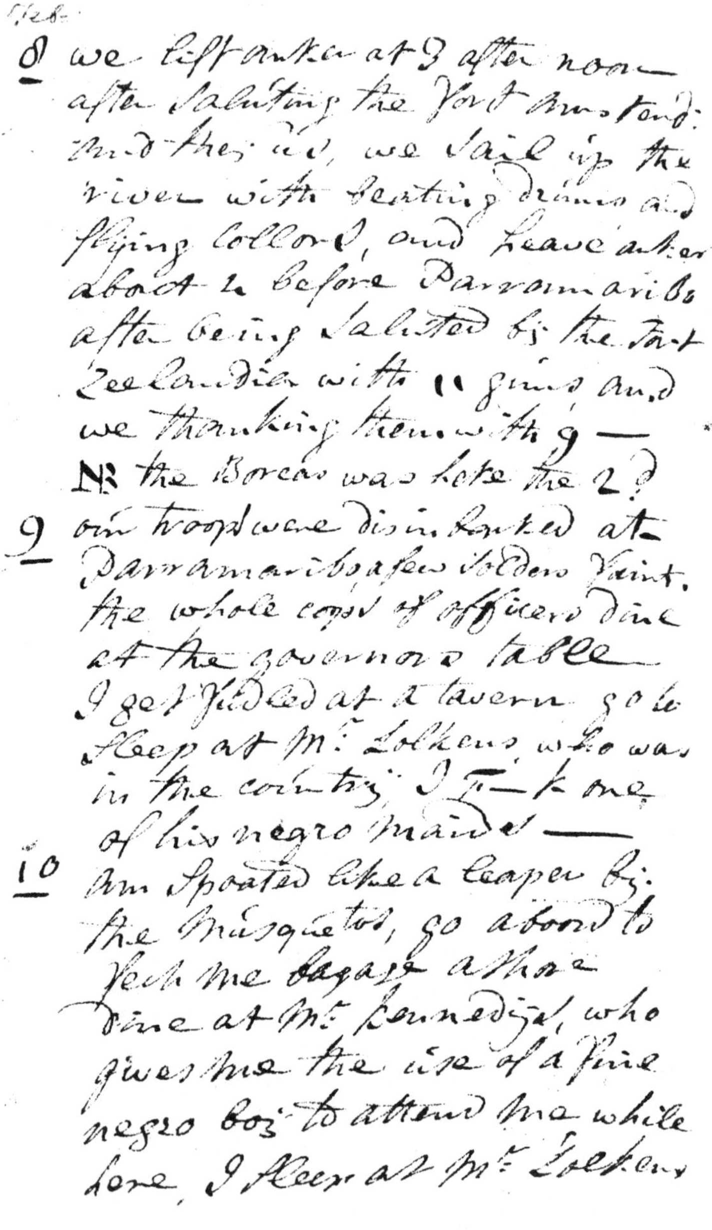

8 we left anker at 3 after noon
after Saluting the Fort Amsterdam:
and their &c, we Sail up the
river with beating drums and
flying collors, and Leave anker
about 2 before Parramaribo
after being Saluted by the Fort
Zeelandia with 11 guns and
we thanking them with 9 —
N: the Boreas was here the 2d

9 our troops were disimbarked at
Parramaribo a few soldiers Faint.
the whole corps of officers dine
at the governors table
I get Yiddeed at a tavern go to
Sleep at Mr Lolkens who was
in the country I f—k one
of his negro maids —

10 Am Spotted like a Leaper by
the Musquitos, go abord to
fech me bagage ashore
dine at Mr Kennedys who
gives me the use of a fine
negro boy to attend me while
here, I Sleep at Mr Lolkens

Figure 3. Page from Stedman's Suriname diary (8–10 February 1773). James Ford Bell
Library, University of Minnesota.

siveness, and there are some years (e.g., 1779–83) for which no materials have been found at all.[15]

As we set out to reconstruct the stormy publication history of Stedman's book, we first worked with these materials in the form in which they had been published by the English antiquarian Stanbury Thompson (1962, 1966), who had bought them from a London junk dealer about 1940.[16] However, it quickly became apparent that Thompson's work confused as much as it elucidated. Examination of the original notebooks and papers that Thompson had used (which are now in the James Ford Bell Library at the University of Minnesota) revealed that, not only had he inserted his own commentary into that of Stedman without in any way distinguishing the two, but he had changed dates and spellings, misread and incorrectly transcribed a large number of words, translated Dutch words (and mistranslated Sranan words) into English, reordered words and even whole passages, rephrased column lists as prose, included passages that had been carefully crossed out by Stedman, and deleted other passages without apparent reason—all this without indicating in his publication where the alterations had been made.

Thompson also took it upon himself (perhaps mimicking eighteenth-century practice, perhaps from his own personal post-Victorian sensibilities) to insulate his readers from shock. He published Stedman's Suriname diary entry for 12 March 1773, for example, as "Dine at Kennedy's," but discreetly omitted to print Stedman's next sentence, "3 girls pas the night in me room." He reworded Stedman's entry for 8 January 1774 at many points and deleted the observation that the piranhas that infest the creeks and rivers of Suriname were known locally as "p——k biters."[17] Thompson obscured an allusion to the inebriated state of the publisher of the "Narrative" at the time he wrote Stedman "an insolent epistle" in September 1795 by transcribing the (clearly written) word "wine" as "w——," and he modified in similar fashion Stedman's frequent references to "turds." More significant, Thompson took Stedman's characteristic and unambiguous diary references to having "f——d" one or another woman (or having been "f——d" by same) and printed them as "fooled," altering the interpretation of several key incidents.[18] It should be clear, then, why, in preparing our new edition of Stedman, we have relied exclusively on those manuscript diary pages now at the University of Minnesota, rather than on Thompson's flawed book.

According to his diary, Stedman began working on the "Narrative" on 15 June 1778—just a year after returning to the Netherlands from Suriname, and only a few days after receiving from Sir George Strickland (the man to whom he dedicated the 1790 "Narrative") an offer "to get my West Indies voyage published, which I promised to write" (*10 June 1778*).

In September 1784, having married a young Dutch woman, he moved to England, and in May 1785 they settled at Tiverton in Devonshire, where he continued the writing and began enlisting the support of subscribers for the publication.

His diary entries for these years were dominated by mundane domestic matters, such as financial worries, children's and animals' health, gardening activities, the weather, trips with his wife, problems with servants, attendance at church and social events, horseback riding, moving his family from one rented house in Tiverton to another, thefts in the neighborhood, taxes, births and birthdays, minor marital disputes, and his own ill health. Family responsibilities were a constant burden; as he commented on 20 November 1789, soon after the birth of his third child, "between wives and children—nurses and maids—dogs and cats—mice and rats rats and mice—fleas and lice, I am plagued out of my senses." The diaries we have for these years are incomplete and erratic and contain almost no mention of the progress of his projected book. He seems to have worked at it steadily throughout the period, however, and—in spite of his numerous travails—made clear in 1787 that "My only ambition remaining is to se my little wrytings made publick" (*18 January 1787*).

The daily log that Stedman kept during his "five years" expedition in Suriname reflected the perspective of a bright and independent young officer—unattached, adventurous, and barraged with new physical, emotional, and social experiences. By the time that he had married and settled down in England, however, he had become committed to a family-oriented existence that could not have contrasted more dramatically in its bourgeois domesticity to the heady experiences he had had in Suriname. From this perspective, both geographically and culturally distanced from Suriname, he exhibited a strong tendency to romanticize the personal relationships of that period of his life. The "Narrative," then, should be read in part as Stedman's retrospective and somewhat idealized vision of his youth in Suriname, written from the perspective of a significantly changed personal situation. Surprisingly, perhaps, the events of the 1790 text closely follow the diaries that Stedman kept in Suriname. Although the diary entries tend to be brief and cryptic, compared to the more elaborated descriptions in the "Narrative," discrepancies or contradictions are rare. However, one major transformation did take place: the depiction of his relationship with his "Suriname wife," Joanna.[19] This in turn had significant repercussions for his treatment of interracial sexual relationships in the "Narrative" more generally.

Stedman's daily log from his early months in Suriname leaves no doubt about the frequency of his sexual encounters with slave women (continuing his pattern of frequent transactions with Dutch prostitutes in the

Figure 4. "John Gabriel Stedman. Capt. Scotch Brig. Stuarts Regt." Oil portrait by C. Delin, 1783 (when Stedman was thirty-nine years old). Stedman Archive, Haus Besselich, Urbar, Germany. Courtesy of Hilda von Barton Stedman.

years before). On 9 February 1773, the very first night after his arrival in Paramaribo, Stedman laconically recorded in his diary, "sleep at Mr. Lolkens . . . I f——k one of his negro maids." During the following months, his notes about dinner companions were frequently complemented by mention of his sleeping partners.

> a negro woman offers me the use of her daugter, while here, for a sertain soom[.] we dont agre[e] about the price. (*22 February 1773*)

> soop in me room with two mallato girls. (*25 February 1773*)

> B——e comes to me and stays the whole night. (*26 March 1773*)

> J——a, her mother, and Q—— mother come to close a bargain [of formalized concubinage] we me, we put it of for reasons I gave them. (*11 April 1773*)

> Dine and soop at Lolkens—B——e and J——a both breakfast with me, I call meself Mistire. (*12 April 1773*)

> B——e sleeps with me. (*13 April 1773*)

> J——a comes to stay with me. (*23 April 1773*)

The rather different account that Stedman gave of this same period in his 1790 "Narrative" minimized the frequency of everyday, quasi-commercial sex between white men and slave women and strongly romanticized his own relationship with Joanna. While not actually denying in the 1790 manuscript that Mr. Lolkens' "negro maid" (whom he depicts there as being extremely insistent) stayed with him that first night, he discreetly chose to "draw a Sable Curtain" over the climactic scene (1790/1988, 43; cf. p. 19); his disagreement about the price of the girl who was offered to him by her mother was transformed, in the 1790 version, to a curt refusal based on his shock and moral disapproval of a mother offering her daughter "to be what she pleased to call my Wife"; and neither his activities with "B——e" nor those with the other, unnamed mulatto girls were ever mentioned in the 1790 text. Also removed, between the diaries and the 1790 depiction, were important aspects of Joanna's role as a sexual partner. There is no mention of her sleeping with Stedman (either alone or with "B——e") until well after they became good friends; the very telling scene in which her mother offers her to Stedman for a price is deleted wholesale; and in general, the early stages of their relationship are rephrased by Stedman to elevate Joanna from the role of a slave girl providing routine sexual services, as part of a commercial transaction, to the status of a pure and noble beauty, a true Sable Venus, whom Stedman first began to worship from afar.

Emblematic of this shift is the fact that Stedman's early diary refer-

Figure 5. "The Voyage of the Sable Venus, from Angola to the West Indies." Colored engraving by W. Grainger, after a painting by T. Stothard. Also published in Edwards 1794, 2:27, to illustrate Edwards's dreadful seven-page "The Sable Venus, An Ode (Written in Jamaica)." The iconography is characteristic of the years when Stedman was writing the "Narrative." Courtesy of Judith Johnston, New York.

ences to Joanna usually identify her (along with other slave women who slept with him) by her first initial only, while in the 1790 manuscript she joined the ranks of more respectable characters in the "Narrative," being referred to by her full name. In the course of the 1790 text, Stedman developed the romantic image fully; a passage from chapter 13 conveys the characteristic tone of his retrospective portrait of Joanna and includes an example of his frequent practice of "adapting" well-known verse (in this case from *Paradise Lost*).

> Not Adam and Eve in Paradise could Enjoy a greater Share of felicity, than we now did—free like the roes in the forest and disintangled from every care and fashion, we breathed the purest Ether in our walks, and refresh'd our limbs in the Cooling limpid Streams, health and Vigour were now again my portion, while my Mulatto flourished in youth and beauty, the envy and admiration of all the River Comewina—

> —Here in close recess,
> With flowry Garlands and sweet Smelling herbs,
> Espoused Eve did deck her nuptial bed,
> And heavenly Quires the hymenaean Sing;
> What Day the genial Angel to *her friend*
> Brought her in naked Beauty more adorn'd,
> More lovely than Pandora, whom the Gods
> Endow'd with all their Gifts. (1790/1988, 260)

These alterations and embellishments were clearly important to Stedman in projecting an image of his own conduct in the colony that now seemed appropriate, from the perspective of his life as a middle-aged gentleman established with his wife and children in the English country-side, and in preserving the memory of a woman whom he had indeed come to love. Motivated by very personal considerations, these alterations had the effect of distorting Stedman's descriptions of an important aspect of contemporary Suriname life. While his diaries depicted a society in which depersonalized sex between European men and slave women was pervasive and routine, his 1790 manuscript transformed Suriname into the exotic setting for a deeply romantic and appropriately tragic love affair.

In terms of social and cultural description, the major distortion these changes produced was the treatment of a local institution that had come to be referred to as "Suriname marriage" (see van Lier 1949, chap. 3). The features that distinguished this arrangement from traditional European marriage were its commercial dimension (with the European man paying an agreed-upon sum to a member of the slave woman's family), its temporal limitation (to the period of the man's residence in the colony), the nature of its initiation (through a secular rather than a religious ceremony), and its ready availability to already married men. Stedman alluded to this kind of arrangement in speaking of Joanna's own mother, a slave named Cery, who had "attended [Joanna's white father] with the Duties of a Lawful Wife" (1790/1988, 88; cf. p. 42). And in the 1790 "Narrative," he also outlined the terms of the institution more generally, though never in any way associating it with his own relationship with Joanna:

> I must describe this Custom which I am convinced will be highly censured by the Sedate European Matrons—and which is nevertheless as common as it is almost necessary to the batchelors who live in this Climate; these Gentlemen all without Exception have a female Slave /mostly a creole/ in their keeping who preserves their linnens clean and decent, dresses their Victuals with Skill, carefully attends them /they being most excellent nurses/ during the frequent illnesses to which Europeans are exposed in this Country, prevents them from keeping late Hours knits for them, sows for them &c*—while these Girls who are sometimes Indians sometime Mulattos and often negroes, naturally pride themselves in living with an European whom they serve with as much tenderness, and to whom they are Generally as faithfull as if he were their lawfull Husband to the great Shame of so many fair Ladies, who break through ties more sacred, and indeed bound with more Solemnity, nor can the above young women be married in any other way, being by their state of Servitude entirely debard from every Christian priviledge and Ceremony, which makes it perfectly lawfull on *their* Side, while they hesitate not to pronounce as Harlots, who do not follow them /if they can/ in this laudable Example in which they are encouraged as I have said by their nearest Relations and Friends.
>
> *—of this Habit even the Clergymen are not Exempt witness the Rev. Mr. Snyderhaus, Mr. Talant, &c. (1790/1988, 47–48; cf. pp. 20–21)

"Suriname marriage" was both well defined and widespread in the colony, and from the perspective of those who knew Stedman and Joanna, it clearly served to delineate the terms of their relationship. It was at once the framework for the most meaningful personal relationship in Stedman's life and the embarrassing reminder of Joanna's servile status. A decade after he left Joanna, and several years after her death, Stedman seems to have dealt with this awkwardness simply by denying that his situation fit the mold of other "marriages" between Europeans and slaves in the colony. In the 1790 "Narrative," he repeatedly stressed that he had intended to make Joanna his legal Christian wife in Europe; and at the same time, he chose not to mention the special "Suriname wedding" that he celebrated according to local custom on 8 May 1773. In denying that his relationship with Joanna was the product of its colonial time and place,

Stedman drew on then-current European sentimental ideals to elevate it, in retrospect, to an example of pure and faithful love (which effectively captivated European audiences—see below). "Suriname marriage," meanwhile, became a vague, hastily discussed abstraction in the 1790 "Narrative," even though it was being reported by a man whose personal life had centered on it for more than four years.

"To Make Them Publick"

In the spring of 1787, Stedman's diary began to mention the reactions of the friends to whom he showed parts of what he was then calling his "Journal" (later to become the 1790 "Narrative") and his efforts to secure their financial backing for its publication. On 8 February 1791—almost thirteen years after he had begun its composition—he sent a copy of the full manuscript as well as a list of seventy-six subscribers (for ninety-two copies) to his publisher, Joseph Johnson, in London. At the same time, he posted "proposals" to potential subscribers in London, Edinburgh, York, Liverpool, Bath, Bristol, Exeter, Portsmouth, and Plymouth. During the next several weeks, his correspondence (presumably regarding subscriptions for publication) continued to expand dramatically; on 28 February 1791 he noted that he had by then sent out proposals "to Cambridge and Oxford Coledges [and] to about 30 towns at home and abroad. Besides to a number of Private English gentlemen."

Stedman's financial arrangements with Johnson are not fully clear,[20] but he seems to have sold Johnson the complete rights and, during the six years the book was in press, his role vis-à-vis Johnson was not dissimilar to that of a modern author whose manuscript has been accepted by a publisher: ultimately dependent about all decisions regarding production details (typeface, illustrations, print run, pricing), as well as about matters of editorial modification.

Johnson was a prominent figure in radical British political and intellectual circles during the late eighteenth century. A shy, taciturn bachelor, he nevertheless entertained a particularly active social group in his home over his bookshop, regularly bringing together men and women interested in art, literature, and politics for dinner and discussion on Sundays and occasional Tuesdays (Tyson 1979: xv, xvii). His regular guests included authors whom he published, such as Thomas Paine, Joseph Priestley, William Godwin, Erasmus Darwin, Richard Price, Mary Wollstonecraft, and Henry Fuseli. Between 1790 and 1796, Stedman often participated in these evenings when he was in London.

Johnson's interests ranged widely, and he published works of theology, medicine, moral philosophy, science, poetry, children's literature, feminism, and politics, as well as *The Analytical Review*. Of particular importance—both in his general publishing career and in his treatment of Stedman's "Narrative"—were his political views, which have been characterized as "moderate radicalism" (Tyson 1979: 139), but which often grazed the edge of official acceptability. "Both lucky and shrewd, he managed for a time [during the mid–1790s] to pick politically sensitive books that espoused radical sentiments while staying within the law against seditious writings" (135). But though he managed to walk this thin line for several years, Johnson was finally arrested in 1798, ostensibly for selling a pamphlet by Gilbert Wakefield (a reply to the Bishop of Llandaff's patriotic, anti-French *An Address to the People of Great Britain*), which concluded, "Great revolutions are accomplishing: a general fermentation is working for the purpose of general refinement through the universe" (158). It seems clear that Johnson's handling of Stedman's "Narrative," which he published just two years before his arrest for sedition, was affected by his general concern during this period about staying within the law.

"80 Engravings Design'd from Nature on the Spot"

Johnson began to work on Stedman's manuscript as soon as he received it in early 1791, focusing his attention first on the formidable logistics of getting Stedman's approximately 106 "drawings" (mainly watercolors) engraved for eventual inclusion in the book. At the time Stedman submitted his manuscript and artwork, he envisioned eighty-three engraved plates (many consisting of two separate images on a single page) including a frontispiece, and in fact Johnson eventually published all but two.[21] Johnson, like other contemporary publishers, "had to employ the best engravers he could afford, and he had to match the genius of the engraver to that of the painter whose work he was to recreate" (Bentley 1980, 64). He also had to match engravers to appropriate subject matter and, in Stedman's case, to decide which original works merited the extra expense of "name" engravers.

Johnson seems to have sorted Stedman's artwork according to such criteria and to have farmed it out quickly to his engravers. Thirty-five of the published plates are unsigned and remain unattributed. Of these, all but three seem to have been executed in 1791, soon after Johnson commissioned them; they include most of the fish, bird, and plant depictions and are, for the most part, uninspired journeyman work. Two similar natural history plates are dated 1791 and signed by A[nker] Smith. Fourteen plates, mainly depicting animals and the majority also dated 1791, were executed and signed by [Inigo] Barlow, a frequent engraver of natural history subjects. The seven plates that include Stedman's most important maps and plans were engraved by a cartographic specialist, T. Conder, all but one in 1791. And a single plate depicting a "Female Quadroon Slave" was engraved by Perry in 1794, rather late in the book's production; though executed in stipple, it seems otherwise to have been directly modeled on the engraving of Joanna that had been produced by the better-known Holloway the previous year.

Johnson engaged four "name" engravers to execute the remaining twenty-two plates. In 1796, when his own *Analytical Review* announced the imminent publication of Stedman's book, there was special mention of the eighty [*sic*] plates "executed by Bartolozzi, Blake, Holloway, Benedetti, &c. &c.," and an early review of the work praised these engravings as being "in a style of uncommon elegance" (*Critical Review,* January 1797, 60). Francesco Bartolozzi, a Royal Academician and undoubtedly the most expensive of the engravers who worked on Stedman's plates, signed three—two full-page, rather stylized figures executed in characteristic stipple, and the more compositionally ambitious Stedman self-portrait that serves as the frontispiece (chronologically the final plate to be produced for the book).[22] Michele Benedetti was engaged early in the project to engrave the two Amerindian depictions, which he accomplished in 1792 in a style similar to that of Bartolozzi. And T. Holloway was given the task of engraving a single important plate, Stedman's beloved Joanna, which he executed in 1793 in a style reminiscent of Blake's work for the book.

William Blake's sixteen plates "have long been recognized as among the best executed and most generally interesting of all his journeyman work . . . [and] particularly in the large paper copies with the engravings colored by hand, are some of [his] most interesting and important book illustrations" (Keynes 1971, 98; 1969, 10). Undoubtedly, they include the most arresting visual images in the *Narrative.* Each of Blake's engravings successfully blends his own inner vision with Stedman's, producing works that express, for example, in the case of slave tortures (pls. 11, 35, 71) extraordinary power and pathos, in the case of his wonderfully humanoid monkeys and the skinning of the giant anaconda (pls. 18, 42, 19) sprightly humor, and in the case of his emblematic representation of the three interdependent continents (pl. 80) demure but unmistakable sensuality.

Blake effectively matched his engraving techniques to Stedman's subjects. His moving depictions of slaves were viewed by one scholar as "figures shaped by heavy linear nets placed against [contrastive] landscapes etched in a notably free and open style . . . their representations bound to the pictorial equivalent of the social system which imprisons them" (Essick 1973, 503–6; see also Essick 1980, 52–53). In contrast, his *finis* page engraving of "Europe supported by Africa & America" manages an almost airy representation of what another scholar glossed as "three comely nude women tenderly embracing each other, the Negro and the European clasping hands in sisterly equality" (Erdman 1952, 244). Thirteen of Blake's plates are signed by him and dated December 1792 and 1793; three others are almost certainly his and are dated December 1793 and 1794 (pls. 25, 55, 71—Keynes 1921; Erdman 1952, 244; Bentley 1977, 622). In addition, his signature on the very ordinary plate 52, combined with Stedman's expressed satisfaction with Blake's work for the book as early as 1 December 1791, suggests that some of the other unsigned and routine journeywork in the book may also be his.

As Bentley has written, "Engraving is always a work of translation in which the graphic conventions are different from those of the artist with a brush or pencil" (1980, 63), but Blake often "overstep[ped even] the usual barriers between designer and engraver," imprinting his own vision on his journeyman graphic works (Essick 1980, 51). Consequently, there has been lively scholarly interest in the relationship between Stedman's original "drawings"—long presumed to be lost—and Blake's engravings modeled after them. Essick (drawing on Smith 1960) has made an ingenious argument by analogy about "the subtle alterations that Blake probably brought to the Stedman designs" by introducing the better-documented transformations that Blake effected in 1792 (the same year he worked on many of the Stedman plates) upon a preliminary wash drawing by Governor King of "A Family of New South Wales." As Essick notes, "The family is a scruffy little group in the drawing, and the faces seem more like simplified caricatures than careful representations. Not only has Blake altered the disposition of the figures, but he has transformed poor and naked aborigines into noble savages" (Essick 1980, 53).[23]

In a similar fashion, Erdman suggests that Blake must have taken liberties with Stedman's intentions. Referring to the *finis* page, he notes that while Stedman, in the 1796 text, "expresses an 'ardent wish' that all peoples 'may henceforth and to all eternity be the props of each other' since 'we only differ in colour, but are certainly all created by the same Hand' . . . [in Blake's plate] Europe is *supported* by her darker sisters, and they wear slave bracelets while she has a string of pearls—a symbolism rather closer to the historical fact" (1952, 244). But this interpretation, clever as it is, seems wide of the mark: the beautiful contemporary hand-colored versions of this plate (in which Blake and/or Stedman may even

Figure 6. "A Family of New South Wales." Left: *Wash drawing by Governor King.*
Right: *Blake's engraving, made after King, for Hunter,* An Historical Journal of the
Transactions at Port Jackson and Norfolk Island, *1793 (plate dated 1792). From
Essick 1980, figs. 40, 41.*

have played a supervisory role—see below) suggest that Blake's and Stedman's intentions were both more egalitarian and more similar. For what
Erdman calls "slave bracelets" are represented in color as shining gold
ornaments, and his "pearls" become, in color, simple blue beads.

During the mid–1790s, the relationship between Stedman and Blake
was quite close; they repeatedly dined together, Stedman entrusted his
business affairs to Blake when not in London, Stedman sent gifts (geese,
a sugar cruse) to the Blakes, and they had a very active correspondence
(all, apparently, now lost). Yet Stedman did not know Blake personally
before 1792 at the earliest, and the fruit of their relationship, in terms of
practical influence on their respective published works, was strictly one-
way; while Stedman had completed his work on the "Narrative" well
before he met Blake, Stedman's manuscript and drawings, as well as his
various meetings with Blake, seem to have exerted a significant influence
on Blake's own thought. For example, "The persons and problems of
Stedman's *Narrative* reappear, creatively modified, in the text and illustrations of Blake's [1793] *Visions [of the Daughters of Albion]*: the rape and
torture of the virgin slave, her pride in the purity and equality of her soul,
and the frustrated desire of her lover and husband" (Erdman 1952, 245).

And there are numerous detailed textual and visual parallels between Theotormon's love in this poem for the gentle Oothoon, whom he is unable to set free, and Stedman's love for the enslaved Joanna (ibid.; see also Paulson 1983, 89–95).

Stedman's influence extended to other Blake works as well. Though Blake "shrank from signing his engraving of this bloody document, 'The Execution of Breaking on the Rack' [Stedman's pl. 71] . . . the image of the courageous rebel on the cruciform rack bit into his heart, and in the Preludium of *America* [1793] he drew Orc in the same posture to represent the spirit of human freedom defiant of tyranny" (Erdman 1969, 231). Likewise, the plate for Blake's "A Poison Tree" in *Songs of Experience* (1794) seems to echo the Stedman/Blake "Rack" (Davis 1977, 56). Stedman's graphic description and depiction of the South American vampire bat (1790/1988, 206, 428, pl. 57; cf. pp. 110, 231)—which he also calls the "Spectre of Guiana"—seem also to have impressed Blake, whose own haunting Spectre in *Jerusalem* takes on many of its specific characteristics (Erdman 1969, 234; Bogan 1976; but see also Stedman 1790/1988, Appendix A, s.v. *Vampier*). The snake that three figures sit astride in Blake's *America* (1793, 11) seems to be an imaginative ninety-degree transposition of the anaconda he engraved that same year for Stedman's plate 19—with similar neck harness and straddling figure and the same overall contours. And even Blake's famous "Tyger! Tyger! burning bright / In the forests of the night" and its accompanying illustration from the 1794 *Songs of Experience* may well be related to Stedman's "Tiger-Cat . . . its Eyes Emitting flashes of Lightning" (1790/1988, 359) or his *"Red* Tiger . . . Eyes Prominent, and Sparkling Like Stars" in the nighttime forest (1790/1988, 359), as well as to Stedman's drawings for plate 48 (see also Paulson 1983, 97–110).

Stedman's diaries and his few surviving works bear witness that he worked in several graphic media—pen and ink, watercolors, and oils—and he often used "drawings" as a generic term. We believe, however, that most or all of his originals for the "Narrative" were watercolors, which he sometimes referred to as "paintings" (see, for example, 1790/1988, 10). In the absence of evidence to the contrary, Stedman's artistic skills have generally been presumed to have been negligible. For example, Ray writes of Stedman's "modest ability as a draftsman," based on the two works known to him (Ray 1976, 9), and Keynes thinks that "it seems probable that they [Blake's prints] were not very exact copies" (1971, 100). Such judgments may, however, be overly hasty. Stedman himself took special pride throughout his life in his artistic aptitudes and accomplishments. Writing of his early artistic promise, he commented that

my talents for drawing were so universally admired that my parents were
advised not to neglect them—but to Encourage me since I would make a
figure by proper cultivation not inferiour even to Rubens or van Dyk.*

*This was the real and general opinion. (*1786, 5 bis*)

His later writings report frequent praise for his drawings and paintings
from critics in many walks of life—from poets and playwrights to some
of the finest painters of the age, including the miniaturist Richard Cos-
way, the Royal Academicians John Francis Rigaud and Ozias Humphry,
and, apparently, Sir Joshua Reynolds himself, "who Signalized it [Sted-
man's collection of drawings, especially those later engraved as pls. 4, 8,
53, and 61] With a verry high Compliment as Verry Expressive, And
upon the whole an Excellent Performance" (1790/1988, 392; see also *10
December 1786, 4 April 1787,* and *22 October 1789*). Without question, Stedman considered himself a far better artist than writer, and his contemporaries seem to have shared his opinion.

We have been able to uncover 15 drawings and paintings by Stedman.
Unfortunately, they do not permit a full assessment of his artistic skills
nor, therefore, of the role he ultimately played in shaping the major engravings for his book. None of them served as models for the full-page
figures that constitute the book's most powerful images; only one was
used at all, and that for a half-page engraving. Nevertheless, they do attest that his own work was ethnographically careful and accurate—considerably more so than many of the engravings modeled after it. In addition to the 15 works that we have found and to the 104 (or perhaps 105)
others that he submitted to Johnson in 1791, Stedman produced a large
number of others whose locations (in spite of our several years' intensive
search on three continents) remain unknown to us.[24]

A comparison of Stedman's watercolor entitled "Manner of Sleeping
&c. in the Forest," made in 1776, with the 1791 half-page engraving that
Barlow modeled on it for the 1796 *Narrative,* reveals a number of significant changes. In reorienting the scene from vertical to horizontal, Barlow
transformed Stedman's excellent depiction of the multilayered tropical
forest into a bare savanna, adding the edge of a river or creek in the foreground; he omitted the slave who is offering Stedman a calabash con-
tainer as well as the slave who is diligently blowing on the fire; he altered
the characteristically African squatting-relaxing posture of another slave
into a typically European head-in-hands sitting position; he eliminated
the tobacco pipes that Stedman and one of his slaves were enjoying at the
end of a long day of campaigning; he turned the pieces of clothing drying
over the fire as well as the two pet parrots, which Stedman had carefully
delineated, into vaguely defined forms; he altered Stedman's accurately

Figure 7. *"Manner of Sleeping &c. in the Forest."* Top: *Stedman's original 1776 watercolor. 14.6 by 10.5 cms.* Bottom: *1791 engraving by Barlow, after the watercolor, for the 1796 first edition of the* Narrative *(pl. 73 [top]).*

drawn carrying chests into coffinlike boxes, moved the saber, and deleted the powder pouch and wallet hanging from the roof; he moved the fire off to one side, apparently not understanding that it served to keep Stedman warm and hold mosquitoes at bay during the chilly tropical nights; and he smoothed out the rough palm leaf roof of the shelter to resemble English thatch.

Stedman first recorded his reactions to seeing what Johnson's engravers had produced when he noted that, shortly before 1 December 1791, he had received "above 40 Engravings from London some well some verry ill." These included several by Blake that particularly pleased Stedman: "I wrote to the Engraver blake to thank him twice for his excellent work but never received any answer" (*1 December 1791*). Stedman soon began sending "corrections" to the engravers, via Johnson, and he participated actively in the platemaking by sending such corrections even after the text had begun to be printed: on 5 June 1795, six months after he had received his final plate (the frontispiece) from Bartolozzi, he noted in his diary, "take home My Spoilt M. Script & repair all plates." We can surmise that Stedman was quite exacting in his attention to the way his "drawings" were engraved; on his 1790 manuscript "Directions for the Plates," he kept a running log in penciled symbols of plates still "to correct," and these included at various times at least eight of Blake's sixteen, all three of Bartolozzi's, Holloway's "Joanna," and many others. This log also offers the only indication that it was Stedman himself who supplied the drawing of five ships sailing into the distance—even though they are not included in the 1790 manuscript—that appears as a vignette on the title page of each of the 1796 volumes.

Johnson printed an unknown (but apparently very small) number of 1796 first editions on large paper with "the plates admirably coloured by hand" (Keynes 1971, 103). During the 1790s, the first great age of English illustrated book publishing, hand coloring was already common practice for illustrated works. "Printshops sold their merchandise either colored or plain, depending upon the tastes and pocketbook of the purchaser" (Essick 1980, 121). Often, the colorists were political refugees from the Continent, and it was common for these workers (usually women) to work at long benches, assembly line fashion, each applying a single color. Publishers constantly experimented with ways to cut the costs of coloring; just around the corner from Blake's house during the 1780s, one publisher set up a school to train boys to color, to avoid the expense of adult miniaturists (Bentley 1980, 65). We do not know the details of how the Stedman plates were colored.[25] However, a comparison of his original watercolor for plate 73 [top] with contemporary hand-colored examples suggests that either Stedman or a master colorist with

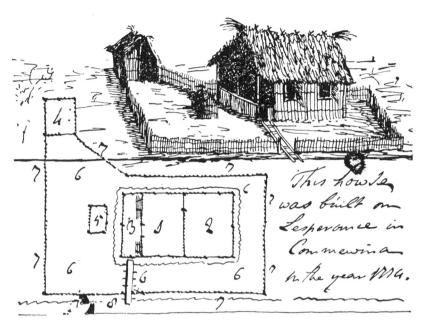

Figure 8. Stedman's house at Plantation L'Esperance (The Hope). Top: *Stedman's pen-and-ink sketch, 1776, to which he affixed the following key:* "1. The room where I dined, painted, and wrote letters &c. 2. Joanna's room, where we slept &c. 3. Was the gallery. 4. Was the kitchen for Quaco. 5. Was the hen-house. 6. The yard for ducks, and 2 sheep, a hog &c. 7. Palisades all round. 8. The entry and bridge" *(Thompson 1962, 194).* Bottom: *Engraving by Barlow, 1791 (probably after a Stedman watercolor based on this sketch), for the 1796 first edition of the* Narrative *(pl. 73 [bottom]).*

Figure 9. Two examples of Stedman's maritime watercolors, and the vignette from the title page of the 1796 Narrative. Left: "A Ship at Anker." Right: "A Dutch Frigate." Watercolors, Stedman Archive, Haus Besselich, Urbar, West Germany. Courtesy of Hilda von Barton Stedman. Bottom: Vignette.

access to Stedman's original watercolors made the specimens that the other colorists used as models. For there is a remarkably close correspondence between the colors of the original and the engravings, which would have been unlikely without direct copying; in both, for example, Stedman's shirt is precisely the same shade of pink, his jacket the same blue, and his trousers the same gray. We know nothing, either, of the financial arrangements between Johnson and his engravers, but one not-uncommon contemporary arrangement was for the engravers to be paid in kind with copies of the book. In this case, it is even possible that Blake—who was close to both Johnson and Stedman during the period—had a hand in coloring copies for his own benefit. But we have no hard evidence either way.

"THE BOOK GOOD FOR NOTHING"

Although the production of engravings for the *Narrative* spanned the entire period 1791–95, editorial work on the text seems to have started only in 1794, when Johnson quietly engaged William Thomson to serve as *"literary dry-nurse"* to the "Narrative." At Johnson's behest, Thomson rewrote Stedman's manuscript sentence by sentence, producing a new text "with a celerity unequalled, perhaps, on the part of any other man" (Anon. 1818, 2:110). Though Stedman came to regard Johnson as "the demon of Hell" (*May 1796*) because of the many changes wrought on his manuscript, Stedman apparently remained unaware—right up to his death soon after publication—that it was actually Thomson, a professional editor and ghost writer, who was directly responsible for causing his book to be "mard intirely" (*24 June 1795*).

William Thomson (1746–1817) was described in an obituary written by a lifelong acquaintance as

> one of the most extraordinary men of letters of the present age. . . . with an exception to poetry, [his name] is connected with almost every species of composition, and it would be impossible to write the history of the literature of the reign of George III. without assigning him a place, if not very elevated, at least somewhat conspicuous among the authors of that period. (Anon. 1818, 2:74)

After completing theological studies in Scotland, Thomson was given his own parish, in a presbytery renowned for its "religious gloom and fanatical austerity" (ibid., 86–87). In this setting of "puritanical orthodoxy," he "acquired the character of a *bon vivant* and pleasant companion, rather than that of a godly minister" (87), and his employment there was, by mutual agreement, short-lived. Thomson then moved to London (ca. 1780), where he sought to become a man of letters and was eventually enlisted to "revise, correct, and finish" a manuscript on King Philip III of Spain, following the death of its original author (93). As a result of the favorable response to this work (and his being awarded "the unsolicited degree of LL.D. from the University of Glasgow"), his reputation grew, and, among other literary activities, he was "not unfrequently employed either to revise or review the works of living authors" (94). During the next several decades, he wrote professionally in an astonishing variety of formats—from pamphlets and newspaper articles to novels and plays, as well as works of biblical commentary, military tactics, political and scientific history, and world travel, under both his own name and pseudonyms. By the time he made the acquaintance of Joseph Johnson during the early 1790s and had begun to frequent his literary evenings (once falling asleep and snoring aloud during a *tête-à-tête* with Mary Wollstonecraft), Thomson was devoting himself largely to writing travel accounts on, for example, the Western Hebrides and on Norway, Denmark, and Russia—working from notes provided by the "authors" to produce the final texts (102–6). Johnson's selection of Thomson to edit Stedman's "Narrative" was, then, hardly surprising.

On 25 May 1795, Stedman got his first glimpse of the manuscript he had given Johnson in 1791, noting laconically in his diary, "12 chapters printed & mard." Thenceforth until his death two years later, Stedman's life became a tormented struggle to repair what he saw as the damages inflicted upon his work. His relations with Blake and with Luke Hansard (Johnson's printer for the *Narrative*) remained friendly throughout the period; he entrusted his business affairs to Blake when he was away from London and parts of his manuscript to Hansard, as a way of keeping it out of Johnson's hands. But Stedman's irritation with Johnson knew few limits, and he was often consumed by anger and frustration at the publisher's stubborn and "uncivil" refusal to respect his wishes. By June 1795, he was referring in his diary to "My Spoilt M. Script" (*5 June 1795*); "on Midsummer day" he complained of receiving "the 1s. vol. of my book quite mard[,] oaths and sermons inserted &c" (*24 June 1795*); and shortly after, he remarked, "My book mard intirely[.] am put to the most extreme trouble and expence . . . . ba[w]dy oaths lies & preachings in my unhappy book" (ibid.). He also mentioned "a hot quarl with Johnson" (ibid.). In August the problems continued: "Johnson uncivil all along"; in December, after Johnson had sent him a "blur'd index," he concluded that "the book good for nothing"; and on 17 January 1796, he wrote what was probably his final letter to his brother's wife in Holland: "My book was printed full of lies and nonsense, without my knowledge.

I burnt two thousand vols., and made them print it over again, by which they lost 200 guineas. You have no idea of the villainy and folly I have to deal with." In this same month, Stedman sent his printer new front and back matter for the book:

> I sent besides to London Hansard—
> a compleet index above 650 names
> a compleet list of 200 subscribers
> a compleet direction for 80 plates
> a compleet errata with 60 faults
> a compleet table of 30 chaps. contents
> a compleet form for a title page
> a compleet preface—and
>
> a compleet Dedicn. to Prince of Wales of which he was made acquainted by General S = Leger who was wrote to by Major Wemyfs of II Regimt[.] I charged Hansard not to trust the above papers with Johnson who I would now not save from the gallows with only one of them so cruelly was I treated—and I declare him a scoundrel [i.e. challenge him to a duel?] without he gives me satisfaction. (*1796*)

In May, Stedman was still complaining: Johnson "again torments me by altering the Dedication to the P. of Wales &.—he being a d——nd eternal Jacobin scoundrel" (*May 1796*). But by the middle of the month, Stedman's travails were over: "the whole or most of my publication of which I send away the last cancels so late as the middle of May 1796—having been in hand no less than 7 or 8 long years" (*May 1796*).[26]

From the summer of 1795 until early 1796, Stedman spent much of his time in London, negotiating with Johnson about the differences between the text he had completed in 1790 and the altered version. Stedman's diary and related evidence make clear that what emerged as the 1796 first edition was an unhappy compromise. Stedman, like many battered authors, eagerly waiting to have his work published and to receive royalties (and buffeted by rapidly declining health), felt it necessary to concede on many of the points of difference in order to reinstate those passages he cared about most (and which Johnson was willing to publish). Stedman's insistence on not simply accepting the version that Johnson had printed allegedly cost the publisher two hundred guineas, presumably in printer's fees and paper costs. In the end, Stedman seems to have come to terms with Johnson, settling for a book that was rather different from the one he had written. Just before the complete 1796 first edition was to appear (in its final, "negotiated" form), he wrote, "I have overcome them all, and at last, in one month's time, the book comes out, and so soon we can make up accounts" (Thompson 1966, 75).

A Comparison of the Texts of 1790 and 1796

Although Stedman was quite unprepared for the massive revisions that were made in his 1790 manuscript, he had always expected some professional editing to take place. In his 1790 "Advertisement to the Reader" he implied that his manuscript might benefit from being "properly prepared for the Eye of the Publick by the able Pen of a candid and ingeneous Compiler" and that, before publication, it would need to be "Maturely and fully digested" (1790/1988, 25). The actual editing that Thomson did at Johnson's behest ranged from this expected kind of minor rephrasing— often designed to "improve" Stedman's direct, sometimes coarse soldier's language—to substantial alterations of Stedman's views on race, slavery, and social justice, obliterating or warping significant aspects of his Suriname experience and the social commentary he had intended to share with his readers. In this section, we attempt to describe and analyze these editorial modifications, providing sufficient examples to establish the relationship between the Minnesota manuscript, which Stedman finished in 1790 (and which was published for the first time in 1988), and the well-known and much-published version first brought out by Johnson in 1796.

Purely stylistic changes—in spelling, punctuation, and phrasing— were effected throughout. We offer two characteristic examples, to illustrate the extent of this type of general editing. The first forms part of Stedman's description of the encounter between government troops and the rebels of Boucou; the second is part of the account of his own arrest in the forest for insubordination.

1790 (1988, 84–85; cf. pp. 37–38). To through a *facine* bridge over the Marsh was then projected but this Plan after several weeks had been spent in the attempt and a great many Men shot dead in the execution was also frustrated and drop'd—during which time the two little armies kept popping and black-guarding each other at a shocking rate. Having desisted from carrying over the above bridge, and no hopes of getting through the Marsh into the Fortress, besides the ammunition and victuals growing considerably less. . . .

1796 (1:82–83). It was then projected to throw a fascine bridge over the marsh, by the troops; but this plan, after several weeks had been spent in the attempt, and a number of men shot dead while employed upon it, was of necessity laid aside. Thus every hope of passing through the marsh into the fortress being frustrated, and the food and ammunition being considerably lessened. . . .

1790 (1988, 433–36). we Proceeded on till we Entered the Camp; at

1796 (2:148–49, 154). The reader may judge of my mortification, when I in-

Which Moment I was met by the Adjutant, And put Under an Arrest by the Commanders Orders to be tried by a Court Martial Under Pretence of having quitted the Rear Guard Without his orders. . . . No Sooner Was I Sat Down at this Place /where was Also kept a Post of the Society Troops/ than I was Accoasted by Several deputies sent me from Col: Seybourgh With an Offer of being set at Liberty Providing I Would Acknowledge before two Commisarys, that I had been Justly arrested Which I Refused.	form him, that, instead of receiving the approbation of my commander, as I certainly deserved, I was immediately on my arrival in camp put under an arrest, to be tried by a court-martial for disobedience of orders. . . . We were scarcely arrived at this post, than I was accosted by several deputies from Colonel Seyburg, who earnestly intreated that I would only acknowledge myself to have been in fault, assuring me that I should then be set at liberty, and all would be forgotten. As I was conscious, however, of my own innocence, I could not in common justice criminate myself.

There were many other types of largely stylistic alterations. In a number of cases, the order of paragraphs was shifted, footnotes were incorporated into the text, textual material was placed in footnotes, the selection of poems was altered, verse was rephrased as prose, foreign-language quotations were translated (in both directions; e.g., Fourgeoud's "I am Undone" became *"Nous sommes perdus!"* [1790/1988, 413; 1796, 2:120; cf. p. 219] and *"vincere out mory"* became "victory or death" [1790/1988, 116; 1796, 1:128; cf. p. 56]), and there was, throughout, an extensive weeding out of Stedman's Latin quotations and biblical allusions.

Some of the rephrasing designed to "correct" Stedman's occasional coarseness caused alterations mainly in tone or color, lending a certain flatness to Stedman's lively and picturesque descriptions. For example, his reference to a "Smouse" was changed to read "Jew" (1790/1988, 116; 1796, 1:127; cf. p. 56), his "Quacks" were transformed into "surgeons" (1790/1988, 176; 1796, 1:249), "a Couple of hungry whores" became "a brace of the frail sisterhood" (1790/1988, 616; 1796, 2:393), and a portion of his description of a dalliance with a slave woman was changed from "[she gave me] such a hearty kiss—as had made my Nose nearly as flat as her own" to the briefer and more delicate "[she] imprinted on my lips a most ardent kiss" (1790/1988, 43; 1796, 1:20; cf. p. 18). Likewise, scatological references were systematically purged. For example, the 1796 publication omitted the passage that described Colonel Fourgeoud's joy, after a discouraging day of vainly pursuing his rebel slave foes through the forest, at finding a pile of "reeking S—— [declaring] he was now perfectly sure of following the Enemy," upon which a grenadier embarrassedly stepped forward to admit *"this was me and please your Honour"* (1790/1988, 214; 1796, 1:264; cf. p. 113); and Stedman's report that "some suppose" that the unusual sound produced by the bird called the *trumpeter* "is made by the nose . . . and others that it comes forth through the Anus" was edited to omit the latter phrase (1790/1988, 213; 1796, 1:262).[27]

For related reasons, no doubt, a number of sexual allusions were deleted by the editor. For example, Stedman described how the sadistic mistress of a plantation "from a Motive of *Groundless* Jealousy . . . put an end to the Life of a young and beautiful Quadroon Girl, by the infernal means of plunging a red hot Poker in her Body, by those parts which decency forbids to mention," but the 1796 version removed the final phrase (1790/1988, 115; 1796, 1:126; cf. p. 56). Likewise, when Stedman related how "the pious Mother of the Charity-House [in Paramaribo] Nephariously Kept Flogging the Poor Slaves dayly because they were She said Unbelievers," the editor deleted his accompanying observation: "the Men she Always Strip'd *Perfectly* Naked, that not a *Single* Part of theyr Body might Escape her Attention—to what is Religion Come at Last?" (1790/1988, 472; 1796, 2:198; cf. p. 246). Similarly, his claim that howler monkeys are so lascivious that they "sometimes Attack the female of the Human Species" was censored (1790/1988, 502; 1796, 2:236);[28] his statement that not only are Negroes' "Necks . . . Thicker than Ours . . . [but] their Genitels Conspicuously Larger" was also excised (1790/1988, 512–13; 1796, 2:252; cf. p. 258); the fact that a "Cowskin" with which "during Breakfast 7 Negroes were Again tied up and Flogg'd" was in fact "the Dried Penous of a Bull" was omitted (1790/1988, 555; 1796, 2:307; cf. p. 290); and even his personal, deeply felt statement about the "pleasure [of] rambling naked when the occasion will permit it" apparently overstepped bounds of conventional propriety and was deleted (1790/1988, 138; 1796, 1:160; cf. p. 69).

Stedman's editor also made a consistent effort to mute evidence of his "wilder" side (which Stedman himself had already toned down considerably between his diaries and his 1790 "Narrative"), and much of the wenching, hard drinking, brawling, and dramatic temper tantrums reported in the 1790 manuscript was altered or simply deleted. A representative example, describing an incident during the outward voyage to Suriname, may illustrate the more general process:

1790 (1988, 34; cf. p. 14): Having received a severe fall on the Quarter deck by its being wet and Slippery and finding myself otherwise exceed-	**1796** (1:14): Becoming extremely low-spirited towards the close of our voyage, I now had recourse to daily sea-bathing, and to a chearing glass

ingly low spirited I had recourse to daily bathing in sea water, and also made use of a Cheering Glass of Claret with two *anchors* of which /being about 20 Gallons/ each Officer was provided, besides his own Stock /but part whereof had been industriously filshed from me and which I deteckted from the back of a hencoop/. by these Means I found such a considerable benefit that in a few days after, I was perfectly recover'd of my Complaint but so exasperated that I took revenge on a locker with above 300 Consealed Eggs, which I stove in and bedaubed the whole Cabin with Yolks.

of claret, two ankers of which had been provided for each officer, independantly of his own stock. These means proved efficacious, and I found myself in a few days perfectly recovered from my complaint.

Sometimes this type of editing, though apparently minor, caused the loss of significant descriptive information. Stedman reported graphically, for example, how on board the ship bound for Suriname, "dinners were sometimes served up in the very Tubs employed by the Surgeons to void the filth of the Seek" (1790/1988, 33; cf. p. 14), but in published form the tubs were more politely characterized simply as being "of not the most cleanly appearance" (1796, 1:12). Likewise, Stedman's reference to the "overgrown Widows, Stale Beauties, and overaged Maids" of Suriname (1790/1988, 49; cf. p. 22) who mistreated their young female slaves out of jealousy was discreetly deleted. And even the telling observation that "All the mulatta-, negroe- and Indian Slaves in the Colony go bare footed—and naked above the waist" was excised (1790/1988, 41; 1796, 1:18). Moreover, in the course of such minor editing, a number of careless errors were introduced—misspellings of foreign words, alterations of dates (with those in the 1790 version corresponding to Stedman's diary entries), and so on. And Stedman's editor was not above exaggerating facts for effect—for example, increasing the size of the weight attached to a female slave as punishment from "3 score pounds or upwards" to "at least a hundred pounds" (1790/1988, 39; 1796, 1:15; cf. p. 15).

Stedman himself was responsible for making two changes between the versions of 1790 and 1796—the Dedication and the final pages of the work. Stedman dedicated the 1790 manuscript to Sir George Strickland, who "from . . . first seeing my Original drawings seem'd to patronize them" and who had been the first to encourage him seriously to write up and publish his Suriname experiences (*10 June 1778*). By 1796, for reasons that are nowhere spelled out, Stedman had sought and received permission to dedicate the work instead to the Prince of Wales (*1796*). Johnson, apparently objecting to the new dedication on political grounds, attempted to alter it (*May 1796*), but we have no indication of the precise nature of the argument nor which of the two antagonists won out in the end.

The final pages were also changed, at least partly by Stedman. In the 1790 "Narrative," after describing the untimely death of his dear and virtuous Joanna, Stedman added a long memorial poem, mentioned his marriage that same year to "a young Lady . . . of a very Respectable Family in Holland" and the birth of their first "English" children, and then proudly commented that Johnny Stedman (his son by Joanna) was "at this moment on board of the *Southampton* Frigate . . . ready to Strike a blow at the Spaniards should they dare to Quarrel with the Kingdom of Great Britain" (1790/1988, 626). In contrast, the 1796 version omits all but the barest mention of Joanna's death (a change probably effected by the editor) and then adds a poem to the recently drowned Johnny, Stedman's "An Elegy on my Sailor" (2:402–3, previously published in a 1795 issue of the *Weekly Entertainer* [Thompson 1962, 375]).

A third such alteration remains mysterious, and Stedman himself makes no direct reference to it in his diaries. The 1790 title page clearly lists the author as "Lieut: Col: J: G: Stedman." (The same designation appears both on the title page of the manuscript autobiography he completed in 1786 and in his formal instructions about his return address that same year [Thompson 1962, 287].) We know that Stedman was promoted by the Prince of Orange from captain to major, and from major to lieutenant colonel in the Scots Brigade in 1777 and 1783, respectively (1796, 2:395; 1790/1988, 622).[29] Indeed, the prepublication announcement of the book in Joseph Johnson's own *Analytical Review* (February 1796, 223) listed the author of the *Narrative,* which "in a Short Time will be published," as "LIEUT. COL. STEDMAN." Yet the title page of the 1796 book styled him, rather, "Captn. J. G. Stedman."

In the 1790 preface, Stedman defiantly defended his right to criticize others freely "till I shall have found out the Reason why Vice ought not to be Expos'd to the World as well as Virtue made Conspicuous" (1790/1988, 10). Yet, being aware of the risks of libel, and afraid that some of his criticisms "might tend to expose him both to great Confusion, and even Danger," he expressed his intent for the published version, rather than "omitting publick or private transactions . . . to insert both the one and the other . . . [but] with initial Letters" (1790/1988, 25).[30] In accord with these instructions (and, undoubtedly, with an eye on Fox's recently passed libel law), the names of many individuals mentioned pejoratively in the 1790 "Narrative" were abbreviated in the 1796 publication. For

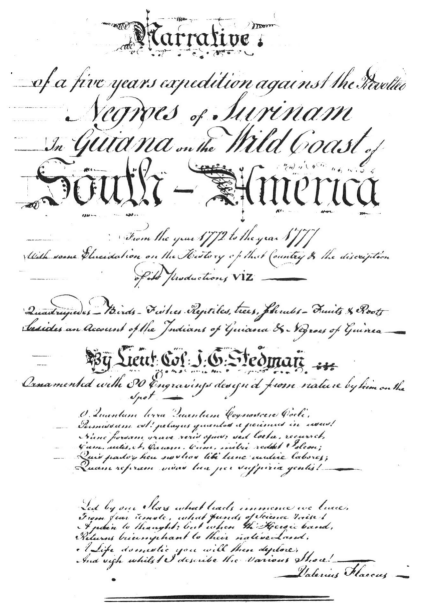

Figure 10. Title page of Stedman's 1790 "Narrative." James Ford Bell Library, University of Minnesota.

example, Mrs. Stolker, who reportedly drowned a baby for crying and then gave the mother 300–400 lashes for trying to retrieve its body from the river, was referred to in 1796 as "Mrs. S——lk——r" (1790/1988, 267; 1796, 1:329; cf. p. 148). Similar abbreviations are used in the 1796 first edition for the names of two clergymen who kept slave concubines (1796/1988, 47; 1796, 1:26; cf. p. 20), for the captain "who in 1781 threw 132 living Slaves into the Sea to perish" (1790/1988, 81; 1796, 1:78; cf. p. 34), for the plantation owner whose clandestine flight from Suriname caused Joanna and her fellow slaves to be put up for sale to pay his debts (1790/1988, 175; 1796, 1:208; cf. p. 96), and many others. And some personal criticisms were deleted altogether, for example, the acquittal of an officer (identified only by an initial even in the 1790 manuscript) whose cruelty resulted in his lieutenant "leaping out at the Cabbin Window and ending his Existence" (1790/1988, 81; 1796, 1:78; cf. p. 35).

Stedman, no more hesitant to find fault with the scientific observers who preceded him than with cruel slave owners or military officers he knew in Suriname, frequently criticized the misleading reports of "too many Authors . . . among whom are Men of genius and Learning," and suggested that "some indeed may have erred from Ignorance or wrong information, but numbers from a motive of Pride, and presumption, have been with impunity permitted to vend of their shamefull impositions on the too Credulous Public" (1790/1988, 164; cf. 1796, 1:198). Many of the controversies he addressed in this realm—with Merian, Buffon, Fermin, Bancroft, and others—were printed in the 1796 book, but others were suppressed. For example, in his assessment of a report by *"Alexander Garden* M[.] D. F. R. S." on the electric eel, the following passage was excised: "nor have I ever heard of any ones being kil'd by them according to this Gentlemans Account," as was the general statement that followed: "and in this manner I shall make it my business to Confute all the Errors that come within the Circle of my Compass, by whatever Author they may be Stated without exception, as a Duty to Myself in Particular, and to the World in General" (1790/1988, 115; 1796, 1:126).

Stedman's sharpest personal criticisms in the 1790 manuscript were reserved for his commanding officer, Colonel Fourgeoud, and it is here that the 1796 publication was most extensively edited. Frequent allusions to the sausages, hams, claret, and other delicacies on which "the old Gentleman" dined while his soldiers were forced to subsist on the most meager (and often worm-infested) staples are consistently toned down or deleted (1790/1988, 209, 229–30, 274; 1796, 1:258, 282, 339). Also carefully edited were reports that Fourgeoud systematically neglected the well-being of his troops (1790/1988, 164; 1796, 1:197), invented tasks "for the mere purpose of thus persecuting me to Death" (1790/1988, 225; 1796, 1:277; cf. p. 122), and "having found every means to kill me ineffectual," tormented Stedman by confiscating his cartridges and slandering his friends (1790/1988, 226; 1796, 1:278). The rough edges of Stedman's similarly adversarial, though briefer, relationship with another commanding officer, Lieutenant Colonel Seybourgh, were also systematically smoothed over in the 1796 publication. For example, the descriptions of Seybourgh's sadism toward his troops and much of the detail and emotion surrounding Stedman's false arrest by Seybourgh ("my infamous Foe") in the forest were simply deleted, as was the general remark that "Col: Fourgeoud, Lieut: Col: Seybourgh & Myself by this Time so Effectually hated each Other that no Triumvirate was ever more Compleat" (1790/1988, 339, 433; 1796, 2:24, 149).

Stedman's reactions to Fourgeoud's sadism and favoritism, which ranged from fantasies about murdering him (1790/1988, 210; 1796, 1:259) to images of relinquishing himself to Hell for the "Satisfaction of seeing him [Fourgeoud] burn" (1790/1988, 281; 1796, 1:349 cf. p. 155), were generally deleted from the 1796 publication, as were his thoughts about reporting the colonel's "neglect of duty" directly to the Prince of Orange or other authorities (1790/1988, 285; 1796, 1:355; cf. p. 156). Similarly deleted was Stedman's disclosure that Fourgeoud had actually received his commission on the basis, not of merit, but of financial gain to the men who nominated him: "those who Recommended this man to Such a distinguished Rank, & Office . . . proceeded from self interest Alone to be Reinburs'd the money that he Was in theyr debt" (1790/1988, 617; 1796, 2:394). And sarcastic as well as simply disrespectful allusions to Fourgeoud (e.g., as "the Hero" [1790/1988, 284; 1796, 1:354; cf. p. 156] or "this Sod" [1790/1988, 188; 1796, 1:227; cf. p. 101]) are converted to more polite forms of reference, as are Stedman's many pejorative comparisons of Fourgeoud to, for example, tyrants, bedlamites, or reptiles (1790/1988, 225, 227; 1796, 1:277–78). Not all of Stedman's criticisms of Fourgeoud were deleted in the 1796 publication, and there are even a few cases in which they were slightly embellished (1790/1988, 571; 1796, 2:332). But in general, the muting of the adversarial relationship between these two strong-willed soldiers probably represents the single most frequent alteration of Stedman's manuscript for publication.

Stedman's descriptions of sexual relations between European men and African women were subtly but systematically changed between 1790 and 1796. The frequency and importance of such relations were diminished, at the same time that the social distance between the partners was

emphasized. Emblematic of these changes is the 1790 passage that elabo-
rates on Stedman's diary entry for his first night in the New World ("sleep
at Mr. Lolkens . . . I f——k one of his negro maids" [*9 February 1773*]):

> having knocked once or twice at the door—it was opened by a Masculine
> young *Negro-woman,* as black as a coal . . . I was fatigued and longed for
> some rest—thus made a signal that I wanted to sleep—but here I was truly
> brought into great Distress—for she again misunderstanding me had the
> unaccountable assurance to give me such a hearty kiss—as had made my
> Nose nearly as flat as her own—I knew not what to do or how to keep my
> Temper and disentangling myself with some resentment flung into
> my sleeping apartment but here *wousky*[31] pursued me again—and in Spite
> of what I could say pulld of[f] my Shoes and my Stockings in a Moment.
> Heavens, I lost all patience. This Young Woman to be sure was as black as
> the Devil, to be short as the rest of this adventure can afford but little in-
> struction or entertainment to the reader. I shall beg leave to draw a Sable
> Curtain over it. (1790/1988, 42–43; cf. pp. 18–19)

In contrast, the 1796 publication related the incident until the removal of
Stedman's shoes and stockings, but carefully avoided any direct or indi-
rect reference to the sexual encounter itself, and it added a comment—not
present in the 1790 "Narrative"—about the characteristic servility of "female negro slaves . . . [in all] the West India settlements" (1796, 1:21).[32]

Stedman's relationship with Joanna, one of the leitmotifs of the book,
was changed in a similar direction by means of a large number of subtle,
individual alterations. Descriptions of the deep emotional bonds between
Stedman and his mulatto lover were in general either deleted or elevated
to a purely literary plane, and the text was repeatedly rewritten to stress
the inequality of their respective positions in society.[33] A single example
may convey some idea of these changes. In the 1790 "Narrative," Stedman described his chagrin at learning that Joanna was about to be transferred to a new plantation

> at the mercy of some rascally Overseer—Good God; I flew to the Spot in
> Search of poor Joanna and found her bathing with her Companions in the
> Garden*—

> But lo! with graceful Motion there she Swims
> Gently removing each Ambitious Wave
> The crowded waves transported Clasp her Limbs
> When, When, oh when shall I such freedoms have
> In vain ye envious Streams So fast he flow
> To hide her from a lovers ardant Gaze
> From every touch you more transparent grow
> And all revealed the beautious Wanton plays

But perceiving me She darted from my presence like a Shot, when I returned to Mrs. Demelly and declared without the least hesitation no less than that it was my intention /if such could be/ to Purchase to Educate & to make even my lawfull Wife *in Europe,* the individual Mulatto Maid *Joanna* which I relate to the World without blushing or being ashamed of while Mrs. Demelly gazed upon me with Wild Astonishment.

*—This is here regularly done twice a Day by all the Indians Mulatto's Negroes &c— and which Constitutes so much to theyr health and to their Cleanliness—while by the Europeans /some few excepted/ this Salutary Custom is never put in *practice.* (1790/1988, 98; cf. p. 46)

But Stedman's editor substituted for this passage, simply:

Good God!—I flew to the spot in search of poor Joanna: I found her bathed in tears.—She gave me such a look—ah! such a look!—From that moment I determined to be her protector against every insult. (1796, 1:99)

Stedman's own version, characteristically, dwells on Joanna's beauty and clearly states his intention to raise her to his own status by education and by making her his lawful wife. The edited version, saying nothing of her beauty,[34] emphasizes Joanna's pitiable condition (bathed in tears rather than bathing with her companions) and makes Stedman her protector and patron, rather than her lover-aspiring-to-be-her-husband. These changes seem to have been just what the reading public wanted: the *British Critic* noted with approval, "The tale in particular of Joanna, and of the author's attachment to her, is highly honourable to both parties" (November 1796, 539).

Stedman's views on slavery, the slave trade, social justice, and organized religion were also substantially and systematically altered for the 1796 publication. At the time that he was writing the "Narrative" during the 1780s, his positions were well within the mainstream of contemporary educated British opinion—ambivalence and equivocation about slavery and the trade as institutions, combined with genuine compassion for oppressed humanity (see, for example, Anstey 1975, 91–153; Davis 1966, 391–421; 1975, 420–21, passim; Lewis 1983, 94–238). While Stedman was far from being (like Johnson, Blake, and others of that circle) a republican or abolitionist sympathizer, within the contemporary spectrum of public opinion he was equally far from being a political conservative. With his feet firmly planted in the middle of the political road, Stedman saw himself as arguing equally against men such as Clarkson who exhibited the "enthusiasm of ill placed Humanity [Humanitarianism]" and against those who would "persevere in the most unjust and diabolical barbarity . . . for the sake of drinking rum, and eating Sugar" (1790/ 1988, 168; cf. p. 88).[35]

In his 1790 "Narrative," Stedman rehearsed the whole panoply of already well-worn arguments in favor of the continuation of slavery and the trade, including (among others) the Lockean claim that captives in just wars may legitimately be enslaved (1790/1988, 170; cf. p. 91; see Sypher 1942, 76–83); the commonplace apologetic that, with just laws, Africans "may live happier in the West Indies, than they ever did in the forests of Africa," and far happier than the oppressed hordes of laborers, prostitutes, soldiers, and others, in Europe (1790/1988, 171; cf. p. 91; see also Goveia 1956, 78–79); the argument that sailors, "the props, and bulwarks of every Mercantile-Nation," are far better off working on slave ships than having to be "hang'd to keep them from Starving" in times of peace (1790/1988, 171; cf. p. 92); the political-economic warnings about the advantages France would gain, and the attendant doubling of the price of sugar and rum, should the trade be abruptly ended (1790/1988, 172; cf. p. 92); and even the semantic reminder that "slavery" was a mere word that had come to have misleading connotations and that it might better be replaced by "Menial Servant," since many slaves were in fact better off than "Prentices in England" (1790/1988, 173; cf. p. 93; see also Davis 1966, 395). Motivated, he claimed, by a dual concern for "the *African*" (whom he explicitly said he "loved") and for "this *glorious Island*," Stedman urged Parliament to focus on amelioration—the passage and rigid enforcement of laws that would protect the rights of enslaved Africans as human beings—and thus "make the Slaves in our West India Settlements perfectly happy, with even an Accumulation to the Wealth of their Masters" (1790/1988, 173; cf. p. 94). The key for Stedman was to enforce the rule of just law, and he styled a "Cancer" those current West Indian "laws which are deaf to the cry of the Afflicted Dependants, While the Master is invested With that unbounded de[s]potism Which ever ends in a Tirannical Usurpation" (1790/1988, 534, 542; cf. pp. 273, 281).

Stedman's editor made a consistent attempt to slant his "moderate" opinions, as expressed in the 1790 "Narrative," in the direction of a rigid proslavery ideology for the 1796 first edition, at the same time deleting many of his observations that suggested the common humanity of Africans and Europeans. And he often altered Stedman's middle-of-the-road humanitarianism and strong penchant for cultural relativism to read almost like Edward Long's (1774) acidulous proslavery apologetics. In the 1790 "Narrative," Stedman frequently depicted the African as Natural Man, exactly like a European but for the mixed blessings of "civilization": "the *Africans* in a State of nature, Are not that Wretched People Which they are by too Many ignorant European Wretches Represented" (1790/1988, 369; cf. p. 189); "the africans are not so intirely destitute of morality and even Religion as a number of ignorant Europeans imagine"

(1790/1988, 72–73; cf. p. 30); "their own Religion being much more Comodious [than ours], and not so much divested of Common Sence as numberless Stupid Europeans imagine" (1790/1988, 171; cf. p. 92); and yet more forcefully, "the African Negroes though by Some Stupid Europeans treated as Brutes Are made of no Inferior Clay but in every one Particular are our Equals" (1790/1988, 514; cf. p. 259). By 1796, all of these passages (and others like them) had been expunged and, in their place, the "national character of [the African] people" was now described as being "perfectly savage" (1796, 1:203).

Likewise, Stedman's occasionally ambivalent but generally laudatory assessments of the character of the Saramaka and Ndjuka Free Negroes, whom he depicted as carefree, state-of-nature forest dwellers in 1790 (1988, 172; cf. p. 93) were transformed in 1796 to make them brute savages. While the "Narrative" admitted that they "have indeed behaved indifferently well ever since the foregoing treaty" (1790/1988, 73–74; cf. p. 31), even though the Society of Suriname had repeatedly reneged on "Sending the Yearly *Presents*" according to the treaties (1790/1988, 510; cf. p. 254), the 1796 edition deleted both these observations and asserted flatly that there are no "marks of civilization, order, or government among them, but, on the contrary, many examples of ungovernable passion, debauchery, and indolence" (1796, 1:203).

Realizing that "the anti-slavery writer accents every trait that identifies the Negro with the white man" (Sypher 1942, 5), Stedman's editor tried to weed out his frequent and, in themselves, seemingly minor comments to this effect. To cite but three examples: Stedman at one point credited the rebel Negroes with what he called "humanity" for sparing the lives of his own men, but by 1796 the editor had completely altered his intentions by simply changing the word to "hurry" (1790/1988, 154; 1796, 1:183; cf. p. 81); Stedman's footnote explaining that "the word *negroish* is verry ill applied when meant to discribe greediness or Self interest" was deleted by the editor (1790/1988, 524; 1796, 2:265; cf. p. 264); and while Stedman had directly compared "Black Women [with] theyr Sparkling Eyes.—Ivory Teeth, and remarkable Cleanliness All over" to "the to[o] many Languid Looks, Sallow Complexions, deform'd Bodies, And Broken Constitutions, of European Contriwomen," this passage (like others on the physical beauty of Africans) was deleted wholesale (1790/1988, 369; 1796, 2:62; cf. p. 189).

Similarly, many of Stedman's blunt general remarks about the pervasiveness of misconduct and debauchery among European planters were muted or deleted, as were his several statements of this sort: "those planters who dare so inhumanely to persecute theyr Slaves without a Cause deserve in my opinion no better treatment [than to have their slaves revolt]" (1790/1988, 75; 1796, 1:69; cf. p. 32). More generally, Stedman's editor tried to sharpen the thrust of what he apparently viewed as the book's incipient antiabolitionist message by adding new, topical, and un-equivocal statements against immediate abolition to the 1796 preface:

> it must be observed that LIBERTY, nay even too much lenity, when *suddenly* granted to illiterate and unprincipled men, must be to *all* parties dangerous, if not pernicious. Witness the *Owca* and *Sarameca* Negroes in Surinam—the *Maroons* of Jamaica [who had rebelled in 1795], the *Carribs* of St. Vincent [who had also just rebelled], &c. (1:v)

And, just to be sure, he added a still more explicit and longer passage arguing, in contrast to the thrust of Stedman's 1790 "Narrative," that slavery in Suriname is far worse than that in the British West Indian colonies, where "our [British] planters have by their own laws most hu-manely restrained . . . [the] unlimited infliction of punishment . . . ex-ercised so commonly in Surinam" (1796, 2:289–90).

Stedman's Voltairean skepticism about organized religion apparently offended his editor as well. As with slavery and the trade, Stedman took pains to make clear that he was not opposed to the institution itself (1790/1988, 525; cf. p. 265), but rather to its widespread corruption—in this case by "hypocrites," among whom he seems to have numbered most British clergymen as well as the Moravian missionaries sent out to con-vert the Indians and Africans in Suriname. Here is a characteristic pas-sage, excised by Stedman's editor, who had, after all, once been a min-ister:

> As for the moravian missionary's that are Settled Amongst them to Pro-mote theyr faith &c. I have no Objections, Providing their morals go hand in hand with theyr Precepts, but without Which they ought /like a Pack of Canting Hypocritical Rascals deserve/ to be Strip'd naked, then tar'd & Feathered by the negroes, & flog'd out of the Colony. (1790/1988, 595; see 1796, 2:363; cf. pp. 309–10)

Some of Stedman's views on other social issues seem to have been al-tered in response to rapidly shifting political currents (and with an eye on the recent sedition law). For example, his lengthy and inflammatory crit-icisms of conduct in the British navy, with direct comparisons of sailors to slaves (and the identical conclusion that just treatment would lead to both greater efficiency and happiness), were very largely deleted (see, for example, 1790/1988, 77–78; 1796, 1:73). And, similarly, his political pas-sages relating to British-American relations were consistently altered (1790/1988, 182; 1796, 1:218; cf. p. 99).

We now believe that the alteration of Stedman's "Narrative" to make it less radical (and more proslavery) was matter-of-factly effected by his editor, William Thomson, largely on his own initiative. We know that at the same time Thomson was rewriting the "Narrative" line by line, he was also "actively engaged in writing tracts in defence of the slave-trade," commissioned by proslavery groups "holding forth *golden temptations* to needy men of letters" (Anon. 1818, 2:108). And the period immediately after 1792 witnessed a broad public reaction against the antislavery movement—in part an anti-Jacobin backlash following the French Revolution, in part horror at the 1791 slave rebellion in Saint Domingue and bitterness at the subsequent death of more than forty thousand British soldiers sent to quell the nascent Haitian Revolution. Thomson's political alterations of the "Narrative," then, not only may have squared with his own views; they also seem to have been in step with changing public opinion and to have protected the book against the new sedition law, and they might even have been expected to help sell a few additional copies of the work.

We suspect that Johnson, who must have focused more on the overall impact he thought the book would have, paid little attention to what he assumed to be largely technical editing on Thomson's part, and that he gave Thomson's text to the printer without first having compared it carefully to Stedman's original. Only after Stedman saw the printed pages in 1795—when it was too late to restore most of the altered text (much of which, after all, had been changed quite subtly)—would Johnson have realized, from Stedman's complaints, the extent of the changes. And Johnson probably argued to Stedman, in fact with some justice, that the overall message of the book had not really been changed at all. Although Thomson had systematically edited out such explicit passages as "thus in 20 Years two millions of People are murdered to Provide us with Coffee & Sugar" (1790/1988, 533; see 1796, 2:279; cf. p. 273), Johnson understood that the *Narrative* (with its numerous chilling eyewitness accounts of barbaric tortures of slaves and its graphic accompanying illustrations) would, even in its edited form, stand as one of the strongest indictments ever to appear against plantation slavery. And public reaction bore him out: upon publication, the *Analytical Review* claimed:

> It will be impossible to peruse the numerous relations of shocking cruelties and barbarities contained in these volumes without a degree of painful sympathy, which will often rise into horrour. Many of the facts are indeed so dreadful, that nothing could justify the writer in narrating them, but the hope of inciting in the breasts of his readers a degree of indignation, which will stimulate vigorous and effectual exertions for the speedy termination of the execrable traffic in human flesh, which, to the disgrace of civilized society, is still suffered to exist and is, even in christian countries, sanctioned by law. (September 1796, 225–26)

And the influential *Critical Review* (January 1797, 53) observed, similarly, that "we have never opened any work which is so admirably calculated to excite the most heart-felt abhorrence and detestation of that grossest insult on human nature,—domestic slavery."

A History of the Minnesota Manuscript

Despite several years of research (in England, Germany, the Netherlands, France, and Suriname), we cannot trace the complete path of Stedman's manuscript "Narrative" from the house in Tiverton where he died in 1797 to its present home in the James Ford Bell Library at the University of Minnesota. But certain phases of its life history have been possible to reconstruct.

A major bundle of clues turned up in England, but it was via a roundabout German route that we came upon them. Through a literary connection, we had learned that an eccentric elderly descendant of Stedman lived in what was described to us as a "castle on the Rhine," and that she kept there a great deal of material relating to his life and work. In 1980 RP traveled to Germany to see for himself. Hilda von Barton Stedman, then ninety-two years old, greeted him in overalls and mud-covered boots; she had been working in her vineyards on a beautiful hillside facing Koblenz am Rhein. (Her magnificent home, Haus Besselich—a medieval abbey, part of which she had turned into a family archive—had been bought in 1834 by her grandfather, himself the grandson of John Gabriel's brother [Schlegel 1980, 76].) After inviting RP to sample her fine Rhine wine, she led him to her library, and they chatted about her illustrious ancestor, who turned out to be her father's father's father's father's brother (see fig. 11).[36]

Hilda quickly made clear that she felt special affinities to the man she referred to casually as John Gabriel. She also offered a lead in our search for traces of the original "Narrative": among many interesting anecdotes, she recounted how, not long after World War II, she had visited a distant cousin in England and found that the latter possessed a large stack of John Gabriel Stedman's papers and manuscripts. This woman vigorously disliked the Stedman side of her family, however, calling John Gabriel "a terrible man," vehemently denying any interest in the papers, and not even allowing Hilda to see them except from across the room. Not only had John Gabriel married a "black" woman, the cousin explained, but his side of the family was much less distinguished than her own ("The Earl of Such-and-Such and Lady So-and-So," Hilda mimicked her). Hilda also mentioned that this English cousin was *much* older than she. A

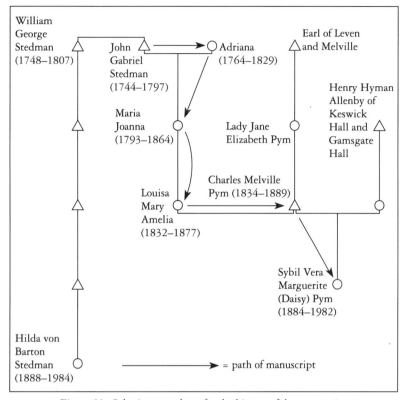

Figure 11. Selective genealogy for the history of the manuscript

many-month-long attempt to retrieve the name and address of this distant Stedman relation from Hilda's lively but erratic memory, and a second pilgrimage to her abbey on the Rhine by the two of us, finally bore fruit through the good offices of her niece, who found written in an old address book in Hilda's desk: "Miss S. V. M. Pym," with an indication that she was a Stedman descendant, and an address in Louth, Lincolnshire.

When a ninety-two-year-old talks of a long-past encounter with someone who she says was "Much, much older than I," one tends to entertain little hope of interviewing the person in question. So, on advice from an English friend, we wrote to the vicar at Louth, Miss Pym's last known address, to ascertain the date of her death and find out whether she had any descendants. What we received by return mail was a message from the manager of the Mablethorpe Hall Old People's Home, near Louth, saying that Miss Pym (or "Daisy"), who was ninety-eight years old, would be delighted to receive us. Not wishing to press our luck, RP hurried out to buy a fine box of Dutch chocolates (we were living in Holland at the time) and set out posthaste across the Channel.

Although Daisy proved considerably more charming than informative during the teatime visit, information provided by her solicitors and her two closest friends in Louth, combined with information from Hilda as well as with other oral and documentary sources, permitted us to reconstruct a trajectory for Stedman's manuscript "Narrative" that we consider highly probable, beginning at the house in Tiverton where he died in 1797 and ending at its present home in Minneapolis.

The genealogical information in Figure 11 helps explain Daisy's negative attitude toward Stedman. Not only did her ancestry indeed include earls and ladies, but her connection to the Stedman family was solely through her father's childless marriage to John Gabriel's granddaughter, who had died a certified lunatic, presumably with considerable disgrace to the family, before Daisy's mother became his second wife.

This same genealogy helps us trace the path of the manuscript itself. During the early 1790s, while the "Narrative" and its accompanying illustrations were in press, Stedman kept the original manuscript with him at Tiverton (apparently traveling with it while correcting proofs in 1795 in London). After Stedman's death in 1797, his widow, Adriana, took possession of his papers. Though she changed residence several times, she finally settled down in Maastricht, where she lived with a servant, close to the house of their youngest daughter, Maria Joanna, and her husband. In 1829, Adriana died there; Maria Joanna handled her mother's affairs, and we presume that she took possession of her father's manuscripts and papers at that time. Years later, one of Maria Joanna's daughters, Louisa Mary Amelia, married Charles Melville Pym and moved to his estate at Woodpark (Ballyclough, County Cork, Ireland), bringing Maria Joanna to live with them. When Maria Joanna died there in 1864, Louisa Mary Amelia in turn took over her affairs, including the papers originally belonging to her own grandfather, John Gabriel. Soon thereafter, Louisa Mary Amelia and Charles moved to Yorkshire, where he assumed the post of rector of Cherry Burton, and where she became mentally ill, eventually dying, childless, of "Acute Mania" in the "Lunatic Hospital St. Giles." After his wife's death, Charles remarried and in 1884 had a daughter, Sybil Vera Marguerite ("Daisy") Pym, who we now have reason to believe was the last legitimate private owner of the manuscript of the "Narrative."

Daisy Pym was orphaned at about age five and lived her entire active life at Louth. Along with two younger brothers, she was raised by servants, and she later lived with a single servant, never marrying. It was upon the premature death of Daisy's own parents (about 1890) that she became the grudging keeper of John Gabriel's papers, including his manuscript of the "Narrative." In the mid-1960s, Daisy—who was then an octogenarian—moved into the Mablethorpe Home, leaving her own house, with its contents intact, in the care of two close friends who lived nearby. Soon thereafter, two younger relatives independently visited the house, removing "a chest of drawers and some other things," according to Daisy's friends.[37]

Sometime in late 1965 or early 1966 (according to our oral sources), "two Brighton knockers, very disagreeable chaps," appeared at the door of a well-known London bookseller, peddling a bound manuscript, cheap.[38] Within a few weeks of its purchase, and despite the fact that the very knowledgeable bookseller's assistant suspected that the manuscript was the original copy of Stedman's *Narrative,* "the guv'nor" (his boss) insisted on selling it at a low price to a Danish bookseller then making his London rounds. These transactions occurred in sufficiently quick succession so that the London bookseller failed to notice the existence of a small original watercolor by Stedman (see fig. 9), which lay between two leaves in the middle of the volume. In March 1966, not long after the manuscript had been removed to Copenhagen, Dr. John Parker, curator of the James Ford Bell Library, was shown the manuscript by Rosenkilde & Bagger, Booksellers, and arranged for its purchase. Some twelve years later, Professor Stuart Schwartz of the Department of History, University of Minnesota, apprised us of the existence of a Stedman manuscript that he had seen in the James Ford Bell Library and that he thought might be of interest. RP arranged to examine it in the fall of 1978; at that time, he confirmed the identity of the manuscript and began the research that led to the 1988 edition and the present abridgment.

THE PRESENT EDITION

In abridging our critical edition of the 1790 "Narrative" (1988) to include about 50 percent of the original text and 33 of the original 81 plates, we have attempted to leave intact as much as possible of Stedman's first-hand observations about the daily life of slaves, planters, soldiers, and maroons. We have deleted large portions of the text devoted to historical background and Amerindian ethnography (most of which Stedman borrowed from unreliable secondary sources), as well as many of his botanical and zoological descriptions and a substantial number of the literary passages (mostly verse) that he incorporated into his manuscript. We have also omitted most of Stedman's own poetry.[39]

The text of this abridged edition is "normalized"; that is, we have reg-

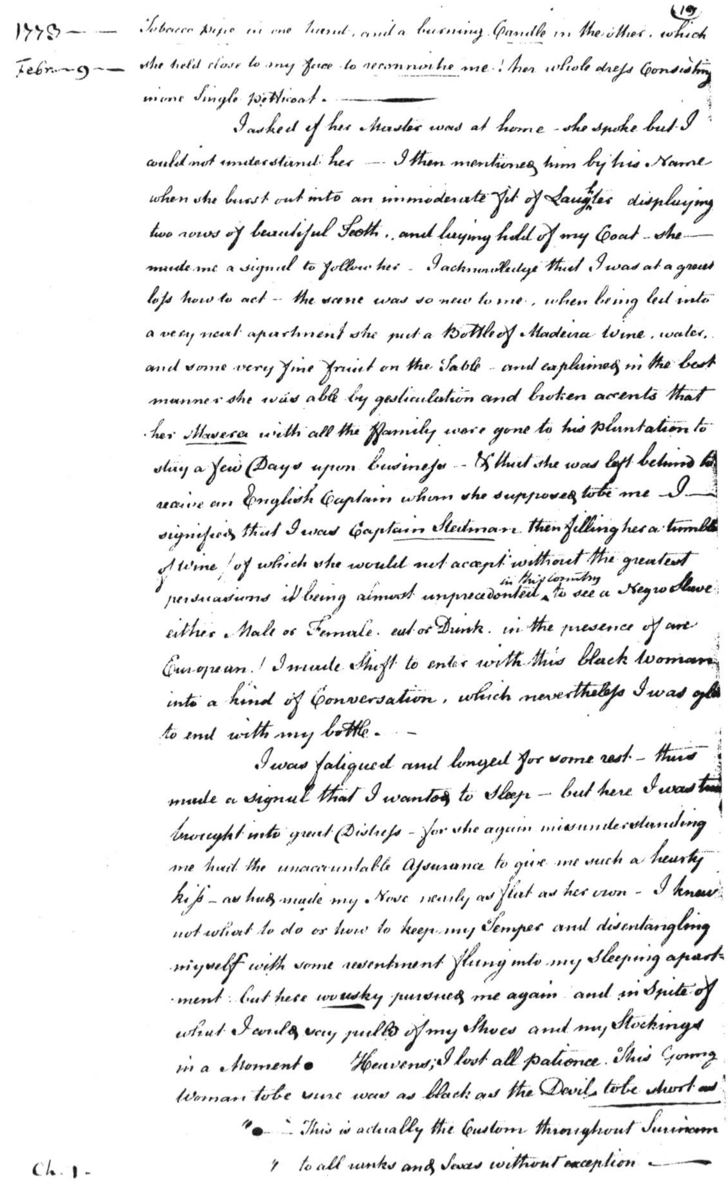

Tobacco pipe in one hand, and a burning Candle in the other. which
she held close to my face to reconnoitre me! her whole dress Consisting
none Single petticoat. ———

I asked if her Master was at home — she spoke but I
could not understand her ——— I then mentioned him by his Name
when she burst out into an immoderate fit of laughter displaying
two rows of beautiful teeth, and laying hold of my Coat — she —
made me a signal to follow her — I acknowledge that I was at a great
loss how to act — the scene was so new to me, when being led into
a very neat apartment she put a Bottle of Madeira wine, water,
and some very fine fruit on the Table — and explained in the best
manner she was able by gesticulation and broken accents that
her Master with all the family were gone to his plantation to
stay a few Days upon business — & that she was left behind to
receive an English Captain whom she supposed to be me — I
signified that I was Captain Stedman, then filling her a tumbler
of wine, / of which she would not accept without the greatest
persuasions it being almost unprecedented in this country to see a Negro Slave
either, Male or Female, eat or Drink, in the presence of an
European! I made Shift to enter with this black woman
into a kind of Conversation, which nevertheless I was glad
to end with my bottle. ——

I was fatigued and longed for some rest — thus
made a signal that I wanted to Sleep — but here I was
brought into great Distress — for she again misunderstanding
me had the unaccountable Assurance to give me such a hearty
kiss — as had made my Nose nearly as flat as her own — I knew
not what to do or how to keep my Temper and disentangling
myself with some resentment flung into my Sleeping apartment but here wusky pursued me again and in Spite of
what I could say pulled of my Shoes and my Stockings
in a Moment ● Heavens; I lost all patience. This young
Woman to be sure was as black as the Devil to be short and

● ¯ This is actually the Custom throughout Surinam
† to all ranks and Sexes without exception ——

Ch. 1.

Figure 12. A page from Stedman's 1790 "Narrative." James Ford Bell Library,
University of Minnesota.

ularized Stedman's inconsistent, idiosyncratic, and often charming spelling and punctuation, rectified a few incorrect word choices, and changed word order in some places for greater clarity.[40] Our intent throughout has been to effect the kind of light copy editing Stedman envisioned when he expressed the hope that his manuscript would be "properly prepared for the Eye of the Publick by the able Pen of a candid and ingeneous Compiler" (1790/1988, 25). A brief example may serve to illustrate the sorts of editorial changes we have made; we present here Stedman's initial description of his lover Joanna from the beginning of Chapter 5—on the left as it appeared in his 1790 manuscript, and on the right as it appears in our abridgment:

Having before said that from our Arrival till for several Weeks after, we seem'd to be landed in Guiana for nothing but idle dissipation till viz. Feb–27–I shall now proceed from March 1st the same Year, and just about the beginning of the rainy-Season, when our Life of Mirth and Joviality still continued, and diversify the mind of the reader after the preceeding Scenes of Horror by giving of a Description of the beautifull Mulatto Maid Joanna—

This fine young Woman–I first saw at the house of a Mr *Demelly* Secretary to the Court of Policy where I daily breakfasted, and of whose Lady, *Johanna* aged then but 15 Years was a verry remarkable favourite—

Rather more than middle Size–She was perfectly streight with the most elegant Shapes that can be view'd in nature moving her well-form'd Limbs as when a Goddess walk'd— Her face was full of Native Modesty and the most distinguished Sweetness–Her Eyes as black as Ebony were large and full of expression, bespeaking the Goodness of her heart. With Cheeks through which glow'd /in spite of her olive Complexion/ a beautiful tinge of vermillion when gazed upon–her nose was perfectly

Having said before that from our arrival till several weeks after, we seemed to be landed in Guiana for nothing but idle dissipation, I shall now proceed from March 1st of the same year, just about the beginning of the rainy season, when our life of mirth and joviality still continued, and diversify the mind of the reader after the preceding scenes of horror by giving a description of the beautiful Mulatto maid Joanna.

This fine young woman I first saw at the house of a Mr. Demelly, secretary to the Court of Policy, where I daily breakfasted, and of whose lady, Joanna, aged then but fifteen years, was a very remarkable favorite.

Rather more than middle-sized, she was perfectly straight with the most elegant shapes that can be viewed in nature, moving her well-formed limbs as when a goddess walked. Her face was full of native modesty and the most distinguished sweetness. Her eyes, as black as ebony, were large and full of expression, bespeaking the goodness of her heart. With cheeks through which glowed (in spite of her olive complexion) a beautiful tinge of vermilion when gazed upon, her nose was perfectly well-formed and rather small, well formed rather small, her lips a little prominent which when she spoke discovered two regular rows of pearls as white as Mountain Snow—her hair was a dark brown–next to black, forming a beauteous Globe of small ringlets, ornamented with flowers and Gold Spangles—round her neck her Arms and her ancles she wore Gold Chains rings and Medals– while a Shaul of finest indian Muslin the end of which was negligently thrown over her polished Shoulder gracefully covered part of her lovely bosom–a petticoat of richest Chints alone made out the rest bare headed and bare footed she shone with double lustre carrying in her delicate hand a bever hat the crown trim'd rown with Silver—The figure and dress of this fine Creature could not but attract my particular notice, as she did indeed of all who beheld her, which induced me to ask of Mrs Demelly in the name of wonder who she was that appeared so much distinguished above all the rest of her Species in the Colony, and which request this Lady obligingly granted—

her lips a little prominent which, when she spoke, discovered two regular rows of pearls as white as mountain snow. Her hair was a dark brown, next to black, forming a beauteous globe of small ringlets, ornamented with flowers and gold spangles. Round her neck, her arms, and her ankles she wore gold chains, rings, and medals, while a shawl of finest Indian muslin, the end of which was negligently thrown over her polished shoulder, gracefully covered part of her lovely bosom. A petticoat of richest chintz alone made out the rest. Bareheaded and barefooted, she shone with double luster, carrying in her delicate hand a beaver hat, the crown trimmed round with silver. The figure and dress of this fine creature could not but attract my particular notice, as she did indeed of all who beheld her, which induced me to ask of Mrs. Demelly, in the name of wonder, who she was that appeared so much distinguished above all the rest of her species in the colony, and which request this lady obligingly granted.

Notes to the Introduction

1. In our Introduction, all references in italics are to Stedman's manuscript diaries, now at the University of Minnesota. Most such references list day, month, year (e.g., *2 February 1792*), but for those cases in which Stedman did not specify day and month we simply list the year (e.g., *1795*). During 1785–86, Stedman wrote a series of retrospective diary entries—in effect, an autobiography covering the period 1744–72—which we refer to here as *1786;* our page references to this manuscript correspond to the complex handwritten numeration system employed by Stedman (see also n. 15, below). In transcribing Stedman's diaries, we retain the slashes (/) that he used throughout in lieu of parentheses.

2. Stedman's letter was considered sufficiently admirable to be published during his lifetime in the *Weekly Entertainer* and several other such periodicals and, in 1819, in R. Turner's *The Fashionable Letter Writer* (Thompson 1966, 62–63); the full text was also published by Thompson (ibid.).

3. During the course of the eighteenth century, the idea of the Great Chain of Being was invoked both to emphasize the differences between Europeans and Africans (Thomas Jefferson's famous argument that Negroes stood exactly halfway between whites and the highest apes [see Jordan 1968, 490] or Long's lengthy proof of "the natural inferiority of Negroes" that was capped by the rhetorical question of whether they were not "a different species of the same GENUS" [1774, 2:352–77]) and to stress their common humanity (as Stedman often did—sometimes invoking Linnaeus's nonhierarchical principles of natural classification [e.g., p. 259]). For an excellent discussion of these issues, see Jordan 1968.

4. Stedman refers to *"Bampfield-Moore-Carew"* in the "Narrative" (1790/1988, 229) and seems to have regarded him "as a kindred spirit . . . [for whom he] felt particular esteem and admiration" (Snell 1904, 138). Carew (born in either 1693 or 1703) was the son of a Devonshire rector who ran off and joined the gypsies at an early age, was accused of swindling and fled to Newfoundland, and returned to England where he eloped with the daughter of an apothecary and was chosen King of the Gypsies. Convicted of vagrancy, he was transported as a prisoner to Maryland, escaped to the Indians, successfully posed as a Quaker in Pennsylvania, returned to England, won prizes in the lottery, and died in either 1758 or 1770 (Stephen and Lee 1967–68; Thompson 1966, 80; van Lier 1971, xii). Stedman was, in fact, buried near the Gypsy King at Bickleigh, according to his own "odd" wishes (Snell 1904, 138).

5. Stedman's position regarding the expression of unvarnished truths was characteristic of contemporary authors of illustrated travel accounts.

> A further consequence of the scientific (that is, factually motivated) travel description is its favoring of a plain, rhetorically unornamented, and seemingly artless style. . . . The struggle to find an innocent mode of literary and visual expression that would convincingly do justice to the novelty of the material circumstances encountered is discussed in the preface to every notable relation of a voyage of discovery published between the middle of the eighteenth century and the middle of the nineteenth. (Stafford 1984, 28)

6. Excellent analyses of the internal structure of these groups, with rich, previously unpublished supporting documents, may be found in de Beet 1984 and Hoogbergen 1985. The reader interested in military aspects of Stedman's "Narrative," which we have chosen not to cover in detail, is urged to consult those works. Considerable further military data relating to these wars may be found in the voluminous correspondence of Stedman's commander, Colonel Fourgeoud, now in the Algemeen Rijksarchief (Coll. Fagel); although we have read through many of these materials, their level of detail places them beyond the scope of this essay.

7. Stedman's "translations" of the names of maroon villages, which he "thought so *verry Sentimental*" and which have been taken at face value by many readers of the "Narrative" (e.g., Bubberman et al. 1973, 62; Counter and Evans 1981, 272), are in fact the fanciful products of a romantic sensibility. "Kebree me," which Stedman renders as "Hide me O ye Surrounding Verdure," means simply "Hide me"; "Boucou," which Stedman translates as "It shall moulder before it Shall be taken" means, rather, "fog" or "mold" (and most likely referred to the swampy location of the village); and so on (1790/1988, 400; cf. p. 208). More accurate accounts of the names and locations of the villages to which Stedman refers in the "Narrative," including excellent maps, may be found in de Beet 1984 and Hoogbergen 1985.

8. Blacks had long provided the numerical core of antimaroon military expeditions in Suriname, but during the early and mid-eighteenth century they had always been nonmanumitted plantation slaves, used in unarmed support roles (R. Price 1983b). In 1770, for the first time, a corps of free "coloureds" and blacks (not specially manumitted for this purpose) was formed (the so-called Corps Vrije Mulatten en Neegers), but they met with little military success. In contrast, the Neeger Vrijcorps, or corps of Rangers, formed in 1772, was unusually effective and became especially feared by Boni and his allies, as various testimonies of captured maroons attest (de Beet 1984). Stedman himself had no doubts about the superiority of the Rangers over his European troops, "*one* of these free negroes . . . [being] Preferable to half a Dozen White men in the *Woods* of Guiana" (1790/1988, 396; cf. p. 204). For comparative materials on the use of black troops by Caribbean colonial governments during slavery, see Buckley 1979.

9. Stedman describes the siege and fall of Boucou from second-hand sources (pp. 35–39). The documents in de Beet 1984 provide far richer eyewitness descriptions, by both soldiers and members of Boni's group. See also de Groot 1975 and Hoogbergen 1985.

10. Fourgeoud, a personal friend of the Prince of Orange, was a rather eccentric, obsessive Swiss-born professional officer who had earlier served the Dutch in putting down the great Berbice slave rebellion of 1763 (Hartsinck 1770).

11. A much smaller cordon path had already been constructed in 1770 in the eastern coastal region. Nepveu's more ambitious cordon was, in fact, built between 1774 and 1778, and it soon had more than one thousand men stationed permanently at its various posts (Bubberman et al. 1973, 64; Essed 1984, 52–53; see also pp. 282 and 303). This cordon, maintained at least in part until 1842, did not, however, achieve its purpose.

12. These figures are taken from van Lier (1971, xiv). Stedman claimed that a total of twelve hundred troops were sent to Suriname, with less than one hundred returning (p. 315; but see also p. 254).

13. It was not until 1789 that Boni's people once again commenced hostilities in Suriname territory, initiating what has come to be called the Second Boni War (1789–93); see Hoogbergen 1984, 1985.

14. Years later, Stedman wrote of the "small green almanack that I Carried in my pocket during the Expedition through Danger—Disease, Famine, water, Smoak & Fire—& which long & Constant Hardships having so much defaced the Above little Green Book that its most Recent Contents became to all but to myself unintelligible" (1790/1988, 8). This notebook and other Suriname fieldnotes are now at the James Ford Bell Library, University of Minnesota. Though some passages are difficult to read, they are on the whole legible.

15. The autobiographical sketch, though written in 1785 and 1786, often adopted a presentist perspective, taking on the style of diary entries written contemporaneously with the events reported. The diaries also include at least some comments written well after the dates under which they were entered, though this is apparent only from a careful reading. Thus, in the entry dated 21 April 1778, Stedman reported giving his mother "Security for 50f per annum. . . . I payd til 6 May 1779." In the entry for 24 February 1785, he noted receiving "news that W. Macbeath was drownd which was afterwards proved to be falce"; this comment was followed by one dated 27 June stating, "the raport of W. Macbeaths being drownd contradictid." And for 1 December 1791, he recorded that "I wrote to the En-

graver blake to thank him twice for his excellent work but never received any answer."

16. Thompson relates how,

> about the year 1940 . . . I acquired the journal from a junk dealer in Pimlico, London. The man submitted the sheets (the journal comprised of about one hundred loose pages, letters, etc.) to me as a job lot, all mixed, all jumbled together, creased, and partly torn, for a few shillings. . . .
>
> "'Ere guv'nor! a pile o' old letters cheap. A dollar the lot. Tek 'em out a mi' road," were his words.
>
> A quick glance at a few sheets assured me of the fact that I had in my possession an original old 18th century manuscript journal. (1966, 131–32)

In the late 1960s, before Thompson's death, John Maggs visited him and arranged to purchase Stedman's diaries and letters; in 1981, we were able in turn to arrange for them to be acquired from Maggs Brothers by the James Ford Bell Library. We do not know the path by which these materials traveled from Stedman's house in Tiverton, upon his death in 1797, to the Pimlico junk dealer in 1940. But we suspect that they may have been passed down, along with the manuscript of the "Narrative" itself, to Miss Pym, who may have simply disposed of them as worthless clutter in the late 1930s (see pp. lxii–lxv).

17. This image had also apparently troubled the editor of Stedman's "Narrative" who, during the 1790s, excised the final six words of the author's comment about the piranhas snapping off "the fingers and breasts of Women and the private Parts of Men" (1790/1988, 131; 1796, 1:149).

18. Sometimes, instead of "fooled," Thompson printed "***" (e.g., 1962, 115); and once he replaced Stedman's clearly written "fuk" with a dash and an explanatory footnote that read "Become intimate" (1962, 185).

19. Stedman's European marriage took place on 2 February 1782 (Thompson 1962, 234). Joanna died, possibly from the effects of poison, on 5 November 1782; Stedman did not learn of her death until August 1783. In spite of his sentimentality about Joanna throughout the "Narrative" (and despite his fudging of this chronology there—pp. 316–18), he seems to have decided well before her death to keep her simply as a precious memory and not to seek to bring her to Europe. Similarly, soon after his return to Holland from Suriname, Stedman divested himself of his personal slave, "my true & Faithful Black boy *Quaccoo*," by making a present of him to the Countess of Rosendaal (1790/1988, 620).

20. Stedman was able to guarantee a sum to Johnson by having raised, as of early 1791, ninety-two subscriptions at a guinea each. By date of publication in 1796, the list of subscribers had grown to two hundred (for 208 copies), in large part due to Stedman's incessant letter writing and personal solicitations, drawing on his Dutch, Scottish, and Suriname connections (including some of the participants in the events of the "Narrative"), on his acquaintances in Devonshire and London, and on career military officers elsewhere. Johnson had apparently agreed, upon accepting the manuscript in 1790, to pay Stedman "£500 & chance for 1000" should the book prove successful (*2 February 1792*), and in 1793 Stedman requested and received an advance of £212.10.0 (*25 December 1793*). Production of the plates would have cost Johnson at least £5 each and probably a good deal more, making a total of £400 at the very least (G. E. Bentley, Jr., personal communication, 1984). When the book was finally published in two quarto volumes in 1796, its price was quoted variously as £2.12.6, £2.14.0, and £3.3.0 (*British Critic*, November

1796, 536; *Critical Review,* January 1797, 52; *Analytical Review,* September 1796, 225).

21. The two exceptions are labeled in Stedman's 1790 "Directions for the Plates" as "Snake" or "Slake," intended for manuscript page 234 and apparently related to the description there of a wounded maroon named Snakee (see pp. 110–11), and "The Chastisement call'd Spanso Bocko," a punitive torture described in detail on manuscript page 720 (p. 291), where the reader is referred to a plate that Johnson may have deleted because of its particularly grisly character, anticipating such commentary as appeared in the *British Critic* (November 1796, 539): "The representations of the negroes suffering under various kinds of torture, might well have been omitted, . . . for we will not call them embellishments to the work."

22. Stedman lavished special care on this portrait of himself. Since the publication of the 1988 critical edition, we have learned that, apparently dissatisfied with his own depiction of his face, Stedman engaged the academician John Francis Rigaud to make a portrait which could serve as a model for the engraver. Rigaud describes having produced

> A small oval portrait of Mr. Stedman . . . intended to direct the engraver in regard to his likeness and expression, in a frontispiece to his book. . . . I only did the head. . . . I did it in one day, and was particularly successful in the character [of] the expression. (Rigaud 1984, 82)

Rigaud incidentally makes clear that, in 1790, Stedman had not yet chosen the verse that graces the frontispiece, at that time intending instead to use simply "My hands are guilty, but my heart is free" (ibid.).

23. Smith, who was the first to make this comparison, concluded that "there is no finer expression of the idea of the noble savage in visual art than Blake's engraving." Smith also suggested that the male Loango slave in Blake's engraving for Stedman's plate 68 was "a graceful and dignified . . . embodiment of youthful masculine beauty [that] may be compared with the striding male figure in *A Family of New South Wales*" (Smith 1960, 128–29).

24. We describe the fifteen surviving artworks by Stedman that are known to us in Stedman 1790/1988, LXXXIX–XC. We list there also all versions of those artworks produced by him about which we have any information (Stedman 1790/1988, XCI–XCII).

25. We believe (as, apparently, did Keynes [1971, 103]) that all the original 1796 hand-colored copies are on large paper, which distinguishes them from copies colored later—often a century after publication. Likewise, all large paper copies we have seen (or corresponded about) are hand colored.

26. A close reading of Stedman's diary makes clear that Thomson must have produced an entirely new manuscript (now lost) from Stedman's 1790 text, and that it was from this new manuscript that Johnson, in 1795, had Luke Hansard print what he then thought would be the first edition. We now believe that the often-faint pencil "cancellation" marks across many passages on Stedman's personal copy of the manuscript (now at Minnesota) were made by him during the summer of 1795, as he read in anger through the printed pages for the first time, noting to himself what Johnson (actually Thomson) had deleted or altered. Comparison of Stedman's marks with the 1796 first edition suggests both the extensiveness of the changes that Johnson/Thomson had expected to be able to make in Stedman's text and Stedman's success in getting a certain number of the alterations reinstated.

27. Stedman's book, even in its edited (1796) form, still falls squarely within the sty-

listic temper of his age and exhibits the characteristic rhetoric of its genre. In her study of the contemporary illustrated travel book, Stafford points to an "emphatically masculine" style and notes that "a hardy virility thus became a peculiar prerogative of the traveler's scientifically educated eye" (1984, 49). After citing various supporting examples, she singles out one author who "captures this attitude best, stating [in 1821] that he composed in a 'natural and manly language as it would become an English naval officer to write'" (ibid., 50).

28. Tales of lascivious monkeys, apes, and orangutans ran rampant through eighteenth-century travel literature. It is an indication of Stedman's lack of racialism, relative to his contemporaries, that he depicts the potential mate of his howler monkeys as the (generalized) female of the *human* species, rather than specifying— as was common practice—the female African or Hottentot (see, for example, Jordan 1968, 229–30, 490–93).

29. His corresponding promotions in the British Service culminated in his appointment to lieutenant colonel in May 1796 [*14 May 1796*].

30. Stedman's fears were not merely abstract; among the subscribers to his book, for example, were two people bearing the same surname as Mrs. Nagel, whom Stedman had originally described as "a hott bich" (*5 March 1776*) but who appears more anonymously and decorously in 1790 (1988, 483) and 1796 (2:211) simply as "Mrs N."

31. See note to page 19, below.

32. Stedman's descriptions of this encounter clearly touched on themes that fascinated the European audience. A passage from a contemporary satirical account, describing a visit to a Barbados plantation, displays similar concerns:

> Towards the evening the gentleman [the narrator's planter host] asked me if I would look at his hen negroes. I accepted the proposal, and we walked along a rank of about thirty females of that species. He then asked me how I liked them. I said that perhaps it was owing to prejudice that I did not think them very amiable. After supper he conducted me to my apartment, where I was surprised to find a very pretty mulatto girl. My friend told me, that as I did not seem to like any of his hen negroes, he had sent to a planter of his acquaintance to borrow a beauty of a somewhat lighter hue. I thanked him, told him there was no occasion for such an attention, and expressed my sorrow at his incurring such an obligation on my account.
>
> "Oh!", answered he, "that is nothing; I shall lend him one of my people to work at his sugar-mill tomorrow, which you know is much the same thing." Though this extraordinary attention of the West-Indian shocked the morality of my ideas, yet, as I have always made it a rule to conform to the customs of the countries I visit, I invited the young mulatto girl to get into bed.
>
> "Ki, Ki!" cried the tawny beauty, starting back with the greatest marks of astonishment. Upon my renewing my solicitations, she told me that it was a liberty she could never think of taking; that the mat at the bed-side was destined for her bed; and, "if massa," said she, "want ee chambepot, he will put he hand out of bed; if he want me, he will puttee out he foot."— There was something droll in this arrangement, but however, it was convenient, and I thought it a thousand pities that Providence should visit so hospitable a country with such frequent hurricanes. (Corncob 1787, 70–71)

33. Changes in the Joanna story between the 1790 and 1796 versions are somewhat less

consistent than other substantive editorial alterations. The motivation for one addition—the mention of Stedman's "wedding" to Joanna (1796, 1:106)—remains
unclear to us, as it seems inconsistent with most of the other changes. We would
speculate, however, that the editor's attempts to depersonalize the relationship
throughout the text may have caused Stedman, when he first saw the edited version in 1795, to insert this passage as a step toward righting the balance. And the
fact that he referred to a "decent wedding," rather than to "Suriname marriage,"
may have been his way of circumventing the problems that had caused him to
leave out any mention of the ceremony in 1790 (see p. xxxiii).

34. The deletion of references to the beauty of African or mulatto slaves, as well as to
their personal cleanliness relative to local Europeans, was frequent throughout the
work (as was the complementary deletion of Stedman's various comments about
the unattractiveness of European women in Suriname).

35. Stedman himself, of course, had not only been "married," Suriname-style, to a
slave (Joanna), he had owned the young slave "Qwacco" (whom he had purchased
for 500 florins) until 1777, when he bestowed "my true & Faithful Black boy"
upon the Countess of Rosendaal to become her butler (1790/1988, 340, 620). And
on 20 February 1792, Stedman's diary unequivocally records, "I refuse Mr. Sam-
son & parson Land to put my name on the petition for the abolution of slaves"
[i.e., for the abolition of the slave trade].

36. Our genealogical evidence comes from family papers and interviews kindly provided by Hilda Emge–von Barton Stedman and her aunt Hilda von Barton Stedman, as well as from Thompson (1966).

37. We have been able to contact the person who is said, by the custodians of the
house, to have removed the chest of drawers, but he denies any knowledge of
Stedmaniana; the other relative in question, who lives in the south of England not
far from Brighton, has not replied to our repeated inquiries. Unfortunately, the
solicitor who handled Miss Pym's affairs until the 1960s, and who—it is said—
would have known exactly what she did and did not own in the way of Stedmaniana, is (like so many of Miss Pym's contemporaries) now deceased.

38. In British parlance, "knockers" are sharp-eyed men who, getting a foot in the door
by one fast-talking means or another, offer to buy a painting, book, or other un-
suspected valuable for a pittance from an innocent, usually elderly, person in need
of cash, and then unload it quickly in another town, no questions asked. "Brighton knockers" are said to be "the worst of the lot."

39. The complete critical edition includes (in addition to the full text of the 1790 "Narrative") Stedman's Dedication, Preface to the Manuscript, and Advertisement to
the Reader, all omitted here. More extensive editors' notes (including the identification of flora, fauna, and literary citations) are also given there. Moreover, the
introduction to that edition describes in detail the 1790 manuscript itself (which is
available to scholars at the James Ford Bell Library of the University of Minnesota), includes a descriptive listing of all published editions, translations, and re-
prints of the "Narrative," and provides a comparison of the plates in various editions.

40. Our choice of spellings for names of persons and places has, of necessity, been
somewhat arbitrary, as Stedman—like other contemporary sources in Suriname—
often used several variants. In each case, our decision results from a consideration
of the identity of the most frequent speakers of the name (slaves, masters, JGS),
whether it comes from Dutch, English, French, or Sranan, which spelling JGS

preferred, what spelling is now generally accepted (on maps, in histories, etc.), and so forth. For words and phrases in Sranan, we have retained Stedman's own spellings; in his orthography, both *oe* and *oo* represent the vowel sound in English "food." Note that in some cases we adopt different orthographic conventions for Stedman's eighteenth-century text (e.g., Surinam, Marawina) and our own twentieth-century prose (Suriname, Marowijne).

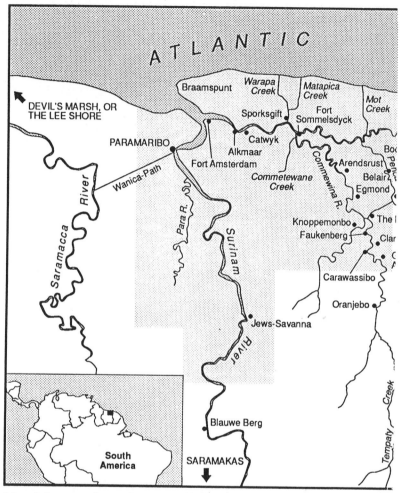

Map of places most frequently mentioned by JGS in his 1790 "Narrative."

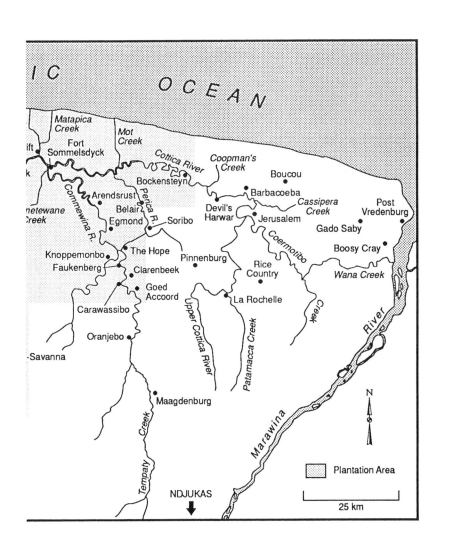

AT
LANTIC
OCEAN

Matapica
Creek

Mot
Creek

Fort
Sommelsdyck

ift

k

Cottica River

Coopman's
Creek

Boucou

Bockensteyn

Commewina R.

Arendsrust

Perica R.

Barbacoeba

Cassipera
Creek

Post
Vredenburg

netewane
Creek

Belair

Egmond

Soribo

Devil's
Harwar

Jerusalem

Gado Saby

Boosy Cray

Knoppemonbo

The Hope

Pinnenburg

Coermotibo

Wana Creek

Faukenberg

Clarenbeek

Rice
Country

Goed
Accoord

La Rochelle

Creek

Carawassibo

Oranjebo

Upper Cottica River

Patamacca Creek

Savanna

Maagdenburg

Marawina

River

N

Tempaty Creek

NDJUKAS

Plantation Area

25 km

STEDMAN'S SURINAM

Stedman Pinxt. *Bartolozzi Sculpt.*

"From different Parents, different Climes we came,
At different Periods;" Fate still rules the same.
Unhappy Youth while bleeding on the ground;
'Twas Yours to fall—but Mine to feel the wound.

London. Published Dec.r 1.st 1794. by J. Johnson, S.t Paul's Church Yard.

Narrative
of a five years expedition against
the Revolted
Negroes of Surinam
In Guiana on the Wild Coast of
South-America

From the year 1772 to the year 1777

With some Elucidation on the History of that Country & the
discription of its Productions **viz**
Quadrupedes–Birds–Fishes–Reptiles, trees, Shrubs–Fruits & Roots
besides an Account of the Indians of Guiana & Negroes of Guinea

---

by Lieut: Col: J: G: Stedman

Ornamented with 80 Engravings
design'd from nature by him on the Spot

O Quantum terra Quantum Cognoscere Coeli,
Permissum est! pelagus quantos aperimus in usus!
Nunc Forsam grave reris opus: sed loeta, recurret,
Cum rutis, et, Caram. Cum, mitri reddet Iolcon;
Quis pador heu nostros tibi tunc audire labores;
Quam referam visas tua per suspiria gentis!

Led by our Stars what tracts immence we trace,
From fear remote, what funds of Science raise!
A pain to thought; but when th'Heroic band,
Returns triumphant to their native Land,
A Life domestic you will then deplore,
And sigh whilst I describe the various Shore!
Valerius Flaccus

4

TABLE OF CONTENTS

CHAPTER 28th

CHAPTER 29th

CHAPTER 30th

PLATES

CHAPTER 1st

*Insurrection among the Negroes in Dutch Guiana—An
expedition sets out from the Texel—Short account of the
voyage—The fleet arrives in the river Surinam—Reception of
the troops—Sketch of the inhabitants &c.*

A most dangerous revolt having broken out in the Colony of Surinam
among the Negro slaves who were armed and assembled in the woods
threatening immediate destruction to that settlement, the States of the
United Provinces determined to send out a fresh corps of five hundred
volunteers in 1772, to act conjointly with the troops already there to quell
the insurrection and prevent a general massacre. At this time, I was Lieutenant in the Honorable General Stuart's Regiment of the Scots Brigade
in the Service of Holland and, being impressed by the prospect of preferment usually annexed to so hazardous a service, and in the hopes of grat-
ifying my curiosity in exploring a country so little known, I offered myself to be one of the party. I had the honor to be accepted by His Serene
Highness the Prince of Orange, who immediately advanced me to the
rank of Captain by Brevet in the new corps intended for the expedition
under Colonel Fourgeoud, a Swiss gentleman from Geneva near the Al-
pine mountains, who was invested with the supreme authority and appointed to be our Commander in Chief.

   Having taken the oaths of fidelity on the 12th of November, provided
myself with a case of pistols, and otherwise prepared for the voyage, I
took my last farewell from my old regiment. Three transport ships lay in
the Texel roads to receive us on board and, on the 8th of December, the
troops—being formed into companies and embodied as a regiment of
Marines—were embarked and only waited for the first fair wind to set
sail to South America. At our embarkation we were saluted with seven
guns from each ship in particular, which compliment was again returned

by three cheers from the soldiers, my station being with Colonel Fourgeoud.

On December 24th at eight o'clock in the morning, with a fresh breeze from E.N.E. and the most beautiful weather, our small fleet put to sea in company with above a hundred other vessels, bound for different parts of the globe, and under convoy of the *Westellingwerf* and *Boreas* men-of-war.

On January 2nd, 1773, we had as was expected a very hard gale of wind at N.N.E., with double-reefed topsails and hatches laid fore and aft, which made the poor soldiers very sick. Off Cape Finisterre, we lost sight of the *Boreas* man-of-war and of the transport ship *Vigilance,* which had both parted company with us during the gale. On the 3rd, remaining but two vessels out of five and being now without any convoy, we prepared the ships for defense against the rude African pirates should any of them chance to fall in with us.

The 14th, in the morning watch, we passed the Tropic, where the usual ceremony of ducking was ransomed by tipping the sailors with some silver in an old shoe that was nailed to the mast for the purpose. About this time the convoy most unluckily lost one of her best seamen, the boatswain's mate who, by his too great intrepidity, pitched from the fore yardarm into the waves. His presence of mind in calling to the captain, "Be not alarmed for me, Sir," in the certain hope of meeting with relief, attracted peculiar compassion since no assistance of any kind was offered to him, in consequence of which the unfortunate young man, after swimming a considerable time within view, went to the bottom.

We now were got into the trade winds, which blow perpetually east and differ with the monsoons in that these latter are only seasonal.

The weather here became from day to day more warm, which made it very comfortable. I generally spent my time mast-high above my shipmates, reading a book for amusement in the roundtops, or hauling a rope for exercise. Their company in the cabin was not very desirable owing to seasickness and other complaints, most of them being fresh-water sailors, one or two who had belonged to the navy excepted, as well as a few of those gallant officers who had helped to quell the Negro insurrection in the colony of Berbice in 1763, of whom Colonel Fourgeoud was one. The whole ship's company, officers included, lived on salt provisions alone, a pig and a couple of lean sheep excepted, whose legs had been broken by the rolling and pitching of the vessel. These dinners were sometimes served up in the very tubs employed by the surgeons to void the filth of the sick; we must impute this abominable negligence to Monsieur Laurant, Colonel Fourgeoud's French *valet de chambre.*

On the 22nd, having received a severe fall on the quarter-deck by its being wet and slippery, and finding myself otherwise exceedingly low-spirited, I had recourse to daily bathing in sea water and also made use of a cheering glass of claret with two ankers of which (being about twenty gallons) each officer was provided, in addition to his own stock—part whereof had been industriously filched from me, which I detected from the back of a hencoop. By these means I found such considerable benefit that after a few days, I was perfectly recovered of my complaint but so exasperated that I took revenge on a locker with more than three hundred concealed eggs, which I stove in, and then bedaubed the whole cabin with yolks.

On the 30th, in hazy weather, the ships brought-to and hove the lead in thirteen fathoms foul water.

On the 31st, we passed several large black rocks to windward, called the Constables, and cast anchor near the Euripice, or Devil's, Islands off the coast of South America.

On February 1st, we weighed anchor and, having kept course till the evening, we came to an anchor again, off the River Marawina. This place has been fatal to many ships that have mistaken it for the River Surinam, to which its entry bears a very great resemblance, since this river is so very shallow even at high water that ships of any burden immediately run aground.

On the 2nd, the fleet entered the beautiful River Surinam with a fine breeze, and at three o'clock P.M. dropped anchor before the new fortress called Amsterdam, where the transport ship *Vigilance* had arrived two days before us. The fortress immediately saluted the ships from the batteries and got the compliment returned, and soon after, a longboat with one of our captains was dispatched to Paramaribo to give the Governor notice of the troops having arrived in the Colony.

Here the air was perfumed with the most odoriferous smell in nature, by the many lemons, oranges, shaddocks, &c., with which this country abounds.

When stepping on land, the first object I met was a most miserable young woman in chains, simply covered with a rag round her loins, which was, like her skin, cut and carved by the lash of the whip in a most shocking manner. Her crime was in not having fulfilled her task, to which she was by appearance unable. Her punishment: to receive 200 lashes and for months to drag a chain several yards in length, one end of which was locked to her ankle and at the other end of which was a weight of three score pounds or upwards. She was a beautiful Negro maid, and while I was meditating on the shocking load of her irons I myself barely escaped being riveted by fascination. I now took a draft of the wretched

A Female Negro Slave, with a Weight chained to her Ancle.

Plate 4

creature upon paper, which I here present to the sympathizing reader, and which inspired me with a very unfavorable opinion of the humanity of the planters residing in this colony toward their Negro slaves.

On the 3rd, several officers of the Society or Colony troops, with a number of other gentlemen, came to visit us on board and to welcome us to the Colony, complimenting us with a great quantity of fruits, vegetables, and other refreshments. They were rowed in the most elegant barges or tent-boats by six or eight Negroes, mostly accompanied by flags and small bands of music, which vessels I shall afterwards more amply describe. But what astonished me most of anything was to see all the bargemen as naked as when they were born, a small strip of check or other linen cloth excepted, which was passed between their thighs to cover what decency forbids us to expose and was simply drawn before and behind over a thin cotton string tied around their loins. These men looked very well, being healthy, strong, and young, their skin shining and almost as black as ebony. The colonists generally use their handsomest slaves to row their boats, serve at table, &c. How different from these were one or two canoes filled with half-starved, emaciated wretches that came alongside our ships, begging bits of salt beef or dried fish from the soldiers, and who would even fight for the value of a bone.

On the 5th, a Mr. Rynsdorp came on board and introduced to Colonel Fourgeoud, our Commander in Chief, two black soldiers who were manumitted slaves, part of a recently formed corps numbering three hundred. Mr. Rynsdorp showed us these two men as samples of that valiant body, which had a short time before so gallantly distinguished itself for the welfare of the Colony, and which I shall in proper place make mention of.

On the 6th, I received a most polite invitation from a Mr. Lolkens (a planter to whom I had been recommended) to accept of his house and table at Paramaribo, which is the capital of the Colony.

On the 8th, we at last once more weighed anchor, taking leave of the fortress with nine guns each, which it returned. Sailing up the River Surinam with beating drums, flying colors, and a guard of Marines on the quarter-deck, we finally dropped anchor before the town of Paramaribo at four o'clock P.M., within pistol shot of the shore, having been saluted by the citadel *Zeelandia* with eleven guns on our arrival, which compliment was returned by the man-of-war and by the transport ships.

At this time, all the inhabitants of Paramaribo ran out and flocked together to see the newly arrived troops. And well they might, for a finer corps was never seen in any country—flourishing young men, the eldest scarcely past thirty, all neat and clean, dressed in new uniforms and caps ornamented with twigs of orange blossom.

Having thus paraded on a large green plain between the citadel and the town, in front of the Governor's house, during which time several soldiers fainted from the heat (it being still in the dry season), the companies marched into quarters which were provided for their reception, while the officers were entertained with a most elegant repast by the Governor. The choicest delicacies of Europe and America mixed together were served up in silver plate by a score of the handsomest Indian, Negro, and Mulatto maids in the world, dressed in the finest India chintzes but all naked above their middles, according to the custom of the country, and adorned in the richest manner with golden chains, medals, beads, bracelets, and sweet-smelling flowers. Meanwhile, the most delicious wines sparkled in gilded crystal and were poured out with profusion, and the fruits presented on richest Japan at the dessert were a composition of charm and ambrosia.

Having enjoyed this superb entertainment till about seven o'clock, I went in search of the house of Mr. Lolkens, the gentleman who had so kindly come to invite me while I was on board. I soon discovered the place of his residence, where my reception chanced to be so ludicrous that I beg leave to relate the particulars in full. Having knocked once or twice at the door, it was opened by a masculine young Negro woman, as black as a coal, holding a lighted tobacco pipe in one hand and a burning candle in the other, which she held close to my face to reconnoiter me. Her whole dress consisted in one single petticoat.

I asked if her master was at home. She spoke, but I could not understand her. I then mentioned him by his name, at which she burst into an immoderate fit of laughter, displaying two rows of beautiful teeth and, laying hold of my coat, she made me a signal to follow her. I acknowledge that I was at a great loss how to act—the scene was so new to me—when I was led into a very neat apartment. She put a bottle of Madeira wine, water, and some very fine fruit on the table, and explained in the best manner she was able, by gesticulation and broken accents, that her *massera* with all the family were gone to his plantation to stay a few days upon business, and that she was left behind to receive an English captain whom she supposed to be me. I signified that I was Captain Stedman and then filled her a tumbler of wine, which she would not accept without the greatest persuasion, it being almost unprecedented in this country to see a Negro slave, either male or female, eat or drink in the presence of a European. I made shift to enter with this black woman into a kind of conversation, which nevertheless I was glad to end with my bottle.

I was fatigued and longed for some rest, and thus made a signal that I wanted to sleep. But here I was truly brought into great distress for, again misunderstanding me, she had the unaccountable assurance to give me such a hearty kiss as had made my nose nearly as flat as her own. I knew not what to do or how to keep my temper and, disentangling myself with some resentment, I flung into my sleeping apartment. But here Wowski pursued me again, and in spite of what I could say pulled off my shoes and my stockings in a moment.[1] Heavens, I lost all patience. This young woman, to be sure, was as black as the Devil. To be short, as the rest of this adventure can afford but little instruction or entertainment to the reader, I shall beg leave to draw a sable curtain over it, only observing that from this small sample the general character of the Negro girls may be decided, which may serve to put young Europeans on their guard who may chance to visit the West India settlements, and who do not always escape with impunity.

On the 10th, having breakfasted on a dish of chocolate, and with no appearance of the planter's soon returning, I took my leave of his house and his black maidservant, and having visited the soldiers in their quarters, I was conducted by the quartermaster to a very neat house of my own, which even if unfurnished was not uninhabited. Leaving my captain's commission (which was of parchment) in the window, it was eaten by the rats during the first night, which animals and mice are exceedingly plentiful in this country.

I no sooner got my baggage carried on shore, and began to put my little house in some order, than the ladies sent me tables, chairs, mirrors, plate, china, glasses, and all other furniture that I needed, while the gentlemen (who gave me a general invitation) overloaded me with presents such as Madeira wine, porter, cider, rum, sugar, and lemons—besides some delicious fruits.

On the morning of the 11th, my face, breast, and hands were spotted all over like a leopard, occasioned by thousands of mosquitoes which, flying in clouds, had kept me company in my new quarters during the night, and to the stings of which vermin I had actually been rendered insensible by the fatigues of a sea voyage of which I had not yet got the better, by a scorching climate, &c. The inhabitants burn tobacco in their apartments just before they shut the windows, which ought to be at sunset (six o'clock). The tobacco smoke sets them a-flying and the Negro girls help to drive them out by the wind of their petticoats, which they throw off without the least reserve every evening, thus *in cuerpo* to battle with the gnats or mosquitoes. Some people have slaves to fan them the whole night during their sleep—especially the ladies—except such as have green gauze doors to their beds. The generality of the inhabitants usually sleep in hammocks which are covered with a large sheet suspended on a

---

1. This is actually the custom throughout Surinam for all ranks and sexes without exception.

tight line straight over them, something in form of an awning of a ship, the lack of which convenience was the cause of my distressed situation.

About this time Colonel Fourgeoud was acquainted by the Governor and Council that the Rebel Negroes now seemed so quietly disposed, without offering any more injury to the planters &c., that the Colony had no further use for our troops, which could be very well defended by those of the Society and by the new corps of Black Rangers, and in consequence of which we were at liberty to return to Europe when we thought proper, without deviating from our duty. Some received this news with pleasure, and others with reluctance. Meanwhile, the transports which had still been kept in commission were ordered to be put in ballast for our departure. However, by a petition signed by most of the inhabitants in opposition to the Governor and Council, we were again desired to remain, which after some canvassing it was agreed to by all parties, and the wooding and watering of the ships was ordered to be stopped.

The 19th. Today, I was invited to dine with a Mr. Kennedy, who was remarkably civil to me. He not only told me that his carriage, riding horses, and table were entirely at my service, but gave me the use of a fine Negro boy to carry my umbrella while I remained in the Colony.

The 22nd. What was my astonishment at seeing an elderly Negro woman enter my room this morning, who did no less than present me her daughter to be what she pleased to call my wife. Being recovered from my surprise, I had so little gallantry as to refuse the old lady's offer, which I however did in a civil manner. A trifling present ended the ceremony to their satisfaction and, curtsying decently, they both departed.

Having still nothing to do, I must describe this custom, which I am convinced will be highly censured by the sedate European matrons but which is, nevertheless, as common as it is almost necessary to the bachelors who live in this climate. These gentlemen, all without exception, have a female slave (mostly a Creole) in their keeping, who preserves their linens clean and decent, dresses their victuals with skill, carefully attends them (they being most excellent nurses) during the frequent illnesses to which Europeans are exposed in this country, prevents them from keeping late hours, knits for them, sews for them, &c.[2] These girls, who are sometimes Indians, sometimes Mulattoes, and often Negroes, naturally pride themselves in living with a European, whom they serve with as much tenderness, and to whom they are generally as faithful, as if he were their lawful husband, to the great shame of so many fair ladies, who break through ties more sacred, and indeed bound with more so-

---

2. Of this habit, even the clergymen are not exempt, witness the Reverend Mr. Snyderhaus, Mr. Tallant, &c.

lemnity. Nor can the above young women be married in any other way, being by their state of servitude entirely debarred from every Christian privilege and ceremony, which makes it perfectly lawful on their side, while they hesitate not to pronounce as harlots those who do not follow them (if they can) in this laudable example, in which they are encouraged, as I have said, by their nearest relations and friends.

Many of these sable-colored beauties will, however, follow their own penchant without restraint whatever, even refusing with contempt the greatest acknowledgments offered by the champions on whom they bestowed their favors, and which they proffer without any kind of ceremony to the first other favorite who may chance to strike their fancy. These are the disinterested daughters of pure Nature, but there are others who must be rewarded for their charms, and will go so low as a dram or a broken tobacco pipe.

Having apologized to the modest reader for this ingenious sample of the Surinam way of living, I shall go forward.

At more than twenty families my board was now daily spread, to partake of their hospitality when I thought it convenient, so that notwithstanding our gentlemen having formed a regimental mess, I had very seldom the honor to profit by their company. In short, all seemed to vie with each other over who was to show the newly arrived troops the greatest marks of politeness, and entertainments went round like the guns go round the Tower on a day of public rejoicing. A Mr. Rynsdorp invited no less than the whole corps without exception to a very superb dinner, accompanied with music &c. Nor did it stop here—balls, card assemblies, and cavalcades were daily recreations, continuing even upon the river, for Captain Van de Velde invited us the same evening on board the *Boreas* man-of-war and gave the company a very genteel supper in the cabin, after which we danced on the quarter-deck under an awning or large sail spread over it in the form of a tent till six o'clock in the morning, and after that we took an airing with the ladies in their carriages.

Thus, in place of fighting the enemy, we seemed to have come over for nothing else but idle dissipation, which was carried to such a length that it absolutely knocked up several of our officers.

Luxury and dissipation in this country are carried to the extreme and, in my opinion, must send thousands to the grave. The men are generally a set of poor, withered mortals, as dry and sapless as a squeezed lemon, owing to their intemperate way of living—such as late hours, hard drinking, and particularly their too frequent intercourse with the Negro and Mulatto female sex, to whom they generally give the preference over the Creole ladies. Indeed, many of them really deserve that preference because of their remarkable cleanliness and youthful vigor when compared to the fair women of this colony, who are a poor, languid generation, with complexions not much better than that of a drumskin, a very few perfect beauties set aside, whose delicate features, elegant shape, and graceful air are certainly exceptional.

But all things may be carried to excess, and from this excess it is that I have known many wives to outlive four husbands but never a man to wear out two wives. Is it then to be wondered that the poor ill-treated ladies should be jealous of their spouses and so bitterly take revenge on the causes of their disgrace, the Negro and Mulatto girls whom they persecute with the greatest bitterness and most barbarous tyranny? Or is it to be wondered that the unmarried, with so little reserve, should snap at any newcomer from Europe? It certainly is not, and I myself have already been persecuted by overgrown widows, stale beauties, and overaged maids till I have lost my temper on the occasion, notwithstanding they were possessed of opulent fortunes.[3] Nay, it was even publicly reported that two of them had fought a duel on account of one of our officers.

During all this fine piece of business, having nothing better to do in my retirement, I resolved for my amusement to write a short "History of the Colony of Surinam" and to take such drawings upon paper as I thought worth my attention. In the pursuit of this plan (besides consulting the best and most modern authors) I was much befriended by the Governor, Mr. Nepveu, who not only himself gave me a great deal of information and showed me several manuscripts, but also sent me regularly every morning such shrubs, animals, &c., as I desired to copy.

---

3. It is a true observation that the tropical maids and mosquitoes generally attack the newly arrived Europeans by instinct, in preference to the West India settlers.

CHAPTER 2nd

*General description of Guiana—Of the Colony of Surinam
in particular*

The face of this country is in some places mountainous, dry, and barren, but in general the soil is exceedingly fruitful and luxurious, being the whole year overspread with a continual verdure, while the trees bear both blossom and ripe fruit at the same time and present an everlasting spring. This general vegetation, in Surinam particularly, must not only be attributed to the rains and warmth of the climate, but also to its low and marshy situation, particularly where it is cultivated by the Europeans, which situation (though not so healthy) answers best for the purposes of the planter. The fields flooded by the swelling rivers produce crops of sugar cane, without replanting, that are sometimes ten times those that are produced in the West India islands, and thus may not improperly be compared to the banks of the River Nile in Egypt.

The uncultivated parts of Guiana[1] are covered over with immense forests, rocks, and mountains (some impregnated with minerals of different kinds), intermixed with very deep marshes or swamps, and large heaths or savannas. The stream along the coast runs continually northwestwards, as I have mentioned, and the shore is almost inaccessible because of rocks, banks, quicksands, bogs, prodigious bushes, and impenetrable brushwood, by which it is lined and closely interwoven.

Guiana abounds with very beautiful rivers, witness the Orinoco and Amazon, by which it is bordered, and which rivers may with justice pass for two of the largest in America, if not in the whole world.

---

1. Surinam is less cultivated than formerly owing to the frequent insurrections of the Negro slaves, who have ruined most of the distant plantations.

This part of Terra Firma is occupied only by the Portuguese, Spaniards, and Hollanders, a small settlement called Cayenne excepted, which is situated between the River Marawina and Cape Orange, and which belongs to the French. The Portuguese dominions in Guiana stretch along the River Amazon, and those of Spain line the banks of the River Orinoco. The Dutch settlements, which are spread along the seaside—along the western or Atlantic Ocean from Cape Nassau to the River Marawina—are Essequibo, Demerara, Berbice, and Surinam. Of all these, the last is the best and largest, and the description of which, as I have promised, I intend to make the principal subject of my narrative.

The principal rivers that belong to this settlement are the River Surinam, from which the Colony takes its name, the Corantyn, the Coppename, the Saramacca, also the Marawina. But of all these rivers, the first alone is navigable. The other three, and even the River Marawina, are indeed very broad and long, but at the same time they are so shallow and so crowded with rocks and small islands that they are of little consequence to Europeans, nor are their banks inhabited, except by some of the Indians, or natives of the country.

Along the higher parts of the rivers Surinam, Commewina, and Cottica are also continually kept advanced guards to protect the inhabitants from inland invasions by the Indians or runaway Negroes. In these consists the principal defense of this settlement, besides a small armed bark or *garda costa* which cruises to and fro between the rivers Marawina and Berbice to give intelligence in case of any threatening emergency to the Colony.

I had almost forgotten to mention that a path fortified with military posts had been projected and was actually begun from the upper part of the River Commewina till the River Saramacca, but the plan did not take, and the above line, which was called the Orange Path, is at present overgrown to a wilderness.

Having thus fully described the surface of the country in general, with its boundaries, rivers, &c., I shall now proceed by giving an account of the earliest discovery and most remarkable revolutions of this once so flourishing colony, Surinam.

[Editors' note. The original manuscript includes here a history of the colony taken from secondary sources, which Stedman glosses in his chapter heading as follows: "Account of its earliest Discovery—is possest by the English—by the Dutch—Murder of the Governor Lord Somelsdyk—The Settlement taken by the French & ransom'd." See the unabridged 1988 edition, pp. 58–65. For further historical background, see R. Price 1976.]

CHAPTER 3rd

History of the first Negroes revolting—Causes thereof—
Distracted state of the Colony—Forced peace concluded with
the Rebels

No sooner was this unfortunate colony delivered from its outward enemies than it was attacked by inward ones of a more fierce and desperate
nature. In former times, the Carib and other Indians had often disturbed
this settlement, but ever since a peace was established after the arrival of
Governor Sommelsdyck in this colony, they have inviolably kept it, living in the greatest harmony and friendship with the Europeans.

The revolted Negro slaves are the foes I now intend to speak of, who
may with truth be called the terror of this settlement, if not the total loss
of it. From the earliest remembrance, some runaway Negroes had
skulked in the woods of Surinam, but these were of very small consideration till about the year 1726 or 1728, when with their hostile numbers
increasing, and mostly being armed with (in addition to bows and arrows) lances and firelocks which they had pillaged from the estates, they
committed continual outrages and depredations upon the coffee and
sugar plantations. These they did both from a spirit of revenge for the
barbarous and inhuman treatment which they had formerly received
from their masters and with a view toward carrying away plunder such
as gunpowder, balls, hatchets, &c., in order to provide for their subsistence and defense. These Negroes were mostly settled in the upper parts
of the rivers Coppename and Saramacca, from which last they take the
name of the Saramaka Rebels, which distinguishes them from other
gangs that have since revolted.

Several commands of military and plantation people were now sent
out against them but were of very small effect in bringing them to reason

by promises, or in getting them rooted out by blows. In 1730, a most shocking execution of eleven poor captives was experimented—to terrify, if possible, their companions, and thus to make them return to their duty. One man was hanged alive upon a gibbet with an iron hook struck through his ribs, and two others, being chained to stakes, were burnt to death by slow fire. Six women were broken alive upon the rack, and two girls were decapitated, through which tortures they went without uttering a sigh. In 1733, three Indians were also decapitated, for having killed three French deserters, which shows how far the civil law now extends in this country.

But I must return to the Negroes, on whom it appears the inhuman carnage that I have mentioned above had very little effect, indeed quite the reverse, since it enraged the Saramaka Rebels to such a degree that they became dreadful to the colonists. This lasted for several years successively until the colonists—no longer being able to support the expense and fatigue of sallying out against them in the woods, besides the great losses and terrors which they so frequently sustained by their invasions—at last resolved to treat for peace with their sable enemies.

Governor Mauricius, who was at this period at the head of the Colony, accordingly sent out a strong detachment to the rebel settlement on the Saramacca River for the purpose of effecting, if possible, the so much wished-for peace. After some skirmishing with the struggling Rebel parties, the detachment at last arrived at their headquarters, where they demanded and obtained a parley. At this time, in 1749, a treaty of peace consisting of ten or twelve articles was actually concluded between them, as had been done before in 1739 with the rebels on the island of Jamaica.

The chief of the Saramaka Rebels was a Creole Negro called Captain Adu, who now received from the Governor as a present a fine large cane with a massive silver pommel, on which were engraved the arms of Surinam, as a mark of their further independence and a preliminary to the other presents that were to be sent out the following year, as stipulated by the treaty, particularly arms and ammunition, once the peace was finally concluded. To the Governor, Adu then returned a handsome bow with a complete case of arrows, which had been manufactured by his own hands, as a token that during that time, on his side, all enmity was ceased and at an end.

This affair gave great satisfaction to some, indeed to most of the inhabitants of Surinam, who now thought themselves and their effects perfectly secure, while others looked on this treaty as a most hazardous resource, nay, as a sure step to the Colony's inevitable ruin. Be that as it may, I cannot help thinking, with the latter, that regardless of Governor

Mauricius' good intentions, nothing can be more dangerous than making a forced friendship with people who, by the most abject slavery and bad usage, were provoked to break their chains and shake off the yoke to seek revenge and liberty, and who by this trust being put in them have it in their power to become from day to day more formidable. Nor can I help thinking, on the contrary, that the insurrection having already risen to such a pitch, the colonists ought to have continued fighting against it while they had a nerve to strain, or a hand left to draw a trigger—not from a motive of cruelty, but for the political good of so fine a settlement. After all, if taken at the worst, it is still better to lose one's life with one's fortune, sword in hand, than to live in the perpetual dread of losing both by one general massacre.

That the best of all would be never to have driven these poor creatures to such extremities by constant ill treatment speaks for itself. At the same time, it is certainly true that to govern the Coast-of-Guinea Negroes well, nay, even for their own benefit, the strictest discipline is absolutely necessary. But I ask: Why in the name of humanity should they undergo the most cruel racks and tortures, entirely depending upon the despotic caprice of their proprietors and overseers, which it is well known is too generally the case throughout the West Indies? And why should their bitter complaints be never heard by the magistrate that has it in his power to redress them? Because His Worship himself is a planter and scorns to be against his own interest. Such is most truly the case, and such is no less truly lamentable, not only for the sake of the master and the man, but also and chiefly for that of one of the finest colonies in the West Indies being, by such unfair proceedings, put in the utmost danger and difficulty. However, it is to be supposed that exceptions do here take place, as they do in all other circumstances—God forbid they should not—and I myself have seen and even at different times been eyewitness where plantation slaves were treated with the utmost humanity, where the hand of the master was seldom lifted but to caress them, and where the eye of the slave sparkled with gratitude and affection.

Let us now step forward and see what were the fruits of making peace with the Saramaka Rebels. In 1750, which was the year thereafter, the promised presents were dispatched to Captain Adu, but the detachment that carried them was attacked on their march and every soul of them murdered on the spot by a desperate Negro called Zamzam who, not having been consulted at the peacemaking, had since put himself at the head of a strong party. He now carried off the whole stock (consisting of arms and ammunition, checked linens, canvas cloth, hatchets, saws and other carpenter's tools, besides salt beef, pork, spirits, &c.) as his own private property. Moreover, Adu, not having received his presents, suspected that the delay was intended to cut their throats, by means of a new supply of troops which he was told was coming from Europe.

By this accident the peace was immediately broken, cruelties and ravages increased more than ever, and death and destruction once more raged throughout the Colony. In 1757, things were come from bad to worse (while one Mr. Crommelin was Governor of this colony), a new revolt having broken out in the Tempaty Creek among the Negroes, owing to nothing but their being so cruelly treated by their masters. This fresh insurrection was of such serious consequence—they having joined themselves to 1600 other runaway Negroes already settled in eight different villages between the Tempaty and the River Marawina, along the banks of the Djuka Creek—that after repeated battles and skirmishes (they being all well armed, as I have mentioned) without much success for the colonists or any hopes of quelling it, they saw themselves once more reduced to suing for peace with their own slaves, as they had done in 1749 with the Rebels of Saramaka (but which peace was, as I have said, broken in 1750 by the irascible conduct of the Rebel Negro Zamzam).

To let the whole world now see that black men are not such brutes as the generality of white ones imagine, I must beg leave to mention a few of the principal ceremonies that attended the ratification of this peace. In 1760, the first thing was another parley, proposed by the colonists. This was, to be sure, agreed to by the Rebels, and these latter not only desired but absolutely insisted that the Dutch should send them yearly (among a great variety of other articles) a handsome quantity of firearms and ammunition, as specified in a long list made up in broken English by a Negro whose name was Boston and who was one of their captains.

Next, Governor Crommelin sent two commissioners, Mr. Sober and Mr. Abercrombie, who marched through the woods escorted by a few military &c., to carry some presents to the Rebels preliminary to the ratification of the peace. At the arrival of the above gentlemen in the Rebel camp at the Djuka Creek, they were introduced to a very handsome Negro called Araby who was the chief of them all, and born in the forest among the last 1600 that I have mentioned. He received them very politely, and taking them by the hand, desired they would sit down by his side upon the green, at the same time assuring them they needed not be under any apprehensions of evil, since coming in so good a cause, no one intended or even dared to hurt them.

But when the above-mentioned Captain Boston perceived that they had brought a parcel of trinkets—such as knives, scissors, combs, and small looking-glasses—and had forgotten the principal articles in question, viz., gunpowder, firearms, and ammunition, he resolutely stepped up to the commissioners and asked in a thundering voice if the Europeans imagined that the Negroes could live on combs and looking-glasses, adding that one of each was fully sufficient to let them all see their faces with satisfaction, while a single gallon of *mansanny,* viz., gunpowder, should have been accepted as a proof of their trust. But since that had been omitted, they should, with his will, never more return to their countrymen till every article of his list should be fulfilled. A Negro captain called Quacoo now interfered, saying that these gentlemen were only the messengers of their Governor and Court, and as they could not be answerable for their masters' proceedings they should certainly go back to where they came from without hurt or molestation, and not even he, Captain Boston, should dare to oppose them.

The chief of the Rebels then ordered silence and desired Mr. Abercrombie to make up a list himself of such articles as he, Araby, should name him, which that gentleman having done, the Rebels not only gave him and his companions leave peaceably to return with it to town, but their Governor and Court a whole year to deliberate on what they were to choose—peace or war. They swore unanimously that during that interval all animosity should cease on their side, after which, having entertained them in the best manner their situation in the woods afforded, they wished them a happy journey to Paramaribo.

Upon this occasion, one of the Rebel officers represented to Mr. Sober and to Mr. Abercrombie what a pity it was that the Europeans, who pretend to be a civilized nation, should be so much the occasion of their own ruin by their inhuman cruelties towards their slaves.

> We desire you (continued this Negro) to tell your Governor and your Court that in case they want to raise no new gangs of Rebels, they ought to take care that the planters keep a more watchful eye over their own property and not so often trust them to the hands of a parcel of drunken managers and overseers, who by wrongfully whipping the Negroes, debauching their wives and children, neglecting the sick, &c., are the ruin of the Colony and willfully drive to the woods such quantities of stout, handsome people who by their sweat got your subsistence and without whose hands your colony must drop to nothing, and to whom at last in this pitiful manner you are glad to come and ply for friendship.

Mr. Abercrombie now begged of them to be accompanied with one or two of their principal officers to Paramaribo, where he promised they should be vastly well treated &c., but the chief, Araby, answered him with a smile that there would be sufficient time a year thereafter, once the peace was thoroughly concluded, and that then even his youngest son should be at their service to receive his education among them. And as for his subsistence and even for that of his descendants, he should take the sole care upon himself without ever giving the Christians the smallest trouble. After this, the commissioners left the Rebels and all arrived safe and sound at Paramaribo.

The year of deliberation being ended, the Governor and Court sent out two fresh commissioners to the Negro camp to bring the so much wished-for peace to a thorough conclusion. After a great deal of canvassing and ceremonies on both sides, with the presents being promised to the Negroes according to their wishes (as some nations pay tribute to the Emperor of Morocco), at last it was finally agreed on. And as a proof of their affection for the Europeans, the Negroes indiscriminately insisted that, during their remaining stay in the Rebel camp, each of the commissioners should take for his constant companion one of their handsomest young women. They also treated them with game, fish, fruit, and the best of all that the forest afforded, entertaining them without intermission with music, dancing, and cheering, besides firing one volley after another, after which they returned contented to town.

This done, the above presents were sent to the Negroes near the River Marawina by Mr. Mayer, escorted by six hundred men, soldiers and slaves, and which gentleman had nearly baffled the whole business by—contrary to his orders and from a pusillanimous principle—delivering all the presents to the Rebels without receiving the hostages in return. Fortunately, however, Araby kept his word and sent down four of his best officers as pledges to Paramaribo. By this the peace was perfectly accomplished, when a treaty of twelve or fourteen articles was signed by two white commissioners and sixteen of Araby's black captains in 1761, which ceremony took place on the Plantation Auka on the River Surinam where all the parties met—this being the spot of rendezvous appointed for the purpose, after four different embassies had been sent by the Europeans to the Negroes.

But signing this treaty alone was still not looked on as sufficient by the Rebel chief Araby and his people, who all immediately swore an oath, and insisted on the commissioners doing the same, after the manner in practice by themselves, not trusting entirely, they said, in that made use of by the Christians, which they had seen too often broken, whereas for a Negro to break his oath is absolutely without example (of this, at least, I never saw or heard of an instance during all the time that I lived in the Colony), which plainly argues that the Africans are not so entirely destitute of morality and even religion as a number of ignorant Europeans imagine, and which I hope still more clearly to demonstrate on other occasions.

The solemnity made use of on this day consisted in both parties, with a lance or penknife, letting themselves a few drops of blood from the arm into a calabash or cup with clean spring water, into which were also mixed a few particles of dry earth, and of which all present were obliged to drink a draught upon the spot, Europeans and Africans without exception, which they call drinking each other's blood. This was done after having first scattered a few drops upon the ground, when their *gadoman* or priest, with upcast eyes and outstretched arms, took Heaven and Earth as witness, and with a most audible voice and awful manner, invoked God's curse and malediction on all such as should first break this sacred treaty made between them, from that moment henceforth to all eternity, to which the multitude answered *"Da so,"* which signifies in their language "Amen." The solemnity being ended, Araby and each captain was presented with a fine large cane and silver pommel on which were engraved the arms of the Colony (to distinguish them from other Negroes, as had already been done with the Saramaka captain, Adu, in 1749).

The above-mentioned Negroes are called Aukas [Ndjukas], after the name of the plantation where the peace articles were signed, by which name they are distinguished from the Saramakas, whom I have already described.

The Auka Negroes have indeed behaved indifferently well ever since the foregoing treaty—fortunately for the Colony of Surinam, from which they must yearly receive (as I have said, among a number of other articles) a handsome quantity of ball and gunpowder.

This same year, 1761, a peace was also a second time concluded with the Saramaka Rebels who were at present commanded by a Negro called Wii instead of their former chief, Adu, who was dead. But, unfortunately, this second peace was broken by a Rebel captain called Musinga, who had received none of the presents, and which presents had been again on their way to the chief, Wii, as they had been formerly on their way to the chief, Adu, cut off and captured by the individual and enterprising devil, Zamzam. However, with this difference: this time none of the detachment that were sent with them were murdered as on the preceding time, or even one single person hurt.

The above Captain Musinga now fought desperately against the colonists. He gave battle face to face and beat back above 150 of their best troops, which were sent out against him, killing numbers and taking away all their baggage and ammunition. However, very soon after this, when the real cause of Musinga's discontent became known, means were found and adopted to pacify this gallant warrior, by making him receive and share the presents sent out by the colonists on an equal footing with his brother heroes, when peace was a third and last time concluded in

1762 between the Saramaka Rebels and the Colony, which has providentially been kept sacred and inviolable, the same as with the Negroes of Auka, to this day.

On their arrival at Paramaribo, the hostages and chief officers of both the above-mentioned Negro cohorts were entertained at the Governor's own table, having previously paraded in state through the town, accompanied by His Excellency, and in his own private carriage.

By their capitulation to the Dutch, the above Auka and Saramaka Rebels must yearly receive, as I have mentioned, a handsome quantity of arms and ammunition from the Colony, for which those have received in return the Negroes' promises of being their faithful allies, to deliver up all deserters (for which they receive proper bounties), never to appear armed at Paramaribo above five or six at a time, and also to keep their settlements at a proper distance from the town or plantations—the Saramaka Negroes at the River Saramacca, and the Auka Negroes near the River Marawina, where one or two white men called Postholders were to reside among them as a species of envoy. Both these tribes were now supposed to be in all some three thousand people. However, only several years later their numbers were computed by those who were sent to visit their settlements to be no less than fifteen or twenty thousand people (including wives and children). They have already become overbearing and even insolent, brandishing their silver-headed canes under the noses of the inhabitants by way of derision and independence, forcing from them liquors and very often money and, if they refuse, putting them in mind how (when they were their slaves) they murdered their parents and their husbands. From what I have just mentioned, and with their numbers increasing from day to day, I must conclude that should ever the peace be once more broken, the above new allies will become the most dreadful foes that ever the Colony of Surinam will have to deal with. I would mention besides the example and encouragement these treaties give other slaves to revolt even without provocation against their masters, and obstinately fight for the same privileges. At the same time, those planters who dare so inhumanely to persecute their slaves without a cause deserve, in my opinion, no better treatment, and this, most assuredly, too often is the consequence.

CHAPTER 4th

*Short interval of peace and plenty—The Colony plunged in
new distress by a fresh insurrection and nearly ruined—
Review of the troops for its defense—An action with the
Rebels—Gallant behavior of a Black Corps till the arrival of
Colonel Fourgeoud's Marines*

The Colony seemed now in a prosperous and flourishing way since the
peacemaking with the Saramaka and Auka Negroes, and everything was
peaceful and in good order. The inhabitants, as I mentioned, thought
themselves and their effects now perfectly secure, so nothing but mirth
and dissipation was thought of, which was even pushed to lavishness and
profusion. Surinam looked like a large and beautiful garden stocked with
everything that nature and art could produce to make the life of man both
comfortable to himself and useful to society. All the luxuries and necessities for subsistence were crowding upon the inhabitants, while the five
senses seemed intoxicated with bliss and, to use an old expression, Surinam was a land that overflowed with milk and honey.

But alas, this delusive felicity, this life of wantonness and thoughtless
dissipation, lasted not long. The planter wanted to get rich too soon,
without taking into consideration the wretchedness of the slave, till finally drunkenness, luxury, riot, and all manner of vice and debauchery
became predominant. Even the cruelties of several masters towards their
slaves rather increased than diminished (notwithstanding the destruction
that so lately threatened them), and at the same time (as I have mentioned
before) the bad example of the peacemaking with the Saramaka and Auka
Negroes stimulated the other slaves to revolt in the same way, in hopes of
meeting with the same success. Such were the complicated causes of the
Colony again being plunged into its former abyss of difficulties. Some of
the most beautiful estates (in this settlement called plantations) were
again seen blazing in flames, and others laid in ashes, while the reeking

and mangled bodies of their inhabitants were scattered along the banks of the River Cottica, and their effects pillaged by their own Negroes, who all fled to the woods—men, women, and children without exception. These new revolters were distinguished by the name of the Cottica Rebels, where their hostilities had begun, and their numbers augmenting from day to day, they soon became as formidable to the settlement as the Saramaka and Auka Negroes had been before them, and were just about to give the finishing blow to the Colony of Surinam in 1772.

Now all was horror and consternation, and nothing but a general massacre was expected by the greatest majority of the inhabitants, who fled from their estates and crowded into the town of Paramaribo for protection. In this dilemma the inhabitants were now obliged to come to the distracted resolution of limiting the game upon itself, that is to say, of forming a regiment of manumitted slaves to fight against their countrymen, thus setting Negro to battle against Negro, which providentially had the desired effect. These brave men acted wonders above expectation in conjunction with the Colony or Society troops, whose strength alone was no longer thought sufficient to defend this settlement at present. In addition, the Society of Surinam made application to His Serene Highness the Prince of Orange for assistance, and in consequence of which a corps of Marines (all volunteers) was immediately embodied, drafted from the different regiments in Holland. Of this, as I mentioned, the command was given to Colonel Fourgeoud, and it was in this corps that I had the honor to be appointed a captain.

I shall now give some account of the Surinam army, white and black, and then proceed to a detail of their gallant behavior before our fleet arrived to their assistance.

The regular troops that belong to the Society of Surinam are intended to be twelve hundred men when complete, divided into two battalions paid partly by the Society and partly by the inhabitants. But they never can produce that number in the field, owing to many complicated reasons, such as their dying on the passage, their seasoning to the climate, their dangerous and fatiguing duty, their being shot, lost in the woods, &c. Besides this number, a reinforcement of three hundred more was now sent from the town of Amsterdam, but of these unlucky wretches scarce fifty were landed fit for service, having shared a fate on their passage by the inhumanity of their leader, Mr. H——, little better than that which the poor African Negroes later experienced at the hand of the barbarous Captain Coolingward, who in 1781 threw 132 living slaves into the sea to perish. Mr. H—— starved and tortured to death, by unnecessary hardships, almost the whole of his reinforcement, and forced his lieutenant (who was no longer able to bear or be witness to the infliction of his tyranny) to seek redress in the waves, by leaping out the cabin window and ending his existence. Mr. H—— was honorably acquitted.

The military in Surinam are composed of several very good and experienced officers, well inured to the service. But for their private men I can indeed say little to boast of, being a composition of scum composed of all nations, ages, shapes, and sizes, by chance wafted together from all the different corners of the globe. Yet notwithstanding, they fight like little devils and have on many different occasions been of infinite service to this settlement.

Here is also a small corps of artillery, being part of the twelve hundred, which I must acknowledge to be very fine in all respects. As for what they please to call their militia, they are, a few gentlemen who command them excepted, such a set of dastardly scarecrows that they will absolutely not bear to be mentioned as fighting men. But now for the newly raised corps of manumitted slaves who, though in number only three hundred, have proved to be of as much service to the Colony as all the others put together, greatly owing to the strength of their constitutions, their wonderful activity, perseverance, &c. These men were all volunteers, mostly stout, strapping, able young fellows, picked from the different plantations, whose owners received for them their full value in money. None were accepted but such as were reputed to be of a very good character, and indeed they have since in my own presence given astonishing proofs of their fidelity to the Europeans and their valor against the revolters. Their chief leaders are three or four white men called *conductors,* to whom they pay the strictest obedience, and one or two of whom generally attend them when they set out on any enterprise or march of consequence. Every ten privates have one captain who commands them in the forest by the different sounds of his horn, as the boatswain commands the sailors or as the cavalry of Europe are commanded by the trumpets in the field, by which they advance, retreat, attack, or spread, &c. They are armed only with a firelock and saber but of both weapons they understand the management in the most masterly manner. They generally go naked by preference in the woods, excepting trousers and a scarlet cap on which is their number, and which (besides their *parole,* or watchword, which is "Orange") distinguishes them from the Rebels in any action, to prevent disagreeable mistakes.

Having thus described the forces of Surinam, I shall now proceed in order with my narrative. I have already said that the newly revolted (called the Cottica) Rebels were just going to give the finishing blow to the Colony in 1772, and I shall now relate how this catastrophe was prevented.

These Negroes, being commanded by a desperate fellow named

A Coromantyn Free Negro, or Ranger, armed.

Plate 7

Baron, had erected a strong settlement between the River Cottica and the seacoast, not far distant from the River Marawina, from where they sallied forth to commit their depredations on the plantations. I call it strong because, like an island, it was naturally surrounded by a broad unfordable marsh or swamp which prevented all communication except by private paths under water, known only to the Rebels, and before which Baron had placed loaded swivels which he had plundered from the neighboring estates. Besides, it was fenced and enclosed on every side by several thousand strong palisades, making it no contemptible fortification. To this spot Baron gave the name of Boucou, or Moldered, intimating that it should perish in dust before ever it should be taken or even discovered by the Europeans. However, after many marches and counter-marches this nest was at last discovered[1] by the vigilance and perseverance of the Society troops and that of the black soldiers, or *Rangers* (as I shall call them for the future, their service being chiefly like that of the Rangers in Virginia, who are sent out against the Cherokee Indians). It now being determined that these sable foes should be besieged and rooted out, a strong detachment of white and black troops was sent against them, under the command of one Captain Meyland to head the first, and Lieutenant Friderici, a spirited young officer with the conductors, to lead the latter, and which detachment on their arrival at the above marsh was obliged to encamp upon its borders, not being able to pass through it on account of its unfordable depth.

On the discovery of the troops, the bold Negro Baron immediately planted a white flag within their view, which he meant as a token of defiance and independence, when an incessant firing began on both sides, which was of very little effect. To throw a fascine bridge over the marsh was then projected, but, after several weeks had been spent in the attempt and a great many men shot dead in the execution, this plan was also frustrated and dropped, during which time the two little armies kept popping

---

1. Another settlement of the Rebels was well known to exist in a corner of the Colony known by the name of the Lee Shore and situated between the rivers Surinam and Saramacca, but its situation, surrounded by marshes, quagmires, mud, and water, is such that it fortifies them from any attempts of Europeans whatever. Nay, they are even undiscoverable by Negroes, except by their own, so thick and impenetrable is the forest on that spot, and overchoked with thorns, briars, and underwood of every species. From under these covers nevertheless these sable gentry sally forth in small parties during the night to rob the gardens and fields surrounding Paramaribo and carry off the young women they chance to meet with. In this diabolical wilderness was once lost for two or three days and nights, as he went out a-shooting, a young officer called Friderici, of whom I am in a little time to take further notice, and who would probably never more have been heard of had not Governor Crommelin's precaution of ordering one gun to be fired after another given him an opportunity to find his way back and thus restore him once more to his friends.

and blackguarding each other at a shocking rate. Having desisted from carrying over the above bridge, without hopes of getting through the marsh into the fortress, with the ammunition and victuals growing considerably less, and with the loss of a great many men, things were come to such a crisis that the siege must have been abandoned and the troops marched back to Paramaribo had not the Rangers, by their indefatigable efforts and (however strange to think) implacable bitterness against the Rebels, found out and discovered to the Europeans the underwater paths of communication to Boucou, several being shot and drowned in the execution of this material piece of service.

Captain Meyland with the regulars now forded the swamp on one side and, designedly making a *feint attack* on the fortress, drew Baron with all his Rebels to its defense, as was expected, while Lieutenant Friderici (having with the Rangers crossed the marsh on the other side) had the opportunity of leaping with his black party (who were eager like so many bloodhounds) over the palisades, sword in hand without opposition.

A most terrible carnage now ensued, with several prisoners being made on both sides, and the fortress of Boucou was taken. But Baron,[2] with the greatest number of the Rebels, escaped into the woods, having first found means to cut the throats of ten or twelve of the Rangers who had lost their way in the marsh and whom he seized sticking in the mud, cutting off the ears, nose, and lips of one of them, whom he in this condition returned living to his friends where, however, the miserable man soon expired. Nor could Lieutenant Friderici himself have so well escaped during the action that took place within the fort, where in the first onset no one but Negroes were engaged, had he not been favored by darkness, smoke, and a black crepe being covered over his face, which prevented him to be distinguished by the Rebels from out among his dusky companions.[3]

---

2. This Baron, who (as I mentioned) was the head of all the Cottica Rebels, had formerly been the Negro slave of one Mr. Dahlberg, a Swede who had made him a favorite on account of his genius, who had taught him to read and write and bred him a Mason. He had also been with his master in Holland and was promised his manumission on his return to the Colony. But when Mr. Dahlberg broke his word in regard to his liberty and sold him to a Jew, Baron obstinately refused to work, in consequence of which he was publicly flogged below the gallows, which the Negro resented so much that from that moment he swore revenge against all Europeans without exception and flew to the woods. Putting himself at the head of all the Rebels, his name became dreadful to the Colony and in particular to his former master, Dahlberg, and he declared solemnly he should never die in peace till he should have washed his hands in the tyrant's blood.

3. A few of the Negroes indeed wear trousers, shirts, and jackets in the woods. The regulars are but seldom seen to wear more, both the officers and private men dressing alike, and as light, and as plain, as possible.

Such was the war we were come to wage in Surinam and in which I frankly declare I should never have engaged had I known any other way to push my fortune.

That the Rangers and Rebels must be the most inveterate enemies can very well be accounted for, since notwithstanding the first are useful and true to the Europeans, they are certainly looked upon by the second as traitors and betrayers of their countrymen, being both the one and other party originally Africans from the coast of Guinea or Creoles born in the Colony of Surinam.

The taking of Boucou was now greatly spoken of and deemed a very severe crush for the Rebels, in which both the regulars and Rangers indeed behaved with unprecedented intrepidity and courage, while independent of Captain Meyland's gallant conduct, Lieutenant Friderici was particularly taken notice of and was presented by the Surinam Society with a beautiful saber, firelock, and brace of pistols mounted in silver and ornamented with the marks of his merit, besides the rank of captain.

Indeed, the whole detachment without exception, white and black, met with the greatest marks of content and approbation.

In this state were the public affairs of this settlement in 1773, when our fleet dropped anchor before the town of Paramaribo.

CHAPTER 5TH

*The scene changes—Some account of a beautiful female
slave—The manner of traveling in Surinam—Barbarity of a
planter—Sensibility*

Having said before that from our arrival till several weeks after, we
seemed to be landed in Guiana for nothing but idle dissipation, I shall
now proceed from March 1st of the same year, just about the beginning
of the rainy season, when our life of mirth and joviality still continued,
and diversify the mind of the reader after the preceding scenes of horror
by giving a description of the beautiful Mulatto maid Joanna.[1]

This fine young woman I first saw at the house of a Mr. Demelly,
secretary to the Court of Policy, where I daily breakfasted, and of whose
lady, Joanna, aged then but fifteen years, was a very remarkable favorite.

Rather more than middle-sized, she was perfectly straight with the
most elegant shapes that can be viewed in nature, moving her well-
formed limbs as when a goddess walked. Her face was full of native modesty and the most distinguished sweetness. Her eyes, as black as ebony,
were large and full of expression, bespeaking the goodness of her heart.
With cheeks through which glowed (in spite of her olive complexion) a
beautiful tinge of vermilion when gazed upon, her nose was perfectly
well-formed and rather small, her lips a little prominent which, when she
spoke, discovered two regular rows of pearls as white as mountain snow.
Her hair was a dark brown, next to black, forming a beauteous globe of
small ringlets, ornamented with flowers and gold spangles. Round her
neck, her arms, and her ankles she wore gold chains, rings, and medals,

---

1. A Mulatto is between white and black.

Joanna.

Plate 8

while a shawl of finest Indian muslin, the end of which was negligently thrown over her polished shoulder, gracefully covered part of her lovely bosom. A petticoat of richest chintz alone made out the rest. Bareheaded and barefooted, she shone with double luster, carrying in her delicate hand a beaver hat, the crown trimmed round with silver. The figure and dress of this fine creature could not but attract my particular notice, as she did indeed of all who beheld her, which induced me to ask of Mrs. Demelly, in the name of wonder, who she was that appeared so much distinguished above all the rest of her species in the Colony, and which request this lady obligingly granted.

> She is, Sir (said she), the daughter of a respectable gentleman named Kruythoff who has, besides this girl, four children by a black woman called Cery, the property of a Mr. De Borde on his estate called Faukenberg in the upper part of the River Commewina. Some few years ago, Mr. Kruyt-hoff made the offer of above one thousand pounds sterling to Mr. De Borde to obtain manumission for his offspring, which being inhumanly refused, it had such an effect upon his spirits that he became frantic, and died in that melancholy state soon thereafter, leaving in slavery and at the discretion of a tyrant, two boys and three beautiful girls, of which the one now before us is the eldest.[2] The gold medals &c., which may seem to surprise you, are the gifts which her faithful mother (who is a most deserving woman to-wards her children, and of some consequence among her own caste) re-ceived from her father before he expired, and whom she ever attended with the duties of a lawful wife. Mr. De Borde, however, got his just reward for, having since driven all his best carpenter Negroes to the woods by his in-justice and severity, he was ruined to all intents and purposes, obliged to flee the Colony and to leave his estate &c. to the disposal of his creditors, while one of the above unhappy deserters, a Samboe,[3] had by his industry been the protector of Cery and her children. His name is Jolicoeur and he is now the first of Baron's captains, whom you may have a chance of meet-ing in the Rebel camps, breathing revenge against all Christians.
>
> Mrs. De Borde is still in Surinam, being arrested for her husband's debts till Faukenberg shall be sold by execution to pay them, which lady now lodges at my house where the unfortunate Joanna attends her, in whom she prides and treats with much tenderness and distinction.

Having thanked Mrs. Demelly for her relation of Joanna, in whose eye was started the precious pearl of sympathy, I took my leave and went to my lodging in a state of sadness and stupefaction.

---

2. In Surinam all such children go with the mother; that is, if she is in slavery her off-spring are her master's property, even if their father be a prince, unless he obtains them by purchase.

3. A Samboe is between a Mulatto and a Negro.

However insignificant and like the style of a romance this account may seem to some, it is nevertheless a genuine fact, which I flatter myself may not be uninteresting to many others.

When reflecting on the state of slavery altogether, and my ears being stunned with the clang of the whip and the dismal yells of the wretched Negroes on whom it was inflicted *sling-slang* from morning till night, and when considering that this might one day be the fate of the unfortunate Mulatto maid I have above described, should she chance to fall into the hands of a tyrannical master or mistress, I could not help cursing the barbarity of Mr. De Borde for having withheld her from a fond parent who, by bestowing on her the education of a lady, would have produced in this forsaken plant (now exposed to every rude blast without protection) an ornament to civilized society.

I became melancholy at all this and, as it were, to counterbalance the general calamity of the miserable slaves that surrounded me, I began to take more delight in the prattling of my poor Negro boy Quacoo than in all the fashionable conversation of the polite inhabitants of this colony. My spirits were depressed and in the space of twenty-four hours I was very ill indeed, when a cordial, a few preserved tamarinds, and a basket with some fine oranges were sent me by an unknown person. This, and letting about twelve ounces of blood, recovered me so far that on the 5th I was able for a change of air to accompany a Mr. Macneyl, who gave me a most pressing invitation to his beautiful coffee plantation, Sporksgift, in the Matapica Creek.

Let us now proceed to the estate Sporksgift, for which plantation we set out from Paramaribo on the 5th in a tent-boat, or barge, rowed by six or eight of the best Negroes belonging to Mr. Macneyl, everybody as I have said traveling by water in this country. These barges I cannot better describe than by comparing them with those that accompany what is usually styled the Lord Mayor's Show on the River Thames, only being less in magnitude—though some are very little less in magnificence, if gilding, flags, music, and every convenience can be called such. They are often rowed by ten and sometimes by twelve oars, and are lightly built, with a most astonishing swiftness, while the rowers never stop from the moment they set off till the company is landed at the place of destination, continuing to tug night and day, sometimes for twenty-four hours together, and singing a chorus all the time to keep up their spirits when (their naked bodies dripping with sweat like post horses) they one and all plunge headlong into the river to refresh.

We now passed a number of fine plantations, but I could not help taking particular notice of the cacao estate called Alkmaar, situated on the right side in rowing up the River Commewina, which is no less conspicuous for its beauty than for the goodness of its proprietor, the invaluable Mrs. Elizabeth Danforth, now Widow Godefrooy, as shall be seen on many different occasions.

At our arrival on the estate Sporksgift, I had the pleasure to see a maneuver which gave me the greatest satisfaction, as also to an American, one Captain Bogard, who was our companion on this jaunt. The scene consisted in Mr. Macneyl, the moment after we had landed, turning the overseer out of his service and ordering him to depart from the plantation in an inferior boat called a *ponkee*[4] to Paramaribo, or to wherever he thought proper, which was instantaneously put in execution—he having, by bad usage and cruelty, caused the death of three or four Negroes. After which all the slaves got a holiday and a present of some rum, which was spent in festivity by dancing and clapping hands in a green before the dwelling-house windows.

The overseer's sentence was the more ignominious and galling as, at the time of his receiving it, a Negro foot-boy who was buckling his shoes was called back and he was desired to buckle them himself, which verifies the old proverb—set a beggar a-horseback and he rides to the Devil.

But I should be guilty of partiality did I not relate one instance which throws a shade over the humanity of my friend Macneyl. Having observed a handsome young Negro go very lame while the others were capering and dancing, and inquiring for the cause of it, this gentleman told me himself that, the Negro being accustomed to run away from his work, he had been obliged to hamstring him, which was that he had with a knife cut through the large tendon above one of his heels. However severe this despotic sample of bad usage may appear, it is nothing compared to what I will make appear in the sequel.

March 28th. I took another trip with a Mr. Charles Rynsdorp, who rowed me in his barge to five beautiful coffee estates and to one sugar plantation in the Matapica, Paramarica, and Warapa creeks, the description of which last, called Schoonoord, I must also defer to another occasion, but where I saw one scene of barbarity which I cannot help to relate.

The victim was a fine old Negro slave who, having been (as he thought) undeservedly sentenced to receive some hundred lashes by the lacerating whips of two Negro drivers, had during the execution pulled out a knife which (after having made a fruitless thrust at his persecutor, the overseer) he plunged up to the haft in his own bowels, repeating the blow till he dropped down at the tyrant's feet. For this crime he was (being first recovered) condemned to be chained to the furnace that dis-

---

4. A *ponkee* is a flat-bottomed boat of four or six oars, something like a square-toed shoe. Sometimes it has a tent and sometimes not.

View of the Estate Alkmaar, on the River Commewine.

Representation of a Tent Boat, or Plantation Barge.

Plate 10

tills the kill-devil,[5] there to keep in a perpetual fire night and day, by the heat of which he was all over blistered, till he should expire by infirmity or old age, indeed of which last he had but little chance. He showed me his wounds with a smile of contempt, which I returned with a sigh and a small donation, nor shall I ever forget the miserable man who, like Cerberus, the dog of Hell, was loaded with irons and chained to everlasting torment. As for everything else that I met on this little tour, I must acknowledge it to be elegance and splendor, and my reception was hospitable above my expectation. But these Elysian Fields could not dissipate the gloom that the infernal furnace had left upon my spirits, a damp of such a dusky nature that no faint sunshine can evaporate.

Today, dining at the house of my friend Mr. Lolkens, to whom I had been (as I first mentioned) recommended by letters, I was an eyewitness to the unpardonable contempt with which Negro slaves are treated in this colony, by his son, a boy not more than ten years old. When sitting at table, he gave a slap in the face to a gray-headed black woman for, by accident, having touched his powdered hair as she was serving a dish of curry. I could not help blaming his father for patronizing the action, who told me with a smile that the child would not longer offend me as he was the next day to sail to Holland for education, to which I answered that I thought it was high time. At the same moment a sailor passing by broke the head of a Negro man with a bludgeon for not having saluted him with his hat. Such here is the state of slavery.

I now inquired of Mrs. Demelly what was become of the amiable Joanna. She told me that her lady, Mrs. De Borde, had escaped to Holland on board the *Boreas* man-of-war under the protection of Captain Van de Velde, who, like a true Perseus, had broken her chains and rescued this Andromeda from the jaws of the monster Persecution, and that her young Mulatto was now at the house of an aunt, a free woman, from where she expected at any moment to be sent by the creditors to the estate Faukenberg, friendless and at the mercy of some rascally overseer. Good God, I flew to the spot in search of poor Joanna and found her bathing with her companions in the garden.[6]

But perceiving me, she darted from my presence like a shot, after which I returned to Mrs. Demelly and declared without the least hesita-

---

5. Kill-devil is a species of rum which is distilled from the scum and dregs of sugar cauldrons. It is much drunk in this colony and is the only spirits allowed the Negroes, when they get any at all. Many Europeans also, from a point of economy, make use of it—to whom it proves no better than a slow and pernicious poison.

6. This is here regularly done twice a day by all the Indians, Mulattoes, Negroes, &c., and contributes much to their health and to their cleanliness, while by the Europeans (some few excepted) this salutary custom is never put in practice.

tion no less than that it was my intention (if such could be) to purchase, to educate, and even to make my lawful wife in Europe the individual Mulatto maid Joanna, which I relate to the world without blushing or being ashamed of, while Mrs. Demelly gazed upon me with wild astonishment.

I next went to the house of my friend Mr. Lolkens, who happened to be the administrator of Faukenberg Estate and, asking his assistance, I intimated to him my strange determination. Having recovered from his surprise and stared at me, an interview at once was proposed and the beauteous slave produced trembling in our presence. Reader, if you have perused the fate of Lavinia with applause (though the scene admits of no comparison), reject not the destiny of Joanna with contempt. It was she who had sent me the cordial and oranges in March, when I was nearly expiring, which she now modestly acknowledged before us both was in gratitude for having pitied her situation. But as to live with me on any terms she absolutely refused—not, she said, from a want of friendship or insensibility of the honor I did her, but from a sense that she must be parted from me soon, should I return to Europe without her, as well as a conviction of her inferior state in that part of the world should she ever accompany me there. In which sentiments firmly persisting, she was permitted decently to withdraw and return to the house of her aunt. I recommended her from my soul to Mr. Lolkens, and begged that she might at least be continued at Paramaribo (which privilege this gentleman humanely was pleased to grant her), and now I once more, yet only to some, apologize for this wonderful digression. Here it ends.

On the 30th came the news that the Rangers, having discovered a Rebel village, had attacked it and carried off three prisoners, leaving four others shot dead upon the spot, whose right hands, chopped off and barbecued or dried in smoke, they had sent to the Governor at Paramaribo.[7]

On receiving this news, Colonel Fourgeoud immediately left the River Surinam and on the 1st of May returned to town in expectation of his regiment being employed on actual service. But there it ended, and we still were allowed to linger away our time, each after his own private fancy, while the Rangers were reviewed on the 4th in Fort Zeelandia, at which ceremony I was present, and must confess that this corps of black soldiers had a truly tremendous appearance—warriors whose determined and open aspect could not but give me the greatest pleasure to behold. They received the thanks of the Governor for their manly behavior and faithful conduct, besides which they were entertained with a rural feast at

---

7. For every Rebel prisoner a reward is paid of twenty-five florins and for every right hand fifty, being nearly five pounds.

the public expense at Paramaribo and, having invited their wives and children, the day was spent in mirth and conviviality, without the least disturbance, nay, even with decorum and propriety, to the great satisfaction of the inhabitants.

The *Westellingwerf* under Captain Crass now sailed for Holland, stopping first at the colony of Demerara. Thus, both our convoys having left us, things began to look as if we should still be employed on actual service, and we began to have great reason to wish for either that or our returning to Europe. Not only our officers but our private men were beginning to be debilitated by the relaxation of the climate, and some by a continued debauchery so common to all ranks in this settlement, the latter dying by half dozens every day, just as hard labor and bad treatment had killed the poor sailors, which clearly demonstrates that all excesses are mortal to Europeans in Guiana. But men will give lessons that they do not imitate, since I myself, notwithstanding my former resolution of living retired, now relapsed into the vortex of dissipation, not only becoming a member of a club, and partaking of all the polite amusements, but plunging into every extravagance without exception. However, I got the reward that I deserved and all at once became so ill with a fever that I was no more expected to recover.

In this situation did I lie in my hammock till the 17th, with only a soldier and my black boy to attend me, and without another friend, sickness being so common in this country. This morning entered my apartment, to my unspeakable joy and surprise, the valuable Mulatto slave Joanna, accompanied by one of her best friends. She said she was acquainted with my forlorn situation and that if I still entertained the same good opinion of her, her only request was that she might be allowed to wait upon me till I should be recovered, which I readily granted, and by her unremitting care and attention had the good fortune to regain my health and spirits so far as to be able, in a couple of days, to take an airing in Mr. Kennedy's carriage.

I now renewed with the greatest sincerity my wild proposals of purchase, of education, and of transporting her to Europe, but these were now all once more rejected with this humble declaration:

> I am born a low, contemptible slave. To be your wife under the forms of Christianity must degrade you to all your relations and your friends, besides the expense of my purchase and education. But I have a soul, I hope, not inferior to the best European, and blush not to acknowledge that I have a regard for you who so much distinguishes me above the rest. Nay, that now independent of every other thought I shall pride myself (in the way of my ancestors) to be yours all and all, till fate shall part us or my conduct shall give you cause to spurn me from your presence.

This was spoken with downcast looks and tears dropping upon her heaving bosom, while she held her companion by the hand. From this instant the beauteous maid was mine, nor had I ever after cause to repent it, as shall be seen more particularly in the sequel. Now, pale envy, do thy utmost, while I shall continue to glory in this action, as much as this virtuous slave did pride in making me her choice. Having only added that I this day made her a present of different articles to the value above twenty guineas, I shall drop the azure theme.

But the day following, what was my very great surprise at seeing my gold all returned upon my table, this enchanting creature having carried every article back to the merchants.

> Your generous intentions alone, Sir (said she), are sufficient. But allow me to tell you that I will look on any superfluous expense on my account as diminishing that good opinion which I hope you have, and will ever entertain, of my disinterestedness, and upon which I shall ever put the greatest value.

Such was the genuine speech of a slave who had simple Nature for her only education, and the purity of whose refined sentiments stand in need of no comment, which I was now determined to improve by every care. I shall now only add that gratitude for her superior virtues and particular attention to me, and my duty to the world in general by producing such a slave upon the stage, could alone have induced me to dwell on a subject which I am convinced must attract me so much censure, while if but with a few my motive will plead for my presumption, I shall lay easy under the burden.

This evening I visited at Mr. Demelly's, who, with his lady, congratulated me on my recovery from sickness while at the same time, however strange, with a smile they wished me joy with what (by way of good humor) they were pleased to call my conquest, which Mrs. Demelly assured me was not a little spoken of in Paramaribo, as censured by some and applauded by others, but she believed in her heart envied by all. Now, Reader, prepare for scenes of a more dusky nature.

CHAPTER 6th

Account of a dreadful execution—Fluctuating state of political affairs—Short glimpse of peace—An officer shot dead—His whole party cut to pieces and a general alarm renewed throughout the Colony

May 21st. Now died our lieutenant colonel, Lantman, while a number of our officers lay sick, among whom at last (in place of joy and dissipation) pale mortality began to take place, and which from day to day increased among the private men at a most lamentable rate.

Next day the remains of the deceased lieutenant colonel were interred with military honors in the center of Fortress Zeelandia, where all criminals are imprisoned and all field officers buried, and where I was not a little shocked to see the captive Rebel Negroes, and others, clanking their chains and roasting plantains and yams upon their graves. This could not help putting me in mind of so many hellish fiends in the shape of African slaves, tormenting the souls of their European persecutors (in which number those in the navy or army ought with justice not be included, as they come not to inspire revolts but to quell them). From out these gloomy mansions of despair, this very day seven captive Negroes were selected, and being led by a few soldiers to the place of execution, which is in the savanna where the sailors and soldiers are interred, six were hanged and one broken alive upon the rack; besides which in front of the courthouse one white man was scourged by the public executioner, who is in this country always a black. But what makes me take particular notice here was the shameful injustice of showing a partiality to the European, who ought to have known better, by letting him escape with a slight corporal punishment, while the poor African, who is destitute of precepts and laws, lost his life for the same crime—stealing money out of the town hall—under the most excruciating torments, through which he manfully went without heaving a sigh or complaining. Meanwhile, one of his companions, with the rope about his neck and just going to be turned off, gave a hearty laugh of contempt at the magistrates who attended the execution. I ought not to omit that the Negro who flogged the white man inflicted the punishment with the greatest marks of commiseration, all of which almost induced me to decide that, between the Europeans and Africans in this colony, the first were the greater barbarians of the two, a name which tarnishes Christianity and is bestowed on them in too many corners of the globe—with what real degree of justice I will not take on myself to determine.

Having testified how much I was hurt by the cruelty of the above execution, and surprised at the intrepidity with which the Negroes bore their punishment, a decent-looking man stepped up to me.

Sir (said he), you are but a newcomer from Europe and know very little about the African slaves, without which you would testify both less feeling and surprise. Not long ago (continued he) I saw a black man hanged alive by the ribs, between which an incision was first made with a knife, and then an iron hook clinched with a chain. In this manner he kept living three days, hanging with his head and feet downwards, and catching with his tongue the drops of water (it being in the rainy season) that were flowing down his bloated breast, while the vultures were picking in the putrid wound. Notwithstanding all this, he never complained and even upbraided a Negro for crying while he was flogged below the gallows,[1] by calling out to him *"You man? Da boy fasi."* ("Are you a man? You behave like a boy.") Shortly after which he was knocked in the head with the butt end of a musket by the more commiserating sentry who stood over him. Another Negro (said he) I have seen quartered alive and, after four strong horses were fastened to his legs and arms, and after having had iron sprigs driven home underneath every one of his nails, on hands and feet, without a motion he first asked a dram and then bid them pull away, without a groan. But what gave us the greatest entertainment (continued he) were the fellow's jokes, by desiring the executioner to drink before him in case there should chance to be poison in the glass, and bidding him take care of his horses lest any of them should happen to strike backwards. As for old men being broken upon the rack and young women roasted alive chained to stakes, there can be nothing more common in this colony.

---

1. All Negroes cry out for mercy while they are being flogged, in hopes of having thereby the lesser punishment—but never, no never, where no mitigation is expected.

A Negro hung alive by the Ribs to a Gallows.

Plate 11

I was petrified at the inhuman detail and, breaking away with a curse from the damnable spot of laceration, made the best of my way home to my own lodgings.

May 24th. Having now received a supply of provisions from Holland, and absolutely doing no service in the Colony, it is resolved on all sides that we shall go home. Notwithstanding that our regiment is being paid partly by the United Provinces, it is still exceedingly chargeable to the Society and the inhabitants, who conjointly paid all other expenses. Thus, in the hopes of sailing in the middle of June, the transports were ordered a second time to wood, water, and otherwise prepare. I must say nothing of what I felt on this occasion.

But only the next day, getting intelligence that a plantation was demolished and the overseer murdered by the Rebels, we were a second time desired to stay by request of the Governor and the inhabitants. In consequence, the three transport ships which, since February 9th, had been kept waiting at a great expense (eighty florins per day, coming to more than two thousand guineas each) were finally put out of commission and the victuals stowed at the headquarters in temporary storehouses erected for the purpose.

Now the minds of the people began to be quieted, witnessing the enactment of what the troops were come here for, viz., to go on actual service and protect the inhabitants, which was certainly much better for both than to linger away an idle life at Paramaribo.

On the 7th, to our unutterable surprise, we were actually for the third time officially acquainted that, things seeming quiet and tranquillity reestablished, the Colony of Surinam had no further use for our services. These sudden changes did not fail to cause a great deal of discontent among the military and among the inhabitants. Cabals were formed that threatened to break out in a civil contest, some charging the Governor as jealous of the unlimited power that was vested in Colonel Fourgeoud—who by many people was blamed as abusing that power by not treating the Governor with that civility which he might have done without deviating from his own consequence. Thus, while one party swore we were the bulwarks of the settlement by keeping the Rebels at bay, the opposition hesitated not to call us the locusts of Egypt who were come to live on the fat of the Colony.

On the 15th, we received news which was no less than that an officer of the Society troops was shot dead by the Rebels, and that his whole party, consisting of about thirty men, had been cut to pieces, which threw the whole colony once more into confusion and consternation. The above gentleman, whose name was Lepper, and only a lieutenant, was much the cause of this misfortune by his too great courage and intrepidity, without either temper or conduct[2] of which I cannot omit relating the particulars.

It being now in the heart of the short dry season, this officer—being informed that between the rivers Patamacca and upper Coermotibo a village of Negroes had been discovered by the Rangers some time before—now insisted with this small party, which was only a detachment from the Patamacca post, to sally through the woods and attack them. But the Rebels, being apprised of his intention by their spies (which they never lack), immediately marched out against him, laying themselves in an ambush near the borders of a deep marsh through which Lieutenant Lepper with his party were to pass on their way to the Rebel settlement. No sooner were these unfortunate men got in the swamp till near their armpits than their black enemies rushed out from under cover and shot them dead in the water at pleasure, without their being able to return the fire more than once, their situation preventing them from reloading. They indeed might have strove to get upon the shore had not a general confusion taken place by the sudden death of their over-gallant commander, who (being imprudently distinguished by a gold-laced hat from among the rest) was shot through the head in the first onset. The few that scrambled out of the marsh upon the banks were immediately butchered in the most barbarous manner, while five or six were taken prisoner and carried alive to the settlement of the Rebels. I shall in proper place describe their melancholy fate, as I had it from those that were eyewitness to it, and which ends this dismal catastrophe.

June 16th. Now all Paramaribo was in an uproar—some parties so vehement that they were ready to tear the Governor and Council to pieces for having dismissed Colonel Fourgeoud with his regiment, while others ingeniously declared that if we were intended for no more use than we had hitherto proved to be, our company could without ceremony be dispensed with. All this could not but be exceedingly galling for our officers, who wished nothing more than to be employed on actual service for the good of the Colony of Surinam. Thus, while on the one side our chief did not escape from censure, on the other side the most bitter lampoons were spread through the town against the Governor and his Council, libels of such a black and inflammatory nature that no less than a thousand gold ducats were offered as a reward to the discoverer of their author, with a promise of maintaining the secrecy of his name if he required it. But the whole was to no purpose, and neither author nor informer made their appearance. Meanwhile, the general clamor still continuing, the

---

2. This gentleman formerly belonged to the Life-Guards in Holland, from where he had fled after stabbing his antagonist through the heart with his sword in a duel.

Governor and Council were forced (as they had desired us a third time to sail for Europe) now a third time to petition us to remain in Surinam and protect the distracted situation of the Colony. To this petition we once more condescended, and the ships were actually a third time put out of commission.

We, however, still continued doing nothing, to the unspeakable surprise of everyone, the only duty hitherto having consisted in a subaltern's guard at the headquarters to protect the chief, his colors, his storehouses, pigs, and poultry (which parade regularly mounted every day at half past four o'clock and to which our gentlemen squired the ladies), and another guard on board the transports, till the provisions were stowed ashore in the magazines, a few field days excepted, when the soldiers were drilled for pomp alone in a burning sun till they fainted.

I cannot continue any further without giving some sample of these two extraordinary men who, by their inveteracy and opposition to each other, were the principal cause of our undecided and fluctuating manner of proceeding, and the outlines of which two characters may assist in unraveling the riddle: Why in the name of wonder were we so plagued in Surinam?

Governor Nepveu was said to be a man of sense more than learning and was indebted alone to his artful and cunning manner for having risen from sweeping the hall of the courthouse to this present dignity. At the same time, he also, from nothing, found means to accumulate a most capital fortune and to command respect from all ranks who had any dealings with him, they never daring to attack him but at a distance. His comportment was affable but ironical, without ever losing the command of his temper, all of which gave him the appearance of a man of fashion, able to carry everything before him as he wished. He was generally known by the appellation of Reynard, and was most certainly a fox of too much artifice to be run down by all the hounds in the Colony.

Colonel Fourgeoud was quite the reverse. Impetuous, passionate, self-sufficient, and vengeful, he deserved not the name of cruel to individuals but was a tyrant to the generality and the death of hundreds, by his sordid avarice and oppression. With all this, he was partial, ungrateful, and confused, but the most indefatigable man for hardships and fatigue that ever yet was known, which like a true buccaneer he bore with the most heroic courage, patience, and perseverance. He was also affable to the private soldiers, but of his officers he was the bane. He had read, but had no education to digest it. In short, few men could talk better but on many occasions none acted worse.

Such were the characters given of our two commanders, which I shall not contradict, and whose opposition to each other could not miss to gall the happiness of the troops and, as I have said, promote the fluctuating state of political affairs in this dejected colony, where by appearance we were still come to do nothing.

June 29th. At last the hour arrives, and all the officers and men are ordered to be ready at a minute's warning to set out on actual service. Now all was in a stir, and each now preparing to do wonders, while our little corps was already melted from 530 able men to about three-fourths of that number, by death and sickness, the hospital being crowded with invalids of every kind.

June 30th. This day I was also informed of some cruelties which I must relate before my departure, as motives to deter others from abominable practices, at which humanity must shrink and sicken. What reader will believe that a Jewess, from a motive of groundless jealousy (for such her husband made it appear)—I say, who can believe that this unprecedented monster put an end to the life of a young and beautiful Quadroon girl by the infernal means of plunging a red-hot poker into her body, by those parts which decency forbids to mention, while for a crime of such a very hellish nature, the murderer was only banished to the Jews-Savanna, a village I shall afterwards describe, besides paying a trifling fine to the fiscal, who is a magistrate.

Another young Negro woman, having her ankles chained so close together that she could hardly move her feet, was knocked down with a cane by a Jew till the blood streamed out of her head, her arms, and her naked sides.

Still a third Israelite had dared to strike one of my soldiers for having made water against his garden fence. On this rascal I took revenge for the whole fraternity by wresting the offending weapon out of his hand, which I instantly broke to a thousand pieces on his guilty naked pate.

I nevertheless was just enough to flog another of my men out of the regiment, for picking a Smouse's pocket. So jealous are the Dutch soldiers of what they please to call a point of honor, that were a thief to be known in the ranks, the whole regiment would lay down their arms. This etiquette is not amiss and would be of no bad consequence to be introduced into some other armies, where a thief is as good as another if he is born to be six feet high.

And now for *vincere aut mori,* on board the wooden walls of the Colony, the props of Surinam, viz., half a dozen crazy old sugar barges, such as are used by the colliers on the Thames, only being roofed over with boards which gave them more the appearance of so many coffins. How well they deserved this name, I am afraid, I shall too soon make appear by the number of men they have buried.

With one of these vehicles of destruction, departed this very day for the Jews-Savanna up the River Surinam Major Medlar, two subalterns, one sergeant, two corporals, and twenty-eight men. Thus, after having been kept fiddling, dancing, and dying for five months at Paramaribo, the maneuvers were fairly begun.

July 1st. Today departed for the River Commewina one captain, two subalterns, one sergeant, two corporals, and eighteen men. Today departed also another barge to the River Perica, with two subalterns, one sergeant, one corporal, and fourteen men commanded by Lieutenant Count Randwyck.

On the evening of the 2nd, having entertained some select friends at my house, I took my last farewell from the lovely Joanna, to whose care I left my all, and herself to the protection of her mother and aunt, with my directions for putting her to school till my return. After which I at last marched on board, with four subalterns, two sergeants, three corporals, and thirty-two men under my command, to be divided into two barges and bound for the upper part of the River Cottica. The above barges were all armed with swivels, blunderbusses, &c., and provided with allowance for one month. Their orders were—that which went to the Jews-Savanna excepted—to cruise up and down the rivers. Each barge had a pilot and was rowed by Negro slaves, ten of which were on board for the purpose, which made my complement, including my black boy Quacoo, exactly thirty-six.

CHAPTER 7th

*Armed barges are sent up to defend the rivers—A cruise in
the upper parts of Rio Cottica and Patamacca—Great
mortality among the troops—View of the military post at
Devil's Harwar*

July 3rd. At four o'clock in the morning the fleet cast off from their
moorings and with the ebb tide rowed down as far as the fortress New
Amsterdam where, being wind-bound, we dropped anchor off the battery.

I hope it will not be out of character to describe here the dress of our
Marines, which was blue turned up with scarlet, short jackets, leather
caps, armed with a musket, saber, and pistol, a large wallet or knapsack
across one shoulder, and their hammocks slung over the other. In the
woods, they wore trousers and check shirts with short linen frocks, as
more adapted to the climate. Indeed, they still looked as if each soldier
could devour a tiger by himself. But how in a little time these strong and
flourishing young men were metamorphosed into a parcel of smoke-
dried scarecrows, my pen is not sufficient to describe.

I now reviewed my forces, viz., myself, four subalterns, two sergeants, three corporals, thirty-two privates, two pilots, twenty Negroes,
and my black boy Quacoo, being altogether sixty-five. I next numbered
them, placed the arms (consisting in blunderbusses, swivels, &c.),
stowed the luggage, and slung the hammocks with propriety. I then perused my orders, which consisted of cruising up and down Rio Cottica
between the Society posts, La Rochelle at Patamacca and s'Landswelvaren above the last plantation, to prevent the rebels from crossing
the river, to seize or kill them if possible, and to protect the estates from
their invasions—in all which (if necessary) I was to be assisted by the

A private Marine of Col. Fourgeoud's Corps.

Plate 13

troops of the Society on the above posts, with whom I was also to deliberate on the proper signals to be given in case of any alarm.

July 4th. In the morning, up anchor and, having doubled the cape, rowed with the flood till we arrived before Elizabeth's Hope, a beautiful coffee plantation where the proprietor, Mr. Klynhams, invited us ashore and showed us every civility in his power, besides loading my barge with refreshing fruits, vegetables, &c. He pitied our situation from his heart, he said, and foretold the miseries we were going to struggle with, the rainy season being just at hand or, indeed, already commenced by frequent showers, accompanied by loud claps of thunder. "As for the Enemy," said he,

> you may depend on not seeing one single soul of them, they knowing better than to make their appearance in public, while they may have a chance of seeing you from under cover. Thus, Sir, take care to be upon your guard. But the climate, the climate will murder you all. However (continued he), this shows the zeal of your commander, who will rather see you killed at any rate than allow you any longer to eat the bread of idleness at Paramaribo,

which he accompanied with a squeeze by the hand when we took our leave, and the beautiful Mrs. Dutry, his daughter, shed tears at our departure. This evening we anchored before the Matapica Creek.

July 5th. I here converted my two barges to men-of-war and christened them the *Charon* and the *Cerberus*,[1] by which names I shall distinguish them during the rest of the voyage. We now kept rowing up the River Cottica, having passed, since we entered Rio Commewina, the most enchantingly beautiful estates of coffee and sugar, which line the banks of both these rivers at the distance of one or two miles from each other.

My crew having walked and cooked their dinners ashore on the plantation L'Aventure, we anchored in the evening before Rio Perica.

July 6th. We rowed still further up Rio Cottica and went ashore on the estate Alia. At all the above plantations we were most hospitably received, but these now began to diminish as the river here begins to grow narrower. This evening anchored before the estate Lunenburg.

July 7th. We continued to keep course and, having walked ashore on the estate Bockensteyn (being the last plantation up the River Cottica on the right, except one or two small estates in Patamacca), at night we cast

---

1. The *Sudden Death* and *Willful Murder* would not have been out of character or less applicable, but with these epithets I had at that time not yet the honor of being acquainted.

anchor at the mouth of Coopman's Creek. Today the *Charon* was on fire but it was soon extinguished.

July 8th. We again kept rowing upwards and at eleven o'clock A.M. cast anchor off the post s'Landswelvaren, which was guarded by the troops of the Society. Here I stepped ashore with all my officers to wait on Captain Oorsinga, the commander, and deliver three of my sick men into his hospital, where I saw such a sight of misery and wretchedness as baffles all imagination. This place was formerly called Devil's Harwar, on account of its so very great unhealthiness—a name by which alone I shall again distinguish it as much more suitable than that of s'Landswelvaren, which signifies the Welfare of the Nation.

Here I saw a few of the wounded wretches who had escaped from the engagement in which Lieutenant Lepper, with so many men, had been killed. One of them told me the particulars of his own miraculous survival, which were so very wonderful and at the same time so authentic that I think them highly worth relating, to show what, in this climate, a soldier is exposed to.

> I was shot, Sir (said he), with a musket bullet in my breast. To resist or escape being impossible, I threw myself down, as the only means left me to save my life, among the deadly-wounded and the dead, without moving hand or foot. Here in the evening the Rebel chief, surveying his conquest, ordered one of his captains to begin instantly to cut off the heads of the slain, in order to carry them home to their village as trophies of their victory. Which captain, having already chopped off that of Lieutenant Lepper and one or two more, said to his friend *"Son de go sleeby caba. Mekewe liby den tara dago tay tamara."* ("The sun is just going, we must leave the other dogs till tomorrow.") Saying which (continued the man), as I lay upon my bleeding breast with my face resting upon my left arm, he dropped his hatchet into my shoulder by way of gesticulation and made the fatal wound you see and of which I shall perhaps no more recover. I, however, lay quite still till they went away, carrying along with them the mangled heads of my comrades and five or six prisoners, alive with their hands tied behind their backs, who never more since have been heard of. When all was quiet and it was very dark, I found means to creep out on my hands and feet among the carnage and get under cover in the forest, where I met another of our soldiers who was less wounded than myself and with whom, after ten days wandering in torment and despair, without bandages and not knowing which way to go, and with only one single loaf of black bread for all subsistence between us, we at last arrived at the military post of Patamacca, emaciated, and our wounds creeping in live worms and corruption.

I gave the miserable creature half a crown, and having agreed with Captain Oorsinga upon the signals, we left this pesthouse of the human species and, stepping on board my man-of-war, rowed up till before a place called Barbacoeba, where we once more came to an anchor.

July 9th. We rowed still further up the river till we came before the Coermotibo Creek, where we finally moored the fleet, as being the spot of my head-station, by Colonel Fourgeoud's command. Here we saw nothing but water, wood, and clouds which had an extremely solitary appearance.

July 10th. I detached the *Cerberus* to her station, viz., upper Patamacca, for which place she rowed immediately with a long list of paroles, according to my orders, but which were never of any service.

July 19th. Now also getting information that on the spot where we had dressed our victuals in the Coermotibo Creek, which is on the Rebel side of the river, a strong detachment had lately been murdered by the enemy, I ordered the cooking shed to be burnt to the ground and the meat to be dressed on board the barge. Here all the elements now seemed to oppose us: the water, pouring down like a deluge by the heavy rains, forced itself fore and aft into the vessel, where it set everything afloat; the air poisoned by myriads of mosquitoes that from sunset to sunrise regularly kept us company and prevented us from getting any sleep, besides besmearing us all over with blood and blotches; the smoke of the fire and the tobacco (which we burnt on their account) ready to choke us; and not a footstep of land to cook our salt provisions in safety. To all this misery may be added that discord broke out between the Marines and the Negroes, with whom promises or threats having no weight, I was obliged to have recourse to other means, viz., I tied up the ringleaders of both parties and, after ordering the first to be well flogged and the latter to be horsewhipped for an hour, I pardoned them all without one lash—which had equally the effect of the punishment, and peace was perfectly reestablished.

July 20th. We now rowed down till the mouth of the Cassipera Creek in hopes of meeting some relief, but it was equally as bad. So very thick were the mosquitoes now that by clapping my two hands against each other I killed in one stroke to the number of thirty-eight, upon my honor.

July 29th. We again rowed down to Barbacoeba, during which we saw one or two beautiful snakes swim across the river and where, by stepping ashore under the shade, we met with a little relief. I now had recourse to the advice of an old Negro. "Cramaca (said I), what do you do to keep your health?"

> Swim in the water twice or thrice every day, Sir (said he). This, *Massera,* not only serves for exercise where I cannot walk but keeps my skin clean and cool, while the pores being open, I enjoy a free perspiration. Without

this, the pores are shut by unperceivable filth, the juices stagnate, and corruption must inevitably follow.

Having recompensed the old gentleman with a dram, I instantly stripped and plunged headlong into the river. I had, however, no sooner taken this leap than he called to me for God's sake to return on board which, having done with much astonishment, he put me in mind of the alligators, besides a fish which is here called *pery*.

> Both these, Sir (said he), are exceedingly dangerous, but by following my directions you will run no hazard. You may swim as naked as you were born, but only take care that you constantly keep in motion, for the moment you are quiet you run the risk not only of their snapping off a limb but of being dragged yourself to the bottom.[2]

This Negro also advised me to walk barefooted and thinly dressed.

> Now is the season, *Massera* (said he), to get your feet used to becoming hard, by walking on the smooth boards of the vessel. The time may come when you will be obliged to do so for want of shoes in the middle of thorns and briars, as I have seen some others. Custom (said he), *Massera,* is second nature. Our feet were all made alike. Do as I advise you, and in the end you will thank old Cramaca. As for being thinly dressed (continued the Negro), a shirt and trousers is fully sufficient, which not only saves trouble and expense, but the body wants air as well as it does water. Thus, bathe in both when you have the opportunity.

From that moment, I followed his wise counsel, to which—besides being cleanly and cool—I in great part ascribe the preservation of my life.

July 23rd. This being the day appointed between Captain Oorsinga and me to try the signals, at twelve o'clock precisely the whole number of blunderbusses and swivels were fired at Devil's Harwar on board the *Charon* and on board the *Cerberus,* still stationed at Patamacca—which afterwards proved to be ineffectual and to no purpose, no one having been able to hear the report of the guns fired by the other. During this, however, I met with a small accident, viz., by firing one of the blunderbusses myself, having placed it like a musket against my shoulder, I received such a violent stroke by its repulsion as threw me backwards over a large hogshead of Irish beef and nearly dislocated my right arm. This, it seems, was owing to my ignorance of the maneuver, as being since told that all such weapons ought to be fired under the hand (especially when they are heavily charged), and when by swinging round the body at once with the

---

2. This is confirmed by Dr. Bancroft, who says the Indians, in swimming, take care to continue in motion, by which means the fish are frightened and keep at a distance.

arm, the force of the repulsion is broken without effect. I insert this only to show in what manner heavily loaded musketoons ought always to be fired, especially since without any aim the execution of their wide mouth is equally fatal.

July 26th. Getting now an account by a canoe that came down from Patamacca that the *Cerberus* was in danger of being attacked by the enemy, who had been spied hovering round about her, and the river where she was moored being very narrow, I immediately (having rowed the *Charon* up till the mouth of the Pinnenburg Creek) manned the yawl as being the most expeditious, and went myself with six men to her assistance, but the whole proved to be a false alarm, and in the evening we returned back to our station. In rowing down, I was surprised to be hailed by a human voice, which begged me, for God's sake, to step ashore. This I did with two of my men, when I was accosted by a poor old Negro woman imploring me for some assistance. It seemed she was the property of a Jew, to whom belonged the spot of ground where I found her, and where the poor creature lived quite alone, in a hut not larger than a dog's nest, surrounded by a wilderness except a few plantain trees, yams, and cassava for her support. She was of no more use to work on the great estate and was banished here only to support her master's right to the possession, since this spot had been ruined by the Rebels. Having left her with a piece of salt beef, some barley, and a bottle of rum, I took my leave, when she offered me in return one of her cats, but to no purpose, the row-Negroes firmly insisting that she was a witch—which shows that superstition reigns not only in Europe.

July 27th. We now returned to Coermotibo Creek, where this day my Negroes, having been ashore to cut wood for the furnace, brought on board a poor animal alive, with all its four feet chopped off with the bill-hook, and which lay still in the bottom of the canoe. Having freed it from its torment by a blow in the head, I was acquainted that this was the sloth, called *loyaree* or *hiaey* by the natives, on account of its plaintive voice. It is about the size of a small water spaniel, with a round head something like that of a monkey, but its mouth is remarkably large. Its hind legs are much shorter than those in front to help it in climbing, being each armed with three tremendous sharp claws, which are all its defense and which had induced my slaves to commit the above amputation. Its eyes are languid, and its motion is so slow that it takes two days to get to the top of a moderate tree from which it never descends while a leaf or a bud is remaining, beginning its devastation first at the top to prevent its being starved in coming to the bottom, when it goes in quest of another, making incredible little way when on the ground. Of these animals, there are two species in Guiana, distinguished by the names of *sicapo* and *dago loy-*

The Ai, & the Unan; or the Sheep & Dog Sloth.

Plate 16

aree, viz., the sheep and the dog sloth, which some authors call the *ai* and the *unan*. The sloth has a soft, squeaking voice like a young cat; it is different in its generative parts from all other quadrupeds and is eaten with avidity by the Indians and Negroes.

July 28th. Now came down from Patamacca in an open canoe and burning sun Lieutenant Stromer, the commander of the *Cerberus,* in a violent fever, drinking cold water from the river for all relief. Came down also a Jew soldier of the Society post La Rochelle, with the account that the Rebels had actually passed the creek above the last estate two days before, as had been reported, viz., from east to west, at the same time delivering me a Negro woman and sucking child who had formerly been stolen by the Rebels and now had found means to make her escape. From below, I received also the news that Major Medlar had sent to town from the Jews-Savanna two barbecued hands of the enemy, killed by the Rangers; that an officer and ten men were landed at Devil's Harwar with provisions under my command; and that one of my sick men there had died; also an order from Fourgeoud to seek out, if possible, a dry spot to build a magazine. Now having detached my Lieutenant, Mr. Hammer, to take command of the *Cerberus* at Patamacca, I instantly weighed anchor and rowed down till the mouth of the Cassipera Creek, where we passed such a night as no pen can describe, being crowded with all sorts of people. The sick groaned, the Jew prayed, the soldiers swore, the Negroes begged, the woman sang, the child squeaked, the fire smoked, the rains poured down, and the whole stank to such a degree that I vow to God I began to think myself little better off than in the black hole of Calcutta. Heaven and earth all seemed now to conspire against us. However, at six o'clock next morning, the joyful sun broke through the clouds, and I dropped down with the *Charon* till before Devil's Harwar.

July 29th. Here I now delivered my sick officer and five sick men, besides my other passengers, for whom I had done all that was in my power (but that was very little). Having also stowed the newly arrived provisions in a proper place, I once more returned to my cursed station, where I came to an anchor on August the first.

August 2nd. Now, between the showers, we saw great quantities of monkeys, of which I shot one, and having had no fresh meat for a long time I got it dressed and ate it with a good appetite. We were at this time really in a shocking condition, not only wanting refreshment but with all the men's shoes and hammocks rotting from day to day, being (besides mostly wet) composed of the very worst ingredients sent from Holland.

August 3rd. Got the account that Lieutenant Stromer was dead at Devil's Harwar. The next day, we dropped down till before that place to bury him decently, but such was utterly impossible, since having contrived to

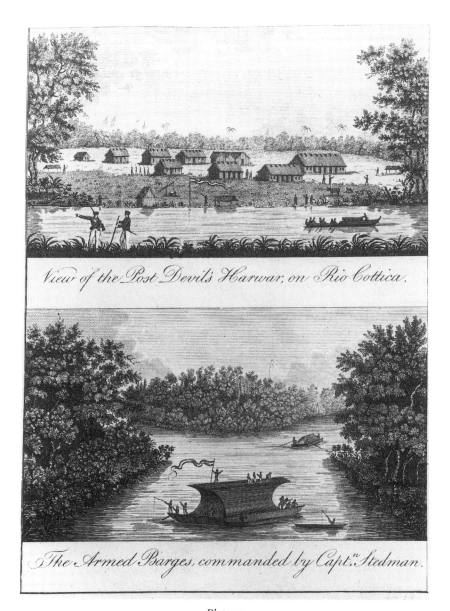

View of the Post Devil's Harwar, on Rio Cottica.

The Armed Barges, commanded by Capt.ⁿ Stedman.

Plate 17

make a coffin of old boards, the corpse dropped through it before it reached the grave and afforded an absolutely shocking spectacle. We nevertheless found means to go through the rest of the interment with some decorum, having covered it over with a hammock by way of a pall, and fired three volleys by all the troops that had strength to carry arms. This over, I regaled the officers with a glass of wine and once more took farewell of Devil's Harwar on the 6th, having first written Colonel Four-geoud that the Rebels had passed above La Rochelle and that I had found a spot for a magazine at Barbacoeba. Reported also the death of my lieu-tenant, Mr. Stromer, and recommended my sergeant (who had been an officer of hussars) for advancement.

August 7th. I now arrived again at Coermotibo Creek, where I re-solved to make a landing on the west shore at every hazard, so that my own soldiers could cook their beef and barley (it being just as well to be shot by the enemy at once as to be killed on board the *Charon* by inches). However, this was a difficult task, all that shore being so very marshy and overgrown with every kind of underwood that we could hardly put our new project in execution. But at last, my Negroes having made a tem-porary kind of bridge (to step from the yawl upon a small speck of dry ground), and having formed a slight shade of manicole leaves to keep off the rain, we found means to keep up a fire and be a hundred times better than we were on board the *Charon*.

But here our danger was certainly also much greater, since an old Rebel settlement was not very far from this place, which was called Pin-nenburg (from a neighboring creek, though others say it got this name on account of the sharp pins stuck in the ground, like crow-feet or *chevaux-de-frise,* with which the Rebels had formerly fortified and de-fended it). Notwithstanding this village had been demolished, it was well known that the Rebels still often visited the spot, to pick up some of the rice, yams, and cassava which the ground continued (in its uncultivated state) to produce for a temporary subsistence. And I was almost abso-lutely convinced that the Rebels who had lately passed above La Rochelle in Patamacca were at this moment encamped at the above spot, Pinnen-burg, ready to commit some depredations on the estates in the rivers Cottica or Perica, if not to attack us. For this reason, I always kept double sentinels round the landing place, with orders that no man should be al-lowed to speak or make any manner of noise while on that spot, in order to hear even the smallest rustling of a leaf, and prevent danger by vigi-lance and alacrity.

On the 8th, my other officer, Macdonald, fell sick but refused to be sent to Devil's Harwar, on account of leaving me thus quite by myself. I have said that we had no surgeon but a parcel of medicines, which consisted of emetics, laxatives, and powders (of which I knew not the proper use). I also had some plasters on board the barge, but these were indeed very soon expended by the running ulcers which covered the crew all over, and which was easily accounted for, since in this climate (where the air is impregnated with myriads of invisible animalcules) the smallest scratch immediately becomes a running sore, and scratching must be a daily occupation, where one is covered over with mosquitoes &c. I have said the best antidote and cure was lemon or lime acid, but this we had not; the next is never to expose an open wound or even the smallest scratch to the air, but the instant they are received to cover them up with a gray paper wetted with spirits or any kind of moisture, so that it may stick to the skin. For my own part, no man could still continue to be more healthy, wearing nothing but my long trousers and check shirt loose at the collar and turned up in the sleeves, nay, even when the sun was not too hot, I stripped altogether to the buff, and every day twice continued to plump into the river. By this I was always cool and clean; besides, there is a kind of pleasure in rambling naked when the occasion will permit it, which I always envied the Indians and Negroes, and of which only those few can have any idea who have tried the experiment, and delight in following these rules, which kind Nature, by an unerring precept, has prescribed. I also daily used a cheering glass of wine, having first hung it a few fathoms under water, which made it much more cool and agreeable.

This evening, we heard the sound of a drum, which we could suppose to be no other than that of the Rebels. Nevertheless, we determined to continue dressing our victuals ashore, keeping on our guard (according to the advice of Mr. Klynhams, who had exactly foretold what now befell us).

August 9th. This day Mr. Macdonald was much worse. However, by seeing me receive a letter from Colonel Fourgeoud, he seemed to revive (as did we all), expecting now to be relieved from our horrid situation. But what was our mortification at reading that we were still to continue on the cursed station (by his order who, like a true general, was relentless of our misery and complaints). This letter was accompanied by a present of fishhooks and tackle, to make up for the deficiency of other refreshments and indeed salt provisions, which began daily to grow both worse and less. And so it was, while the whole crew bore distraction in their countenances, declaring they were sacrificed for no manner of purpose, while the Negroes sighed, pronouncing the words *"Ah, poty backera."* However, by a few tamarinds, oranges, lemons, and Madeira wine, which were by this occasion sent me by my best *friend* at Paramaribo, I found means to give not only to my officers, but also to my drooping soldiers, some relief. But this cheering sunshine could not last long, and the day following we were as much distressed as ever. I once more had recourse to the nimble fraternity of the forest, and brought down two monkeys with my gun from the top of the mangroves, where they were skipping not by dozens but by hundreds.

August 11th. Sent two men sick to the hospital. This evening again heard the drums.

August 22nd. I at last fell sick myself, and upon the whole I was now truly in a pitiful condition, deprived of both my officers and my sergeant, my men upon the three stations (viz., the two barges and Devil's Harwar together) melted down to only fifteen from forty-two, without a surgeon or refreshment, surrounded with a black forest, and exposed to the mercy of a relentless enemy, should he be informed of our defenseless situation. The remaining few declared that they were doomed to destruction, and could hardly be prevented from rising in rebellion and going down the River Cottica with the *Charon* against my orders. But how little reason is there in a common soldier. Had they only considered that our Commander in Chief had other fish to fry at Paramaribo, where he made wise plans for his ensuing campaigns and wrote letters to Holland with an account of his already begun exploits, which to be sure had a much better grace, and more martial appearance because of the number of dead (no matter in what manner they were killed) that were mentioned in their bloody contents. Indeed, I myself was not altogether free from making some unfavorable reflections, such as that the enemy having crossed the Patamacca Creek, a few troops from all quarters ought to have marched against them, that is from La Rochelle, Devil's Harwar, and the River Perica when, betwixt the three, the enemy might have been (if not entirely routed) at least called to a very severe account for their presumption. Not to speak of the happy effect which such a check must have in saving the lives and property of those victims, who, after such incursions, are generally devoted to their rage. But all such reflections, and many more, we must impute to the effects of a frenzy fever, which seemed already to have affected my pericranium.

August 23rd. I was rather a little better this day, and between the fits of the fever shot a couple of large black monkeys, to make some broth by way of refreshment, which (however uncommon and strange it may appear to the reader) I had nevertheless found to be extremely good—while this may be owing, in part, to my being in want of other fresh provisions.

But as the killing of one of these was attended with such circumstances as almost deterred me forever after from going a-monkey hunting, I must beg leave to relate them as they happened. Seeing me on the side of the river in the canoe, the creature made a stop from skipping after his companions and, being perched on a branch that hung over the water, examined me with attention and the greatest marks of curiosity, no doubt taking me for a giant of his own species, while he showed his teeth, perhaps by way of laughing, chattered prodigiously, and kept dancing and shaking the bough on which he rested with incredible strength and velocity. At this time I laid my piece to my shoulder and brought him down from the tree, plump in the stream, but may I never again be witness to such a scene. The miserable animal was not dead but mortally wounded, so taking his tail in both my hands to end his torment, I swung him round and knocked his head against the sides of the canoe with such a force that I was covered all over with blood and brains. But the poor thing still continued alive, and looked at me in the most pitiful manner that can be conceived. I knew no other means to end this murder than by holding him under water till he was drowned, while my heart felt sick on his account. Here his dying little eyes still continued to follow me with seeming reproach till their light gradually forsook them and the wretched creature expired. Never poor devil felt more than I on this occasion, nor could I taste of him or his companion when they were dressed, though they afforded to some others a delicious repast, which ended the catastrophe.

That monkeys are no bad food, especially when young, may easily be accounted for, since they feed on nothing but fruit, nuts, eggs, young birds, &c., they being both fructivorous and carnivorous. Indeed, in my opinion, all young quadrupeds are edible, but when one compares those killed in the woods to those filthy, disgusting creatures that disgrace the streets, no wonder that they should turn the stomach of the most famished. As for the wild ones, I have eaten them boiled, roasted, and stewed, and found their flesh white, juicy, and good—the only thing which disgusted me being their little hands and their heads, which when dressed, and being deprived of the skin, look like the hands and the skull of a young infant. I have already observed that there are in Guiana many different species, varying according to Dr. Bancroft from a large *orangoutang* to the very small *saccawinkee*. However, I never heard speak of the former while I was in this country and, as for the latter, I shall describe him in his turn, when he shall give me the opportunity, and now only give an account of those whom I have met with on this cruise.

That which I shot the second instant is what is called in Surinam *meecoo*. It is near the size of a fox and of a reddish-gray color with a black head and very long tail. Those I killed on the 10th were indeed exceedingly beautiful, and much more delicate when dressed than the former. They are called *keesee-keesee* by the inhabitants, and are about the size of a rabbit and most astonishingly nimble. Their color is reddish all over the

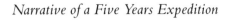

body, and the tail, which is long, is black at the extremity, but its four feet are orange. The head is very round and the face milk-white, with a round black patch in the middle, in which are the mouth and the nostrils, and which give it a masklike appearance; its eyes are black and remarkably lively. These monkeys we saw pass daily along the sides of the river, skipping from tree to tree, but mostly about midday, and in very numerous bodies, regularly following each other like a little army, with their young ones on their backs not unlike little knapsacks. Their manner of traveling is by the foremost walking to the extremity of a bough, from which it bounds onto the extremity of that belonging to the next tree, at a most astonishing distance, and with such wonderful activity and precision that it never once misses its aim. Then, all the others one by one (and even the females with their little ones on their backs, which stick fast to the mother like burrs) perform the same leap, with the greatest seeming facility and safety. They are also remarkable in climbing up along the *nebees,* or natural ropes, with which many parts of the forest are interwoven, and make it look like the rigging of a fleet at anchor. The monkeys, I am told, sometimes have two young, and of their suckling them like the human species I have been a witness. Towards sunset, this kind clamber up to the tops of the palm trees (some of which are above one hundred feet in height), where they sleep safe in the large diverging branches. The *keesee-keesee* is such a beautiful and delicately formed creature that it is by many people kept as a pet on a silver chain—besides for its mimicry, drolleries, its good nature, and chirping voice, which pronounces *peeteeco-peeteeco* without intermission. They are easily tamed, and the way to take them is by a strong glue, made by the Indians, and which is something like our European birdlime.

The other species of which I gave the horrid account were called by my Negroes *monkee-monkee.* The only thing further that I can say of them is that they are in size between the two former described, and black all over. One thing I ought not to omit, which is very remarkable, viz., that one morning I saw from my barge a monkey of this kind down at the water's edge, rinsing his mouth and appearing to clean his teeth with one of his fingers. He was first discovered by one of the slaves, who pointed him out to me to my astonishment. The last thing I shall now say further upon this subject (without the smallest pretensions of being a connoisseur in natural philosophy, as may too easily be perceived throughout the descriptive parts of this no less laborious work) is that the wonderful Chain of Gradation, from Man to the most diminutive of the above species, is too conspicuous not to inspire me with humility, and think more of these wandering little objects, who if wisely viewed and dissected, bear such general resemblance with (nay, little difference from) myself, not only in

The Mecoo & Kishee-Kishee Monkeys.

Plate 18

their external and internal form but in many of their actions and pursuits, which are by us called instinct, and by following which they never err. Meanwhile, Man—the proud Lord of the Creation with all his reason—is so many times mired in a bog, from where he can no more be extricated. Does not the face, shape, and manner of the African Negro (whom in every respect I look on as my brother)—I say, does this not often put us in mind of the Wild Man of the Woods or orangoutang? While, on the other hand, what is *this* [what am I?] stilled more than a large monkey? I acknowledge the theme almost too delicate to bear investigation. Here I shall end it for the present, after still adding that the above animals are sociable, that they are very tenacious of life, as I have shown, and that the usual distinction between what are called monkeys and apes consists in this: that the first all have tails, of which the latter are divested, and which (never having met with one in Guiana) I believe more to be the inhabitant of Asia and Africa than of that part of the New World distinguished by the name of South America. The monkeys are often mischievous near the plantations, where they commit depredations on the sugar canes &c., yet of which I but one time have been a witness.

August 26th. Resting in my hammock between the paroxysms of my fever, about halfway between Coermotibo and Barbacoeba, while the *Charon* was floating down, the sentinel called to me that he had seen and challenged something black and moving in the brushwood on the beach which gave no answer, and which from its thickness he concluded must be a man. I immediately dropped anchor and, having manned the canoe, ill as I was, I stepped into it. We rowed up to the place mentioned by the sentinel, where we all stepped ashore to reconnoiter, I suspecting this to be no other than a Rebel spy, or straggling party detached by the enemy. Suddenly, one of my slaves named David declared it was no Negro but a large amphibious snake which could not be far from the beach, and that I might have an opportunity to shoot it if I pleased. But to this I had not the smallest inclination from its uncommon size, from my weakness, and the difficulty of getting through the thicket, which seemed impenetrable to the water's edge, and I ordered all to return on board. The Negro then asked me liberty to step forwards and shoot it himself, assuring me it could not be at any distance, and warranting me against all danger. This spirited me so much that I determined to take his first advice and kill it myself, providing he was to point it out to me, and bail the hazard by standing at my side, from which I swore that if he dared to move I should level the piece at himself and blow out his brains without judge or jury, and to which he agreed. Thus having loaded my gun with a ball cartridge, we proceeded, David cutting away a path with the billhook, and a Marine following with three more loaded firelocks to keep in readiness.

We had not gone above twenty yards through mud and water (the Negro looking every way with an uncommon degree of archness and attention) when starting behind me he called out, *"Me see snakee,"* viz., that he saw the snake coiled under the fallen leaves and rubbish of the trees. "D——n you, rascal (said I). Then stand before me till I also see him, or you are dead this instant." And this he did, when with very much difficulty I perceived the head of this monster distant from me not above sixteen feet, moving its forked tongue, while its eyes seemed to emit fire by their brightness. Now resting my piece upon a branch to take a proper aim, I fired, but missing the head the ball went through the body, when the animal struck around with such astonishing force as cut away all the underwood around him with the facility of a scythe mowing grass, and by flouncing his tail he made the mud and dirt fly over our heads at a considerable distance. During this maneuver we all ran to the river and crowded into the canoe, but the Negro now entreated me to renew the charge, assuring me he would be quiet in a few minutes, and at any rate persisting in the assertion that the snake was neither able nor inclined to pursue us (which he undertook to prove by walking before me till I should be ready to fire). I again undertook to make the trial, the more since he said that his first starting backwards had only proceeded from a desire to make room for myself. I now found him a little removed from his former station but very quiet, with his head as before, out among the fallen leaves, rotten bark, and old moss. I fired at it immediately, but with no better success than the other time, the snake sending up such a cloud of dust and dirt as I never saw but in a whirlwind, and making us all once more betake to our heels for the canoe, where now being heartily tired of the exploit I gave orders to paddle[3] for the barge. But the slave still entreating me to let him kill the animal, I was actually induced to make a third and last attempt in company with himself. Thus having once more discovered the snake, we discharged both our pieces at once (not unlike the story told of Robinson Crusoe with Friday), however with this good effect, that he was now by one of us shot through the head. David, the slave (leaping with joy before the monster, as his namesake, the king, had done before the ark), fetched the painter, or boat rope, in order to drag him to the canoe. But this again was a difficult job, since the creature, notwithstanding its being mortally wounded, still continued to make such twists and writhes as made it dangerous for anyone to come very near him. However, the Negro, having made a running noose, threw it over his head with much dexterity, after a few fruitless attempts to make an approach, and now all taking hold of the rope we hauled him to the

---

3. In all canoes, paddles are used instead of oars.

beach and tied him to the stern of the canoe to take him in tow, being still alive, where he kept swimming like an eel. I had no relish for taking such a shipmate on board, whose length (notwithstanding to my astonishment all the Negroes declared it to be but a young one, come to about its half-growth) I measured to be twenty-two feet and some inches, and its thickness like that of my black boy Quacoo, who might then have been about twelve years old and around whose waist I since measured the creature's skin.

Being arrived alongside of the *Charon,* the next thing was what now to do with this huge animal, when it was determined to bring him ashore at Barbacoeba, to have him skinned, take out the oil, &c. This we did, the Negro, David, having climbed up a tree with the end of the rope, let it down over a strong forked branch, and the other Negroes hoisted the snake up. This done, David—with a sharp knife between his teeth—now left the tree and clung fast upon the monster, which was still twisting, and began his operations by ripping it up and stripping down the skin as he descended, which though the animal could now do him no hurt, I acknowledge had a terrible appearance, viz., to see a man stark naked, black and bloody, clinging with arms and legs around the slimy and yet living monster. However, his labor was not in vain, since he not only dexterously finished the operation but provided me with (besides the skin) above four gallons of fine, clarified fat, or rather oil, losing perhaps as much more. This I delivered to the surgeons at Devil's Harwar for the use of the wounded men in the hospital and for which I received their hearty thanks, it being deemed—particularly for bruises—a very excellent remedy. At signifying my surprise to see the snake still living after he was deprived of his intestines and skin, Cramaca, the old Negro, assured me he would not die till after sunset. The Negroes now cut him in slices in order to dress him and eat part of him, they all declaring he was exceedingly good and healthy, which to their great mortification, I refused giving my assent to, and we rowed down with the skin to Devil's Harwar.

Having thus described the manner in which he was killed, I shall now give some account of the animal itself, which is mentioned by many different authors, and of which several skins are preserved in the British and Mr. Parkinson's museums. It is called by Mr. Wesley *lyboija,* and *boa* in the British Encyclopedia, to which I refer the reader for a perfect account and an excellent engraving of this wonderful creature, which is in the Colony of Surinam called *aboma.* Its length, when full grown, is sometimes forty feet and more than four feet in circumference. Its color is a greenish black on the back, a fine brownish yellow on the sides, and a dirty white under the belly, the back and sides being spotted with irregular black rings, of a pure white in the middle. Its head is broad and flat,

The skinning of the Aboma Snake, shot by Cap. Stedman.

Plate 19

small in proportion to the body, with a large mouth beset with a double row of teeth, a forked tongue, and two bright prominent eyes. It is all covered over with large scales, some about the size of a shilling, and under the body near the tail armed with two strong claws like cock spurs, to help its seizing its prey. It is an amphibious animal, that is to say, it delights in low and marshy places where it lays coiled up like a rope and concealed under all kinds of moss, rotten timber, and dried leaves to seize its prey by surprise, which from its great bulk it has no activity to pursue. This consists, when hungry, in anything that comes within its reach, no matter what—a sloth, a wild boar, a stag, or even a jaguar, around which having twisted itself by the help of its claws, so that it cannot escape, it next breaks by its irresistible force every bone in the animal's body, which it then covers over with a kind of slime or saliva from its mouth to make it slide, and at last gradually sucks it in till it disappears. After this, the *aboma* cannot shift his station on account of the great knob or knot, which the swallowed prey occasions in that part of the body where it rests, till it is digested, which would hinder him from sliding along the ground, and during which time the *aboma* wants no other subsistence. I have been told of Negroes being devoured by this animal, to which I willingly give credit should they chance to come within his reach during the time of his affamishment, and which properties of seizing their prey, long fasting, &c., I believe to be common in many (if not in most) other snakes. Nor do I apprehend that its flesh, which looked beautifully white and had the appearance of fish, is in any way pernicious to the stomach, and I should never have refused the Negroes eating it had I not observed a kind of dissatisfaction among the remaining Marines when I went to give the Negroes the use of the kettle to boil it. The bite of this snake is said not to be venomous, nor do I believe it bites at all from any other impulse than hunger.

I shall only add that, having nailed its skin on the bottom of a canoe and dried it in the sun (sprinkling it with wood ashes to prevent it from corruption), I sent it to a friend at Paramaribo from where it was since sent to Holland as a curiosity.

In short, this job being ended, we also made an end of the cruise by dropping down in the night for the last time till before the Society post Devil's Harwar, in order next day to take possession.

CHAPTER 8th

*Three estates burnt and the inhabitants murdered by the
Rebels—Real picture of misery and distress—Specimen of a
march through the woods of Surinam*

On August 27th, I stepped ashore to relieve Captain Oorsinga and his
men and take the command of this place, having been on board the
Charon exactly fifty-six days, or eight weeks, in the most wretched condition that can be described. Hoping now to get the better of my complaint by the help of a few refreshments, such as milk &c., and with the
Society troops (above one hundred in number) ready to set off the next
day with my empty barges to La Rochelle in Patamacca, I now reviewed
my Marines. I found that I had but two out of five officers left, both sick,
the other three being dead, besides one sergeant, two corporals, and only
fifteen privates, being the remainder of fifty-four people who had been
healthy on the 2nd day of last July. This army was sufficient only to defend the hospital crowded with sick, the ammunition and victualing
magazine, &c., on a spot where lately had been kept three hundred soldiers, particularly while the enemy were lurking not far off; in consequence, the Society captain reinforced me with twenty of his men, and
all was well.

On the morning of the 28th, the Society troops at last rowed up to
Patamacca, when, examining the twenty soldiers they had left me, they
proved to be the refuse of the whole party, with agues, wounds, ruptures,
and rotten limbs, and most of them next day were obliged to enter the
hospital.

On the 29th, having bastonaded my late pilot for stealing from the
soldiers, I sent a report to Colonel Fourgeoud that I had taken post, and
acquainting him of my weak situation, I asked for a proper reinforce-

ment. This evening again two of my men died. All things now being regulated and settled, I thanked Heaven in the expectation of at last getting some rest, still being weak, and with these cheering hopes I retired at ten o'clock at night to my hammock. But this tranquillity was of short duration, since having scarcely shut my eyes, I was awakened by my sergeant and the following letter put in my hands, sent by an express from the captain of the militia in Cottica.

Sir,
This is to acquaint you that the Rebels have burnt three estates by your side, De Suynigheid, Du Perou, and L'Esperance, the ruins of which are still smoking, and that they have cut the throats of all the white inhabitants who fell into their hands. As on their retreat they must pass close by where you are posted, be on your guard. I am in haste.

Yours &c.
(Signed) Stoelman

Conscious of my defenseless situation, I immediately started up; and the express who brought the letter having spread the news the moment of his landing, I had no need to turn out the soldiers, since not only the few that were well but the whole hospital burst out, several of whom in spite of my opposition crawled on hands and feet to their arms, and dropped dead upon the spot. Nor may I ever behold such a scene of misery and distress: lame, blind, sick, and wounded, in the hopes of preserving a wretched existence, rushed upon certain death.

I was myself in a very weakly condition indeed. However, we continued to lie all night upon our arms, during which time I pressed the messenger to add one to the number, being determined to sell our lives as dearly as possible. But no enemy appearing in the morning, we buried the dead in their hammocks, not a board to make a coffin to be met with on the whole post. I now lost all patience, and had the audacity to write to my commander (besides what had happened) that my last men stood upon the brink of the grave, by hardships and for want of being properly supported (the very waiters of the hospital having deserted the moment of my arrival here and gone to Paramaribo). Indeed, our whole number was now melted down to but twelve men, to protect twelve buildings, while we had no more than two very small chests of ammunition to defend them, and no retreat for the sick, since all the barges were gone to Patamacca and the last canoe with my letter to Colonel Fourgeoud (I having set adrift that belonging to the express, who was bookkeeper of a neighboring plantation, to prevent him or any other from making their escape). In this situation, I was now obliged to make slaves to soldiers, whom I armed with a hatchet, not daring to trust them with a firelock.

In short, I acknowledge I found myself in great difficulty, while this whole night we again watched under arms, and in the morning found two more of my poor soldiers dead on the ground.

I now began really to think we were all devoted to destruction, while the men, regardless of all order (self-preservation excepted), threw out aloud the most bitter invectives against their persecutor, the gallant Fourgeoud, which I could not prevent. Nor can I help remarking the generalship of the Rebel Negroes, who had kept lying on the lurch just till the removal of the Society troops from Devil's Harwar, and who seized the very first day of their departure, convinced of its being guarded only by my sick and emaciated soldiers, in order to commit their depredations on the Cottica estates, well knowing that my force was not sufficient to pursue them, nay, hardly to stand in my own defense. However, all this was much according to my expectation, while on the contrary, had my strength timely been sufficient, they could never have escaped at least from being cut off in their retreat, especially if the troops in Rio Perica had acted conjointly with those in Cottica by patrolling the cordon or path between the two rivers, and across which the Rebels were unavoidably obliged to pass twice.

We now waited once more till morning and then buried another of my poor men, while I still cannot conceive how anyone could survive such toil, in such a debilitated state, and in a tropical climate. Yet some did, though few, while I at last being persuaded that the Rebels must have passed the cordon, without having thought proper to pay us a visit on their retreat, determined to let those few stand watch no longer but let them die their own natural deaths. At last in the evening, when all was too late, came down by water from the post La Rochelle to our assistance one officer and ten men, I having had but nine left to do the duty. But to what purpose now?

On September 2nd, another man died. At this time, I once more reviewed my forces, which amounted to exactly seven Marines, the few scarecrows of the Society excepted. However, the chance of our getting our throats cut was at this time over, thanks alone to the pusillanimity, perhaps even to the humanity, of the Rebel Negroes, against whom, by Heavens, we could have made little more resistance than a field of grasshoppers against a flock of carrion crows.

September 3rd. I now received a letter from Colonel Fourgeoud, condoling with me on the loss of so many good officers and acquainting me that I was to be reinforced and that, at my recommendation, my sergeant, Mr. Cabanes, was appointed an ensign, which gave me pleasure, and happened apropos, since today poor Ensign Macdonald was sent down very sick to Paramaribo. I answered to all this that I was obliged to him, as I could no longer be accountable for whatever consequence happened, where I was left to defend a whole river with none but sick people, without even sufficient ammunition, and who were hourly expiring for want of proper medicines or even so much as a surgeon to attend them—there being none here but one or two surgeon's mates belonging to the troops of the Society, who could do little better than draw blood and cut off a beard or a corn upon occasion, but nothing else of any consequence, and this letter immediately departed.

September 4th. I buried another of my Marines.

Next day, another one died, and I had not one remaining who was not ill or his feet swollen with the insects called chigoes, all these poor men (being mostly Germans) having been accustomed to a healthy climate in their own country. In short, I began now to be reconciled to putting my last man under ground, and to leaping into the grave after him myself, when finally arrived from Paramaribo a barge with the proper reinforcements, ammunition, provisions, medicines, a surgeon, &c., &c., and an order from my chief for me to trace out the track of the Rebels immediately, on the quondam path of communication called the cordon, between Cottica and Perica, and to write him the result of my discovery, also that he intended to keep his magazines at Devil's Harwar and was not to make use of the spot I had found for that use at Barbacoeba.

As the manner of marching in this country is so very different from that in Europe, I shall here, before we set out, accurately describe its proceeding.

In the first place, in Surinam no such thing is practicable as three or even two ranks, thus no marching by divisions, platoons, or even by files—but the whole party being dressed in one rank, face to the right, and every man follows his leader, the Negro slaves being interspersed between the men to be guarded themselves, as well as what they carry, and which manner of marching is called Indian-file. For instance, for a detachment of sixty men, consisting of one captain, two subalterns, two sergeants, four corporals, one surgeon, and fifty privates, at least twenty Negro slaves ought to be employed, for the use of whom their masters are paid at the rate of two shillings sterling per day by the Colony; and this is a much greater expense than would be horses or wagons, which in this country cannot be employed for military service.

The manner of interspersing them among the troops is as follows: the first or foremost are generally two pioneers, viz., two Negroes with billhooks to cut a way, so as to make a practicable path, with one corporal and two men to reconnoitre the front, and in case of necessity to give the alarm; and then one subaltern, six privates, and a corporal, which forms the van or advance guard. Then follows, at some distance, the corps or main body, in two divisions, being in the first, one captain, one corporal, twelve privates, one surgeon, and two Negroes to carry the powder; in the second are one sergeant and twelve privates; and then again follows at some distance the rear guard, or *corps de reserve,* consisting of one subaltern, one sergeant, one corporal, eighteen privates, and sixteen Negroes, to carry the medicines, beef, bread, spades, axes, kettles, kill-devil or rum, the officers' boxes, the sick, &c., the three last of all being one corporal and two men at some distance, to give the alarm in case of an attack by the enemy, as the others had orders to do in the front; which ends the train.

September 7th. Everything being ready, as much as possible according to the above rules, for my small party—consisting of myself, Subaltern Officer of the Society Mr. Hertsbergh, one surgeon's mate, one guide, two sergeants, two corporals, forty privates, and only eight Negro slaves to cut open the passage and carry the luggage—we faced to the right at six o'clock in the morning and sallied forth into the woods, keeping course directly for the Perica River.

Having marched till about eleven o'clock on the cordon, I discovered, as I had expected, the track of the Rebels in their retreat, by the marks of their footsteps in the mud, broken bottles, plantain shells, barbecued fish, and fresh ashes where they had made a fire, bearing by appearance towards Pinnenburg, already mentioned.

I had now, to be sure, found the nest, but the birds were flown—and to whom to attribute this mistake I must leave to the decision of the judicious. In short, we continued our march till 8 o'clock, when we arrived at the Society post Soribo in Perica, in a most shocking condition, having waddled through water and mire above our hips, climbed over heaps of fallen trees, crept underneath them on our bellies, scratched and torn by the thorns or *macas* that are here of many kinds, stung all over by the *patat* or *scrapat* lice, ants, and *wassy-wassy* or wild bees, fatigued to death by marching in a burning sun, and the last two hours in Hell's darkness, holding each other by the hand, and having left ten men behind—some with agues, some stung blind, and some with their feet full of chigoes. Being received at Soribo in the most hospitable manner by the commanding officer, I went to my hammock with a fever.

September 9th. Being now sufficiently refreshed to renew my march, we left Soribo at four o'clock in the morning, and at four o'clock P.M. arrived (after indescribable sufferings, like so many miserable wretches) at Devil's Harwar, torn to rags, covered over with mud and blood, and our thighs and legs cut and scratched from top to bottom by the prickles and flogging of the branches, most of the men being without shoes and stockings by necessity; while I, who had done this march in the same condition from choice, absolutely had suffered the least of the whole party, by having inured myself gradually to walking barefoot on the barges.

September 12th. Now came the news from Patamacca that the Rebels, on their repassing the river above La Rochelle, had again destroyed a small estate and murdered its proprietor, a Mr. Nyboor. It was either this time, or it happened since, that an overseer escaped by the help of a Negro boy, who desiring him to leap into a canoe, and lie down in it flat upon his belly, leaped himself into the water, where by swimming with one hand and guiding the canoe with the other, he ferried his master safe over the Creek Patamacca, through a shower of musket bullets, the Rebels firing upon them all the time but without execution. However, for this material piece of service, he was recompensed the week after with three hundred lashes by the same master, for having forgotten to open one of the sluices or floodgates. On this act of gratitude, I shall make no comment, but proceed. Resting upon a Negro's shoulder, at twelve o'clock noon I walked to the waterside, where stepping in the boat, I left this human butchery, where I had buried so many brave fellows, and rowed with six Negroes and my black boy to the town of Paramaribo.

Here I arrived on the 14th, at two o'clock in the morning, but having no residence of my own, I was most hospitably received at the house of a Mr. De Lamarre, a merchant, whose wife was Joanna's sister, and for which last he immediately dispatched a servant to the house of her aunt, as well as another for a physician, I being extremely ill indeed, which was the end of this brilliant, this fruitful expedition. After an absence of two months and twelve days, during which time I am convinced that the sympathizing reader has often felt for us, and to whom I renew my most unfeigned apology for dwelling so long upon my own subject; yet which I could not very well avoid, and keep up the connection, while far from glorying in any one of my private actions, I only state them to expose the weakness of human nature, and as a guide for others, in like circumstances (in some measure) to rule their conduct with more propriety.

CHAPTER 9th

*Some diseases peculiar to the climate—Group of newly
imported Negroes going to be sold—Reflections on the slave
trade—Their voyage from Africa—Manner of selling them in
the Colony*

September 15th, I found myself in an elegant and well-furnished apartment, encouraged by the hopes given to me by the physician, caressed by my friends, and supported by the care and attention of the inestimable Joanna.

One Captain Brandt, having at this time the command in Colonel Fourgeoud's absence, sent me this morning my trunks and baggage, which had been sealed up. But when looking into them, I found that I had enemies at home as well as abroad, since most of my shirts, books, &c., were now eaten to molders by the blatta or cockroach, called *cakrelaca* in Surinam. Nay, even my shoes were destroyed, of which I had brought over twelve pairs new from Europe, they being extremely dear and bad in this country.

September 20th. My fever now began much to abate, but I was infected with another disorder peculiar to this climate and which, I am afraid, I shall be able but indifferently to describe. It is called in Surinam the ringworm and consists in large, scarlet, irregular spots, particularly on the under parts of the body, which increase in magnitude from day to day, unless prevented by timely application. These spots are surrounded with a kind of hard, scrofulous border that makes them look, in my opinion, something like land maps and which are as troublesome by their itching as the itch called prickly heat or the sting of the mosquitoes, and so very infectious that if one chances to sit on a chair immediately after another who has the disorder, one is almost certain to catch it. It is, I believe, endemic, very ill to get rid of, and the best cure is to rub it with a composition of refined saltpeter, benjoin, flowers of brimstone, and white mercury mixed with fresh butter or hog's lard. Inconceivable are the many troubles to which one is exposed in this climate.

September 26th. I now again relapsed, and was twice drawn blood in one day.

October 3rd. I now for the first time did take the air on horseback, in company with young Mr. Heneman, though we could not ride above three English miles distance out of town, on a species of gravel that leads to the Wanica-Path, which communicates with the River Saramacca and forms the only practicable road in the Colony. During this little jaunt, which (on account of the dry season being commenced) we did at six o'clock in the morning, we saw a great many of those large, fine-looking birds called macaws, and in Surinam called ravens, from their proportion to the parrots, and which may be looked on as a kind of tropical crow. The macaws are divided in different species, all of which fly in couples, have a shrill, disagreeable shriek, and bite severely, their bill being very hard and sharp, and which is of great use to them in climbing. They are easily tamed, and may be taught to speak like other parrots. The Indians frequently bring them to Paramaribo, and sometimes part with them for a bottle of rum or a few fishhooks.

October 6th. The fever had now left me and the ringworm began to abate, but the misery and hardships which I had so lately undergone still affected my constitution, two enormous boils breaking out on my left thigh, which entirely prevented me from walking. However, my physician ordering me daily to take the air when I had the opportunity, I waited today on His Excellency the Governor of the Colony by the help of my friend Kennedy's chaise. And while returning homewards, I stopped the carriage at the waterside, to behold a group of human beings who had deservedly attracted my particular attention, and which group I shall circumstantially endeavor to describe. They were a drove of newly imported Negroes, men and women with a few children, who had just landed from on board a Guineaman that lay at anchor in the roads, to be sold for slaves to the best bidder in the Colony. They were such a set of living automatons, such a resurrection of skin and bones, as justly put me in mind of the last trumpet, seeming that moment to be risen from the grave, or deserted from Surgeon's Hall at the Old Bailey, and of which no better description can be given than by comparing them to walking skeletons covered over with a piece of tanned leather.

Before these wretches (who might be in all about sixty in number) walked a sailor, and another followed behind, with a bamboo rattan; the one serving as a shepherd to lead them along, and the other as his dog to bite them occasionally should anyone lag behind, or wander away from

The Blue & Yellow & the Amazon Macaw.

Plate 21

the blessed flock. At the same time equity claims of me to acknowledge that, in place of all those horrid and dejected countenances that are with so much industry described in pamphlets and newspapers, I perceived not one single downcast look among them all, and the bite of the bamboo was inflicted with the utmost moderation by the sailor who, nine times out of ten, changed it to a bark or a grin. Having viewed this sad cluster of my fellow creatures with amazement, I drove home to my lodgings with no less humiliation, where I noted down what I could learn from the best authority, both white and black, what is really the fate of these people, from the last moment of their liberty in Africa to the present period of their slavery in America, which I shall endeavor to relate, together with a few of my own unbiased sentiments upon the slave trade (which is now so much in agitation) with that becoming candor and impartiality which not only every gentleman, but every man, should pride himself in being possessed of.

I have since read Mr. Clarkson's essays, and read them with pleasure, I have read all the debates and newspaper controversies, and I have heard still more arguments on the subject, but I find myself obliged to say (with that same bluntness which is perhaps too conspicuous throughout this whole work) that most of the learned gentlemen, in many cases, have erred on both sides, some by misinformation and prejudice, and others by stubbornness and passion; and which errors I will point out with manliness even should I be damned by them altogether. It is idle, from a principle of humanity alone, to persist in supporting such arguments as are confutable by common sense, especially when founded principally on information (providing people's ears will be open to conviction, by those who ought to know better by experience, and if not, then it is only spending their lungs to no purpose, and firing their powder at the sparrows), while it is equally absurd, for the sake of drinking rum and eating sugar, to persevere in the most unjust and diabolical barbarity—the enthusiasm of ill-placed humanitarianism, being in my opinion equally as pernicious to society on one side as the practice of ill-grounded cruelty is wickedly destructive on the other. In short, in the evening those Negroes who were not sold were returned to their companions on board the Guineaman, to be paraded in the same manner next day.

Here we will leave and take a retrospective view of those people in their own country. All the world knows the extent of Africa, and that the greatest part, nay almost the whole, is what the Europeans call uncivilized. Nevertheless, not only the African Negroes but all the rest of the human species, nay even the animal creation, live under a species of government, to where they flock, either prompted by fear for protection or influenced from a motive of avarice, to augment their wealth. These gov-

Group of Negros, as imported to be sold for Slaves.

Plate 22

ernments in Africa are small, and each ruled by a private king or prince (who, like in all other governments, counterbalances the lower class of his subjects in the scale of misery, while the middle station alone enjoy real happiness), their little kingdoms increasing so fast in population that like other great ones they clash together, and millions are destroyed on both sides, and well it is (however little our narrow conception to see it) that the all-wise Creator has ordered war this generally, and from all times, just as throughout all the other links of the Creation, as one fish lives upon another, man would eat man and prey upon his brother without it. I acknowledge the many arguments in favor of waste lands and industry, but I may as well use the argument of waste water or waste air, and which human remarks come not in the smallest competition in the scale of omnipotence. Man can and ought but see at a certain distance and no farther. And it would be just as absurd to ask the question why, as it is in Pope's lines to ask:

Why has not Man a microscopic eye?
The reason's plain, because Man's not a fly.

No more is he a God, thus let him keep within his limited bounds, judge the small circle allotted to be within his compass and conception, but leave a universe to be governed by the great fountain of nature alone, submitting to its events with resignation. Nay, I will even venture to say that war is just as necessary to prevent a general stagnation on the globe, as are our passions, nay the circulation of the very blood that is in our veins to keep us healthy. Does not the whole Creation, from the invisible insect, go to war and make way for each other? Nay, do not the very elements clash together, and enter in tremendous convulsions, as the one proceeds from natural causes to thin and purify the air, so does the other to thin and preserve the human species, who ever have and ever will be thinned, if not by war, by hurricanes, pestilence, scarcity, &c., and whom it is just as necessary to diminish as it is to weed vegetables or plants in a garden, in order to give room to some by destroying others, and prevent (as I said before) one general stagnation, which arguments I shall end by observing, with the author above quoted, that in my humble opinion, *whatever is, is right,* whatever dreadful the apparent consequences.

If it is then allowed that war is a necessary evil proceeding from natural causes, and that its horrors and devastations are, at times, as necessary among the sable Africans as among the fair Europeans (who even derive from it honor and glory), the question remains, on which of the two continents are felt the greatest calamities and the most people destroyed by its effects? The answer is evident, if we compare the magnitude of uncivilized Africa to the dimensions of hostile Europe (bursting from every corner with smoke and fire, and which even carries its dire and pestilential effects to every other quarter of the globe). And I candidly ask whether, in fifty such battles as are described by the ingenious Mr. Clarkson (kindled for the capturing of slaves, and of which but few examples can be produced), there is committed half the ravage and destruction that sometimes rages in one of our British sea engagements, both in regard to friend and foe? Certainly not. Then, what is the result of the Africa wars? The result is that great numbers of prisoners are taken on both sides, who are either doomed to be killed afterwards, or to be sold for slaves on the coast, and the latter, however despicable, is still to most men preferable to death.

This clears their country, I say, and these (said to be) one hundred thousand people transported yearly are surely but a very small proportion, compared to the millions that in all Europe annually expire under the name of Liberty, loaded with the pangs of want and disease, and crushed under the galling chains of oppression. Nay, while the very oppressors themselves bend under the weight of that gold, extorted from the brow and distilled by the sweat of their drooping subjects. From all this I must conclude that this trade, or buying of Negro slaves, is not so bad a thing as some try to support, while it is the effects that follow from it alone that are the complicated evils, under which lie groaning the too-helpless African Negroes, whose lives, if properly looked after, might (at the same time without being less useful) be made incomparably more happy than those of either our sailors or soldiers. These latter are obliged to go, and be drowned or shot abroad, to get a pernicious subsistence for their little starving families at home, and to which they are too often dragged, locked short in irons, contrary to their capacity or inclinations, not to speak of above fifty thousand helpless young women who, independent of their genius and beauty, must, for the sake of a loathsome temporary subsistence, parade the streets of our metropolis in all weathers, exposed to all that's horrid, till they die unpitied upon a dunghill, in the middle of their own countrymen, starved, detested, kicked, and wallowing in corruption.

How dreadful this account, yet all this bustle (viz., what happens in Africa, the same as what happens in Europe) seems so perfectly necessary to me, that it stands not in need of the smallest investigation, as it is a perfect truth that from a private evil is derived a general good. While still more I am surprised that that humanity, which induces people to plead across the Atlantic Ocean, till in the internal parts of Africa and America, should not inspire them to begin at home with their own countrymen and countrywomen, where the needy who steal to support the cries of nature and the relentless assassin are equally punished, and thousands of whom (as I have just observed), independent of the many so laudable almshouses and charitable institutions (erected as lasting monuments of honor throughout the Island of Great Britain) stand much more in need of their assistance and protection than the Negro slaves of Guinea, the greatest number of whom, under a well-regulated government, may live happier in the West Indies than they ever did in the forests of Africa. And as to their becoming Christians, they may (a few of them excepted) have a chance of becoming a parcel of canting hypocritical rascals, like too many of their protectors, and use it as a cloak to impose upon the ignorant, but will never choose to know more of that sacred institution than they already do of snow, their own religion being much more commodious, and not so much divested of common sense as numberless stupid Europeans imagine. Besides, I cannot help thinking it ungenerous, thus wishing to deprive the West India planters of their property by a sudden abolition of the slave trade, who after their many hazards, and their loss of health, wealth, and time, have no other method of procuring a subsistence for their families and which when cheapest is always too dear bought. As for the sailors employed in it, great numbers of them perish, I acknowledge, but who, if they did not die in this way, would possibly have been obliged to pick your pockets for a subsistence and, in company with too many of their unfortunate shipmates, have been hanged to keep them from starving, it being very well known that these poor men (who are the props and bulwarks of every mercantile nation) have no provisions made for them in times of peace, and that the brave tar, who has escaped a watery grave during the war (to protect your life and property) is often only saved to exchange it for an airy one when it is over. Thus, better to go to the coast of Guinea to buy Negroes.

And as for the political good of the nation that is to be derived by this humane abolition, it is too conspicuous to pass over in silence. Great Britain, it is observed, has already lost her thirteen American colonies (as some say) by wishing to make a free people into slaves, and is now about to lose all her West India settlements by, in reverse, wishing to make slaves into free people—for all which loss her sons now have (at the hazard of peeping through a halter) nobly emigrated to Botany Bay which, being a new thing to be sure, is preferable to old baubles and gewgaws, and will no doubt in time not only make up for the loss of all America, but prove a most blessed acquisition for the nation. And besides forcing us to go to foreign markets to buy at double price, this has the good effect of showing our generosity to our French and Spanish neighbors, of keeping our men from getting drunk at home with Jamaica rum, and our women from spoiling their teeth by eating sugar. These are the complicated advantages which are likely to result should an abolition of the

Guinea slave trade take place, while should an emancipation in the islands have happened, one Negro would have cut another's throat for hunger.

But if we really wish to keep our remaining anti-Atlantic possessions that lie between the tropics, I in that case do maintain that they can never be cultivated but by Negroes alone, neither the fair European nor the American Indian being adequate to the task. Then the grand question that remains to be solved is: Are these Negroes to be slaves or a free people? To which I answer, without hesitation, *dependent* and under proper restrictions (a few very industrious individuals only excepted), not so much even for the sake of the European as for that of the African himself, with whose passions, debauchery, and indolence I am perfectly acquainted, and who, like a spirited horse, when unbridled, often gallops to destruction himself, while he tramples under his feet all that he meets with. They would indeed in time provide for their immediate subsistence but would no more think (at least for ages to come) of amassing wealth by industry than their countryman the orangoutang. Indeed, the twenty thousand Auka and Saramaka Free Negroes who are settled in Surinam, and which I have before mentioned, are a glaring instance, for they want neither land, time, hands, nor the proper tools for cultivation, but will ten times sooner be employed in dancing, drinking, and catching fish, or killing a boar or a jaguar, than in planting either coffee, sugar, cacao, cotton, or indigo, and by which their wealth in a short time might be increased, not only beyond a possibility of want, but even to affluence for themselves and for their descending posterity to many generations. The too much aspiring after which has indeed made as many miserable in the state of civilization as it has made happy, if not more. And I am of Abbé Raynal's opinion that Natural Man (among which class I rank the present generation of Negroes), in a free state, and even in a state of dependence, is the happiest of the two, providing while he is curbed he is also indulged with some liberty, no mortal being perfectly free. And while he enjoys without restraint the complete necessities of life, I think the name of *slave* (with which he is branded, and which sounds so odious to the ears of those not acquainted with the many indulgences which he certainly reaps under a good master) might be exchanged for that of menial servant. Query: What are the apprentices in England?

I love the African Negroes, which I have shown on numberless occasions, and whatever wrong constructions may be placed on what I have said on this subject, I wish from the bottom of my heart that my words may be the anticipation of what shall be pronounced by that illustrious body the British Parliament upon the subject. But should it not be so, I take liberty to prophesy that thousands and thousands shall repent it, and more be ruined by the rash proceeding, while it is not less for the benefit of the African than for that of this glorious Island that I have spoke them, being neither interested the one way or the other, and for which I pledge my honor. While as a further proof, I shall throughout the course of this narrative still take the further liberty of pointing out such measures as may make the slaves in our West India settlements perfectly happy, with even an accumulation to the wealth of their masters.

It is said the West Indies can supply itself with slaves in point of population. I deny it not when, in some course of time, such proper regulations shall have taken place. Then, and not till then, all may be happy and contented together, without loss to the public or to the individual, who first went to settle in these tropical burning climates, under the sanction of the British legislature, and to whom he with justice still looks up for protection. That such an amendment alone for the present may take place, and not a simultaneous emancipation of the Negro slaves, I pray and plead for, and also that it may be crowned with every success, after which time only and not before, I shall feel pride, and glory, in the entire abolition of a trade which is at present certainly carried on with unbounded barbarity and usurpation. This much for Africa in general, and now once more for her sons in particular.

From what I have said above, it clearly appears that numbers of the Negroes offered for sale have been taken in battles and made prisoners, while many others, as Mr. Clarkson wisely observes, have been scandalously kidnapped, and some others transported for offenses &c., of all which I shall produce a few examples in the future.

These groups of people then are marched from every inland part to the factories, erected by different nations upon the coast, where they are sold, or more properly speaking bartered, like the other productions of their country, viz., as gold, elephant's teeth, &c., to the Europeans for bars of iron, firearms, carpenter's tools, checked linens, hats, knives, glasses, tobacco, spirits, &c. Next, they are embarked for exportation, during which time they without contradiction feel all the pangs that mental or corporal misery can inflict, being torn from their country and their dearest connections, stowed hundreds together in a dark, stinking hold, the sexes being separated, while the men are kept in chains to prevent an insurrection. In this manner are they floated over turbulent seas, not certain what is to be their destiny, and generally fed during the passage with horse beans and oil for all subsistence. But all captains are not Coolingwards, and these pangs are often alleviated with better food by the more humane, so much so that none or few of the cargo die during the passage, and the whole crew arrive healthy in the West Indies. I even remember one instance where, the captain, mate, senior mate, surgeon, bosun, and most of the sailors having expired at sea, so that the remaining few could not work the ship without the Negroes' assistance, yet these last, having been well-treated, helped at last to run the vessel upon shore, by which they not only saved many lives, but tamely and even cheerfully allowed themselves to be fetched and sold, as I have above mentioned, to who would please to buy them.[1]

Having wafted them over the Atlantic Ocean, I will now briefly proceed with the manner in which they are disposed of. No sooner is a Guineaman arrived than all the slaves are led upon deck, where they are refreshed with pure air, plantains, bananas, oranges, &c., and being properly cleaned, washed, and their hair shaved in different figures of stars, half moons, &c. (which they generally do the one to the other, having no razors, by the help of a broken bottle and without soap), I say after this, one part of them is sent ashore for sale, decorated with pieces of cotton to serve as fig leaves, armbands, beads, &c., being all the captain's property, while the others spend the day dancing, hallooing, and clapping hands on board the vessel. I having thus sufficiently described their figures after landing, we now shall suppose to see them walking along the waterside and through the streets, where every planter picks out that number which he stands in need of to supply those wanting by death, desertion, &c., and for which he makes a bargain with the captain, good Negroes costing from fifty to one hundred pounds each. Among these, should a woman chance to be pregnant, her price is augmented accordingly, while I have known the captain of a Dutch Guineaman, who acknowledged himself to be the father, possess the unheard-of brutality of doubling the value by selling his own offspring to the best bidder, but for which he was highly censured by his companions, one rotten sheep not disgracing the whole flock. The next thing, before the bargain is struck, is to let the new acquisitions mount upon a hogshead or a table, one after another, where they are visited by a surgeon, making with their arms and legs all the different figures and gestures of a Merry-Andrew upon the stage, to prove their soundness or unsoundness, after which they are adopted by the buyer, or cast off, as he thinks proper. If he keeps them, the money is paid down, and the newly bought Negroes immediately branded on the breast or the thick of the shoulder by a stamp made of silver, with the initial letters of the master's name, as we mark furniture or anything else to authenticate the property. But these hot letters, which are about the size of a sixpence, occasion not that pain that may be imagined, and which blisters being directly rubbed with a little fresh butter, are perfectly well in the space of two or three days. No sooner is this

---

1. This vessel had her captain murdered the voyage before last, and now belongs to Captain Grim.

ceremony over, and a new name given to the newly bought slave, than he or she is delivered to an old one of the same sex and sent to the estate, where each by his guardian is properly kept clean, instructed, and well fed, without working for the space of six weeks, during which period from living skeletons they become plump and fat, with a beautiful clean skin, till disfigured by the lash of the cruel whip, which too generally follows from the hands of the too-relentless overseers. Here I must leave them for some time and continue my narrative, after observing that the Negroes are composed of different nations or castes, such as the

Abo	Congo	Loango	Pombo
Bonia	Gango	N'Zoko	Wanway &c.
Blitay	Konare	Nago	
Coromantyn	Kiemba	Papa	

with most of which I have found means to get acquainted, and of which I shall speak more amply in proper place and season.

October 8th. The surgeon now having lanced my thigh, I scrambled out and once more saw the selling of slaves to the best bidder. Heavens, shall I relate it? Among these was now my inestimable Joanna, the sugar estate Faukenberg with its whole stock being today sold by execution to defray by dividend the creditors of its late possessor, Mr. De Borde. I now felt all the horrors of the damned, bewailing my unlucky fortune that did not enable me to become her proprietor myself, and figuring in my mind her ensuing dreadful situation. Methought I saw her, mangled, ravished, ridiculed, and bowing under the weight of her chains, calling aloud for my assistance. I was miserable, indeed, I was truly wretched, laboring under such emotions as had now nearly deprived me of all my faculties, till restored by the assurances of my friend Mr. Lolkens, who providentially was appointed to continue as administrator of the estate during the absence of its new possessors, Messrs. Passelege & Son at Amsterdam, who had bought it and its dependents for only four thousand pounds. I say, till restored by the assurances of my friend (who brought Joanna again to my presence) that in every service which he could render either to myself or her (and which he had now more in his power than ever, the estate at present belonging to only two masters), no efforts on his side should be wanting, which promise I desired him to keep in remembrance, and in which he since nobly persevered, as shall appear.

October 12th. I now being informed that Colonel Fourgeoud had left Carawassibo Estate and entered the woods just above the plantation Clarenbeek, on his way to the Wana Creek, to try if he could to fall in with the Rebels, I requested, by a letter, that I might join him there so soon as I should be recovered.

This evening departed my friend De Lamarre, with his twenty-five free Mulattoes, to the River Surinam, he being a captain of the militia and they being infinitely preferable to the European scarecrows.

October 24th. Being now perfectly recovered, I resolved to join Colonel Fourgeoud at the Wana Creek, without awaiting his orders, and to accompany him on his excursions through the forest. In consequence of which, having first cropped my hair, as being more convenient and cleanly in the woods, and provided myself with the necessary bush equipage, such as jackets, trousers, &c., I waited on the Governor to ask his commands, who entertained me in a most polite manner and told me that what I was now going to suffer would surpass what I had already undergone. I nevertheless persisted in wishing to go, as I said, without waiting for an order from the chief, and accordingly applied to the magistrates for a boat and the necessary Negroes to transport me, which being promised for the following day, I gave over the colors and regiment's cash, with the command of the remaining sick troops, to a Second Lieutenant Meyer, the only healthy officer then at Paramaribo. Indeed, the colors, the cash, and the sick soldiers were of equal use to us in Surinam, the first never having been displayed except at our landing, the second invisible to all except Colonel Fourgeoud, and the third dying the one after the other.

CHAPTER 10th

Colonel Fourgeoud marches to the Wana Creek—Harasses the enemy—Account of the manicole tree with its various uses—March to the mouth of the Coermotibo Creek—Some Rebels taken—Shocking treatment of a wounded captive Negro

On October 25th, being ready to set out upon my second campaign, I repaired to the waterside at six o'clock in the evening, where in place of a tent-boat, I found a greasy yawl with a few drunken Dutch sailors to row me to an estate in the River Commewina, from where they were going to fetch their captain back to Paramaribo, and from which place I might, if I pleased, beg the rest of my passage upwards, or shift for myself in the best manner that I was able. I already had one foot in the boat when, reflecting that I was going voluntarily on a hazardous expedition without being ordered, and from a motive of wishing to serve a parcel of ungrateful gentry, I repented and stepped back upon the shore where (swearing I should not move to their defense till such time as I should be decently transported, should the whole colony be on fire) I was seconded by all the English and Americans in the town, and a general hubbub took place. The Dutch exclaimed against the expense of a tent-boat, which would cost them thirty shillings, when they could have the other for nothing, while the others declared them a parcel of shabby rascals, who deserved not the smallest protection from Colonel Fourgeoud's troops. A mob now gathered and a riot ensued, in front of Mr. Hardegen's tavern at the waterside, while hats, wigs, bottles, and glasses flew out his window. The magistrates were next sent for, to no purpose, and the fighting continued in the street till ten o'clock at night, when I, with my friends, fairly kept the field, having knocked down several sailors, planters, Jews, and overseers, and lost one of my pistols which I threw after the rabble in my passion. Nor would it have ended here, had not Mr. Kennedy, who was a member of the Court of Policy, and two or three more gentlemen whom he brought with him, found means to appease the whole dispute by declaring that I had been badly used and should have a proper boat the next day, after which we all sat down and drank away the night till the sun rose the next morning.

October 26th. Having now slept and refreshed myself a few hours, I was waited on by four American captains, viz., Captain Timmens of the *Harmony*, Captain Lewis of the *Peggy*, Captain Bogard of the *Olive Branch*, and Captain Minet of the *America*, who insisted on my refusing any vessel whatever from the Colony this time and on their sending me up in one of their own boats, manned by their own sailors only, to which each contributed alike. And I do declare that, independent of the threatening rupture between Great Britain and her colonies (which seemed then upon the eve of breaking out into an open flame), nothing could surpass the warm heart and friendship which these gentlemen proved to possess, not only for me but for every individual that bore a British name or had any connection with that glorious island, for which they all swore to have still the greatest regard that could be—though not for its administration, which they said was a rotten one, and of which I have heard them wish to chop off the head with one blow of the hatchet, rather than they should be the cause of setting a son to fight against his own father, or one brother against another, and upon the whole making go to war two nations that are so nearly allied by the sacred ties of consanguinity, by friendship, and by everything else, but declaring that if it must be so, they would stand till they had spilled the last drops of their blood before they should yield to what they pleased to call a scandalous oppression and usurpation of their rights, their liberties, and their property. In short, I accepted their very polite proposal, when having received a letter from Mr. Kennedy to deliver to one of the militia captains, a Mr. N. Reeder in the River Commewina, with orders to send me further up in a proper tent-boat, and having arranged matters at home so that neither Colonel Fourgeoud nor the cockroaches could hurt me, I shook hands with my Mulatto, and at six in the evening repaired once more to the waterside escorted by my English and American friends, where, having drunk a half-dozen bowls of punch, we separated, and I departed for my station, they having hoisted the colors on board all their vessels in the roads, and at the boat's going off saluted me with three cheers, to my great satisfaction, and the mortification of the gaping scum by which we were surrounded, and which compliment, being returned by the boat's crew, and three volleys from my fusee, we soon rowed out of sight of Paramaribo.

October 28th. I now pursued my voyage upwards as far as the estate Mon Désir.

On the 29th, I came to La Paix, having viewed the ruins of the three estates De Suynigheid, Du Perou, and L'Esperance, which had been burnt when I commanded at Devil's Harwar. Here, one of the overseers gave me an account of the whole catastrophe and particularly of his own miraculous escape, which I shall relate in his own words.

> The Rebels, Sir (said he), had already surrounded the dwelling house in which I was before I knew of their being on the plantation, and were employed in setting fire to the four corners of it, so that running out-of-doors meant rushing on certain death. In this dilemma I fled to the garret, where I lay myself flat upon one of the beams, in the hopes of their dispersing soon and my still escaping before the building was burnt down. But in this I was disappointed, as they remained, and at the same time the flames increased so fast that the heat became insupportable where I was, and I had no other alternative left but to be burnt to death or to leap from a high garret window into the middle of my exasperated enemies. This last, however, I resolved upon and had not only the good fortune to alight unhurt upon my feet, but to escape through among them all without a wound, while they cut and slashed at me with sabers and billhooks and pursued me to the riverside, in which I plunged myself headlong, but not being able to swim immediately sank to the bottom. Nevertheless (said he), I still kept my full presence of mind, and while they concluded me to be drowned I found means, by the help of the *moco-moco* and mangrove roots, to bring myself both under cover of the impending verdure, and just so far above water with my lips, as to continue in a state of respiration, till all was over. They having killed every other body, I was taken up by a boat from my very distressed situation.

These were his very words when, in spite of the aversion I have to overseers in general, I could not help congratulating the poor fellow on his having escaped from the wrath of the four elements.

On October 30th, I arrived at Devil's Harwar, Oh cursed spot.

October 31st. I now at last rowed up the Coermotibo Creek where, having tied the boat to a tree which overspread it by its thick branches, we quietly lay down to sleep for the night, myself and Quacoo in the tent upon the benches, and the Negroes under the seats, whom I ordered alternately to keep watch, and wake me if they heard the least rustling in the woods, forbidding them all absolutely to speak or make any noise to prevent the Rebels, who were hovering at both sides of the creek, from hearing us and cutting all our throats without distinction; at least myself, who was the only white person among them all, I was confident could not escape their fury. I say, after these precautions, we all lay down and I never slept more soundly in my life, from nine o'clock till about three in the morning, when Quacoo and myself were both suddenly thrown down from our benches by the boat all at once keeling upon one side, while all the Negroes leaped overboard into the water. I instantly now cocked my pistol, and jumping out of the tent, called aloud what was the matter, well determined to blow out my own brains sooner than be taken alive by such a relentless sad enemy. For the space of a few seconds I got no answer, when at last the boat again suddenly redressing itself (by the motion of which I was now thrown off my feet), one of the swimming Negroes called out, *"Kay, mi Massera. Da wan see cow,"* and to my great happiness it proved to be no other than the *manatee* or sea cow, which is called in Cayenne the *lamentyn,* but of which animal, for the present, I can say nothing more than that, by the account of the Negroes, it had slept under the boat which by its awakening had been lifted up, and thrown upon one side, and which again redressed itself when the manatee made its escape from underneath it. I not so much as having seen the creature nor indeed hardly they, owing to the darkness of the night which lasted some hours after, but during which time we had no more inclination to go to rest, when at last the sun's bright beams began to dart through the trees and gild the nodding foliage.

We cast off from our moorings, and continued rowing up Coermotibo Creek (which was now very narrow) till near noon, when we saw smoke, and at last came to the mouth of the Wana Creek, which also waters out in the Marawina, and which was the spot of rendezvous, but where the troops were not yet come, and opposite to which were encamped a few of the Rangers, to guard the provisions that were awaiting the arrival of Colonel Fourgeoud and his party from Carawassibo, and last from Patamacca.

November 3rd. One party of the troops now being arrived, and encamped on the southwest side of the Coermotibo Creek about one mile above the mouth of the Wana, I went with a couple of Rangers to pay them a visit. Major Ruhkopf, the commanding officer, informed me that Colonel Fourgeoud had marched last from Patamacca in two columns, of which his was the one, while the other was hourly expected, and that the rest of the regiment was divided between the rivers Cottica, Perica, and Commewina, excepting those that were sick in the hospital at Paramaribo. I was now in excellent health and good spirits and, in the hopes of being reconciled to Fourgeoud by this voluntary proof of my zeal for the service, I returned to the Rangers' camp to await his arrival. I was, indeed, well acquainted with his irreconcilable temper and, at the same time conscious of my own wild and ungovernable disposition whenever I think myself ill-treated, though I soon forget trifling injuries, and was now determined by my active and affable behavior to make this sod become my friend, if such was possible.

On November 4th, the wished-for hour arrived, and being apprised of Colonel Fourgeoud's approaching, I went half a mile from the camp to his rencounter, acquainting him that I was come *pour participer de la gloire* and to serve under his immediate command which, he having answered with a bow, I returned it and we marched together into the Rangers' camp. The news of this march consisted in their having taken from the enemy three villages, particularly one called the Rice Country on account of the great quantity of rice which they here found, some ripe, some in full blossom. Leaving the huts or wigwams entire,[1] they had destroyed all, after driving the Rebels to flight, who were commanded by one Boni, a relentless Mulatto who was born in the forest and had nothing to do with Baron's party that had lately been driven from Boucou. Also, they had found seven skulls stuck upon stakes, under which lay moldering the bodies above ground, and part of the garments, which disclosed them to be the remains of the unfortunate Lieutenant Lepper and six of his men, in consequence of which they were all buried immediately. Also, they had taken prisoner a woman who declared that the white men taken alive at the engagement, as I have related, with Lepper had one by one been stripped by the Negroes as soon as they arrived in the Rebel village or Rice Country, where they had, by Boni's orders, been flogged to death, for the recreation of their wives and their children. This was an act of cruelty in Boni which was quite reverse in the character of Baron, who—independent of all his threats and menaces—it was well known had sent back different soldiers to Paramaribo whom he might have killed, even helping to conceal them from his enraged accomplices and assisting them with provisions, well knowing they were not the cause of the disturbance, while not a Ranger could escape his fury (as I have mentioned before) that had the misfortune to fall into his hands. The other news was that the whole party, nearly being starved for want, had conjointly called out for bread, bread, bread—there still being plenty in the boxes, but which had been kept back three days, in exchange for the rice above mentioned, when the officers, to show their zeal, had rushed in with cocked pistols and drawn swords among the men, and (indiscriminately laying hold of the first in their way) had unluckily seized a poor man named Schmidt who (notwithstanding all the others swore he was innocent) they had, for an example to the rest, bastonaded between two corporals, till the blood gushed out of his mouth like a fountain, which ended the revolt. And one of his conductors, named Mangold, scorning to be under Colonel Fourgeoud's command, had left him without asking his consent,

---

1. This was not necessary, since they are built with so very little trouble.

after which he left the service altogether. These were the particulars of the march in both columns, from Carawassibo in Commewina till the Wana Creek.

November 5th. Being arrived in Major Ruhkopf's camp, where having got a couple of Negroes to serve me, the first thing was to build a hut, or, more properly speaking, a shade over my hammock to keep me free from the rain and the sunshine, and which was done within the space of an hour. As the process of building these huts is of very material consequence throughout this expedition, where we never used any tents, and during which time several thousands of the above huts were erected, I will describe the manner in which it is carried on, the more as being extremely curious, and useful on many other occasions. Curious, because neither hammer nor nails nor, indeed, any kind of carpenter's tools are required, a strong cutlass or billhook only excepted, and useful as they are instantly raised, and form not only lasting, but the most delightful and convenient habitations, with even two stories above each other if required. For all this, nothing is wanted but two things, the first the *manicole*, by the French called *latanie* and here *prasella* or the *pina* tree, and the second the *nebees*, called by the French *lianes*, the Spaniards *bajorcos*, and in Surinam *tay-tay*.

The *manicole* tree, which is of the palm tree species, is mostly found in marshy places, and is always a proof of a rich and luxurious soil. It is about the thickness of a man's thigh, very straight, and grows the height of from thirty to fifty feet from the ground. The manner of using it for building huts or cottages is by cutting the trunk into pieces of as many feet long as you wish to have the partition high, for instance seven feet, which pieces are next split into small boards, the breadth of a man's hand, and divested of their pithy substance, when they are fit for immediate use. Having cut and prepared as many of these laths as you will want to surround your dwelling, you have nothing to do but to lash them in a perpendicular position, and close to each other, to two cross-bars of the same tree, fixed to the cornerposts, all of which is cut and shaped with the billhook alone, and tied together by the *nebees*, or *tay-tay*, which I think have here derived their name from "to tie," since the English had possession of the Colony.

The *nebees* are a kind of ligneous ropes of all sizes, both as to length and thickness, that grow in the woods and which climb up along the trees in all directions. Having only added that some of them are poisonous, especially those that are flat, grooved, or angular, I shall proceed to the roofing of the cottage. This is done by the green boughs or branches of the same manicole tree that made the walls, and in the following manner. Each bough, which I can compare to nothing so well as to the shape of a

The Sculls of Lieut. Leppar, & Six of his Men.

Plate 25

feather and which is as large as a man, must be split from top to bottom in two equal halves, as you would split a pen, when a number of these half-boughs are tied together by their own verdure, and form a bunch. Next you take these bunches and tie them with *nebees,* one above another upon the roof of your cottage, as thick as you please, and in such a manner that the verdure, which looks like the mane of a horse, hangs downwards. This covering, which at first is green but soon takes the color of the English reed-thatching, is very beautiful, lasting, and close, and finishes your house, as I have said, without the help of a hammer or a nail. The doors and windows, tables, seats, &c., are made in the same manner, also enclosures for gardens, or other places for keeping cattle. It is by this convenience that the Rebel Negroes never lack good houses which, if burnt to ashes today, are again perfectly rebuilt tomorrow, however, never in the places where they have been discovered by Europeans. But the hut that I now lie under was not built in the convenient manner above described, which was not requisite for the short time that we generally were in one place, consisting only of a roof or cover without any walls.

The manner of erecting these little shades (which every private soldier does for himself) is simply to plant four forked poles in the ground at such a distance that your hammock can conveniently hang between them, next to rest two short poles strong enough to support your weight in the above forks, the one at the head and the other at the feet, to which are lashed the end knots of your hammock; on the outer extremities of these are laid two long sticks, and on them again two short ones, and thus alternately two long and two short, which all diminish in proportion as you finish, till your skylight looks like the rafter of a ship, on the top of which you scatter the manicole branches as they are, viz., without either splitting or tying them, and as thick as the season may require, when your temporary fabric is completely finished, which keeps you as well as your boxes dry, and under the rafters of which, by the help of the *nebees,* you hang your fusee, sword, pouch, pistols, &c.

November 13th. Colonel Fourgeoud now being determined to scour the north bank of the Coermotibo, we broke up into two columns, viz., his own first and that of Major Ruhkopf, to which last I still belonged, following, leaving behind only a strong guard with the provisions and the sick. Before we set out, I shall specify the essence of our orders to be observed on a march, as issued since by the chief on the 15th August 1774 at Carawassibo, and which (though nine months after this date, thus rather late) are so judicious that they do infinite honor to his adjutant, Captain Van Geurike, who had the chief hand in their composition.

Art. 1—Quietness and sobriety were strongly recommended.
Art. 2—On pain of death none to fire without receiving orders.

Art. 3—Also death to whoever quits or loses his arms.
Art. 4—The same punishment for those who dare to plunder while they are engaging the enemy.
Art. 5—An officer and sergeant to inspect the distribution of the victuals at all times, and
Art. 6—Each officer to be limited in the number of his black attendants.

The other orders were that in case our Marines marched in two or three divisions or columns, they were to mark the trees with a saber or bill-hook, to give notice to each other where they had passed, and which marks were to be cut only in such trees as were on the left side of the path in marching. Also, when the troops marched over large sandy deserts, heaths, or savannas, they were occasionally to drop small twigs or reeds, tied together in the form of a cross; and that at the troops' leaving each camp, was to be left a bottle and blank paper—but in case anything particular should happen, it was to be specified thereon. Next, that in case of the troops being attacked by the Rebels on a march, a small retrenchment was to be formed of the baggage boxes, at the back of which the Negro slaves were to lie down flat on the ground, and which was to be defended by the rear guard only, while the other troops had orders not to linger on the defensive, but vigorously, with screwed bayonets to rush in upon the enemy's fire, nevertheless humanely giving quarter to all such as should be taken alive, or who surrendered themselves to the troops at mercy. These were the stated rules of our future military conduct. But for the present, I beg leave to observe that all was the most unaccountable hurry and confusion. However, in this pickle did we proceed, keeping course toward the mouth of the Coermotibo Creek, each officer provided with a pocket compass, by which we were to steer like sailors through a dark wood, where nothing is to be seen but heaven and earth, as at sea nothing appears but clouds and water. Thus those who were acquainted with navigation were the best off, and ran the least hazard of losing themselves in a black unbounded forest, while those wretches who deservedly most attracted my pity were the miserable Negro slaves, who all were bending under their loads, whose heads (on which they carry all burdens) bore the bald marks of their servitude, who were driven forward like oxen with a stick and, above all, condemned to subsist on half allowance, while they did double drudgery. In short, as our bad fortune would have it, though in the dry season, the rains began to pour down from the heavens like a torrent, which continued all night, and during which deluge (according to Colonel Fourgeoud's order) we were all, like true Trojans, ordered to encamp without huts or other covering of any kind, slinging our hammocks between two trees, under which our firearms were placed upon two small forked sticks, as the only method to keep the priming powder dry in the pan. Above this piece of architecture did I hang, like Mohammed betwixt the two loadstones, with my saber and pistol in my bosom, and independent of wind and weather fell most profoundly asleep.

November 14th. At five o'clock in the morning, I heard the sound of Up! Up! Up! when the rain still continuing, the half of the officers and men were sick, and I rose from my hammock soaked as from a washtub. Having secured the lock of my firelock in imitation of the Rangers, with a piece of the bark of a palm tree, and swallowed a dram with a piece of dry rusk biscuit for my breakfast, we again marched on, but I ought not to forget mentioning the Negroes, who had the whole night slept in the water on the ground, and were in better health than any of the Europeans. Had we now been attacked by the enemy, it is a truth we must have all been cut to pieces, being disabled from resisting with our firearms, in which not only most of the priming but even many of the cartridges were as wet as dung, and which might have been prevented had we, like the buccaneers of America, cased and waxed down our arms, but these were trifles not to be thought of. However, one thing now happened which threatened to be no trifle, and that was that the provisions were gone, and those we expected to meet us in the creek not arrived, having by some mistake been neglected, and by which accident we were now reduced, officers and men, without exception, to subsist on *one* rusk biscuit and water for all allowance for twenty-four hours, to keep us from starvation.[2]

On the 15th, we marched again, through very heavy rains, which by this time had swelled the water so high in the woods that it reached above our knees and prevented us from crossing a small creek in our way, without the help of a temporary bridge, in consequence of which I prevailed on the Rangers to erect one with the help of a few slaves, which they did in the space of forty minutes, by cutting down a straight tree, which fell directly across the creek, and to which they besides made a kind of railing. But even with this, our Commander Ruhkopf was not pleased, whose temper was soured by misery, and whose constitution was already broken by hardships. He called the Rangers "*feegh Shinder-kneghte &c.*," who with a smile of contempt left him swearing, and crossed the creek, some by swimming and others by climbing a tree whose branches hung over it, and by which they dropped down on the opposite shore, in which

---

2. Rusk biscuit is rye bread cut through the middle and baked or dried till it is as hard as a stone. I often broke it with the butt end of my fusee and was glad to have it when moldered, impregnated with worms, spiders, pins, broken bottles, &c., &c.

I followed their example, and there we stopped till the arrival of the poor, trembling, and debilitated Major Ruhkopf, while two-thirds of his command were as bad as himself, but I still continued in perfect health.

On November 16th, we marched again, with better weather, and arrived before noon at Jerusalem, near the mouth of Coermotibo Creek, where I had formerly during my cruise built a shade, but which I had since burnt to prevent a surprise from the surrounding Rebel parties. Here, Colonel Fourgeoud, with his drooping soldiers, was arrived just a little time before us, and here now we made our appearance in such a shocking situation as will hardly admit of a description. It is sufficient to say that the whole little army was knocked up by famine and fatigue, a very small number excepted, while several, unable to walk at all, had been carried upon poles by Negro slaves in their hammocks, and during which time we had discovered *nothing*. One thing is certainly true, viz., that while the Old Gentleman, himself, went through all the above-mentioned hardships (and to which he seemed as invulnerable as a cannon bullet), we had no reason to complain of bad usage. In short, having as usual plunged into the river to wash off the mire and blood occasioned by the scratches, and taken a refreshing swim, I looked for my Negroes to build a comfortable hut, but in this I was disappointed, they being employed by Mr. Ruhkopf to build his kitchen, although he had as yet nothing to dress in it. I for once put up with this piece of politeness, and the Rangers having made me a nice bed of manicole branches on the ground (here being no trees to sling a hammock) and lighted a blazing fire by the side of it, I lay quietly down next to them on my green mattress, where in a clear moonshine night, and no rain, I fell asleep as sound as a rock.

But about two hours before daybreak, I awaked when the moon was down, the fire was out, and I was almost dead by the cold dew and the dampness that exhaled from the earth, being so stiff and so benumbed that I had scarcely strength to crawl on hands and feet, and awake one of my sable companions. However, he having kindled a new fire, I recovered so fast as at six o'clock to be able to rise, but with such excruciating pain in one of my sides that I could not avoid groaning aloud, which to prevent Fourgeoud and the others from hearing, I hid myself in the skirts of the wood, but where the pain augmenting, I soon was prevented from breathing without the greatest difficulty, and at last fell down behind the rotten trunk of an old cabbage tree. Here I was found by one of the Negro slaves who was going to cut rafters, and who, supposing me dead, ran instantly back and alarmed the whole camp, after which I was taken up and carried in a hammock by the care of a Captain Medler, under proper cover, and one of the Society surgeons was instantly sent for to attend me.

By this time, I was surrounded by spectators, and the pain in my side was so acute that, like one in the hydrophobia, I tore my shirt with my teeth and bit whatever chanced to be within my reach, till being rubbed by a warm hand on my side, with a kind of ointment, the complaint immediately vanished like a dream and all at once, when I was recovered and was Stedman again. Nevertheless, to prevent a relapse, the first use that I made of my strength was to cut a cudgel, with which I swore to murder the Berbice ruffian, Gousary, who had the management of the slaves, if he did not instantaneously set them a-building for me a comfortable hut, independent of whoever might order him the contrary, my life being the dearest thing I had to part with. And following him close at his heels with my baton, clubbed upon my shoulder, I had the satisfaction to be well housed in the space of two hours. I must not omit that, during the crisis of my illness, Colonel Fourgeoud had given me an offer to be transported to Devil's Harwar, which I refused.

November 20th. Today were detached a captain with twenty privates and twenty Rangers to reconnoitre the demolished village of Boucou.

November 21st. Major Ruhkopf is also dead at last, and now Fourgeoud himself marches to Boucou, leaving me the command of four hundred men, white and black, but two hundred of whom were sick in their hammocks, and out of which number I transported thirty to die at Devil's Harwar, while I sent sixty Rangers with leave down to Paramaribo, who had disgusted Fourgeoud by swearing his whole operations were neither more nor less than a pack of damned nonsense, and only fit to murder his own troops, in place of the enemy. The nature of the Negroes is such, that where they know nothing is likely to be done, they will not march, and indeed are extremely difficult to keep in proper discipline; but on the contrary, when they expect to see the enemy, no subordination can possibly keep them back, and they are as eager as a pack of bloodhounds, fearless of danger, only panting to rush upon their foe, it being really amazing to see with what degree of skill one Negro discovers the haunts of another, and which can only be compared to a dog upon the scent. And while a European discovers not the smallest sign of a man's foot in the forest, the roving eye of the Negro Ranger catches the broken sprig, and faded leaf trod flat, without ever missing it, and which indicate to him sure marks of approaching his enemy, when, as I said, he can no longer be kept back. This, to be sure, is inconsistent with the modern military tactic, but undoubtedly breathes that spirit of liberty which in ancient times alone completed the valiant soldier. And such was the native and natural spirit still of a people who had but yesterday been slaves, while how wide different from the artificial machinery of their European masters, who please to call themselves the boasted Sons of Liberty, the one flying to victory like the Panting Corviser, to which (with a stick too often) the other is driven like a jackass. However, it belongs not to me to check all Europe which, having degenerated into modern vices, it is meet should be ridden with a modern curb, yet from which I take the liberty to exempt the British soldiers and sailors, a braver and more generous people not existing than compose both its army and navy, and which also is the case in a few more countries where the inhabitants fight from a national principle, witness the Highlanders of Scotland, the Grenadiers of France, &c.

On November 22nd, two slaves were put in confinement, accused of having taken pork from the magazine, and I was addressed by the troops for an exemplary punishment, the common soldiers despising the Negro slaves as being the only people on earth below themselves, and on whom, stupidly, they looked as the causes of their distress. Having found a large piece of pork in their custody, yet having no proof that was sufficient to call them thieves, I found myself greatly at a loss to distribute justice with satisfaction, both parties being so eager against each other, viz., the Europeans unmercifully accusing, and the poor slaves vindicating their starved companions, that the whole camp was in an uproar. In short, the first persisting in that the latter had stolen it, and they in that they had saved it to take to their families. I, like a true despotic prince, first ordered a ring to be formed by the plaintiffs, and next the prisoners to be brought within it, also with a block and a hatchet. Now, the fear of my going to be too rash took the place of resentment in the soldiers, and I was implored, by the very accusers, to show mercy, but now stopping my ears to all entreaty from either side, I relentlessly made a strong Negro slave take up the hatchet and instantly chop—the *bacon* into three equal pieces, when giving one share to the prosecutors, another to the malefactors, and the third to the executioner for having so well done his duty, the farce was ended to general satisfaction, and no more robberies or complaints heard of in the camp.

November 25th. Early this morning I found that I had been attacked by a more bloody enemy, though not so large, which was none other than a bat, by which my hammock was covered with clotted blood, and in which I lay like a cold fowl in jelly. However, as I now could not catch the usurper, I must delay giving a description of his form till I shall have the opportunity of knocking him in the head, only now observing that he had bitten me deep in my great toe.

On the 26th, our Colonel Fourgeoud with his party returned from his trip to Boucou, having surrounded three straggling Rebel Negroes unarmed, as they were cutting a cabbage tree for their subsistence. While one of whom, called Pass-up, had escaped, another was taken alive, and a third with his thigh shot to shivers by a slug cartridge was first lashed hands and feet and thus carried by two Negroes on a pole thrust between them, in the manner of a hog or a beer barrel, bearing all the weight of his body upon his shattered limb, which was dripping with marrow and blood, without a plaster or a bandage to cover the wounds, and with his head hanging downwards all the time, in which manner the unhappy youth—he not having the appearance of being twenty—had been carried without speaking, through thick and thin, for about six miles distance from the camp, while he might have just as well or better been killed all at once, or at least carried in one of the spare hammocks of the soldiers. I was shocked and surprised at this act of barbarity in Fourgeoud, whom I never saw cruel in his cool moments to an individual, indeed quite the reverse, except when he was opposed (as sometimes he was by me), but who on this occasion was so flattered with this trophy of his victory that every spark of feeling and humanity was extinct. The poor young man, whose thigh was now swelled as big as his body, being laid upon a table, I implored one of the surgeons, called Pino, to dress his wounds, on which (by way of play) he put just as many round patches as the slugs had made holes, declaring he could equally never recover and singing *Dragons pour boire* during the operation. Poor Negro! what must have been thy feelings! The fever increasing, he begged for some water, which I gave him myself, clean out of my hat, when he said, *"Thank ye, me massera,"* sighed, and instantly expired, to my inexpressible satisfaction.

His companion, called September, had better fortune, and Fourgeoud, in hopes of making some discoveries, regaled and treated him with more distinction than he did any of his officers, while September looking as wild as a fox newly caught, was put in the stocks during the night and Snakee was interred by the Negro slaves with those marks of commiseration which his unlucky fate seemed to claim from them, spreading his grave with the green boughs of the palm trees and offering a part of their scanty allowance by way of libation.

CHAPTER 11th

*The troops march back to the Wana Creek—The Rebels pass
near the camp—Pursued without success—Great distress for
want of water—Mineral mountains—Sample of wickedness in
a superior—The troops arrive at La Rochelle in Patamacca*

On November 30th, we all broke up together and, leaving Jerusalem,
once more marched back to the Wana Creek, but did not keep exactly the
track that brought us there. Colonel Fourgeoud, independent of his former orders, now allowed his remaining party to sling their hammocks
under cover, for which he saw the great necessity and in which he showed
them the example. Thus were we much more comfortably lodged, but
not more comfortably victualed, and which the Old Gentleman made up
to himself by Bologna sausages, bacon-hams, bullocks' tongues, and a
glass of good claret—stores now carried by six Negroes for his private
purposes.

On the morning of December 4th, discovering a couple of fine *powesas*
on the branches of a high tree near the camp, I asked the chief liberty to
go and shoot one of them which, however, was bluntly refused me, on
the pretense that the enemy might hear the report of my musket (who,
by the by, knew where we were better than we did ourselves). But a little
after, a large snake appearing on the summit of another tree, it was ordered to be shot out of it immediately, whether from fear or from antip-
athy I know not, when plump down it came to the ground quite alive,
sliding instantly into a thicket near the magazine. At this time, I saw the
intrepidity of a soldier who, creeping in after the reptile, fetched it out
among the brambles with his hands, pretending by superstition he was
invulnerable to its bite. Be that as it may, the snake, who was about six
feet long, erected its head and half its body successively to attack him,
which he as frequently knocked down with his fist, and at last severed

him in two pieces with his saber, which ended the battle, and for doing which he was regaled by Fourgeoud with a dram of rum.

December 6th. I now received six gallons of Jamaica rum from Paramaribo, which (except for two) I gave in a present to my friend Fourgeoud, being now determined, in imitation of the Indians, to worship the Devil from fear, not from adoration.

On December 7th, at about six in the evening, two of our slaves who had been out to cut manicoles brought intelligence that a gang of Rebels had passed not more than one mile from the camp, headed by a Captain Ariko, with whom they had spoken on the banks of the Coermotibo Creek, but could not tell which way they steered their course, so much had they been frightened, in consequence of which we got orders to pursue them by break of day. At 5 o'clock the next morning, all was ready, and we again broke up, leaving a detachment with the stores, and repaired to the spot from whence came the information. There we saw a large palm or *mawrisee* tree floating in the river, and moored to the opposite shore by a *nebee,* which plainly indicated that Ariko with his men had crossed the creek, which they do by riding astride the floating trunk the one behind the other, and in which manner they are ferried over, sometimes with women and children, by those who are the best swimmers. Notwithstanding this plain evidence, Fourgeoud swore that it was no more than a trick by the Rebels, whom he said had come from where we supposed they were gone to, and who had only tied the tree across the river to deceive us. I and others did say what we could, but no arguments could prevail with the Hero, and we marched directly from them, viz, east, in place of crossing and pursuing them west, as the Rangers would certainly have done. Thus we kept on till it was near dark, while the bread was forgotten, and the whole day not a drop of water to be met with, marching through high, sandy heaths or savannas. Here the colonel, pointing to a reeking S——, declared he was now perfectly sure of following the enemy, till a grenadier, stepping forward, called out "This was me and please your Honor," to the general mirth of the whole corps.

We now inclined a little to the right, when just before making camp, a Negro called out that we had come to the Wana Creek, which was a welcome sound in my ears. Thus giving him a calabash and the best part of a quart bottle of my rum, I desired him to run to the creek and make me some grog, and this he did. But the poor fellow, never having made grog before in his lifetime, poured in all the spirits but very little water, doubtless thinking the stronger it was the better, which beverage I swallowed to the bottom without taking time to taste it, and when I became instantly so much intoxicated that I could hardly keep my feet, at which accident a sergeant of the Society making merry, I gave him a blow on his meager chops with such force that I cut the very skin of my knuckles upon the jawbone, and he went to complain to one of his officers. We were already slinging the hammocks when this gentleman, named Kellar, with some others stepped up to me, declaring that if I had struck the sergeant with a stick, the matter was nothing, but as I had beat him with my fist, not only the man but the whole corps must be disgraced by it unless I made a proper atonement upon the spot. But I, most unluckily for the present, being in no humor to hear his preaching, threw off my jacket, declaring in my turn that in England, sticks were only made for dogs, and fell a-boxing, helter skelter, men and trees, with so much fury that I accidentally tumbled back into his own hammock, where, however, they most humanely had the civility to let me rest, and where five minutes after, I fell fast asleep. Here I awaked about midnight, in Hell's torments, with my tongue and palate parched as dry and black as my rusk biscuit; and having not only forgotten all that had happened, but even that we had come near the creek, I exclaimed "Good God. Shall we never again see water?" which ejaculation being heard by another Society officer named Graff, he instantly sent for a full calabash of it, which he gave me accompanied by a small piece of his black bread and cheese, and which was so good, surpassing wine and everything I had ever drunk before, that the taste of it shall never be effaced from my memory. Nor would the rich man, when he begged water from Lazarus, have drunk it with greater relish. Having thanked him, and now recollecting all my blunders, in the morning before we marched I went to Mr. Kellar, to whom and to the other officers I (from my heart) made a proper apology, and gave half a crown to the poor sergeant. The whole was ended to satisfaction on all sides.

On the 9th, we returned to our old camp from a fruitless cruise, when Colonel Fourgeoud set the captive Negro September at liberty, who followed like a shepherd dog attending a flock. But our Commander in Chief was indefatigable, and not only crossed and reconnoitred the west side of the creek himself this very day but, filling our knapsacks, the next morning we set out again on the same track we had kept the 8th, he still persisting that he was to overtake the enemy. Having thus marched till almost dark, we altered our course and passed the night in an old camp of the Rebel Negroes, we again having had no water the whole day.

On the 11th, we still proceeded, but no enemies or water was to be met with. The men and officers now began to be very faint, some of whom were already carried in their hammocks. It was now indeed extremely hot, being the very heart of the dry season. In this dilemma, we dug a hole six feet deep, in the bottom of which a ball cartridge being fired, a kind of moisture began to trickle forth, but so slow, and so black, that it proved not to be of any manner of use. Thus we marched on, and now encamped in an old weedy field where the Rebels some time before had cultivated plantains. During the night, it was truly affecting to hear the poor soldiers lament for want of drink, but to no purpose.

In spite of all this misery, Fourgeoud still persisted the third day in going forward, building his hopes on meeting with some creek or rivulet to alleviate this general distress. But he was mistaken, for, having again marched over burning sands till about noon, he dropped down himself among a number of others, a miserable spectacle for want of an opportunity to slacken his raging thirst. And it was well that we now ourselves were not attacked by the Negroes, as it would have been impossible to make any resistance, the ground being strewn with distressed objects that appeared all to be in hot fevers, and despair now seemed to stare wildly even in Fourgeoud's own countenance as he lay prostrate on the earth, with his lips and tongue parched black, and while, independent of what he had done me, he again attracted my pity. During all this, some of the soldiers still devoured salt pork, while others kept creeping on all fours like Nebuchadnezzar, and licking the scanty drops of dew from the fallen leaves that scattered the ground.

Now I found the kindness of a Negro when he is well treated by his master, being presented by the one attending me with a large calabash of as good water as ever I drank in all my life, to my astonishment, and this he had met with after unspeakable difficulty, in the leaves of a few wild pineapple plants, from which it is extracted in the following manner: the plant is held in one hand and a saber in the other, when at one blow it is severed from the root through the thick underparts of the leaves, and is held over a cup or calabash, as you have seen the head of St. John the Baptist held up by the hair after decapitation, and when, as the blood flows from the one, the water flows from the other—pure, cool, and to the quantity of sometimes a quart from each plant—and which has been caught in the time of the rains by its channeled leaves in their proper reservoirs.

Some other Negroes found the *water-withy* to help themselves, but not in sufficient quantity to assist any of the dying troops. This is a kind of very thick *nebee* of the vine species, which grows only in very sandy places, which *nebee* being slashed with the saber in long pieces, and suddenly held to the mouth, produces a limpid stream and affords a cool, pleasing, and healthy beverage in the parching forest.

Being now supplied, I could not help, for my soul, to assist poor Fourgeoud also with water, whose age and spirit pleaded greatly with me in his favor, and who being now refreshed, saw himself at last obliged to turn back, without any more hopes of overtaking the enemy, while the others were carried on long poles in their hammocks, and he still detached (this as his last resource) the Berbician Negro Gousary by himself, to try, if he could, to bring him some intelligence.

On our retreat, we now approached the well or pit we had dug yesterday, and I, convinced it must have clear water by this time, sent Quacoo, my boy, to the front to fill one of my gallon bottles before it should be changed to a puddle, and thus he did, but he was met on his return to me by Colonel Fourgeoud, who with the butt end of his gun relentlessly knocked the bottle to pieces, and doubling his pace, placed two sentinels at the pit, with orders to preserve the water all for himself and his favorites. But at this moment, subordination being dead, the two protectors were forced headlong into the pit followed by several others, who all fought to come at the water, but which being now changed into a perfect mire pool, was good for nothing at all, except (being black) making the divers look exactly like so many shoeblacks. Here it ended, and we slung our hammocks in an old Rebel camp, and this done, a dram of kill-devil was given out to each without distinction, which I, never using, offered my share to my faithful Negro that had given me the water. But here sharp was the word and quick the motion, since being observed by old Fourgeoud, it was snatched out of his hands and returned to the gray-beard, or earthen jar, telling me I must either drink it myself or have none. I was exceedingly exasperated at this mark of ingratitude, and determined in revenge to play him a saltwater trick, which I did that very evening by making Quacoo steal a whole bottle, which I distributed among the poor Negro slave and his companions. At this moment, the good news came that fine water was actually to be found near the camp, when all drank hearty, and Fourgeoud now ordered a warm supper to be boiled for himself, but not so much as a fire to be lit for anybody else, forbidding even the cutting of a stick, while we were now obliged to eat our salt beef and pork *raw* like the cannibals. However, having tied my allowance to a string, I hung it quietly over the side of his kettle to have it dressed.

On the 14th, the Negro Gousary returned from his stroll reporting he had discovered nothing, and was recompensed with a few hearty curses for his trouble.

December 15th. It was feared that Captain Friderici, who had marched the 20th of last month with forty men, white and black, from Jerusalem, and not been heard of since, had met with some bad accident, and in consequence today were dispatched two captains, two subalterns, and fifty men to the River Marawina for some intelligence.

The post at the Marawina, which is called Vredenburg, consists of houses surrounded by palisades in a kind of square, which are all built with manicole trees, with which the woods of Guiana so much abound. On the outer side are a guard and four sentinels, and the fort itself is defended by several cannon. It is situated in an opening on the banks of the river where is placed a large flag, and where the garrison communicates with the French post on the opposite shore, both being situated but a little distance from the Marawina's mouth. To give the best idea of this spot, I here present the reader with a view of it, as also of our situation at the Wana Creek which, however beautiful to behold on paper, was a dreadful limbo to many people. In this the three camps are distinctly perceived, those of Colonel Fourgeoud and of the deceased Major Ruhkopf, on both sides of the Wana Creek, and that late of the Rangers, which was directly opposite its mouth. The barges &c. are to bring up provisions and to take down the sick.

This last was not strictly adhered to, however, as at this very time the whole camp was attacked by that dreadful distemper the bloody flux, which daily carried numbers to the grave, while an emetic or some physic were the only cures for all relief, and there was not a proper surgeon to administer them, they being all with the hospital in Commewina and at Paramaribo. The poor slaves were peculiarly unhappy who (as I have said, getting but half allowance) lived mostly upon the produce of the cabbage tree, seeds, roots, wild berries, &c., which occasioned the first introduction of the above dangerous diseases in the camp, and which had spread like wildfire among all denominations.[1] They were so starved that they tied *nebees* or ropes about their naked bodies, in the vain hopes of thus alleviating their cruel hunger. Myself and a few more escaped the infection, but I was laid up with a miserable bad cold and swelled foot, called here *consaca,* which is not unlike moldy heels in Europe, occasioning a very great itching, particularly between the toes, and issuing a watery kind of substance. The Negroes are much attacked by this complaint, which they cure by applying the skin of a lemon or lime, made as hot by the fire as they can possibly bear it. Now was verified the Governor's prophecy, when he told me, at parting from Paramaribo, that this campaign should be still more disagreeable than my cruise in the barges. God in Heaven knows, they were both disagreeable enough, even to those that were the best treated among us all, but I shall go on.

I have often named what our eating and drinking consisted of, viz., salt beef, salt pork, rusk biscuit (often full of maggots), and water for all allowance, which dainties were dealt out regularly every five or six days (the two former having, perhaps, made the tour of the world after leaving

---

1. The bloody flux is both infectious and epidemic.

The Military Post Vreedenburgh, at the Marawina.

View of the three Encampments at the Wana Creek.

Plate 28

Ireland) and were so green, so slimy, so stinking, and sometimes so full of worms, that at other times, I vow to God, they would have made me cast my stomach. But I have made no mention of what was our furniture. However, this is done in very little time and consisted (besides our huts and hammocks) in a square box or chest for each officer to carry his linen, fresh provisions, and spirits when he had them, but of which one dram in the constitution was worth one gallon in the cellar. These boxes served not only as cupboards but as chairs and tables in the camp, while on a march they were carried on the head of a Negro, but we had no light after six o'clock in the evening, that of the moonshine sometimes excepted, when all was solemn and melancholy beyond description. I in particular, who had expected to find the necessary conveniences, had not so much as a trencher, or basin, fork, or spoon. For the first and second, I made a Negro's calabash serve me, the third I wanted not, and the fourth but seldom, which I then supplied with a folded leaf in imitation of the slaves. As for a knife, each individual carried one in his pocket. I at last also contrived to make a lamp, by breaking a bottle in which, having melted some pork, it served for oil, and a slip of my shirtsleeve for a cotton wick. One becomes exceedingly ingenious when forced by necessity, and every nicety is forgotten. Indeed, could I now have had what formerly I left upon my plate, I should have ardently thanked God for all his mercies. When speaking of ingenuity, I ought not to forget a number of very pretty baskets that were made by the Negroes in the camp and which (they having taught me) I also made to amuse myself, and sent as presents to several friends at Paramaribo.

In the above manner the time was spent for the present, while the whole camp being without stockings, shoes, hats, &c., Colonel Fourgeoud now himself walked a whole day quite barefooted, to give an example of patience and perseverance, and keep the few remaining troops from murmuring. In this respect, I had fairly the start of them all, my skin being (the swelled foot, or *consaca,* and a few scratches excepted) perfectly whole, from my habit of walking thus, while not a sound limb was to be found among the rest, which were running in open sores and corruption, and for which I have already partly accounted but for which I shall still further account in the following manner. While stockings and shoes did remain, they never came off from the feet of many wearers, who after marching through water, mud, and mire, in this dirty pickle, turned into their hammocks where, before morning in fair weather, this dried upon their limbs and, in consequence, occasioned an itching redness on the skin, which scratching having broken in many places, it soon became scrofulous, and ended up as open sores and ulcers. And these, from want of care and proper applications, often changed into mortifications and terrible swellings, by which some lost their limbs and others even their lives, unless a timely amputation took place. Such were the causes and such the effects of what we had to struggle with, while to be sure the reader must think we suffered enough, but I shall in time prove that we still suffered more, and that this was but a sample of the piece.

December 28th. We now got account that Captain Friderici with his command, supposed to be lost, were safely arrived in the River Commewina, and I got a ham and twelve bottles of claret sent me by one of my friends, a Captain Van Coeverden, which I immediately gave all again in a present to Colonel Fourgeoud, only four bottles excepted, three of which I drank with the other officers, and for which in return I was once more kept from sleep by one of his sentinels, who gave me a shake regularly every hour during this whole night, by the commands of his despotic master. Nothing could be more diabolically ungrateful than was this usage, and having cursed myself more than once for my ill-placed generosity, I threw the remaining bottle in the river without a cork, telling them they might now all drink wine and water for as long as they remained at the Wana Creek and be damned, after which I went out on a patrol with Major des Borgnes and forty privates, to try once more, if we still could, to get some account of the Negroes who had crossed the creek, as I have said, on the seventh instant, being only three weeks ago, and who could tell but they would be pleased to wait for us till we should overtake them. However, having dropped down the Coermotibo Creek with a large barge in which we lay all night, we stepped ashore (but still on the north side) the next morning, a few miles below its mouth. We immediately set out upon our march, keeping course due northeast, which march Major des Borgnes, like a hero, was pleased to continue notwithstanding I put him in mind that the chest with all the powder had been forgotten and left behind us in the barge. But what signified cartridges, where we had in reality so little chance of seeing an enemy now? Nothing. Our next distress was in having lost the road, and being without compass, when I, begging to be followed, kept due north in hopes of coming to Rio Cottica, and during which we discovered the track of our own troops (that had marched the 25th instant in search of Captain Friderici and his men) crossing a sandy savanna, and a little after which, now following it, we reentered the wood and slung our hammocks.

The morning of the 31st, we still continued in the same path, till at last it led into a marsh above our middles, when we lost it and, persevering, finally stood in water till under the armpits, each carrying his arms and accouterments upon his head. We were now perforce obliged to return, and marching southwest came once more to the Coermotibo Creek, where we made camp.

January 1, 1775. This morning, we marched again and before noon arrived in the old camp at Wana Creek, where the report was made, having done, as usual, nothing.

January 3rd. At last returned Captain Friderici with his party and a Rebel Negro, called Cupido, in chains, when Colonel Fourgeoud, being finally determined tomorrow to break up this infernal campaign, sent out a detachment of two captains, two subalterns, and sixty privates to cruise before him on the way to Patamacca.

With Captain Friderici came the news, among other trifles, that a poor devil of the Society troops, having received his pardon on the spot, after he had already kneeled to be shot through the head, was gone clean out of his senses. Query: Would he have suffered more if the sentence had been put in full force?

At six o'clock in the morning on January 4th, all was ready to decamp, and having sent down the barges with the sick to Devil's Harwar, we at last crossed Coermotibo Creek and marched directly south for Patamacca, over steep mountains covered with stones and impregnated with minerals, and in the evening we encamped at the foot of a high hill, where we found a small rivulet of good water and a coppice of manicole trees, the two chief ingredients required.

January 5th. We now marched the same course again, over mountains and dales, *cosi va il mondo,* some of which were so steep that one or two of the slaves, not being able to ascend them loaded, threw down their burdens and deserted, not to the enemy, but found their way to their masters' estates, where they were pardoned, while others tumbled down, burden and all, from top to bottom. This evening, however, we found our quarters ready-made, lodging in the *wigwams* or huts that were left standing when the Rice Country had been demolished, and Boni with his men driven to flight. I found in the one where I lay a very curious piece of candle, that the Rebels had left behind, composed of bees' wax and the heart of a bulrush.

Boni's own house, where Fourgeoud lodged, was a perfect curiosity, having four pretty little rooms, and a shade or piazza enclosed with neat manicole palisades.

January 6th. The whole being excessively fatigued, Fourgeoud now ordered a general rest day, only detaching Captain Friderici, as knowing the country best, with six men, to reconnoitre the banks of the Claas Creek, a water that issued from near this place in the upper parts of Rio Cottica. But there is not any peace for the wicked, since this officer had hardly marched off when the chief, his eye by chance falling upon me, ordered me instantly to follow him alone, for the mere purpose of thus persecuting me to death, and to bring him an account of what I had seen, that is, on the other side of the creek.

I was enraged at this injustice and fresh proof of his implacable hatred. However, I affected to go cheerfully, till we were all again in water till under the armpits, but then determined to disappoint my tormentor (by showing him I was proof to the worst that he could possibly invent to plague me), I stripped stark naked and, desiring Friderici with his men to await my return, I plunged headlong into the creek with my saber in my teeth, and swam across by myself alone. Here, having ranged the opposite shore and perceiving not a soul, to my good fortune, I swam back, and we all marched into the camp from whence we came. At noon, making my report to Colonel Fourgeoud, he seemed highly surprised at what he pleased to call my temerity. He said it was a desperate action which he had in reality never intended that I should perform. I was surprised, but he took me by the hand, entertained me with a bottle of my own wine, devising a *vis-à-vis,* and ordered Monsieur Laurant to set some bacon-ham before me. But who shall believe it that this repast was creeping in live worms, while my own—now his—that was fresh was refused me, and which exasperated me so much that I now started up and again left Fourgeoud, his valet, his wine, and his reptiles, with that contempt which they deserved, and alleviated my hunger with a piece of dry rusk biscuit and a barbecued fish called *warapa.*

January 7th. We all marched again. This evening, we encamped near the Patamacca Creek, where the poor captive Negro woman cried bitterly and scattered some victuals and water at the root of an old tree by way of libation, as being the spot where her husband was interred, who had been shot in some former skirmish by the Europeans.

Having now marched a few hours longer, the next morning we at last arrived at the Society post La Rochelle in Patamacca, such a sight of thin, starved, blackburnt, and ragged tatterdemalions, mostly without shoes or hats, as I think were never before beheld in any country whatever. I have already mentioned the prickly heat, ringworm, dry gripes, putrid fevers, boils, consaca, and bloody flux, to which one is exposed in this climate. Also the mosquitoes, patat- and scrapat-lice, chigoes, cockroaches, ants, horseflies, wild bees, and bats, besides the thorns, briars, and alligators and *pery* in the rivers, and to which if added the howling of the jaguars, the hissing of the serpents, and growling of *Fourgeoud,* the dry sandy savannas, unfordable marshes, burning hot days, cold and damp nights, heavy rains, and short allowance, people may be astonished how anyone was able to survive it. But I solemnly declare to have still omitted many other calamities that we suffered, dreading prolixity, of which perhaps I have been already too often guilty, and without which I might have mentioned lethargies, dropsies, &c., &c., besides the many small snakes, lizards, scorpions, locusts, bush spiders, bush worms, and centipedes, nay, even flying lice that one is perpetually tormented with, and in danger of being stung by, but the description of which cursed company I must defer till another opportunity. So famished was I now that, the moment of our coming here, observing a Negro woman supping on plantain broth from a calabash, I gave her half a crown, and snatching the basin from her hands, I devoured the contents with greater relish than I have ever tasted anything before or since during my life.

On January 11th arrived the other party that had left Wana the day before ourselves, having taken or seen according to custom, nothing. Meanwhile the Rebels, knowing best who was their friend and also the proper season, one of them with his wife came to La Rochelle, and surrendered voluntarily to the Commander in Chief, while (to keep from starvation having been their only motive) they were, as usual, delivered to the care of the cook. To the unfortunate Negro, Snakee, alone Colonel Fourgeoud had been cruel, but to September, Cupido, and the captive woman, besides the two last-come volunteers (being the only trophies of our three-months' campaign), he showed every mark of leniency and even friendship—and finally to me, as he this very day acquainted me himself that I was at liberty to go and refit at Paramaribo when I thought proper, which proposal I gladly accepted, and that moment prepared for my departure with some other officers, leaving behind us himself and, as I have said, a gang of such scarecrows as could have disgraced the garden or fields of any farmer in England. Among these was a Society captain named Larcher who declared to me he never combed, washed, shaved, or shifted, or even put off his boots, till all was rotted from his body, and who to be sure looked and smelled like the very Devil in person, while many other Germans ornamented their noses with long whiskers.

On January 13th, at last arrived the happy hour, and taking leave of my tattered companions, I and five more, with a tent-boat and six oars, rowed straight down for Paramaribo, still in good health and in a flow of contentment and high spirits.

At Devil's Harwar I now met a cargo of tea, coffee, biscuit, butter, sugar, lemons, rum, and twenty bottles of claret sent me by my friends, directed to La Rochelle, and which I again (in spite of the barbarous usage that I had so lately met with) gave all in a present to poor Fourgeoud, twelve bottles of wine excepted, which we drank to the health of our wives and mistresses in the barge. Nor could I help pitying Colonel Fourgeoud, whose age (he being about sixty) and indefatigable exertions claimed the attention of the most indifferent, and who during this trip (if few Rebels were taken) had certainly scoured the forest from the River Commewina to the mouth of the Wana Creek, dispersed the enemy, and demolished their support.

On the 15th, at last we arrived before Mr. De Lamarre's door at Paramaribo, when I stepped ashore among a crowd of friends, who all flocked round to see me, and to welcome me to town—and to the land of the living, it having been reported that I was dead so many different times. Next was sent for my dear, my inestimable Joanna, who burst into tears the moment she beheld me, not only for joy at my still existing but from seeing my very distressed situation. However, these precious drops I soon kissed away, and all was happy. Thus ended my second campaign, and with this I put an end to the chapter.

Chapter 12th

*Description of the town of Paramaribo and Fort Zeelandia—
Colonel Fourgeoud marches to the River Marawina—A
captain wounded—Strange execution in the capital—Account
of Fort Sommelsdyck—Of the Hope in Rio Commewina—
Some privates shot*

Being once more arrived at Paramaribo, and having now the leisure, I think it will be high time to give some account of that beautiful town.

Paramaribo is situated, as I have mentioned, on the right side of the beautiful River Surinam, at about sixteen or eighteen miles from its mouth, and is built upon a kind of gravelly rock that is level with the rest of the country, in the form of an oblong square. Its length is above a mile and a half, and its breadth about half as much. All the streets, which are perfectly straight, are lined with trees of oranges, shaddock, tamarinds, and lemons, which appear in everlasting bloom, while at the same time their branches are weighed down with the richest clusters of odoriferous fruit. Neither stone nor brick is here made use of for pavement, the whole being one continual gravel, not inferior to the best garden walks in England, and strewn on the surface with sea shells. The houses, which are mostly two and some three stories high, are all built of fine timber, a very few excepted. Most of the foundations are of brick, and they are roofed with thin split boards called shingles, in place of slates or tiles.

Windows are very seldom seen here, glass being inconvenient on account of the heat, but in place of which are used gauze frames, and sometimes nothing, except the window shutters, which are kept open from six in the morning till six at night. And as for a chimney, I never saw one in the whole colony, no fires being lighted except in the kitchens, which are always built at some distance from the dwelling house, where the victuals are dressed upon the floor and the smoke gotten out by a hole made in the roof. Notwithstanding all this, these timber houses are very dear in Surinam, witness that lately built by Governor Nepveu, which he declared to me had cost him above fifteen thousand pounds sterling. Here is no spring water to be met with, but most houses have wells dug in the rock; yet, affording but a brackish kind of beverage, these are used only for the Negroes, cattle, &c., while the Europeans have reservoirs, or cisterns, in which they catch the rain for their own consumption; while the more polite let it first drop through a filtering-stone into large jars or earthen water pots that are made by the Indians or natives for the purpose, and bartered at Paramaribo for other commodities.

The inhabitants of this country, of whatever denomination, sleep always in hammocks, the Negro slaves excepted, who mostly lie on the ground. Those hammocks of the better sort are all of cotton, with rich fringes, and also made and bartered by the Indians, their value in money being frequently above twenty guineas, and neither bedding nor covering is necessary, an awning excepted, to keep off the gnats or mosquitoes. Some people, indeed, lie in timber beds or mattresses, but in that case they are surrounded with green gauze frames instead of curtains, which let in the air freely, and at the same time keep out the smallest insect. The houses in general at Paramaribo are elegantly furnished, with paintings, gilding, crystal chandeliers, jars of china, &c. The rooms are never papered or plastered but beautifully wainscotted and stocked with the neatest joinery of cedar, brazil wood, and mahogany.

The number of buildings in Paramaribo is computed to be about one thousand four hundred, of which the principal are the Governor's dwelling house or palace, from which through the garden His Excellency can enter Fort Zeelandia. This house and that of the commandant, which has lately been burnt to the ground, were the only brick buildings in the Colony. The town hall is an elegant new building, covered with tiles; here the different courts have their meetings, and underneath this are the prisons for the European inhabitants, the military excepted, who are confined in the citadel called Fort Zeelandia. The Protestant church, where divine worship is done both in Low Dutch and French, has a small spire, clock, and dial, besides which there is a Lutheran chapel, and two elegant Jewish synagogues, the one German and the other Portuguese. Here is also a fine, large hospital for the garrison, that is never empty. The military storehouses, powder-magazines, &c., are kept in the fortress Zeelandia, where the Society soldiers are also lodged in barracks and some officers in proper pavilions.

The town of Paramaribo has a very good road for shipping, the river before the town being above one mile broad, and containing sometimes above one hundred vessels of burden, which are moored within a pistol shot from the waterside. Indeed, there are seldom less than fourscore, which load coffee, sugar, cacao, cotton, and indigo for Holland, including the Guineamen that bring slaves from Africa, and the brigs, schooners, &c., that import from North America and the Leeward Islands flour, salt-herring, and mackerel, Rhine wine, boards, spirits, spermaceti candles, beef, pork, and horses, and for which they export molasses to distill their rum.

This town, which is not fortified, is bounded by the roads and shipping on the southeast, by a large savanna on the west, by an impenetrable wood on the northeast, and is protected by Fort Zeelandia on the east.

This citadel, which is only separated from the town by a large green plain, or esplanade, where the troops assemble on different occasions, is built in the form of a pentagon, with one gate fronting Paramaribo and two bastions commanding the river. It is very small but strong, the whole being made of rock or hewn stone. Round about this is a broad fosse, well supplied with water, besides some outer works, and on the east side fronting the river is a battery of twenty-one pieces of cannon. On one of the bastions is a clock that is struck with a hammer by the sentinel, who is directed by an hourglass, and on the other is planted a large flag or ensign, which is generally hoisted on the approach of ships of war, days of public rejoicing, &c. Having before spoken of its antiquity, I shall only observe that the walls have no kind of parapet but that they are six feet in thickness with embrasures.

Paramaribo is a very lively place, the streets being crowded with planters, sailors, soldiers, Jews, Indians, and Negroes, while the river swarms with canoes, barges, yawls, ships, boats, &c., constantly going and coming from the different estates, and crossing and passing each other like the wherries on the Thames, and mostly accompanied with bands of music. This, and all the different-colored flags perpetually streaming in the wind, while continually some guns are firing in the roads from the shipping, and whole groups of naked girls are playing in the water like so many mermaids, cannot but have a truly enchanting appearance from the beach, and in some measure compensate for the many curses that one is here exposed to daily. I might still add the number of carriages, saddle horses, and profuseness in dress, which is truly magnificent—silk, embroidery, Genoa velvets, diamonds, gold- and silver-lace being daily wear—not so much as a captain of a trading ship appearing in less than solid gold buckles to his stock, breeches, &c., nor are they less refined at their tables, where everything that can be called delicate is produced at any price, and served up in the newest fashioned silver plate and Japan china. But nothing so much displays the luxury of the inhabitants of Sur-

Plate 30 *View of the Town of* **PARAMARIBO,** *with*

the Road & Shipping: from the opposite Shore.

inam as the quantity of slaves that constantly attend them, sometimes in one family to the number of twenty and greatly upwards, a European man- or maidservant being almost never to be met with in the Colony.

The current coin are stamped cards of which some are valued at ten florins, being about twenty shillings, others five shillings, &c., besides which they have notes from the amount of five to fifty pounds. Gold and also silver being very scarce, which is exchanged for the enormous interest of sometimes above ten percent, yet a Danzig base coin commonly called a *bit,* and in value something less than sixpence, is current throughout Surinam. The Negro slaves never receive paper money, which is liable to be burnt, torn by their children, or eaten by the rats, while a Portuguese johannes or an English guinea is sometimes met with, but both these are generally used as ornaments by the Mulatto, Samboe, Quadroon, and Negro girls.

Having this far described the town and its fair inhabitants, who want for nothing, as having, besides butcher's meat, fowl, fish, venison, and vegetables (with which last in particular the country abounds), all other luxuries imported that Asia, Africa, or Europe can afford—I say, having this far gone on with this description, I shall now say that the prices of provisions are excessively dear in general, and in particular those that come from abroad, which are here sold mostly by the Jews and the ship captains, the first enjoying extraordinary privileges in this settlement, and the latter erecting temporary storehouses for the purpose of trade, till their ships are loaded with the produce of the climate. The fair or European inhabitants in this whole colony, who reside mostly in town, are computed (including the garrison) to be five thousand, and the Negro slaves about seventy-five thousand people.

For a better idea of the town of Paramaribo, I shall now say a word or two more of its inhabitants. Here the guard mounts regularly every morning at eight o'clock by the military in the fortress, besides the burghers or militia who keep watch all night in the middle of the town. At six o'clock A.M. and at the same hour P.M., the morning and evening gun is fired by the commanding ship in the roads, when that instant down come all the flags, and all the bells on board the vessels are set a-ringing, while the drums and fifes keep beating and playing the tattoo through the streets. From this time, viz., from sunset to sunrise, the watch is set, and no Negro whatever of either sex is allowed to appear in the streets or on the river without a proper pass, signed by the master or mistress that he belongs to, without which he is taken up and, without further ceremony, flogged the next morning. And at ten o'clock at night, a band of black drums beat the burgher or militia retreat through Paramaribo.

Chapter 12th

white ole
Creole
woman
was

131

But it is after this time that the ladies chiefly begin to make their appearance, who delight (as I have mentioned) above all things to have a *tête-à-tête* in the moonshine, where they entertain you with sherbet, sangaree,[1] and wine and water, besides the most innocent and unequivocal discourse, such as the circumstance of their last lying-in, the mental and bodily capacities of their husbands, and the situation of their young female slaves, of whom they propose you the acceptance, at the price of so much money per week, payable to themselves according to their value in their own estimation. For instance, having ordered half a dozen of the girls to stand in a row, the lady tells you "Sir, this is a *caleebasee* (that is, a maid), and this is not. This has only had one husband, but this had three, &c." Thus are they not only unreserved in their conversation, but even profuse in bestowing their encomiums on the figures and sizes of such gentlemen as have the honor to profit by their entertaining and instructive company. I ought not to omit that, to give a proof of their keeping discipline and good order, they sometimes order the girls to strip as naked as they were born, when you may have a better opportunity of seeing the marks of the whip, which indeed some of them are barbarously covered over with from neck to heel. As for the Negro men, they always go entirely stripped, a small slip of cotton that serves as a fig leaf only excepted, in which dress they attend their mistresses at tea tables, breakfast, dinner, and supper, unless it should happen that some of them had found the means of purchasing a pair of Holland-trousers, but in this case, should they chance to forfeit a flogging, they are by their ladies industriously ordered to take them off in their presence, while the other covering being soon whipped to atoms, she has the better chance of beholding the effects of flagellation, besides the preservation of the poor young man's breeches. Thus much for the humanity, and modesty, of the Creole[2] ladies in this colony, and which, however much it may astonish some readers, is nevertheless an incontrovertible fact, but every country has its customs, yet from these customs exceptions are to be made, and I have seen ladies in Surinam whose polite conversation and delicate feelings would have graced the first circles in all Europe.

I had almost forgotten to mention that, besides the other refined amusements of feasting, dancing, riding, and card playing, they have erected a small theater of late, where the genteelest inhabitants act tragedies and comedies for their amusement and that of their friends. No people can be neater in their dress, and cleanlier in their houses, than the Surinamers are in general, whose fine linens are not only extremely well

1. Water, madeira wine, nutmeg, and sugar.
2. Such as are born in the settlement, of whatever sex or denomination.

sewn and embroidered, but so exquisitely well washed with Castile soap, that their whiteness can only be compared to mountain snow, and next to which the best bleached cloth in Europe looks like canvas. As for the parlor floors, they are always scoured with sour oranges or with lemons, cut through the middle, which gives the house a fine fragrance, and which half a dozen Negro wenches, taking one half in each hand, keep rubbing on the boards, till they are void of juice, and during which time they keep singing a loud chorus. Such is the town, and such are the inhabitants of Paramaribo, the capital of Surinam, and indeed of all the Dutch settlements in the West Indies.

January 28th. Walking this morning by the riverside, I saw brought ashore a fish that well merits to be mentioned, on account of its size and its goodness, being sometimes near two hundred pounds in weight. It is here called *grow-muneck,* or gray-friar, and is said to be of the codfish species, to which it bears no bad resemblance in shape and color. These and all other kinds of saltwater fish are caught by the Negro fishermen, who are trained up and employed only for that purpose by their masters, and who having sold their cargo, are obliged to produce so much money to their proprietor every week. And thus it is with every other trade, and ordained in such a manner, that if the slaves employed in them choose to be industrious, they may reap considerable benefit for themselves, and some even grow rich. But, on the contrary, should they be idle and indolent so as not to fulfill their usual task, in that case, they are sure to be flogged most severely. However, this last is more frequently the case on the plantations than at Paramaribo, where I have known slaves to buy slaves for their own use, and others buy their own liberty or manumission from their masters. Some others keep their money, and if the property of a respectable family, prefer dependence before freedom, having in the first instance nothing to care for but one master, and in the second all duties and taxes to pay, besides being in a manner dependent on all the world. I have known in particular one Negro blacksmith, who was offered his liberty by his proprietor on account of his long servitude and exemplary behavior but who refused to accept it, preferring to be the slave of so worthy a master. This man had several Negro slaves of his own, who worked for himself and no other, kept a decent house, with pretty furniture, and even plate, and when visited by his humane master or mistress, entertained them with sangaree, port, or claret.

However, these are what may be called white ravens, while in general they are treated with too much severity, yet more particularly by the Creole ladies, as I have said. The gentlemen, who are such, making the lives of their Negroes at least comfortable at Paramaribo, where if they do not always allow them to accumulate wealth, they treat them very often even with too much indulgence.

When speaking about slaves, I must here also mention one class of them, called *Quadroons,* that are in general very much respected, on account of their affinity to Europeans, a Quadroon being between a white and a Mulatto, and which are very frequent in this colony. These young men are frequently put to some good trade such as a joiner, a silversmith, or a jeweler, while the girls are employed as waiting women, and taught the arts of sewing, knitting, and embroidery to perfection. They are generally very handsome and well-behaved, and being (both sexes) not divested of pride, they dress with a great degree of neatness, and even elegance. In short, one sees at Paramaribo not only white and black, but meets

> the Samboe dark, and the Mulatto brown,
> the Mesti fair[3]—the well-limbed Quaderoon.

And to give the reader a still more lively idea of these people, I will describe the figures and dress of a Quadroon girl, as they usually appear in this colony. They are mostly tall, straight, and gracefully formed, though generally rather more slender than the Mulattoes, and they never go naked above the waist as do the former. Their dress consists, besides often a satin petticoat covered with flowered gauze, of a close short jacket, made of best Holland chintz or silk, and laced before, showing about a hand-breadth of a fine muslin shift between the jacket and the petticoat. As for stockings, or shoes, none are worn by any slaves in the Colony, but on their head (which is mostly adorned with a beautiful bunch of black hair in short natural ringlets) they wear a black or white beaver hat, sometimes with a feather, or a gold loop and button, while their neck, arms, and ankles are ornamented with chains, bracelets, gold medals, beads, &c.

All these fine women have Europeans for their husbands, to the no small mortification of the Creoles and fair sex, while should it ever be known that a female European had kept a carnal intercourse with a slave of whatever denomination, the first is detested, and the last loses his life without mercy. Such is the despotic law of men in Dutch Guiana, if not in the whole world, over the weaker species.

February 6th. This evening, a poor drummer of the Society brought me a present of some fine *albicata* or avocado pears and oranges, for having supported him, he said, in Holland against my servant, who had

---

3. Between a white and Quadroon, the others I have already described.

knocked him down; this mark of gratitude gave me much pleasure. The avocado pear grows on a tree above forty feet high, and is not unlike our walnut tree, but the fruit, which is about the size and color of a large pear, viz., a purple or pale green, is in my opinion, the most exquisite of any in the Colony, or in the world. It is yellow inside, with a soft stone like a chestnut, and so good is the flesh or pulp of this fruit—so nutritious and salubrious—that it is often called the vegetable marrow (a name given it, it is said, by Sir Hans Sloane), and is usually eaten with pepper and salt. Nor can I approach it to anything so well as to a peach, it melting in the same manner in one's mouth; but though not so sweet it is incomparably more delicious.

> How great thy fame, O vegetable pear.
> What fat, what marrow can with thee compare?
> Long known to fame, till now unknown to song,
> Though Britain sigh, and Britain's monarch long

as this fruit can never be transported.

On February 16th arrived the news that Colonel Fourgeoud with the remaining troops, having marched from La Rochelle in Patamacca to Boucou and Marawina, had been himself attacked by the Rebels, when among others poor Captain Friderici, marching in the front, had been shot through both his thighs. This gallant officer, clapping both his hands on the wounds, remained sitting in water up till his breast to conceal the bleeding (and prevent his situation from discouraging the rear guard from rushing forward), till his wounds were dressed by the surgeon, and he was carried off in his hammock by two Negroes. Indeed, nothing can exceed the zeal that both this young officer and Fourgeoud's adjutant, Captain Van Geurike, showed throughout the whole expedition, who were continually with him wherever he went for five years, whether their constitutions could bear it or not, and the honor of which was the principal profit they derived from their extraordinary and assiduous attendance, since in my opinion Colonel Fourgeoud never yet recompensed them afterwards according to their merit, while he abused the other officers, and even some field officers, worse than ever I did any of my corporals.

To cut the story short, I now once more made an offer to join him myself in the woods, but in place of which he sent me an order to hasten to the estate L'Esperance, in English the Hope, which I will henceforth call it, situated in the upper part of Rio Commewina, there to take the command of that whole river during his absence, and which river, being new to me, I was extremely happy to be sent to.

Thus having provided myself with a complete new camp equipage,

Female Quadroon Slave of Surinam.

Plate 32

and bought provisions, I was soon ready to depart for my new station. But I must not leave Paramaribo without mentioning that, during my stay here, nine Negro slaves had one leg cut off each, for having run away from their work at a plantation. This punishment is part of the Surinam administration of justice, viz., at the master's desire, and was executed by Mr. Greber, the surgeon of the hospital, while the poor devils were deliberately smoking a pipe of tobacco, and for which, he told me, he was regularly paid at the rate of about six pounds per limb. Query: How many would not do the office of Jack Catch for less money? However, independent of his great abilities, four of them died after the operation, while a fifth killed himself by plucking the bandages from the stump, and bleeding willfully to death during the night. These amputated Negroes are frequent in this colony, where they are equally useful in rowing the boats or barges of their masters, while others are sometimes met with that want a hand, but this is for having dared to lift it against any of the Europeans, and this verifies what Voltaire says in his *Candide*.

February 17th. Now for the Hope in the River Commewina, having first astonished all the planters by ornamenting my black boy Quacoo's head with a gold-laced hat, contrary to custom, for his faithful conduct during my last campaign in the woods, and to which place (the Hope) I was this time sent as I ought to be, in a decent tent-boat with six oars, rowed by six Negroes. Adieu, then, once more, my dear Mulatto, and this evening I came to the estate Sporksgift in the Matapica Creek, the next at Arendsrust in Commewina, having passed the Orleana (corruptly called the Whore Helena Creek) and the fortress Sommelsdyck, which, as I have said, at about sixteen miles above the fortress Amsterdam, forms the separation between that and the River Cottica, commanding the two opposite shores by the fire of its cannon. This fortress was built in the year 1684 by Governor Sommelsdyck, whose name it still bears, and lies in the form of a pentagon, having five bastions mounted with artillery and a fosse, besides being well provided with military stores. It is not large but well defended, especially by its so low and marshy situation. Not far above this and on the right hand is a fine creek called Commetewane.

About midday on the 19th I came to the Hope, having found this whole river not less charming than I had found the River Cottica and, as I have mentioned, being lined in the same manner on both sides with enchantingly beautiful estates, particularly of coffee and of sugar, and with the first of which it abounds principally near its mouth. About halfway up both these rivers are also, in each, a Protestant church, where the plantation people resort to hear divine worship, the expense of the parson &c. being paid by the planters.

The estate L'Esperance, or the Hope, where I now took the command, is a very fine sugar plantation, situated on the left in going upwards, and at the mouth of a small rivulet called Bottle Creek, having almost opposite to it on the other side of the river another creek called Cassewinica. The Bottle Creek communicating with both the rivers Commewina and Perica, as the Wana Creek does with Coermotibo and Rio Marawina, thus may they in some degree, rather, be called small channels.

On the Hope, I now found the troops were lodged in temporary houses built of manicole trees, and in such a low and marshy situation that by spring tides the whole was underwater, while the officers were all crammed in one apartment of the same species, which could not miss to be extremely inconvenient, while the planter's fine house was uninhabited (by the overseer or manager of the estate only excepted).

This was rather a disagreeable circumstance, besides its being extremely unhealthy. However, I found those at the estate Clarenbeek in the same condition, where next I visited to examine the state of the hospital, being at best but a cannon shot higher up the river than myself. Indeed, they were rather worse off than we, by the amazing quantity of rats that infested this place, and which were so numerous that they were visible by half-scores at a time, destroying all the clothes and provisions, and galloping over the people's faces while they lay in their hammocks during the night, which cursed inconvenience could only be prevented by stringing quart bottles (having first bored holes in their bottoms) on the ropes or lashings of each hammock, both at the head and the feet, in the manner of glass beads upon a cord, and over which (on account of their polish) it is impossible for the rats to get at the canvas, which shows that *"experientia docet."*

Here the crowded hospital also afforded a melancholy spectacle, by the miserable objects that it presented to my view. And upon the whole, seeing nothing to invite me here, I was glad to return back to the Hope. My orders were here much the same as they had been in Cottica, viz., to protect the estates from the enemy &c., and the paroles or watchwords were regularly sent me by Colonel Fourgeoud.

Having here with me one of the two Berbician Negro captains formerly mentioned, named Akara, he discovered an old decrepit slave called Paulus, belonging to this estate, to be his brother, whom he treated with much kindness, the same being both surprising and affecting. Here I was respected like the Prince of the River, every day invited to dine and visit on the different neighboring estates, and constantly stocked with game, fish, fruit, and vegetables of every kind that were sent me as presents, such that I scarcely knew myself from what I had been so little time before, and had very few wishes remaining. When still to augment my happiness, I was most agreeably surprised by the waving of a white hand-kerchief from a tent-boat that was rowing up the river, and which soon proved to be no other than Joanna herself with her aunt, who now pre-ferred the estate Faukenberg (situated about four miles above the Hope, but on the opposite side) to the town of Paramaribo, and to which plan-tation I accompanied her that instant. Here, she introduced to me a ven-erable old slave, gray-headed and blind, who made me a present of a half-dozen fowls, and was, it appeared, the grandfather of my Mulatto, being now supported comfortably, since many years, by the care and industry of his numerous offspring, and telling me that he was originally from the coast of Guinea, where he had once been more respected than were any of his masters in Guiana.

It must seem wonderful to the world in general to see me so often mention this female slave, and with so much respect, but I cannot help speaking, even with rapture, of that object who was so deserving of my attention, who alone counterbalanced all my other miseries, and who since literally saved my life, as shall be seen in the sequel. While indepen-dent of these considerations, the misfortune of her birth and condition should never be a bar to prevent virtue, youth, and beauty from gaining my esteem, but on the reverse be a stimulant to attract it.

March 8th. Today, having invited some company, we drank the Prince of Orange's health, this being his anniversary, while Colonel Fourgeoud (like a true Trojan) still kept on scouring the bushes, and from whom now came the news of his operations—viz., some shot by the Negroes, some lost in the woods, the Rebel captive Cupido run away with all his chains, &c., but no conquest of any consequence on the enemy, while he sent me two wounded men to put in the hospital at Clarenbeek, the one being terribly cut by the rebels, who had also disarmed him, while he had been obliged to lag behind from necessity. Nevertheless, the chief, for this action, now threatened to take away that life the savages had spared, and from that moment put him under an arrest, till further orders.

CHAPTER 13th

A sugar plantation described—Domestic happiness in a cottage—Further account of Fourgeoud's operations—Dreadful cruelties inflicted by some overseers—Sketch of resentment by a Rebel Negro captain

I have already said that I was happy at the Hope, but how was my felicity now redoubled when, this evening, Mr. Lolkens and his lady came to visit me, and not only gave me the address of Messrs. Passelege & Son at Amsterdam (who, as I have said, were the new proprietors of my Mulatto), but even desired of me to take her to the Hope, where she would be better off than at either Faukenberg or Paramaribo. This request, to be sure, I easily granted, and instantly set my slaves to work to build her a comfortable house of manicole trees, to be ready for her reception and convenience. While during the time of its being erected, I wrote the following letter to Messrs. Passelege & Son.

From the Hope in Commewina. March 22nd, 1774
Gentlemen—
Being informed by Mr. Tierck Lolkens, the administrator of the estate Faukenberg, that you are the present proprietors, and being under great obligation to one of your Mulatto slaves named Joanna, who is the daughter of the late Mr. Kruythoff, particularly for having attended me during sickness, I in gratitude request of you, who are her masters, to let me purchase her liberty without delay, which favor shall be ever thankfully acknowledged, and the ransom money immediately paid, by
Gentlemen,
Your most obedient and most humble servant,
—John Gabriel Stedman—
Captain in Colonel Fourgeoud's Corps of Marines

This letter was seconded by another from my friend Lolkens, who much cheered my expectation with the assurance of success.

Having dispatched these letters to Holland, and having now had the opportunity also to see the whole process of a sugar plantation, I shall here give an accurate account of it.

The buildings usually consist of an elegant dwelling house for the planter, outhouses for the overseer and bookkeeper, besides a carpenter's lodge, kitchens, storehouses, &c., and stables if the sugar mills are worked by horses or mules—which were not required on the Hope, where the wheels went round by water, being saved in canals that surround the estate during the spring tides, by the means of sluices, or floodgates, and which, being let open when the water in the river is very low, the contents run out like a deluge, and set the whole work a-going.

As to the construction of a sugar mill (which is generally built at the amazing expense of from four to seven or eight thousand pounds), I cannot enter into the particular description of it, but shall only say that the large- or water wheel, which moves perpendicularly, corresponds with another large wheel that is placed in a horizontal direction, and this again with three perpendicular cylinders or rollers of cast iron that are under it, supported on a strong beam and placed so close together that, when the whole is in motion, they imbibe and crush to atoms whatever comes between them, and in which manner the sugar cane is bruised, to separate the juice or liquor from the trash.

Those mills that are worked by cattle are also made on the same construction, with this difference only, that the horses or mules answer the purpose of the horizontal wheel by dragging round a large beam, like the hand of a dial.

If the water mills can work the fastest, and are the cheapest, they must wait for the opportunity of the spring tides, whereas the cattle mills have the advantage of always being ready for use, whenever the proprietor thinks it convenient.

Adjoining the mill house is a large apartment (both being built of brick) in which are fixed by masonry the coppers or large cauldrons to boil the liquid sugar, which are usually five in number. On the opposite side are the coolers, being large square flat-bottomed wooden vessels, into which the sugar is put from the cauldrons so that it may cool before it goes into the hogsheads, which are placed next to them on strong channeled rafters that receive the molasses as it drips from the sugar and conduct it into a square cistern underneath the whole, and made for the purpose of preserving it.

Adjoining this apartment is a distillery, where the dross or scum taken from the boiling sugar is converted into a kind of rum, which I have before mentioned and is generally known by the name of kill-devil throughout the Colony.

Having thus far described the buildings (besides which all estates in Surinam keep a tent-boat and several other small craft with a covered dock to keep them dry and repair them), I shall now say something of the grounds, and the cultivation of the cane.

The sugar estates in this colony often consist of more than five or six hundred acres, the parts for cultivation being divided into squares, where the pieces of cane (about one foot long) are stuck in the ground in an oblique position but in straight lines, which is usually done in the rainy season, when the earth is well-soaked and most rich. Here the shoots that spring from the joints grow for a time of twelve or sixteen months, when they become yellow, thick like a German flute, from six to ten feet in height, and jointed, forming a very beautiful appearance, with pale green leaves like those of a leek, but longer and denticulated, which hang down when the crop begins to be ripe for cutting. During all this period, pulling up the weeds is the principal business of the slaves, to prevent the canes from being impoverished by their luxurious progress.

After this, the sugar canes are cut in pieces of three or four feet long, and (being divested of their leaves) tied in bundles or faggots, when they are next transported to the mill by water (which shows the double usefulness of the canals) and where, within the space of twenty-four hours, they ought to be bruised, to prevent the juice from fermenting and becoming sour by the great heat of the climate.

I must not forget to say that some sugar estates have more than four hundred slaves, the expense of buying whom, and erecting the buildings (the ground excepted) frequently amounts to twenty or twenty-five thousand pounds sterling.

We shall now examine the progress of the sugar cane through the mill, where it is bruised between the working cylinders or rollers (which are, as I said, three in number), through which it passes twice, viz., once it enters and once it returns, when it is changed to trash, and its pithy substance into liquid, which is conducted, as it is extracted, through a channeled beam, from the mill to the adjoining boiling house, where it is received into a species of wooden cistern.

So very dangerous is the work of those Negroes who enter the canes in the rollers, that should one of their fingers catch between them, which frequently happens by inadvertency, the whole arm is instantly shattered to atoms, if not part of the body, for which reason a hatchet is generally kept ready to chop off the limb, before the working of the mill can be stopped. The other danger is that should a Negro slave dare to taste that sugar which he produces by the sweat of his brow, he would run the hazard of paying the expense by some hundred lashes, if not by the break-ing out of all his teeth. Such are the hardships, and dangers, to which the sugar-making Negroes are exposed.

From the above wooden cistern, the liquor is let into the first copper cauldron, filtering through a kind of grating to keep back the trash that may have escaped from the mill; here, having been boiled for some time and been skimmed, it is put in the next cauldron, and so forth, till it reaches the fifth or last, where it gets that thickness or consistency which is required to put it in the coolers. It is here to be observed that a few pounds of lime and alum are thrown into the cauldrons to make it work, and granulate, while the whole is well mixed, and boiled gradually stronger and stronger, as it proceeds towards the end, or the last cauldron.

Being next put in the wooden coolers, the sugar is well stirred about so that the grain or body is equally dispersed throughout the vessels where, when it becomes cold, it has the appearance of being frozen, being candied all over, with a brown glazed consistency, not unlike pieces of highly polished walnut tree.

From these coolers, it is next put in the hogsheads (which weigh, at an average, one thousand pounds each), where it then settles and where (through the crevasses and small holes made in the bottoms) it is purged of its remaining liquid contents, which are called molasses (which, as I have said, are received in an underground cistern), after which the sugar has undergone its last operations, and is fit for transportation to Europe, where it is refined, and cast into loaves, &c. I shall only further observe that the larger is the grain, the better is allowed to be the sugar. N.B. the best estates make six hundred barrels.

I will now conclude this account by once more repeating that no soil in the world is so very rich and proper for the cultivation of the sugar cane as is Surinam, or indeed all Guiana, which is in a manner never ex-hausted, and produces at an average three or four hogsheads of sugar per acre.

In 1771 were exported to Amsterdam and Rotterdam alone no less than twenty-four thousand hogsheads, valued at only about six pounds each,[1] which nevertheless returned a sum of nearly one hundred fifty thousand pounds sterling, besides the great quantity of molasses and kill-devil—the first, computed at seven thousand hogsheads, which were sold to the American islands for twenty-five thousand pounds, and the sec-

---

1. It has sometimes been sold for more than twelve or thirteen pounds per barrel of a thousand pounds weight.

ond, which is distilled in Surinam for the Negroes, valued at just as much more, which makes a sum of two hundred thousand pounds benefit for only one year.

The kill-devil is also drunk by some planters, and too much by the common sailors and soldiers, to whom (the more so, as it is always used while it is new) proves to be (as I have said before) no better than a slow and pernicious poison. Yet it never hurts the Negroes, whose constitutions are so much stronger than ours in a tropical climate, but on the contrary does them much good (particularly when at work in the rainy season), if they can have the good fortune to be indulged but with a single dram per day by their masters, which is wide distant from always being the case.

The chaff or refuse of the canes is used for fuel, or manure, and all estates are closely surrounded by the uncultivated forest.[2]

From what I have said on this subject alone, the reader may form an idea of the riches that abound in this country, which nevertheless seemed so little to stimulate its enemies for possessing it during the late war. While I must here make one remark: that is that Surinam, in the possession of any nation other than the Dutch, would instantly cease to be of its present consequence, the Hollanders being indisputably the most patient, persevering, and industrious people that inhabit the globe. While, independent of the great wealth that the West Indies in general afford, it shall ever be my opinion that the Europeans could live as comfortably, if not more healthily, without them, where the want of sugar, coffee, cotton, cacao, indigo, rum, and brazilwood could be amply supplied by honey, milk, wool, geneva, ale, English herbs, British oak, &c. And now once more to my narrative.

I have mentioned that my slaves began to build a small habitation of manicole trees for the reception of my best friend, which, however, was not completed in less than the space of six days, having every convenience, such as a parlor that served also for a dining room, a bedroom (where, besides, I stowed my luggage), a shade or piazza to sit under before the door, a small kitchen detached from the dwelling, and a henhouse, the whole of which was situated in a spot by itself, commanding the most enchanting prospect on all sides, and surrounded with a paling to keep off the cattle. My tables, stools, benches, and seats were all composed of the same identical manicole laths, while my doors and windows

---

2. In the sugar-cane fields, the herds of wild deer often commit very great ravages. The cane pieces are then surrounded by armed Negroes, and the dogs set in to disperse the deer, which are frequently shot.

were guarded with most ingenious wooden locks and keys, which were presented me by a Negro, and which were the work of his own manufacturing.

My house being this far finished and furnished, my next care was to stock it with provisions. Thus, I commissioned from Paramaribo a barrel of flour, another of salted mackerel (which are in this country delicious, as being imported from North America), hams, pickled sausages, Boston biscuit, &c. Also wine, Jamaica rum, tea, and sugar, and a box with spermaceti candles, to which were added two charming foreign sheep, and a hog sent me by Mr. Kennedy from his estate Vriedyk, besides a couple of dozen fine fowls and ducks, given me as a present by Lucretia, Joanna's aunt, while fruit, vegetables, fish, and venison flowed to me from every quarter as usual.

On April 1st, at last my dear Joanna came down the river, in the tent-boat belonging to Faukenberg, and arrived at the Hope. Having communicated to her the contents of my letter to Holland (which she modestly received with downcast looks and a blush, for all reply), I introduced her to her new habitation, where the plantation slaves (as a mark of respect) immediately brought her presents of cassava, yams, bananas, and plantains, and never two people were more completely happy.

On the morning of the 8th, while between six and seven o'clock we were interring one of my sergeants, we heard the report of several minute guns towards the River Perica, in consequence of which I detached an officer and twelve men to give assistance. Next day, they returned with an account that the Rebels had attacked the estate Kortenduur, where having pillaged some powder &c., the plantation slaves (who had been armed by their master) had manfully beaten them back, before he or his men had come up to them.

April 11th. Now a small detachment arrived from Colonel Fourgeoud at Wana Creek (with September, the captive Negro) and related that the Rebels had spoken with, and actually laughed at, Fourgeoud, having overheard him deliver his orders, viz., not to fire on them but to take them alive, while he might as well have taken so many torpedoes; also that among those lost in the woods was the unlucky Schmidt, who had been lately so unmercifully beaten and from which he had never recovered, and that it was forbidden to give him any assistance or even to try to restore him again.

On April 13th, the whole post was under water, occasioned by the spring floods having broken through the dams that were used to keep them off. This accident obliged officers and all to walk in water above the knees, making it the more comfortable for me to be pitched with my cabin upon a dry spot.

April 18th. I have of late said nothing on the subject of cruelty, and am sorry at this time (while all seemed harmony and peace) to be obliged to relate some fresh instances of it, which I am confident must inspire the most unfeeling reader with horror and resentment.

The first object that attracted my compassion while visiting on a neighboring estate was a truly beautiful *Samboe* girl of about eighteen, tied up with both arms to a tree, as naked as she came to the world, and lacerated in such a shocking condition by the whips of two Negro drivers that she was, from her neck to her ankles, literally dyed over with blood. It was after receiving two hundred lashes that I perceived her with her head hanging downwards, a most miserable spectacle. Thus, turning to the overseer, I implored that she might be untied from that moment, which seemed to give her some relief, but my answer from the humane gentleman was, that to prevent all strangers from interfering with his government, he had made it an unalterable rule in that case always to redouble the punishment, which he instantaneously began to put in execution. I tried to stop him but in vain, he declaring the delay should not alter his determination but make him take vengeance with interest upon interest. Thus, I had no other remedy left but to leap into my boat and leave the detestable rascal, like a beast of prey, to enjoy his bloody feast till he was glutted. From that day on I swore to break off communication with all overseers, and implored the curse of Heaven to be poured down upon the whole relentless fraternity.

On my having inquired since for the cause of such barbarity, I was too credibly informed that her only crime had consisted in her firmly refusing to submit to the loathsome embraces of her despicable executioner, which his jealousy having construed to disobedience, she was thus skinned alive. Having hitherto not introduced the *Samboe* caste, I take this opportunity, by here representing the miserable young woman, as I found her, to the sympathizing reader.

A Samboe (as I have said) is between a Mulatto and a black, being of a deep copper-colored complexion, with dark hair that curls in large ringlets. Those slaves, both male and female, are generally handsome, and mostly employed as menial servants in the houses of the planters &c.

At my return to the Hope, I was accosted by Mr. Ebbers, the overseer of this estate, who informed me (with a woeful countenance) that he had just been fined the sum of twelve hundred florins, being about one hundred guineas, for having committed some time before the same diabolical crime, with this difference—that the victim had died during the execution. Telling me of his distress (so far from giving him consolation) gave me the most inexpressible satisfaction, and so I told him.

The particulars of this murder were as follows. During the time that

Flagellation of a Female Samboe Slave.

Plate 35

Captain Tulling commanded here (just before I came to the Hope), it happened that a fugitive Negro belonging to this estate had been taken upon an adjoining plantation and sent back to Mr. Ebbers guarded by two armed slaves. While Mr. Ebbers was reading the letter that accompanied him, this fugitive Negro found means to spring aside and again escape into the forest, which so incensed the overseer that he instantly took revenge upon the two poor slaves that had brought him, whom having tied up in the carpenter's lodge, he kept on flogging at such an unmerciful rate that Captain Tulling thought proper to interfere and beg for mercy. But this (as with me) had just the opposite effect. The clang of the whip, mixed with their dismal cries, was heard to continue for above an hour after, till one of them was absolutely flogged to death, which ended the inhuman catastrophe. A lawsuit was instantly commenced against Mr. Ebbers, for assassination, while paying the above sum was his only sentence and which price of blood is nearly always divided between the fiscal and the proprietor of the deceased slave, it being a rule in the Colony of Surinam that by paying a fine of five hundred florins (less than fifty pounds) per head, you are at liberty to kill as many Negroes as you please, with an additional price of their value should they belong to any of your neighbors, and then the murder first requires to be properly proven, which is extremely difficult in this country, where no slave's evidence is admitted.

Such are the laws of the legislature in Dutch Guiana. The above Mr. Ebbers was indeed peculiarly tyrannical, tormenting a boy of about fourteen, called Cadety, for the space of a whole year, by alternately flogging him for one month, then keeping him laid flat on his back with his feet in the stocks for another, then making him wear an iron triangle called a pot-hook[3] around his neck, to prevent him from escaping or sleeping for a third month, and chaining him to the landing place in a dog's collar night and day without shelter, with orders to *bark* at every boat or canoe that passed, for a fourth, &c., &c., till the youth had almost become insensible to his sufferings, walked crooked and, in a manner, degenerated into a brute.

The above gentleman was nevertheless very proud of his handsomest slaves, and—for fear of disfiguring their skins—I have known him to forgive them with twenty lashes, when by their robberies they had deserved to get the gallows.

---

3. These triangles are frequently put on the Negroes, which being formed with three long, barbed spikes, like small grapples that project from an iron collar, prevent them from entering into the woods without getting entangled, and from sleeping, except in a sitting position.

So much for public and private justice in Surinam, to which I shall only add that the above gentleman, having quitted the Hope on this occasion, his next *humane* successor, Mr. Blenderman, began his reign by, one morning, flogging all the slaves of the estate, male and female, old and young without exception, for having overslept their time by about fifteen minutes.

And now what reader shall believe that the above inhumanities can be exceeded? Yet such they certainly were, only very recently, and by a female, when a Mrs. Stolker, going to her estate in a tent-barge, a Negro woman with her sucking infant happened to be passengers and seated on the bow or fore-part of the boat, but where the child crying (without it could possibly be hushed) and Mrs. Stolker not delighting in such music, she ordered the mother to bring it aft and deliver it into her own hands, with which, forthwith, in the presence of the distracted parent, she thrust it out one of the tilt-windows and held it underwater till it *was drowned*. The fond mother (being desperate from the loss of her helpless baby) instantly leaped overboard in the same stream where floated her beloved offspring, and in conjunction with which she was determined to end her miserable existence. However, in this she was prevented by the care of the Negro slaves that rowed the barge, and was corrected by her mistress for her unnatural temerity with three or four hundred lashes.

April 20th. Now arrived Colonel Fourgeoud with all the troops from Maagdenburg, preferring to establish his headquarters rather nearer the infirmary, for which at this time he indeed had great need, and thus pitched camp upon the estate called Nieuw-Rosenbeek, situated between the Hope and the hospital. To this place I now immediately repaired, where I paid my obeisance to the chief, saw the remainder of his miserable army landed, and got the remaining news of this campaign.

I have already mentioned Captain Friderici's having been shot through both his thighs, one man terribly wounded and disarmed, another lost altogether by neglect, the captives run away with chains and all, the hero scoffed and laughed at by his sable enemies, &c., to which I now shall add that a sick Marine was left behind, to die or recover as he could by himself, that one of the slaves by bad usage had his arm broken, and that the captive Negro woman was also now lost (no more to return to her conqueror) who, carrying back a big belly got among the troops, had the opportunity of thus presenting a recruit to her dusky king, &c.

These were the particulars of the last two months' campaign, while I must not omit to mention the humanity of a poor slave, who at every hazard had deserted Fourgeoud to attend the dying Marine, and having remained alone with him till he expired, returned to the troops to receive his punishment, but where he was most miraculously pardoned.

Let me now do justice to Colonel Fourgeoud by saying that upon such an expedition, and in such a climate, many of these little accidents could not easily be prevented, and that while he killed his troops by scores, without making any captures of the enemy, he nevertheless did the Colony a considerable deal of good by constantly disturbing, and hunting, and harassing them, and destroying their fields with provisions. Indeed, no Negro will ever return to settle in those haunts from which he has been driven, any more than a hare will return to her lair, or a fox to the hole from which he has been unkenneled; to which I may add that his partaking personally in all the dangers and fatigues, and at his age, cannot but help to efface many of the other faults that stained his character, and even serve in some measure to establish his lasting honor.

On the 21st, I entertained several officers who had come to visit me at the Hope with a fish dinner. Among these fish were the *kawiry,* the *lamper,* and a species called *macrely-fisy,* all of which fish are most delicate eating, and taken in great quantities through all Guiana.

However, we had feasted so hearty that one of the officers was ill the same evening, and next morning my poor Joanna, who had herself been the cook, was attacked with such a violent fever that, at her own request, I instantly sent her to the estate Faukenberg, to be attended there by one of her female relations. Nevertheless, she continued to grow worse, and on the evening of the 25th was so extremely sick that I determined now to call upon her in person.

On the morning of April 27th arrived the Mulatto quite recovered, accompanied by a stout black who was her uncle, and whose arm was decorated with a silver band on which were engraved the words "True to the Europeans." This man, who was named Codjo, had voluntarily fought against the Rebels, before his companions had been forced by the inhuman Mr. De Borde to join them in the woods, and of whom he now related to me the following remarkable circumstance. Having a little girl called Tamera by the hand, he told me:

This child's father, whose name is Jolicoeur, is one of them, the first captain belonging to Baron's men, and not without cause one of the fiercest Rebels in the forest, which he has lately shown on the neighboring estate Nieuw-Rosenbeek, where now our colonel commands.

Here one Mr. Schults, a Jew, was the manager at that time (who formerly was the manager of Faukenberg), when the Rebels suddenly appeared and took possession of the whole plantation. Having tied his hands and plundered the house, they next began feasting and dancing, before they thought it proper to end his miserable existence.

In this deplorable situation now lay the victim, only awaiting Baron's signal for death, when his eyes chancing to fall on the above captain, he addressed him nearly in the following words. "O Jolicoeur, now remember Mr. Schults who was once your deputy-master. Remember the dainties I gave you from my own table, when you were but a child and my favorite, my darling among so many others. Remember this and now spare my life, by your powerful intercession." To which Jolicoeur replied, "I remember it perfectly well, but you, O Tyrant, should recollect how you ravished my poor mother, and flogged my father for coming to her assistance. Recollect that the shameful act was perpetrated in my infant presence, recollect this and then die by my hands, and next be damned," saying which, he severed his head from his body with a hatchet at one blow, and with which having played at bowls upon the beach, he next with a knife cut the skin from his back, which he spread over one of the cannon to stop the firing.

Here ended the history of Mr. Schults, when Codjo with young Tamera departed, and left me to anticipate the joyful news that I soon was to expect from Amsterdam, when the deserving Joanna should be unbound from all such rascals.

CHAPTER 14th

April 29th. Having delayed his departure until today, Colonel Fourgeoud, accompanied by a few of his officers, now finally rowed down for Paramaribo, to refresh themselves (of which they had truly great need). Meanwhile, an armed barge was left floating up and down the river, while the remaining emaciated troops (which were melted down to a very small number, and unfit, till recovered in their constitutions, for any further military service) greatly required some rest.

Just before the chief's departure, he sent me (who now commanded the river) the following very curious instructions to observe, which as a proof of his generalship I cannot help inserting; viz., among others, "to ask the planters if the Rebels were come to their estates, in which case to attack and drive them away, but not to follow, unless I was sure that I certainly should conquer them, and for which I should be called to an account," which means in plain English that if I attacked the enemy without success, I must be punished, and if I did not attack them at all, ad idem. However judicious the other articles I had received, I could not help thinking the above so very absurd that I immediately returned them back with an officer, and had the good fortune (at my request) to get them changed into common sense.

Nor were the provisions that he left for the troops (indiscriminately, the healthy and the sick) to be boasted of, which consisted weekly in Irish-horse, viz.,

salt beef	2 lb	besides one spoonful of butter, one half
salt pork	1/2 lb	quart bottle of kill-devil, one quarter

salt fish	1/2 lb	pound of tobacco and a pipe. This was, by
barley	4 lb	Heavens, the whole for seven days allow-
rusk biscuit	6 lb	ance.

—while the wheat flour, peas, cheese, sugar, vinegar, beer, and geneva that had been so plentifully provided by the town of Amsterdam were kept back, as were also the many kegs of preserved vegetables, and hogsheads of excellent claret sent for the officers.

May 1st. Painting, music, bathing, and shooting were now my principal amusements, in which my young Mulatto was my constant companion. But all at once, in the midst of my glory, my truly halcyon days were blasted, and I was almost plunged into despair, by receiving the fatal news of the death of Mr. Passelege at Amsterdam, to whom I had written in order to obtain my Mulatto's manumission, and what could certainly not but redouble my distress was the *situation* in which now she proved to be, who promised fair to become a mother in the space of a few months.

It was now that I saw the wretchedness of my situation, as much as Adam had done by tasting the forbidden fruit. And it was now that I saw a thousand horrors creep all at once upon my dejected spirits, yet which I at first kept concealed from the object that gave them birth, but which when she heard, she received with calmness and with dignity. Heavens, not only my *friend,* but my *offspring* to be a slave, and a slave under such government, Mr. Passelege (my only recourse) buried, and the whole estate going to be sold to a new master. I could not bear it and was totally distracted. Nay, I must have died with grief, had the mildness of her temper not supported me, by the fluttering hopes that Lolkens still would be our friend.

These were my melancholy reflections when, on the evening of the 4th, we heard the report of several alarm-guns towards the northeast.

Thus, by daybreak next morning, I sent a detachment to Rio Perica, who returned about noon with the account of the Rebels attacking the estate Marseille in the River Cottica, but from which they had been beaten back by the plantation slaves, as they had been before by those of Kortenduur. The other news was that they had ill-treated a party of poor Indians, suspecting them to have assisted the estates, in making their defense; also that at Paramaribo, an insurrection was discovered among the Negroes, who had determined to join the Rebels after first having massacred all the inhabitants; however that they were detected, and the most capital ringleaders executed.

May 6th. This morning we again heard several musket shots in the woods, but I, apprehending it to be some European party that had lost their way, made my sentinel answer their signals of distress by firing his piece alternately with theirs, shot for shot, to which I added two drums that kept beating for several hours without intermission, when the report of their arms gradually approached, and finally made their appearance a Society sergeant and six emaciated privates who belonged to Rietwyk in Perica, who had been lost in the forest for three days, nearly starved, without hammocks, meat, or drink, excepting water. Having refreshed them in the best manner I was able, they all recovered, to my very great satisfaction, one of them being stung perfectly blind for several hours by a kind of wasps that go in this country by the name of *marobonso,* of which the only thing that I can say is that they are extremely large, live in hollow trees, are the strongest of the bee kind, and sting so violently that, besides the pain, they always occasion a fever.

May 12th. Having this forenoon swum twice across the River Cottica, which is above half a mile broad, I now came home in a shiver and next day had an intermittent fever.

On the 16th, I was almost perfectly recovered (weakness excepted) when about ten in the morning (as I was sitting with Joanna before my cottage) I got an unexpected visit from a Mr. Steger, who happened to be one of our surgeons, and who having felt my pulse, examined my tongue, &c., declared without ceremony that I was to be *dead* before to-morrow, unless I made use of his immediate prescription. Dead. I acknowledge the sentence staggered me so much that (while at other times I never used medicines at all) I instantly swallowed the dose, which he had prepared for me in a tumbler, without hesitation. But almost as instantly I dropped down on the ground, like a bullock that was struck on the head with a butcher's hammer.

In this manner did I lay till the 20th, being four days before I came to my senses, when I found myself stretched on a mattress in my little house, with poor Joanna sitting by me, all alone, and bathed in tears, who begged of me at that time to ask no questions, for fear of hurting my spirits, but who next day related to me the dismal transaction, viz., that the moment I fell, four strong Negroes had taken me up, and by her direction put me where now I was; that the surgeon, having put blisters on several parts of my body, had finally declared that I was dead and had suddenly left the plantation; when a grave and coffin were ordered to bury me on the 17th, which she had prevented by dropping upon her knees; that she had dispatched a black to her aunt at Faukenberg for wine vinegar and a bottle of old Rhenish, with the first of which she had constantly bathed my temples, wrists, and feet, by (without intermission) keeping five wet handkerchiefs tied about them, while with a silver teaspoon she had found means to make me swallow down a few drops of the mulled wine; that I had lain motionless during all that time, while she had day and night, by the help of Quacoo and an old Negro, attended me, still hoping for my recovery—for which she now thanked her God. To all this I could only answer by the pearl of sympathy that started from my eyes, and a feeble squeeze of gratitude of my hand.

I had, however, the good fortune to recover, but so slowly that (independent of that great care that was taken of me by that heavenly young woman, to whom alone I owed my life) it was the 15th of June before I could walk by myself, during all which time I was carried on a species of chair by two Negroes, supported on two poles like a sedan, and fed like an infant, being so lame, and enervated, that I was not able to bring my hand to my mouth, and while poor Joanna (who had suffered too much on my account) was for several days following very poorly herself. In short, great was the change from what I had been but so shortly before— then the most healthy and most happy in my body and my mind, and now depressed to the lowest ebb, in my constitution and my spirits.

About this time, while the troops were doing nothing, two of the bravest men in the Colony, viz., Captain Friderici and the militia captain Stoelman, entered the woods with the Rangers, who killed three or four of the Rebels and took a few more prisoner, who were starved for want of subsistence, since Fourgeoud had ransacked the surrounding forest.

In the Creek Patamacca, two Rebel Negroes were also shot by Mr. Wine's slaves, where they had tried to plunder some provisions, and who had sent their heads barbecued to Paramaribo, as one of them was conjectured to be that of the famous chief Boni, but which afterwards proved to be a mistake.

On the 17th, being still so weak that I was unfit for any duty, not even at the Hope, I now gave over the command of that post to the next officer in rank, and expecting the change of air would do me good, I (with the previous knowledge of Colonel Fourgeoud) went on a visit to a neighboring estate called Egmond, where the planter, Monsieur de Cachelieu, a French gentleman, had given me a most hearty invitation along with Joanna, my boy Quacoo, and a white servant, Jacobus van der Meer.

At this place I was extremely comfortable, and nothing could be better adapted for my speedy recovery than this Frenchman's good humor, and his frugality—eternally singing, and feeding upon nothing, but which blessings were embittered by his severity and injustice to his slaves.

For instance, two young Negroes, who well deserved a flogging by breaking in and robbing their master's storehouse, came off with a few lashes, while two old ones, for a trifling dispute, were each condemned to receive no less than three hundred. On my asking for the cause of this partiality, I was answered by Monsieur de Cachelieu that the young ones had still a very good skin, and might do much work, whereas the old ones had long been disfigured, worn out, and almost unfit for any service, nay, that killing them altogether would be a profit to the estate.

Some days ago at Arendsrust, a few estates lower down, a poor Negro was sent with a letter from his proprietor to the manager here, of which this last, not liking the contents, gave the messenger four hundred lashes, telling the innocent man at the same time to carry that for the answer to his master. Is not this a truly damnable usage? In the hopes that exercise on horseback might do me good, I determined to take leave of my hospitable French friends and ask a furlough to go for some time to Paramaribo. In consequence, on the 9th of August, Colonel Fourgeoud arriving in the river at the estate Carawassibo, expecting soon to renew his maneuvers, I wrote him a letter on the 10th for the above purpose, and also for above six months' pay that was due me, but which was answered on the 12th not only with a negative to both my requests (which had, however, been granted to other officers), but in such a truly impertinent style as I could not even from himself have expected, such as calling into question my zeal while I was sick, and refusing me my own money or even the proper means of recovering it, &c. This so incensed me that I now not only wished *him* in Hell, but *myself* also, to have the satisfaction of seeing him burn; after which, in a second letter, I let him know that I was incapable of doing, or asking, anything unbecoming my character, but on the contrary (ill as I was) I stood ready to give him such proofs of my honor as should leave him no further room to doubt of it.

August 14th. At our arrival on the estate, I now expected no other than to see him mad with resentment, putting me under arrest, and asking for an explanation of our last correspondence.

However, Monsieur de Cachelieu and I were both disappointed. He not only took us politely by the hand, but solicited us to dine with him, as if nothing had passed between us. But this affectation I despised and refused with contempt to accept of his invitation, in which I was followed by my friend. In my turn, I inquired for the cause of this usage, to which this was the answer, viz., that thirty or forty of the Auka Negroes (who were our allies by treaty) had deceived him in doing nothing while they had been in the woods, and during the time he had been at Paramaribo, and that he was in consequence determined to push on the war with double vigor, on which account he had not only forbid me to go to town, but had since ordered even all the sick officers to come up and to follow the enemy, while they had any strength or breath remaining, not so much as leaving one to keep the colors and the regiment's chest, which had both been left to the care of a quartermaster, and this was literally so, but to which he might safely, and without hurting his conscience, have added, the inveteracy and unforgivableness of his disposition, with which he had sworn to persecute me, and some others, to the last. N.B. It was only about this time that he issued forth his orders to be observed on a march, and previous to which everything was done in hurry and confusion, and which indeed was too often the case even since.

In short, having now spent nearly two months on the estate Egmond, where I could not recover, and not being permitted to go to Paramaribo, I preferred returning back again to take the command at the Hope, where having entertained Monsieur de Cachelieu in the best manner I was able, this gentleman in the evening returned to his plantation.

August 21st. I now received a letter from the Commander in Chief, not an answer to my last, but orders to send up to him at the estate Carawassibo (which was at present his headquarters) all the provisions, kettles, axes, &c., that could be spared at the Hope, he preparing to reenter the woods. These I accordingly dispatched the next day, but they were not very much, a whole barge with beef and pork having been shipwrecked in the river.

September 11th. At last the Hero broke up from Carawassibo, and with all the able troops he could collect (which were now not much more than one hundred) he once more launched into the forest after the enemy, having previously removed the post from the Jews-Savanna, which he placed at the forsaken estate Oranjebo, in the very upper parts of Rio Commewina, leaving the River Surinam to shift for itself, and having opened, and read, all the letters that had been written to the deceased officers from their friends on the old continent.

It must certainly appear singular, in the eyes of the world, that we did so tamely brook all this bad usage and not officially complain to His Serene Highness the Prince of Orange, whose justice and humanity are so conspicuous and generally known, or to the late Duke of Brunswick-Wolfenbuttel, field marshal of the army in Holland, who was equally benign, and indefatigable in fulfilling his office, and who was the father of the deserving soldier and the scourge of those that dared to be neglectful in their military duty. But all things have a reason and so had our bearing Fourgeoud's indignities (if we could) without a murmur, as shall perhaps be explained upon some other occasion. Suffice it to say for the present that neither of the two august personages above mentioned were supposed to be entirely ignorant of his barbarous proceedings, but which their wisdom reserved to check at a more proper opportunity, when the good of a colony should not be dependent on the sufferings of an individual. Also, it would have been indelicate, if not presumptuous, to address the court officially for what, at the present juncture, could not with propriety be mended.

September 28th. This morning we again heard the report of several great-guns towards the River Cottica, where it since appeared the Rebels were a second time beaten back from the plantation Marseille by the fidelity and bravery of the slaves belonging to that estate.

October 8th. Now came the news that Colonel Fourgeoud, having discovered and destroyed some fields belonging to the enemy, had again kept up a distant conversation with him, and having found the mangled remains of poor Schmidt, who had been murdered by the Rebels, was once more come with his troops to Maagdenburg, where he had encamped. On the 11th, he reentered the forest, previously sending the sick and a young officer under an arrest to the Hope, in order to be tried for not being able to undergo the fatigues as well as himself; that is, having been ordered to watch two days and two nights, the youth had been unequal to the task, and had dropped asleep under arms as he was sitting on the ground. The climate, indeed, was such that even without these trials, many were overcome.

What kept Fourgeoud so stout hitherto was his continually drinking a medicine he called *tisane* in large basinfuls, which had a taste sufficient to poison the Devil, and was composed of Jesuits' bark, cream of tartar, and licorice stick boiled together. This he drank as hot as he could bear it and, having accustomed his constitution to it, he could no more be without it than a fish without water. In this, however, he was followed by none of the rest, as they believed that once it should cease to operate, which it must at last, all other medicines in time of real need would be ineffectual. As for my own part, I still continued to be so exceedingly weak that I almost despaired ever more to recover, while my depressed mind, on account of Joanna's critical and helpless situation, greatly contributed to preventing the restoration of my health, particularly when on the 21st, being visited by Mr. and Mrs. Lolkens at the Hope, this gentleman acquainted me that in town it was the general report that we had both been poisoned; that the whole estate Faukenberg, with its dependents, had again been transferred since the death of Mr. Passelege; and that the new proprietor was a Mr. Lude of Amsterdam, with whom he had not the smallest interest. Yet this sentence was greatly alleviated by the civility of his lady, who insisted that my young Mulatto should accompany her to Paramaribo immediately, where at her own house she should meet with every care and attention that her being present could bestow upon her, and that her delicate situation could require, so long till she should be perfectly recovered. To this I made a bow, while poor Joanna cried for gratitude, and having conducted them so far as their estate Killenstyn Nova (where we all dined), I took my leave, and bid my last farewell (for the present time) to that young woman, to whom I was more indebted than to all the universe besides.

At my return to the Hope, my indignation was hardly supportable, when I was even upbraided for taking care of my own offspring by my messmates. "Do as we do (said they), Stedman, and never fear. If our children are slaves, they are provided for, and if they die, may they be damned in the bargain. Thus, keep your sighs in your belly and your money in your pocket, my boy. That is all."

On the 22nd, awakening by daybreak in my hammock, the first thing that I now saw when looking up was a snake about two yards long, hanging with his head downwards like a rope, and straight above my face, from which he was not one foot distant, while his tail was twisted round the rafters under the thatch. Observing his eyes, bright as stars, and his forked tongue in agitation, I was so much distressed that I scarcely had the power to avoid him, which however I did, by running out; after which I heard a rustling in the dry thatch, where the Negroes attempted to kill him but in vain, he having escaped. Thus, I cannot say what species he belonged to.

November 6th. In short, having written to a lawyer, a Mr. Seyfke, to inquire whether it was not in the power of the Governor and Council to relieve a gentleman's child from bondage, providing he paid to its master such ransom as their wisdom should judge adequate, I now received for answer that no money or interest could purchase its freedom without the proprietor's consent since, according to law, it was just as much a slave as if it had been born in Africa and imported from the coast of Guinea. This news perfectly completed my misery, and at last I had recourse to drinking, which temporary relief, like a spring tide, only made my spirits flow higher to make them sink lower after its evaporation.

During this conflict it happened that I was invited with the major to dine, on November 8th, at an estate called Knoppemonbo in the Cassewinica Creek, where a Mr. De Graav, the proprietor, did everything in his power to amuse me, but to no purpose.

At last, seeing me seated by myself on a small bridge that led to a grove of orange trees, with a settled gloom on my countenance, he accosted me and, taking me by the hand, said,

> Sir, I am acquainted by Mr. Lolkens with the cause of your distress. Heaven never left a good intention unrewarded. I have the pleasure to acquaint you that Mr. Lude has now chosen me for his administrator, and that from this

day I shall pride myself in making it my business to render you every service with that gentleman, as well as the virtuous Joanna, whose deserving character has attracted the attention of so many people, while your laudable motive redounds to your lasting honor throughout this colony.

No angel descending from the clouds could have brought me a more welcome message, and no criminal under sentence of death could have received a reprieve with greater joy. The weight of a millstone was removed from my laboring breast, and having made Mr. De Graav repeat his promise, I felt I should yet be happy. Soon after this, I was surrounded by several gentlemen and ladies (to whom my friend had communicated this very romantic adventure), some of whom pleased to call me *Tom Jones,* and others *Roderick Random.* They all indeed congratulated me on my sensibility and my having met with so valuable an acquaintance, and all seemed to partake in the pleasure that I now felt. The day being spent in mirth and conviviality, I returned to the Hope much better pleased than when I left it, where next day the whole company was entertained by Major Medlar, nor did we separate, or cease feasting up and down the river, till the 13th, when we once more spent the day at Knoppemonbo.

Here now Mr. De Graav, having bought some new slaves, gave a holiday to all the Negroes of his estate, and there I had the opportunity of seeing the diversions peculiar to that people, but of which I must reserve the particular account till another occasion, and only now say a word or two of the *Loango-dancing,* which was performed by the Loango Negroes, male and female, and not by any others, and consists from first to last in such a scene of wanton and lascivious gestures, as nothing but a heated imagination and a constant practice could enable them to perform. These dances, which are to the sound of a drum, and to which they strike time by clapping of hands, are more like a play, divided into so many acts, which lasts hours together, and during which pantomime the actors, in place of being fatigued, become more and more active and animated, till they are bathed in a lather like post-horses, and their passions wound up to such a degree that nature being overcome, they are ready to drop into convulsions.

However indelicate the above exhibitions, fashion has rendered them no more so than any other diversions to the European and Creole ladies, who in company with the gentlemen, crowd about them without the least reserve, to enjoy (what they call here) a hearty laugh, and there it ends, while they would color an Englishwoman's face from white to scarlet.

Custom is everything, and peculiar to every country. For instance, in the East Indies (according to the relation of an English officer), the dancing girls will act an amorous adventure with suppleness, dexterity, and precision; sometimes the actresses appear to be penetrated by soft emotions, seized with a flame never before experienced, and sometimes with the powers of life apparently suspended, agitated and panting, they seem to sink under the force of an overpowerful illusion. Thus, by the most expressive gestures and positions, with stifled sighs and languid looks, they express every gradation of passion, from the embarrassment of shame, through desire, fear, and hope, to the trepidations of enjoyment. These girls, says the above author, are almost the only females there that are taught reading, writing, vocal, and instrumental music, while some of them speak three or four languages. Their dress, though light and voluptuous, is yet more decent than that of the others of their sex, and in few countries are social manners purer and more respected than among those Gentoo Indians, who are scarcely acquainted with the name of those horrid vices that prevail in some other countries, while sensual pleasures are considered as a religious duty, and celebrating the praises of their gods. From which he concludes that thus among those Gentoos, there is greater decency and reserve than among the Europeans, into whom it is strenuously inculcated from their infancy that simple incontinence is among those actions subject to the divine anathema, and among which class I take the liberty to rank the Loango dancers, who think that what they are doing is perfectly right, and look on European dancing as the height of insipidity.

November 26th. Colonel Fourgeoud now being once more marched to the Wana Creek after the Rebels (as I have said, after taking the troops from the Jews-Savanna), they availed themselves of this absence and not only pillaged a plantation in the River Surinam, but burnt several dwellings in the Creek Cassewinica. From the above river they were, however, bravely pursued by a feeble Society detachment that chanced to be there, but without success, while two soldiers were killed, and Mr. Neagle, their leader, with several others, wounded.

The major now broke up the new post that was at Oranjebo, which he also dispatched after the enemy, but which having cruised a week in the forest also returned without any manner of success—which shows what a difficult thing it is for European troops to wage war in the forests of South America.

November 30th. This being the anniversary of St. Andrew, and now being in excellent spirits, I roasted a whole sheep with which I entertained all the officers on the Hope, and with a couple of gallons of good Jamaica rum in punch, which we drank to the health of all our friends on the old continent. And which ceremony I repeated on December 4th, upon receiving the tidings that my dear Joanna was delivered of a strong and beautiful boy the 27th past. That very morning I dispatched another letter to Mr. Lude at Amsterdam, to obtain her manumission, couched in much the same terms as that which I had written to his predecessor Mr. Passelege, only praying for dispatch as I was now uncertain how much longer the expedition was to last, and in which request I was again seconded by my new friend Mr. De Graav, as I had been before by my old one Mr. Lolkens, after which I entertained the sick with a dozen bottles of old Rhenish, received from the former gentleman, which had been in his cellar since 1726.

December 10th. Walking round the plantation this morning with my gun, the whole of the slaves of the estate were risen in a mutiny, on account of the cruel usage inflicted by the manager, but which, however, by the interference of the military was presently quelled, to mutual satisfaction.

These frequent disturbances, which I have at different times mentioned, plainly indicate the inclination of the Negroes to break out in an open rebellion, and which would certainly have been often the attempt, had they not been awed at this period by the troops.

December 11th. This morning, the estate Rietwyk in Perica was attacked but the enemy beat back by the military.

Colonel Fourgeoud being now again arrived at Maagdenburg, and I at last being perfectly recovered after an illness of seven months, I proposed by another letter that I might accompany him on his future excursions in the woods, or go for some time to Paramaribo, but neither the one nor the other yet was granted. Mars and Venus were both deaf to my prayers, and I was still doomed to be kept at the Hope like a prisoner of state.

December 14th. Seeing now about noon a molasses boat at anchor before the Hope, in which an English sailor and two Negroes were broiling in the sun, I made the first come ashore, and entertained the poor fellow, to his great surprise, with a bowl of punch and a bellyfull of eggs and bacon, he not having expected this kindness, or to be accosted in his own country's language. What were this man's grateful acknowledgments, whose name was Charles Macdonald, shall be seen in the sequel of this work. A molasses boat is a barge rowed by two oars that fetches the above commodity in large hogsheads from the sugar plantations, and delivers it on board the English-American vessels for transportation, to be distilled into rum, for which they pay the Dutch at an average about three guineas per hogshead.

On the 16th arrived again an officer, sent from our Hero under an arrest (the first was a Mr. Galquin and this was a Mr. Neys) for the crime of disputing with the free Negro Gousary for a bunch of plantains. Both these young men were since sent to Europe by Fourgeoud to have them broken by court martial, but where, after a very short confinement, they were honorably acquitted, to the joy of the whole corps and to his unutterable mortification.

December 18th. Having now obtained my friend Medlar's concurrence, I took a trip *incognito* to Paramaribo, where I found my boy bathing in Madeira and water,[1] and his mother happy and perfectly recovered. Having embraced them and presented Joanna with a gold medal that my father had given my mother on the day of my birth, and also thanked Mrs. Lolkens for her great civility, I immediately returned to the Hope, where I again arrived on the 20th, thus having made extraordinary expedition.

The poor Negro whom I had sent before me with a letter had been less fortunate than I, sinking with his canoe[2] in the middle of the River Surinam, by the roughness of the water. However, having kept in an erect posture (for this man could not swim), the pressure of the boat against his feet had enabled him just to keep his head above the water, while the weight of his body kept the canoe sunk to his full length. In this dangerous attitude he was picked up by a man-of-war's boat, who, taking away the canoe for their trouble, put him on shore at Paramaribo, he having the letter, however surprising, still in his mouth. At this time, being eager to deliver it, he accidently ran into a wrong house where, being taken for a thief (on refusing to let them read it), he was tied up to receive four hundred lashes, but miraculously reprieved by the intercession of an English merchant named Gordon, who was my particular friend and knew the Negro. Thus had the poor devil escaped drowning and being flogged, having been robbed of his canoe in the bargain, either of which he would have undergone sooner than to disclose what he called the secrets of his *massera*. Query: How many Europeans shall we find possessed of so much firmness? Answer: None.

December 25th. But I must once more return to the Commander in Chief, who having drawn breath a few days at Maagdenburg, now again marched with the remaining handful of his men to the Jews-Savanna, from where he returned (having seen nothing) back to Maagdenburg, but with the new title of being called the Wandering Jew himself.

January 5th, 1775. Be that as it may, the major and I renewed our solicitations to accompany him in his peregrinations, but were prevented by his now going to town, where about this time a fresh supply of troops

---

1. This, however uncommon it may appear to a European, is often practiced in Surinam by such as can afford it, and among which class was the hospitable Mrs. Lolkens.
2. A canoe is a very small boat made from a hollow tree by means of fire.

was hourly expected, to arrive from Europe and be murdered as were the former, and where finally he gave me leave to follow him soon, with some other officers, who were literally in want, at a time when fifteen hogsheads of fine claret, and fifteen thousand florins in specie, were obeying his commands at Paramaribo.

CHAPTER 15th

Description of the Aborigines or Indians of Guiana

At last farewell to the Hope, of which I am convinced the reader is by this time as tired as I.

Thus rowing down, on the night of January 19th, I slept at the estate Arendsrust, and next day I dined at the beautiful plantation Catwyk, where I had nearly ended all my travels, for Mr. Goetzee, the owner, having lent me one of his horses to ride round the estate, the animal and I both at once disappeared, not like the Roman soldier who leaped with his horse into an opening or cleft in the earth to save his country, but a wooden bridge over which we passed being rotten, the part under us gave way and we dropped through it into the canal. I, however, with much difficulty got ashore, and having run to call some Negroes, the horse, who stuck in the mud, was extricated barely alive and no more.

Being now arrived in town at my friend De Lamarre's house, I felt extremely happy, and more so seeing my little boy and his mother both well, whom I acquainted with my second request being dispatched to the new proprietor, Mr. Lude, at Amsterdam, for their manumission; and the next day visited the Governor, Mr. Kennedy, Mrs. Lolkens, Mrs. Demelly, &c., who all congratulated me on my acquaintance with Mr. De Graav, and highly honored me, and approved of what I had done for so deserving a young woman and her infant.

On January 25th, a great number of Indians, or natives, being arrived at Paramaribo, and having now the time, I shall with pleasure describe this people, who are the real aborigines of this country. These generations (who are, in my opinion, the happiest creatures under the sun) are divided into many castes or tribes such as these: the Caribbees, Arrowouks, Accawaus, Tawiras, Worrows, and Piannacotaws, besides which there are a great many others whose manners are unknown to us. All these Indians are, in general, of a copper color, while the Negroes of Africa, that live under the same degree of latitude, are perfectly black. And which, however inconceivable at first, is easily accounted for when one considers that the first, viz., the American Indians in Guiana, are constantly refreshed by the cooling sea breeze or easterly wind that blows between the tropics, and that those who dwell in Terra Firma, and Peru, on the west coast, enjoy that same easterly breeze, still kept cool by the great chains of inland mountains over which it passes, and which have their summits perpetually covered over with snow. While the second, viz., the inhabitants of Africa, who live south of the River Senegal, get the same east wind rather heated than cooled, by the prodigious quantity of inland burning savannas, and sandy deserts, over which it passes.

These are the most plausible causes why the Americans are a copper color or red, and the inhabitants of Africa (called Negroes) are black, viz., the one being more burnt by the sun's heat than the other—rather than because they are two distinct sort of people, there being, in my opinion, but one set of people on the globe, who differ with each other only according to the soil and climate in which they live.

A happy people I call them still, whose peace and native morals have not been soiled with mock Christianity. And one thing I know perfectly well, viz., that the native Indians of Guiana possess as few vices as any set of people existing under the sun, and are in their morals but little better for those Moravian preachers that are settled among them on the banks of the Saramacca River, where they also try to convert the Saramaka Negroes.

[Editors' note. Stedman's original manuscript includes here his account of Suriname's Amerindian populations, drawn largely from secondary sources, which he glosses in his chapter heading as follows: "Their food—Arms—Ornaments—Employments—Diversions—Passions—Religion—Marriages—Funerals &c.—Of the Charibee Indians in particular—Their trade with the Europeans." See the unabridged 1988 edition, pp. 304–20.]

CHAPTER 16TH

Reinforcement of fresh troops arrives from Holland—
Encampment on Mount Maagdenburg in Tempaty Creek—
Remarkable instance of lunacy in a Negro—Mountains—
Beautiful views

I have mentioned before that a supply of fresh troops was expected to reinforce our decayed little army, and on January 30th, the news came to Paramaribo that the transport ship *Maastroom,* under Captain Eeg, was arrived in the River Surinam and had come to an anchor before the fortress Amsterdam, with Colonel Seybourgh and two divisions, consisting of one hundred twenty men under his command, two more divisions still being expected.

Next day I went down with a rowboat to welcome them, and having dined with the new-come gentlemen, the ship weighed anchor, and I sailed with them up till before the fortress Zeelandia, where they moored and were saluted by a few guns.

On February 5th, the troops that were so lately landed were already sent to the upper parts of the River Commewina, to be encamped there (viz., the private Marines), while most of the officers still continued feasting and dancing, as we had done in the beginning. Which of the two were really best off was a difficult matter to determine. Nothing could be more pompous than our grand entertainment at the house of a Mr. Mercelius, where to crown the banquet, a half dozen Negroes kept on blowing the trumpet and French horns in the room where we dined, till the company were absolutely deafened by discordancy and noise, and I in particular wished them half a dozen times to go to the Devil. Here the ball continued till six o'clock in the morning, when we were all sent home to our lodgings in stately carriages, never once reflecting on the distressed situation of the poor soldier in the forest.

On the 6th, we all got orders to leave Paramaribo together, to be encamped at Maagdenburg (a mountain in the Tempaty Creek in the upper parts of the River Commewina) to where (as I have just mentioned) the reinforcement was already dispatched.

On the 8th, having prepared myself to set out on my fourth campaign, and taking leave at Mrs. Lolkens's of my little family and friends, I repaired to the waterside, to set out in the same barge with Colonel Seybourgh who, erroneously supposing that the troops come with him from Holland were a distinct corps from those arrived with Fourgeoud in 1773, took with him in his barge none but those he was pleased to call his own officers and his favorites. He made the Negroes shove off the boat in my presence, when I was not a stone's cast from it, and left me on the beach, to my unspeakable surprise and mortification. Meanwhile, Fourgeoud, having sworn he should dance just as much to his pipes as the youngest ensign in the regiment—in which the Old Trojan being perfectly right, I had strenuously supported him against his haughty antagonist—I set off immediately with a sailboat and I soon overtook the *polite* Colonel Seybourgh, and we all slept at the estate Vossenburg in the River Commewina. Next day we came to the estate Arendsrust, having passed the heavy barges that departed from Paramaribo on the 5th, and on the 10th we made the Hope, where having spent so many months, I here present the reader with a view of that estate, and of the estate Clarenbeek, where our hospital was still kept. This day, Colonel Fourgeoud also came up the river and slept at Wayampibo.

On the 11th, we arrived at the plantation Carawassibo, where we passed the night, and where the overseer, a Mr. de Bruyn, was so very impertinent that I (already hating the fraternity of overseers) gave him such a d——nd beating that, with his bloody face, he suddenly decamped from the estate in a small canoe with one Negro and, in this trim, at twelve o'clock midnight, appeared like Banquo, the ghost in Macbeth, before the amazed Fourgeoud, who thought proper to give him no hearing and to dismiss him with a hearty curse.

On the 12th, we all arrived safe at Maagdenburg, viz., Fourgeoud, the officers, and the barges with the privates. From the Hope, the estates begin to appear thinner, and after passing Goed Accoord, about ten or twelve more miles upwards, not a cultivated spot is to be seen, where the plantations were all laid in ashes by the Rebels in 1757, as I have already mentioned, one small place excepted just below Maagdenburg, which I think is called the Jacob, where a few Negroes are kept to cut timber. And the river above Goed Accoord also becomes very narrow, being lined on each side with impenetrable bush wood like the River Cottica between Devil's Harwar and Patamacca, while the Tempaty Creek, which may be

View of L'Esperance, or the Hope, on the Commewine.

View of Clarenbeck, on the River Commewine.

Plate 41

looked upon as the source of the whole River Commewina, becomes still narrower. Maagdenburg, which is about a hundred miles from Paramaribo, was formerly an estate, but now has not a vestige left to show it, a poor old orange tree excepted. It is, at present, neither more or less than a barren mountain.

On the 17th came the news that the transport ship *Maria-Helena,* under Captain Jan Poort, with the remaining two divisions of one hundred and twenty men commanded by one Captain Hamel, had also arrived in the River Surinam the 14th instant. Thus, the reinforcement consisted of two hundred and forty men together, and on the 5th day of March they all arrived in heavy barges at Maagdenburg, where I may now say that Colonel Fourgeoud's whole flock was assembled. Also here arrived today one hundred Negro slaves to carry the loads when we marched &c., &c. One of the row-Negroes being missed on board a military barge, and marks of blood discovered in it, the commanding officer, a Mr. Chatteauview, and the sentinel were both put under arrest to be tried for murder. Also a complaint came upon *me* from the overseer of the estate Carawassibo, for having beaten him, which however ended in nothing. Today also two of our captains fought a duel, in which one of them got wounded in the head (viz., Captain Hamel by Captain Bolts).

March 8th. This being the Prince of Orange's anniversary, Colonel Fourgeoud treated all the officers with a glass of wine. O the wonder of wonders, what a wonder.

On the 13th, a barge with provisions coming up from Paramaribo (shocking to relate) found the Negro who was missed on the 5th at the water's edge, lying in the brushwood with his throat cut from ear to ear, but still alive, the knife having missed the windpipe. This miserable apparition of skin and bone they took on board and brought to Maagdenburg, where by a skillful surgeon (one Mr. Knollard) the wound was all sewn up, and the man miraculously recovered, having lain nine days in that dreadful condition, without any subsistence or covering whatever, and weltering in his own blood, even without a bandage.

The week after, I had nearly lost my own life by an accident. Two Negroes of the estate Goed Accoord, who were employed in hunting and fishing for Fourgeoud—one of them named Philander—proposed to me to accompany them in the wood, where we might chance to meet with some *pingos* or *powesa,* but a heavy shower of rain coming on when we had only walked about two miles, we determined to quit the project and repair to the small spot called the Jacob for shelter, to gain which we had to pass through a deep marsh. Having waded till under our armpits, Philander (who was the finest man, without exception, that ever I saw in all my life) began to swim, as did his companion, with one hand, holding their fowling pieces &c. above the water with the other, while they desired me to follow as they did, and this I tried, having nothing on but my shirt and trousers; when after swimming two or three strokes, I sank to the bottom like a stone with the weight of my musket. But relinquishing it, I immediately rose to the surface and begged that Philander would dive for it, who brought it up in a moment. But we were scarcely again set a-swimming, when a thundering voice called out through the thicket, *"Who somma datty?"* and another, *"Sooto, sooto. Da Boni. Kiry da dago."* ("Who is there? Fire, fire. It is Boni. Kill the dog.") And looking up, we saw the muzzles of six muskets presented upon us, at a very little distance. I instantly dived, but Philander answering that we belonged to Maagdenburg, we were permitted to come ashore, one by one, at the Jacob, where the trusty Negroes, having heard a flouncing in the water, and seeing three armed men in the marsh, took it for granted the Rebels were coming, headed by Boni himself, for whom they had taken me—being almost quite naked and so much sunburned, besides my hair being cut short and curly, that I absolutely looked like a Mulatto. Being here refreshed with some rum, we dried ourselves about a good fire and now returned to Maagdenburg, where I congratulated myself on my escape, though with the loss of the skin of one of my shins.

On March 21st, Fourgeoud reviewed with pleasure his revived little army, where I am sorry the Rangers did not appear, and the five following days he sent out one hundred men on a patrol to reconnoiter the skirts of his new encampment, of which number I had the honor to be one.

During this patrol nothing remarkable happened except that we met with a large company of *quatas*. These being the most remarkable kind of monkeys in the world because of their affinity to the human species, I will here give some account of them. When walking in the evening with my boy Quacoo outside the camp, they came down so low to look at us, throwing small sticks and pieces of excrement at us, that we were brought to a standstill, and I had an opportunity thoroughly to examine them. The *quata* is very large, with an enormous tail and thin arms and legs. Being covered over with long black hair, it has a very hideous appearance, the more so as its face is quite naked and red, with deep sunk eyes, which gives it much the appearance of an old Indian woman. For the rest, they are lascivious, and the females regularly have their menstrua. They are, in short, the most disgustful, dirty animals that I am acquainted with. I shall here only add that they kept on following us till we returned to the camp.

Of the long-haired monkeys, the *saccawinkee* is the smallest. This is a beautiful little animal with blackish gray frizzled hair, a white face, and very bright shining eyes. Its ears are large and naked, yet they are not very perceivable, being covered by the very long and white whiskers that surround the whole visage of this little creature. So very delicate is the *saccawinkee*, and so susceptible to cold, that scarcely one of them is brought to Europe alive and if they are, they very soon pine and die. In the annexed plate I have delineated both these monkeys, the large *quata* and the small *saccawinkee*, thus trying to correct with my pencil the deficiency that may be in my pen.

March 25th. Now I shall once more return to Maagdenburg, before where arriving, I had nearly been crushed to death by an enormous tree, it dropping just at my heels by age, which frequently happens in the forest, and slightly wounded one or two of our Marines. During this trip we had much rain, and crossed over one or two small creeks, which is done by hewing down one of the palm trees on the water's edge, which falling across the river forms a temporary bridge.

On March 27th, I paid a visit to the miserable Negro who had been found with his throat cut, and who was so well as to be able to converse. Having declared that he had done it with his own hands, the unhappy officer and sentinel were acquitted. I asked him what reason he had to commit suicide and he said "None."

> I have (said he) as good a master and mistress as I could wish, and a family of my own that I much love. I had slept sound during the whole night till about four o'clock in the morning, when awakening, I took up my knife to pick my teeth with it, and instantaneously cut my throat without knowing why, the moment after, repenting what I had done; when rising from my hammock, I got in the canoe to wash myself and try to bind up the wound, but stooping over the side and bleeding very fast, I turned faint and fell into the river. Now no longer able to get on board or cry out for assistance, I still, by struggling, made shift to get on shore, where I fell down, and lay helplessly till I was picked up by a boat with provisions going to Maagdenburg, during all which time of nine days I had my full senses, and saw a *tamannoir* or *antbear* come to smell my putrefied blood about my neck, who upon seeing me move retired into the forest.

I gave the poor man some Boston biscuit I had got from Paramaribo, and a large calabash with barley (which we never lacked) to make soup, and also some wine, for which he was very thankful. This Negro appeared to be about sixty years of age, and what is extremely unjust is that the slaves are in general obliged to subsist on but half the allowance of the soldiers, which I think I have before hinted, while they are forced to do double the drudgery.

On March 29th, to my sorrow, I received a letter from Mr. Kennedy, who was preparing to go to Holland, that he desired my boy Quacoo might be returned to his estate, whom I accordingly sent down, but with

The Quato & Saccawinkee Monkeys.

Plate 42

a letter offering to buy him from his master, as I had offered to buy Joanna from hers, while, Heaven knows, I was not master of a shilling to pay the redemption.

On April 2nd, Colonel Fourgeoud ordered all the sick in the Colony to Maagdenburg, where he had erected a hospital and a large victualing magazine. Thus, all the scarecrows from Clarenbeek arrived here, where the air was certainly more healthy, along with surgeons, apothecaries, &c. During this time, the Old Gentleman was peculiarly ill-natured and abused his friends and enemies without distinction, while he swore not a soul should be exempt from duty providing they could but stand on their legs, scoffing at agues and running ulcers as bagatelles and trifles, indeed he possessed neither humanity nor religion.

About this time, a strong detachment was sent to the estate Bruinsberg in Commewina, where an insurrection was expected, the slaves refusing to work upon a Sunday, to which, however, they were driven by the lash of the whip. Is this not barbarous?

April 2nd. It was now in the heart of the rainy weather, when Fourgeoud declared he would henceforth prefer to scour the woods and in consequence gave orders for two strong columns to march next day. The reason for choosing this season was, that by now disclosing the Rebels, they must starve for want, whereas in the dry months the forest is overstocked with fruits of every kind. But this was, in my opinion, a very vague piece of generalship, when considering, on the other hand, how the wet weather murdered his troops, whom he killed, I suppose, twenty to the rate of one Negro. Fourgeoud was himself of a very strong constitution, having been used to hunting and shooting the whole of his lifetime, to which he added temperance and the daily use of his *tisane*. His dress consisted in nothing but a waistcoat, through one of the buttonholes of which he wore his sword. On his head he wore a cotton nightcap, with a white beaver hat above it, and in his hand a cane. But he seldom carried his musket, or his pistols. I have seen him all in rags and even barefooted. In short, at six o'clock this morning, the two columns set out upon their march, the one commanded by Colonel Seybourgh, the other by Fourgeoud, to which last I had the honor to belong, and I expected soon to be put in mind of my former many grievances. Our poor men were now loaded like jackasses, while they were ordered to put their firelocks in their knapsacks, the muzzles excepted, which was intended to keep them dry from the rain which now daily poured in a torrent from the heavens. Our course was south by east, up along the banks of the Tempaty Creek, where we soon were in the water till above our knees.

April 4th, we marched again, course south by east, till two o'clock, when we changed course to south-southwest, and no rain. This day we passed by piles of fine timber that had been left there to rot since 1757, when the estates were demolished by the Negro slaves who rose in rebellion.

April 5th. The word of command being once again, "Take up your bed and walk," we marched south-southeast, and south by east, through deep marshes, up till our breasts in water, and in very heavy rains, in which helpless situation we were suddenly alarmed, not by a party of Rebels, but by a large company of monkeys whom we discovered in the tops of the trees, knocking large nuts (of what species I know not) against the branches of the trees to break them in quest of their contents, with the greatest regularity, keeping time alternately at every stroke, while some of them threw down their burdens, which broke the head of one of our Marines, and which sound of *tuck, tuck, tuck* we had mistaken for the Rebel Negroes' cutting wood with an axe. In the evening, we encamped near the Tempaty Creek, where we had made large fires and comfortable huts, thus sleeping out of the wet. Here, I drank the best water I ever tasted.

April 6th. We now marched again, keeping due west till twelve o'clock, through very heavy rains and deep water, when we changed our course to the north and passed over very high mountains, perhaps pregnant with treasure.

On the 7th, we still continued marching north over mountains, from which we had, to be sure, the most enchanting prospects by the wildness of the country and the beautiful verdure displayed in so many different hues through the forest. Having crossed an arm of the Mapane Creek, in the evening once more returned to our camp at Maagdenburg, one of our officers, a Mr. Noot, and several others being so ill that they were carried in their hammocks upon poles by the Negro slaves, while a great number were so weak that they could hardly support the weight of their emaciated bodies. But to complain of sickness was to revolt, till they dropped down more dead than alive, when they were generally allowed to be picked up. During this expedition (on which we perceived nothing of the enemy) I was remarkably fortunate, having neither suffered by the fatigue nor been persecuted by particular bad usage. The next day Colonel Seybourgh's column arrived, having seen, as we had, nothing.

On the 9th, my boy Quacoo returned from Paramaribo where, to my great joy, his master, Mr. Walter Kennedy, sold him to me for the sum of five hundred Dutch florins, amounting with other expenses to nearly fifty pounds, for which Colonel Fourgeoud civilly gave me a bill for his agent, with which I paid this faithful servant's ransom, wishing to God my dear Joanna and her boy were also mine, from whose new master I had not yet received an answer.

On April 14th was sent a captain with a few men back to the Hope in Commewina, to protect the estates in that river. Now the miserable old Negro who had cut his throat on the 5th day of March, but had since recovered, was seen by some slaves to enter the wood with a knife, from which he no more returned, and where since he was found stabbed to death, while it was afterwards disclosed by his master that two months earlier he had attempted to do the same. Thus regularly, from month to month. Query: Does not this account for the derivation or etymology of the word lunatic?

On the 17th, the command returned from La Rochelle where the troops of the Society are all sick.

April 19th. The poor men were cruelly beaten by Lieutenant Colonel Seybourgh for complaining against the injustice of making them cut wood, which he did to thirty or forty every day only for his amusement, without the least necessity, and which provoked me and some others to treat him with contempt.

On the 20th, Colonel Fourgeoud treated me with the greatest politeness, whom at his own request I presented today with a painting of his own figure marching at the head of his troops in a deep swamp, and which picture he sent to the Prince of Orange and the Duke of Brunswick as a proof of what he and his troops underwent in Surinam—of which, however, he was himself the principal cause. Be that as it may, he gave me leave for fourteen days to go to town to wish Mr. Kennedy a good voyage to Europe. And, availing myself of his good temper, I left Maagdenburg within one hour, and made such dispatch that I came to Paramaribo the 22nd, where I found my little family and friends all very well, and where I put up at the house of Mr. De Lamarre, to which they were finally sent from that of Mrs. Lolkens, who had during all my absence treated them with the greatest attention.

CHAPTER 17th

New samples of unprecedented barbarity—Occurrences on Mount Maagdenburg—Great mortality among the troops in Tempaty and Commewina

April 23rd. The first visit I now did was to Mr. Kennedy, to bid him farewell, and to whom I paid the five hundred florins for the black boy; he gave me a receipt and Quacoo was mine. About this time I got ill with a fever which, however, lasted but a few days.

Walking out on the first day of May, I observed a crowd of people about the waterside in front of the house of Mr. Stolkers, where appeared (dreadful to relate) a beautiful young Mulatto female floating on her back, with her hands tied behind, her throat cut most shockingly, and stabbed in the breast with a knife in more than eight or ten different places. This was reported to be the work of that hellish fiend Mrs. Stolkers who, from a motive of jealousy, suspected her husband might fall in love with this poor young girl, and which devilish woman had before drowned a Negro infant for crying, as I have told the reader. Nay, this monster was accused of still greater barbarity, if greater barbarity could be, viz., arriving one day at her estate to view some newly purchased Negroes, her eye chanced to fall on a fine Negro girl about fifteen years of age, who could not so much as speak the language of the country. Still observing her to have such a remarkably fine figure, and such a sweet face, her diabolical jealousy instantly prompted her to burn the girl all over the cheeks, mouth, and forehead with a red hot iron, and cut off the Achilles tendon of one of her limbs, which not only rendered her a monster, but miserably lame so long as she lived, without the victim knowing what she had done to deserve such a punishment. Some of the Negroes one day representing to this lady the many severities she daily inflicted, and supplicating her to be

of a milder disposition, she instantly knocked out the brains of a Quadroon child, and caused two of the heads of its relations to be chopped off,
being young Negro men who had endeavored to oppose it. When she had
left the estate, these heads &c. were now tied in silk handkerchiefs, and
carried by the surviving friends to Paramaribo, where they were laid at
the Governor's feet with the following speech.

> This, your Excellency, is the head of my son, and this is the head of my
> brother, struck off by our mistress's command for endeavoring to prevent
> murder. We know our evidence is nothing in a state of slavery, but if these
> bloody heads &c. are sufficient proof of what we say, we only beg that such
> may be prevented in time to come, when we will all cheerfully spill our
> blood and our sweat for the preservation and prosperity of our master and
> mistress.

To which the answer was that they were all inhumanely flogged round
the streets of Paramaribo for having told a lie, till the infernal Fury was
glutted with persecution. Had any one *white* person been present at the
above carnage, the evidence would have been good, but never that of a
Negro in the colonies. And even then, she would have escaped by paying
a fine of fifty pounds for each murder. Enough. My soul relents at dwelling longer on the subject.

May 2nd. Being now again as well as ever, I took leave from Joanna
and her Johnny, for thus he was named after myself, though he could not
yet be christened, and who both continued at my friend De Lamarre's
house, after which I once more set out for Maagdenburg in a tent-boat.

On the 3rd, I called at Egmond on my French friend Monsieur Cachelieu, and next day slept at Oranjebo, where I was heartily entertained by
my old adversary Captain Meyland, which gentleman swore he loved me
now better than any man in the Colony. He was just returned from a
cruise of twelve days in the woods. Among his men I reconnoitered one
Cordus, a gentleman's son from Hamburg, in which character I had
known him, but who had been trepanned as a common soldier into the
West India Company service, among which corps, as I have said, are all
nations—Christians, gentiles, and Jews who devoured pork and bacon as
fast as the others when they could catch it.

On May 5th, I arrived once more at Maagdenburg.

On May 9th, an accident had nearly befallen me which must have broken my heart. My black boy, washing my cotton hammock in the Tempaty Creek, it was suddenly carried to the bottom by the rapidity of the
current, and himself entangled in the middle of it, so that both the one
and the other disappeared. However, luckily, the boy extricated himself,
though with difficulty and, after being more than half drowned, appeared

once more on terra firma, when he had the presence of mind instantly to
sink a large fishhook with lead tied to a strong line on the very same spot,
with which he actually brought up the hammock, to all our astonishment, the stream running so swift that rolling over the ground it shifted
its station every moment. The next day, as Captain Hamel was angling
on the waterside, his tackle got fast to the ground when I, diving to clear
it, knocked my ankle with such violence against a rock that it did not
recover in the course of several months.

At the above accidents, Colonel Seybourgh seemed to be so much entertained, and they seemed to make him so very happy, that I in my turn
treated him with that contempt which his malice deserved, which ingra-
tiated me more in the favor of old Fourgeoud, who already hated him,
than if I had destroyed half the Negroes in the Colony. During all this
time, strong patrols cruised between Maagdenburg, La Rochelle, and the
Jews-Savanna, and on the 17th, the Commander in Chief marched to Patamacca himself, with nearly the half of his troops, leaving me the command of those that remained on the mountain, I not being able to accompany him in person, as having by this time a dangerous mortification in
my ankle. As I now had a prospect of remaining some time at anchor, I
dispatched Quacoo to Paramaribo for provisions. Whatever may be
thought of Fourgeoud's maneuvers, and his not being able to bring the
Rebels to a pitched battle, it is no less true that he exerted himself and his
troops to the utmost, and that by his constant cruising about the upper
parts of the rivers (viz., the skirts of the Colony), he prevented the frequent depredations on the estates that had formerly taken place. I now
being here the Commander in Chief, the two Negroes formerly mentioned (hunting and fishing for me) brought me one or two *pingos* (wild
boar) every day, besides fish called *newmara,* some as large as codfish,
with which dainties I regaled all the officers without exception, and never
was a deputy governor more respected; while I gave to the hospital all the
plantains, bananas, oranges, and lemons that were occasionally sent as
presents from the Jacob and the nearest adjoining plantations. Patrols
were also sent out daily to every quarter, and indeed though we could not
expect to find the enemy within several days' marching, the environs of
Maagdenburg nevertheless were so perfectly scoured that no invasion
from the Rebels could be practicable, and which was perfectly necessary,
they having besieged or rather taken by storm or surprise other military
posts, solely for the sake of carrying off ammunition, firearms, &c.
(which is to them of the greatest value and to the Colony of the most
pernicious consequence), and in taking which precautions Colonel Fourgeoud showed as much generalship as he did in constant marching, which
last, however, was the principal part of his duty. And thus, while we were

unsuccessful in taking the Rebels, I availed myself of taking a draft of every animal, reptile, or shrub that I thought could illustrate my little collection of natural curiosity, which I now began to form some idea of exhibiting one day to the public if I was spared to return to Europe.

On May 26th, I was sorry to be informed that all my European letters were sunk in the Texel roads on board *Captain Visser,* who was wrecked among the ice, and still more so that my sincere and very good friend Mr. Kennedy and his lady and his family had taken their final farewell from the Colony and sailed for Holland. This gentleman, Mr. Robert Gordon, and a Mr. Gourlay were the only Scotch inhabitants in the Colony; one Burkland, one Townsend, and Mr. Halfhide were the only Englishmen; and Captain Macneyl was the only one that came from Ireland.

May 28th. Now returned Colonel Fourgeoud with his command from Patamacca, much emaciated, himself and all his people, by fatigue, who left a great number behind him in the hospital at La Rochelle but no account whatsoever of the Rebels. He varied his route every time, thus it was pretty evident that they were routed from this quarter—if of late, they had been settled there at all. But where to find them in this unbounded forest was the question. However, he never despaired and seemed as eager to find the haunts of the Rebel Negroes as he had been formerly in discovering a covey of partridges or a nest of black badgers.

May 29th. The Old Gentleman and I were now extreme friends, at whose board being daily invited, he proposed to me to paint his figure at large, in his bush equipage, which was to be engraved at the expense of the town of Amsterdam. (He now, to be sure, thought himself as great a man as the Duke of Cumberland in England after the Battle of Culloden.) And to this performance I began, on a large sheet of paper with china ink, in his own hut. But one day, looking him full in the face to examine the features of this criterion of wickedness, I burst out in an immediate fit of laughing to think how he and I now sat staring at each other, when all of a sudden the whole mountain was shaken by a tremendous clap of thunder, while the lightning actually scorched Fourgeoud's forehead, and broke all the eggs under a hen that was breeding in a corner of the room where we were sitting.

About June 1st died of a dropsy the captive Rebel Negro September, who had been taken on November 26th, 1773, ever since which time (when his companion was shot), being nearly two and a half years, this poor fellow had followed Fourgeoud like a shepherd's dog through all his rough maneuvers, the Colonel always expecting this Negro would one day surely conduct him to the haunt of the Rebels, but he was mistaken. The other Negro slaves, suspecting he had actually given Fourgeoud some information, attributed his dreadful death to a punishment from

God for his want of trust and fidelity to his countrymen, to whom, they had conjectured, he had sworn to be true, while as I have remarked in the third chapter of this book, it is an invariable supposition among the African Negroes that whoever breaks his oath shall die miserably in this world, and is to be forever damned in that to come.

June 2nd. The Hope in Commewina was now so very unwholesome (in regard to cleanliness and keeping it dry from inundations, being neglected by the new-come troops who now lay there) that the commanding officer and most of his men were unfit for duty because of sickness, and many of them were already buried. Thus Colonel Fourgeoud sent down one Captain Brandt to take the command with a fresh supply and with orders to send, not to town, but to Maagdenburg all the invalids he should relieve. These orders he gave in such a brutal manner to the above gentleman (not so much as allowing him time to pack up his things), while Colonel Seybourgh shamefully deprived him of his servant (whom he took for himself), that Mr. Brandt burst out in tears and declared he wished no longer to survive his ill treatment. He then departed to the Hope with a truly broken heart, where arriving the next day he could not possibly send up to Fourgeoud the late commanding officer, whose name was Captain Brugh, and whom he had found dead as a herring. This poor man had done a few patrols with Colonel Fourgeoud in the woods but, being extremely fat and corpulent, was no longer able to support the fatigues and excessive heat than snow the sunshine, which having melted him down very fast, helped to hasten his dissolution by a putrid fever. Colonel Seybourgh followed Captain Brandt to inspect the sick, and to torment him more if possible.

On June 7th arrived the sick officers and soldiers from the Hope in barges, some of which last, being too ill to be transported, died in the passage, without medicines or assistance, while today also died one of our surgeons in the camp, and a great number of the privates died daily, which were the fruits of having marched so much in the wet season.

CHAPTER 18th

*A jaguar taken in the camp—Fatal rencounter of a party with
the Rebels, who kill several of the troops and force the rest
back—Description of a Surinam planter—Contagious
distempers—Suicide—Scene of primitive nature*

I have mentioned that several officers kept poultry, numbers of which
were now taken away every night without knowing by whom, when one
Captain Bolts (suspecting the *coati mondi* or *crabbodago*) made a trap of an
empty wine chest by supporting the lid with a stick fixed to a long cord
into which (having first secured all the other poultry) he put a couple of
fowls to roost, guarded by two Negroes at some distance. They had not
been many hours on their post when, hearing the fowls shriek, one pulled
the rope and the other ran to secure the invader, by sitting on the lid, and
who proved to be no other than a young jaguar, who would still have
cleared his way out by beating against the box, but which being immediately secured by strong ropes, was dragged with the prisoner in it, to
the river, where being held under water he was drowned, despite the
most amazing efforts, by beating, still to work his escape. Captain Bolts
ordered the skin to be taken off, to be kept as a memorial of so very
strange a circumstance.

On June 9th, availing myself of Colonel Fourgeoud's good temper, I
not only showed great neglect towards Seybourgh, whose occasional caresses I scorned as indeed he deserved, but presented the Old Gentleman
with a plan and bird's-eye view of all the encampment of Maagdenburg,
which pleased him so much that he also sent this (as he had done the first)
to the Prince of Orange and to the Duke of Brunswick, as a proof of his
military maneuvers &c., and which had the desired effect, since I not only
now became one of his favorites, but he declared his highest esteem for
the Scots and English, and even promised to recommend me in particular

at court. God, what a change. I at once took the blame of all former animosity on myself, and could have devoured the Old Carl with caresses, but now all his attention was suddenly attracted by affairs of more consequence.

On the 14th came the news that some Rebels' huts were discovered near the seaside, that Captain Meyland had marched in quest of the enemy with one hundred and forty men of the Society troops who had actually found them out, but (in wading through a deep marsh) had first been attacked by the Negroes, who had killed several of his men (among whom was his nephew, a young volunteer), wounded more, and beaten back the whole detachment, after they had already passed the marsh, and were mounting fast on the opposite beach to storm the village. This news proved that the sable foes were not to be trifled with, though they were discovered; in consequence of which, orders were immediately issued for all the troops that were able to march to keep in readiness, viz., Fourgeoud's Marines, the Society regiment, and my favorite Rangers, who wanted no spur and could now hardly be kept back till the others were prepared, and which troops were to be assembled at a place of rendezvous henceforth to be named, while also a detachment marched to La Rochelle to give information. Now all was alive and in a flow of spirits, some in hopes that this decisive stroke would end the war and their misery, some from hoping to find a little plunder among the enemy, and some from a motive of revenge to these poor naked people, who, as I have related before, originally revolted on account of bad usage and now took every means to retaliate upon their persecutors.

> Some Afric chief will rise, who scorning chains,
> Racks, tortures, flames—excruciating pains,
> Will lead his injured friends to bloody fight,
> And in the flooded carnage take delight;
> Then dear repay us in some vengeful war,
> And give us blood for blood, and scar for scar.

However, let me now do Colonel Fourgeoud the justice to relate till what length went his *humanity* against his enemies, when in my opinion, and in the opinion of many others, he might have attacked and routed them with advantage within a fortnight after receiving the intelligence; but which vengeance he had the good nature to spin out for no less a time than to the 20th of August, being above two calendar months after, and for which remarkable generosity, no doubt, the Rebel chief Boni, and all his black fraternity, were greatly obliged to him, who thus had both the time, and advantage, of the short dry season to look out for a new settlement to where they might retreat when they should be driven from their present habitation by the bloodthirsty Christians. To keep the scales in balance, on the other hand, Fourgeoud treated many of his friends with the greatest barbarity. But I, as mentioned above, was now his favorite and, as such, will faithfully relate how the time was spent during the interval, without partiality to anyone, until the day of the grand attack upon the Negroes.

June 17th. In the first place, while one Captain Perrett-Gentelly had nearly been drowned in one of the neighboring creeks, the account came that Captain Brandt was almost dead with sickness at the Hope (viz., where the troops were quartered), which was at present no better than a pesthouse, and to the command of this place, my being one of his favorites, Fourgeoud now singled me out, declaring I might thank my sound constitution for bestowing on me this honor. I now too evidently discovered that all his friendship was only flattery for my paintings &c., and my natural hatred rekindled against him apace, for thus sending me to be ingloriously killed by inches, when he had such a fair opportunity in view to see me shot.

On June 18th, at my arrival on the Hope, my orders were to send poor Captain Brandt not down, but up to Maagdenburg, but this young man frustrated the tyrannical command, which he, suspecting, had set out with a tent-barge to Paramaribo before I came, where he was no sooner carried to his lodgings than he expired of a burning fever and a broken heart. No one could be more regretted than Captain Brandt, nor ever lost Fourgeoud a better officer or I a better friend, but he, poor youth, was no more. This being the second commander dead in so short a time, I quietly took for my motto

Hodie tibi cras mihi.

But I was happily mistaken, and continued as well as ever I was in all my life, following the advice of old Cramaca, and bathing in the river twice every day, while I despised shoes and stockings as unnecessary lumber.

On June 20th, I received a visit from the Governor, Mr. Nepveu, on his return from his estate Appecappe to Paramaribo, with whom I condoled on the loss of his lady who was lately dead. I also received daily visits from several planters who complimented me with refreshments from their plantations. Did I ever describe the dress and manner of living of these West India nabobs? If not, here it is.

A planter in Surinam, when he lives on his estate (which is but seldom, they preferring the society of Paramaribo), gets out of his hammock with the rising sun, viz. about six o'clock in the morning, when he makes his appearance under the piazza of his house, where his coffee is already waiting on him, which he generally takes with his pipe in place of toast and butter, and where he is attended by half a dozen of the finest young slaves, both male and female, of the plantation to serve him. At this *sanctum sanctorum* he next is accosted by his overseer, who regularly every morning attends at his levee, and having made his bows at several yards' distance, with the deepest respect, informs His Greatness what work was done the day before, what Negroes deserted, died, fell sick, recovered, were bought, or born, and above all things, which of them neglected their work, affected sickness, had been drunk, or absent, &c. They are generally presented, being secured by the bastians, or Negro drivers, and instantly tied up to the beams of the piazza, or to a tree, without so much as being heard, when the flogging begins—men, women, or children without exception—on their naked bodies, by long hempen whips that cut round at every lash, and crack like a pistol, during which they alternately repeat *"Dankee, Massera"* ("Thank you, Master"). Meanwhile, he stalks up and down with his overseer, affecting not so much as to hear their cries, till they are sufficiently mangled, when they are immediately untied and ordered to return to their work, without even a dressing. This ceremony over, the *dressy Negro* (a black surgeon) comes to make his report, who being dismissed with a hearty curse, next makes her appearance a superannuated matron, with all the young Negro children of the estate, over whom she is governess, who being washed clean in the river, clap their hands and cheer in chorus, when they are sent away to breakfast, and the levee ends with a low bow from the overseer.

Now his worship saunters out in his morning dress, which consists of a pair of the finest Holland trousers, white silk stockings, and red or yellow Morocco slippers, the neck of his shirt open and nothing over it, a loose-flowing nightgown of the finest India chintz excepted. On his head is a cotton nightcap, as thin as a cobweb, and over that an enormous beaver hat, to keep his meager visage, which is already the color of mahogany, covered from the sun, while his whole carcass seldom weighs above eight or ten stone, being generally exhausted by the climate and by dissipation. To give a better idea of this fine gentleman, I here represent him to the reader, with a pipe in his cheek (which almost everywhere keeps him company) and receiving a glass of Madeira and water from a female Quadroon slave to refresh him during his walk. Having loitered about his estate, or sometimes ridden on horseback to his fields to view his increasing stores, he returns about eight o'clock when, if he goes abroad, he dresses, but if not, remains just as he is. Should the first take place, having only exchanged his trousers for a pair of thin linen or silk breeches, he sits down and holds out one foot after another, like a horse going to be shod, while a Negro boy puts on his stockings and shoes, which he also buckles &c., while another dresses his hair, his wig, or

A Surinam Planter in his Morning Dress.

Plate 49

shaves him; and a third is fanning him to keep off the gnats or mosquitoes. Having now shifted, he puts on a very thin coat and waistcoat, all white, when under the shade of an umbrella carried by a black boy, he is conducted to his barge, which is awaiting him with six or eight oars, well provided with fruit, wine, water, and tobacco by his overseer, who no sooner has seen him depart, than he resumes the command with a vengeance. But should this nabob remain on his estate, in that case he remains as he is, and goes to breakfast about ten o'clock, for which a table is spread in the large hall, provided with a bacon-ham, hung-beef, fowls, or pigeons, broiled hot from the gridiron; plantains and sweet cassavas, roasted; bread, butter, cheese, &c., with which he drinks strong beer, such as ale and porter, and a glass of Madeira, Rhenish, or Moselle wine, while the cringing overseer sits at the further end, keeping his proper distance, both being served by the most beautiful slaves that could ever be picked out. And this is called breaking the poor gentleman's fast.

After this he takes a book, plays at chess or billiards, entertains himself with music, &c., till the heat of the day forces him to return to his cotton hammock, to enjoy his meridian nap, with which he would no more dispense than a Spaniard with his *siesta,* and in which he rocks to and fro, like a performer on the slack rope, till he falls asleep, without either bed or covering, and during which time he is fanned by a couple of his black attendants, to keep him cool.

About three o'clock he awakes by natural instinct when, having washed and perfumed himself, he sits down to dinner, attended, as at breakfast, by his deputy governor and sable pages, where nothing is wanting that the world can afford in a Western climate, of meat, fowls, venison, fish, vegetables, fruits, &c., while the most exquisite wines are often squandered away in profusion. After this, a cup of strong coffee and a liqueur finish the repast. At six o'clock he is again waited on by his overseer, attended as in the morning by Negro drivers, and prisoners, when the flogging once more having continued for some time, and the necessary orders being given for the next day's work, the assembly is dismissed, and the evening spent with weak punch, sangaree, cards, and tobacco. His worship generally begins to yawn about ten or eleven o'clock, when he withdraws and, being undressed by his sooty pages, he retires to rest, where he passes the night in the arms of one or other of his sable sultanas (for he always keeps a seraglio), till about six o'clock in the morning, when he again repairs to his piazza walk, where his pipe and coffee are waiting his commands, and where, with the rising sun, he begins his round of dissipation like a little king—despotic, absolute, and without control—and which cannot but have the greater relish to a man who, in his own country, viz., Europe, was ten to one a *Nothing.*

In this colony such is too frequently the case, where plantations are sold upon credit, and are left (by the absent proprietor) to the sworn appraisers who, by selling them cheap, find their account in the buyer, and which, while he lives at the above rate under pretense of bad crops, mortality among the slaves, &c., like the upstart rascal he is, he massacres the Negroes by double labor, ruins and pillages the estate of all its productions, which he sells clandestinely for ready money, makes a purse, and goes to the Devil. However, exceptions take place in every circumstance, and I have known as many good gentlemen that were planters in Surinam as I ever would desire to be acquainted with, as I have already mentioned. As for the ladies, they indulge themselves as much after the same manner I have described above as their distinction of sex will admit of, while decency and decorum (nay even compassion, I am sorry to say it) are with them too often terms totally unknown. I say too often, yet there are here such heavenly women as Mrs. Elizabeth Danforth, now Godefrooy, and a few more, whose characters shine with treble luster; and I shall simply draw a veil over all the other imperfections too common to their sex in this climate.

A few words more and I take my leave, which is that hospitality is in no country practiced with less ceremony and greater diffusion, a stranger being everywhere at home, and finding his table and his bed at whatever estate he chooses to step ashore, which is the more convenient, no inns being ever met with in any of the Surinam rivers.

Should the reader be surprised at the above account of a Surinam planter's manner of living, let him peruse Mr. Smith's tour through the United States, where he will find that of a Virginia planter little different, though a Mr. Glen's act of barbarity to his wife in public (as described by that gentleman) is unknown in Surinam, perhaps not from want of inclination but from want of vigor and bodily capacity. And now farewell to the nabobs.

June 23rd. The Hope was now truly a most shocking place of residence, where I much lamented my former cottage and sweet companion, the one in ruins, the other at Paramaribo, and where at present not a man was to be seen without agues, fevers, rotten limbs, &c., and where the bloody flux also began to make its discovery—while they had neither surgeon, medicines, nor as much as a light, and very little bread left. Thus, I distributed all my Boston biscuit, lemons, oranges, sugar, wine, ducks, and fowls among the unhappy sufferers, with a few spermaceti candles. I sent up to the hospital at Maagdenburg today, two sick officers, Orleigh and Fransen, with all the privates that could bear to be transported, and my humble entreaties to be soon relieved from so very disagreeable a situation, for which indeed there was not the smallest glimpse of necessity, and to be one of the party to march against the Rebels. In short, while the accounts came from below that fresh nests of Negroes were discovered, even close to Paramaribo, the news came from above that the troops there were dying away to no manner of purpose, where among others were expired on the 22nd a Captain Seybourgh, brother to the noted colonel, thus the third captain in one month.

June 26th. From Maagdenburg now arrived two fine young officers (one of whom had been page to the Prince of Orange), ruined for their lives by having got ruptures, and which all was occasioned by Fourgeoud's unaccountably persisting to cruise through the woods in the rainy season, when it is so very slippery and he could do nothing. While now it was so dry, he scorned to stir even though he so well knew where the enemy was to be met with. But, as I have said before, he gave for reasons that in the wet season the enemy might more easily be starved. How much he gained by these measures shall be seen in the sequel. This evening one of our Marines, one Spanknevel, was missing and no conjecture could be formed about what was come of him.

On the 29th, one of the Negroes having been out hunting, his dogs brought him to a tree, where this unfortunate man was suspended by the neck to one of the branches (with a *nebee*), as naked as he was born, exhibiting a dreadful spectacle, being swelled like a drowned carrion by the heat of the climate, and already swarming in corruption. He was a German and had hanged himself utterly from despair. But what appeared singular was that not one of his comrades would so much as cut him down to be buried, in spite of what I could say, alleging that to touch him was to become as infamous as he himself. However, the Negroes were exempt from this prejudice and, by my orders, he was interred.

Now came at last, to my great satisfaction, an order for my relief. And another captain having taken the command in my place, I left the miserable situation almost instantly, and that very evening arrived at Goed Accoord in company with Captain Bolts, who had been down, and where the planter, Mr. De Lange, with his lady happened to be. We were received with much hospitality. This sugar estate is, as I said, the last that is cultivated in Commewina. Here, the Negroes are allowed to do just as they please, which indeed was very little, for fear of an insurrection. Here we saw what was to us a novelty, viz., that the young Negro women who attended as servants at table &c., and who were come to the age of puberty, should all be stark naked, without so much as a fig leaf. Had in my cheeks at this time been left any blood, I must have blushed. However, asking the cause of this strange phenomenon, I was answered by the lady that it was intended so, by their mothers and matrons, to promote their growth, by thus being detected in their too early cohabitations with the other sex that otherwise took place. And indeed, finer figures I never beheld, who were a treat to every spectator of real taste. Let prudes say what they will, nature will be nature still, and no stays, gowns or petticoats can ever correct the symmetry and native graces of a well proportioned young woman, but indeed may serve to hide their defects, while the strength, liveliness, and agility annexed to a natural state are great inducements to plead in its favor. And even in the black women, their sparkling eyes, ivory teeth, and remarkable cleanliness all over, fully compensates for the silk ribbons, gold lace, and borrowed feathers that grace the too many languid looks, sallow complexions, deformed bodies, and broken constitutions of our European countrywomen.

At Goed Accoord the men were no less fine, witness Philander (as I have said), and which was all owing to the Negroes here living after their own way, without being crushed under the yoke and mangled by the lash of a relentless European, which proves that the Africans, in a state of nature, are not that wretched people which they are by too many ignorant European wretches represented.

On June 30th, having here dined and drank a hearty glass of wine, we departed for Maagdenburg, an hour before sunset, greatly against the advice of Mr. and Mrs. De Lange, in a small barge with six oars, and covered with a loose awning. We had not rowed above two miles when not only night came on, but we were overtaken by such a shower of rain as had nearly sunk us, the boat's gunwale not being more than two inches above the water. However, with the help of our hats we kept her swimming, while a Negro sat upon the bow with both his arms straight out before him to prevent us from capsizing by inadvertently running against the roots of mangroves &c., which thickly line both the banks of the rivers all upwards. In this pickle and Hell's darkness, at ten o'clock at night we came to the Jacob, being just afloat and no more, where Bolts and I no sooner stepped ashore like drowned cats than the boat sank with all the rest that was in her (the slaves swimming ashore), and among which was my box with my whole journal, and all my paintings, that had cost me above two years' labor, care, and attention. I was truly distracted at this loss, when a skillful Negro, having dived several times to the bottom, before twelve o'clock brought up my little treasure, which, though thoroughly soaked, I was happy to have again in my hands, which ended our shipwreck. And we all fell asleep round a swinging fire, by which I made shift to dry myself and my poor papers.

Next morning we again set out and rowed for Maagdenburg, when coming about half way, our voyage was obstructed by an enormous tree that had accidently fallen across the creek, so that we could drag the boat neither over nor under it. Thus we were obliged to return to the Jacob again, whence we now proceeded to Maagdenburg on foot, through thorns, roots, brambles, and briars, and where we finally arrived, torn and bloody, by the scratches &c., while my ankle—which had been nearly recovered—was now wounded afresh to the bone, the skin and flesh being quite torn away by the numberless inconveniences that obstructed our passage.

There we were now acquainted that Mr. Orleigh (one of the two officers that I had sent up to Maagdenburg from the Hope on the 23rd) was also no more. Thus died most all our gentlemen that had during the last month been upon the Hope, from which scarcely one single private returned in health, and which I will maintain was greatly owing to the dry and burning-hot month of June, when the sun suddenly scorched them, after marching and even sleeping in cool watery swamps, and heavy rains, during the whole wet season. But Colonel Fourgeoud consoled himself with declaring (as he had done before) that the greater his list of mortality, the greater should be his fame when he returned to Europe. But his people thought otherwise, some of whom seeing themselves thus sacrificed to no purpose even cried aloud with despair. However, I still escaped this ceremony, by my fine constitution and great flow of spirits which, God forgive me, I determined now forcibly to keep up from sinking, by laughing, singing, and damning, while all the rest were crying and dying around me.

CHAPTER 19th

The troops march to Barbacoeba in Rio Cottica—Frenzy fevers—Gratitude in an English sailor—Description of the government of Surinam—Scene of unprecedented generosity

The rainy season being now again at hand, and Colonel Fourgeoud having picked out all the remaining healthy people (who amounted to about one hundred and eighty in number), on July 3rd he set out upon his march for Barbacoeba, in the River Cottica, which spot he appointed as the general rendezvous before the grand attack on the Rebels, and at which place the troops of the Society and the corps of free Negroes or black Rangers were to join him. Of this party, I had the honor to be one, but on the surgeon's declaring that I ran the hazard of losing my foot by amputation if I marched in the woods, I was ordered to remain at Maagdenburg, with liberty if I soon recovered to join Fourgeoud at Barbacoeba the best way I could. My limb was now indeed so swollen, and my wound so black by the gangrene or mortification, that I could hardly stand without pain, and of which I shall bear the mark as long as I live. During this confinement, I received daily presents from Philander and the other Negroes, I having always been extremely kind to them.

I have said that all the officers and most of the privates who had been stationed at the Hope lately had died, or had been sent up dangerously ill, while I had escaped the contagion. But, alas, now it became my turn, having only had a reprieve and no more, since on the 9th I was seized with the same burning fever that had carried off the rest. I know not what happened from that time till the morning of the 12th, when I was a little better, and one of our officers, a Mr. Luck, put a paper in my hand that he had written down while he was sitting on his chest under my hammock, and which to be sure was a masterly performance. Here it is. But yet before I presume to transcribe it to the public, who may doom it as savoring of the marvelous, let me ask them the question: How often has it not been remarked that the effects of inebriation have been conducive to the composition of poetry or music, and why may not then the effects of a fever be the same? Thus, here it goes.

Under this stone,
Lies the skin and the bone,
While the flesh was long gone of *poor Stedman*.

Who still took up his pen,
And exhausted his brain,
In the hopes these last lines might be read, man.

Of his life he was tired,
At no more he aspired,
D——nd the rogues, shut his eyes, & went quietly to bed, man.

It has been remarked also that such *frenzies* are very bad omens. Be that as it may, but being come a little to myself again, I determined to confute this pretty elegy, at least at Maagdenburg, from which I took my congee without any ceremony, Fourgeoud &c. being absent, and attended by my poor black boy (who was now also sick from day and night watching at my hammock), I got myself transported in a crazy canoe as far as Oranjebo, on my way to Paramaribo, after giving over the command to another officer. In going down, I met a barge again crowded with sick officers and men from the Hope, which was by this time as dangerous as Smyrna.

The next day I was excessively ill, and Quacoo also. So much so that while we could have no help or refreshment at Oranjebo (which Captain Meyland had left), we were both too sick to be transported any further. I now thought myself in Hell because of the burning heat of the climate and my fever, but I still had the consolation that while Providence may allow one to be so cursed in this world, he will certainly not permit them to be again damned in the other, where he promises that "Should their sins be as scarlet, they shall be white as snow, and though they be red like crimson that they shall be as wool."

In short, on the 14th, once more farewell to this inhospitable spot. However, I could reach no further than Goed Accoord, where I was expected to die, when an old Negro woman found means to make me partake of some buttermilk boiled with some barley and molasses, which was the first food I had tasted since the 9th, and which certainly did me a great deal of good, so that the day following, I was again able to be transported, and the black boy was much better. This evening, I reached Faukenberg, where I was met by a packet of six or eight letters from different friends, accompanied with presents of hung-beef, bullocks' tongues, Madeira, porter, rum, and two gallons of excellent shrub, besides a fine bacon-ham and a beautiful pointer from the identical Charles Macdonald, the English sailor, which he had brought for me from Virginia, in return for the little civility I had formerly shown him so unexpectedly at the Hope, and which mark of this poor fellow's gratitude and generosity (the true characteristic of a British tar) gave me greater pleasure than all the other things I received put together, two letters excepted, the one from Mr. Lude at Amsterdam, and the other from Mr. De Graav, his administrator, at Paramaribo, acquainting me finally, and to my heartfelt satisfaction, that the amiable Joanna and her little boy were at my disposal, but at no less a price than two thousand florins, amounting with other expenses to nearly two hundred pounds, a sum which I was no more able to pay than to fly. And I already owed the fifty pounds that I had borrowed for the black boy Quacoo's redemption. Indeed, Joanna was a charming young woman, and though appraised at one-twentieth share of the whole estate, which had been sold for forty thousand florins, no price could be too dear for one that was so valuable to me.

I now found myself, though exceedingly weak, so much better that on the next day I went down so far as the estate Berkshoven, whence the administrator, a Mr. Gourlay, humanely caused me to be transported to Paramaribo in a decent tent-boat with six oars, and where relapsing, I arrived, just alive and no more, on the evening of the 19th, having passed the last night at the estate called La Jalousie.

Being now in a comfortable lodging at Mr. De Lamarre's, and attended by so good a nurse as Joanna, I recovered apace and was so well that, on the 25th, I was able to scramble out for the first time, and dine with Mrs. Godefrooy, Mr. De Graav not being in town, to finish matters concerning the emancipation of Joanna, who had now once more literally saved my life.

Being now once more at Paramaribo, I will try to give some account of the government of this fine colony, which I am persuaded some of the readers have long ago expected, but having not before now had the opportunity to gratify their curiosity on this subject, was the occasion of my silence.

On July 26th, dining with his Excellency Governor Nepveu, he gave the following information. At present, Surinam belongs two-thirds to the town of Amsterdam and one-third to the West India Company and is governed by several courts of judicature. Thus I shall now proceed to describe them in their proper order, as he gave me the relations. In the first place, the Court of Policy and Criminal Justice consists of thirteen members chosen by the votes of all the inhabitants, each member con-

tinuing for life and of which the Governor is president, and the commandant or deputy governor first counsellor, viz.,

> the Governor,
> the commandant,
> the fiscal,
> the town clerk, and
> nine counsellors.

To this court belongs the decision of all criminal matters, viz., capital
offenses only, while the Governor has the power of reprieving from death
and pardoning any convict, without further ceremony whatever.

The Court of Civil Justice consists also in thirteen members but these
are chosen by the above court only, and renewed every four years, while
the Governor is also president, viz.,

> the Governor,
> the fiscal,
> the town clerk, and
> ten counsellors.

By this court are decided all important lawsuits and petty offenses.

The next is the Subaltern College of eleven members, chosen also by
the Governor and Court of Policy, and as the other, renewed every four
years, the town clerk excepted, who sits for life. The members are selected from the late counsellors of justice, and are

> the deputy president,
> the town clerk, and
> nine counsellors.

The above court supervises the public buildings, streets, canals, orange
trees, &c., and decides all money disputes that are under twenty-five
guineas, any sum above that going to the Court of Justice.

Besides these, there is an Orphan and Insolvent Debtor's College, consisting of

> the commissaries,
> the town clerk,
> the bookkeeper,
> the treasurer, and
> a sworn secretary.

The public revenue officers are

> the office of importation and exportation duties,
> the office of excise and small imposts,

the office for head money, or tax upon heads,
the office for public sales and vendues,
the office for retaking Negro deserters &c.

I have formerly mentioned that the Governor is at the head not only of the civil but of the military law. The other public employments are principally

the secretary to his Excellency the Governor,
the commissaries of the victualing offices,
four inspectors of the exportation of sugars,
one inspector of the molasses hogsheads,
one supervisor of all the North American vessels,
two public auctioneers,
two sergeants or messengers of the court,
two sworn land surveyors,
three measurers of the squared timber,
one inspector of the black cattle &c.,
one sworn overseer of weights and measures,
three Low Dutch clergymen,
one French clergyman
one Lutheran clergyman,
three public schoolmasters &c.

The militia consists of eleven companies, with one captain, one lieutenant, one second lieutenant, one ensign, one secretary, and one cashier each; the captains are generally the sworn appraisers of the estates for sale in the different rivers where they chance to have their department.

These are the principal functions in the government of Surinam, and though thus unconnectedly inserted, are sufficient to give an idea of the civil department of this colony, which is not upon a bad establishment at all, were it not corrupted by sordid avarice, to the great detriment of this beautiful settlement in general, and to that of its inhabitants in particular, especially the miserable Negro slaves, the first being no other at present than a rotten constitution, and the second, the bleeding victims to prevent it from totally expiring. Yet by proper management, this spot might be made the Garden of Eden not only for the European settlers, but also for their African domestics, as I shall clearly demonstrate before I finish this work (according to my promise already made), when I will clearly point out where the cancer lies, and prescribe the means of scooping it out no more to return. Thus, if I cannot, like the Good Samaritan, pour the balm in the wound of anyone, at least I can leave the prescription to cure the deadly wounds of many thousands.

I have just said that at present, by the desperate means of blood was prevented its total annihilation; how much more glorious will it be (by those who have it in their power not only to save this country, but many other valuable West India settlements), by the balm of a well-planned justice and benevolence.

On August 3rd, Mr. De Graav arrived in town, having finally settled affairs with Mr. Lolkens, the late administrator of Faukenberg. I thought I would take the first opportunity to settle matters with him, by proposing to give me credit till I should have it in my power to pay the money for which Joanna and Johnny had been sold to me, and which I was determined to save out of my pay, if I should exist till then on bread and salt and nothing else, and which even then, I could not do in less time than between two or three years. But Heaven interceded and prevented my penurious resolution, by sending that angelic woman, Mrs. Godefrooy, to my assistance, for no sooner was she acquainted with my struggling situation than she sent for me to dine with her, when she addressed me in the following terms.

> I know, good Stedman, too well the present feelings of your tender heart, and the incapacity of an officer's income to alleviate your distress. But know that even in Surinam, virtue will meet with friends. Your manly sensibility for that deserving young woman and her child must claim the esteem of all well-thinking people, in spite of groveling, malice, and folly, and so much have these actions recommended you to my attention in particular, that I should think myself blameable in not patronizing your laudable endeavors. Permit me, then, to participate in your happiness and in the prosperous prospects of the virtuous Joanna and her little boy, by your accepting the sum of two thousand florins, or any sum you stand in need of, with which money go immediately, Stedman, go and redeem innocence, good sense, and beauty, from the jaws of tyranny, insult, and oppression.

Seeing me thunder-struck and gazing upon her in a state of stupefaction, without speaking, she continued with a heavenly smile.

> Let not your delicacy, Stedman, take the alarm and here interfere. Soldiers ought ever to be the men of fewest compliments, and rectitude of mind supplies an incoherent chain of empty words. This I expect from you. Thus say not one word on the subject.

Being now come to myself, however, I replied that I was at a loss how most to express my admiration of such benevolence. I said that Joanna, who had so frequently preserved my life, had certainly merited my eternal affection, but that my gratitude could not be of less duration to one who had so generously put me upon the way to redeem that inestimable woman from slavery, and concluded with observing that I could not now touch a shilling of the money but should have the honor to call upon her the next day, when I retired.

I was no sooner come home than I acquainted Joanna with all that had happened, who bursting into tears called out, *"Gado sa blesse da woma,"* and insisted on she herself being mortgaged to Mrs. Godefrooy till every farthing should be paid, while she indeed wished to see the emancipation of her child, but till which time she absolutely refused to accept of her own liberty. Without here endeavoring to paint the struggle that I felt between love and honor, I shall bluntly say that I yielded to the last, and pressing to my bosom this fine woman, whose sentiments endeared her to me still, I instantly drew up a paper, declaring my Joanna, according to her wish, to be the property of Mrs. Godefrooy, till the last farthing of the money she lent me should be reimbursed. And on the next day, with the consent of her relations,[1] I conducted her to Mrs. Godefrooy's house in person, where throwing herself at the feet of that divine woman, she herself put the paper into her hands. But this lady (having raised her up) no sooner had read the contents than she exclaimed,

> Must it be so? Then come here, my Joanna. I have a spirit to accept of you, not as my slave, but more as my companion. You shall have a house built in my orange garden, with my own slaves to attend you, till Providence shall call me away, when you shall be free as indeed you are now, the moment you shall wish to possess your manumission, and which prerogative you claim both by your extraction and behavior.[2]

On these terms, and no other, I accepted of the money on the 5th, and, carrying it in my hat to Mr. De Graav's, I emptied the contents on his table for a receipt in full, and Joanna was transferred from the wretched estate Faukenberg into the possession of the first woman in the Colony, for which she thanked me with a look that can only be expressed in the countenance of an angel.

Mr. De Graav, on counting the money, addressed me in the following short speech.

> As two hundred florins of this sum belongs to me as administrator, permit me also to have a small share in this very joyful circumstance, by not ac-

---

1. Without the consent of parents, brothers, and sisters, no respectable slaves are *individually* sold in Surinam.

2. I have already mentioned that Joanna was, by birth, the daughter of a gentleman from Holland, while her mother's family were distinguished people on the coast of Africa.

cepting this dividend, while I find myself amply paid by the pleasure of having been instrumental in bringing about what seems so much to contribute to the happiness of two deserving people.

I thanked my disinterested friend with an affectionate shake by the hand, immediately returned the two hundred florins to Mrs. Godefrooy, and all was happy. The next day my praises rang through the town of Paramaribo, and I was crowned for what I had thus far finished, with praises, and congratulations, particularly by Mr. and Mrs. Demelly, and Mr. and Mrs. Gordon, this being indeed the third person (including Quacoo) that I had rescued, within a little more than three months, from the jaws of the monster persecutor, yet to see matters so happily concluded was what I could never have expected.

I ought not to forget, as a further proof of Mrs. Godefrooy's humane character, that hearing of the dejected situation of the sick at Maagdenburg, she sent them as a present a whole barge loaded with fruit, vegetables, and refreshments of every kind that the Colony could afford.

August 7th. Matters being thus far settled, I now wrote a letter to Mr. Lude at Amsterdam, to give him intelligence and to thank him for having parted with the most valuable property of his estate. Since my ankle was now pretty well recovered, I wrote to Colonel Fourgeoud at Barbacoeba that I should have the honor to join him in a few days—for there he was still, while the intrepid and active militia captain, Stoelman, was beating up the woods with a few Rangers at another quarter, and this day sent in four captured Rebel Negroes to Paramaribo.[3]

Being ready once more to enter the forest, I again took farewell from my little family and friends, leaving the first still at Mr. De Lamarre's, at their request, and voluntarily set off with a tent-barge on my fifth campaign, in the hopes of accompanying Fourgeoud, who, having received all his remaining forces about him, with every other arrangement to attack the enemy, was now determined to march in a very few days.

In short, I arrived on the 14th at Barbacoeba in the upper part of the River Cottica, where formerly I was and where I had formerly killed the *aboma* snake, leaving my boxes at Mocha, an estate. I found here the Old Gentleman (who welcomed me civilly), ready to start the very day following. I do declare I never saw the troops in such fine spirits, proceeding from different motives, as I have said before—some in the hopes of plun-

---

3. It is a maxim with the Rangers to chop off the right hand of every Rebel Negro they kill, for which they receive twenty-five florins, and for every one they send in alive fifty florins. Also for finding a town or village, one thousand florins, being a premium of about five pounds sterling.

der, some from revenge, and some from wishing to see the war at an end, while I believe in my soul that others had grown tired of their existence by continual illness and bad usage, and heartily wished for a glorious end of all their miseries, as in general nothing can be more wretched than a military life in a tropical climate, more so under a relentless commander, as old Fourgeoud was thought to be even by his friends.

CHAPTER 20th

August 15th. Whether to dare Fourgeoud or to intimidate his troops, the
Rebels, flushed with their late victory over Captain Meyland and his
party and being well apprised by their spies that Fourgeoud was now at
Barbacoeba, had the assurance lately to set fire to all the huts in two different camps which had been left standing by his circumambulating patrols, while they were shouting and hallooing all the night. But this,
however, proved rather a spur to rouse him than otherwise, and enraged
the old man so much that he now swore he would be revenged on them
coute qui coute. An hour before daybreak, Colonel Fourgeoud, with his
troops, were ready to march and enter the woods—exactly two hundred
Europeans, the others being ill. No Rangers were as yet arrived, who
had, however, been expected but were so much disgusted with being
under Fourgeoud's command that they delayed appearing at all, which
gave the veteran commander an opportunity to call them a pack of pusillanimous rascals. And indeed, I myself was extremely surprised at this
willful absence of my black favorites, who were at other times so eager
and keen to fall upon the enemy, and had declared their utmost satisfaction in the hopes of having a stout brush with their sable countrymen.
This whole day our course was due east, and having proceeded about
eight miles (which is a great deal in this country, where the pioneers must
constantly open a path with billhooks), we erected huts and encamped.

Having frequently mentioned the Rebel Negroes, with whom we
were now certain to have a rencounter, I here present the reader with the

figure of one of these people upon his guard, as alarmed by supposing to hear a rustling among the bushes, and a couple of Rangers at a distance ready to take him by surprise. The first is armed with a firelock and a hatchet, his hair (though woolly) may be observed to be plaited close to his head, by way of distinction from the Rangers, or any other straggling Negroes who are not accepted yet among them, and his beard is grown to a point, like that of all the Africans when they have no opportunity to shave. The whole dress of this man consists of a cotton sheet negligently tied across his shoulders, which protects him against the rain, and serves him as a bed in which to lie down and sleep in the most obscure places he can find. The rest are his *camisa,* his pouch (which is made of some animal's skin), a few cotton strings for ornament around his ankles and wrists, and a superstitious *obia* or amulet tied about his neck, in which case he places all his hope and confidence. The skull and ribs are supposed to be some of his enemies scattered upon a sandy savanna. The two Rangers who make their appearance at a distance may be distinguished by their red caps, while I must observe that the Rebels many times have availed themselves of capturing one of these scarlet distinctions, which by clapping on their own heads in an engagement has not only saved their lives, but given them an opportunity to shoot their enemies.

Another stratagem of theirs has sometimes been discovered, viz., that firearms being scarce among them, numbers have intermixed in the crowd with only a crooked stick, shaped something like a musket to supply it in appearance, which has even more than once had the effect, when they came to ransack the estates, of preventing a proper defense by the plantation slaves, who were thus struck with a panic, and whose courage damped, with the show of such superior numbers, allowing the Rebels calmly (after burning the houses) to carry away even their own wives and daughters.

August 16th, we continued again marching due east upon a ridge or elevated ground, which if I am not mistaken, run in this country generally east and west, as do also most of the marshes or swamps. Having advanced rather less than we had done the day before, we were ordered to sling our hammocks early, and to sleep without any covering, to prevent the enemy from hearing us cut timber. Nor were any fires allowed to be lighted, nor speaking, while a strict watch was kept round the camp, and which were all very necessary precautions. But if we were not discovered by the enemy, we were almost devoured alive by such a cloud of gnats or mosquitoes in this place as I vow to God I had not even met with on board the fatal barges in upper Cottica, and which arose from a neighboring marsh, while we could make no smoke to drive them away.

A Rebel Negro armed & on his guard.

Bartolozzi Sculp.

Plate 53

In this situation, I saw the poor men dig holes with their bayonets in the earth into which they thrust their heads, stopping the entry, and covering their necks with their hammocks, while they lay with their bellies on the ground. To sleep in any other position was absolutely impossible. However, by the advice of a Negro slave, I enjoyed my rest. "Climb (said he), *Massera,* with your hammock, to the top of the highest tree that is in the camp, and there go sleep; not a single mosquito will disturb you, the swarm being too much engaged by the smell of the sweating multitude that is at the bottom." And this I tried, being near a hundred feet above my companions, whom I could neither see by the mist of mosquitoes below me, rolling like the clouds under Blanchard's balloon, nor hear them by the sound of their infernal singing music.

On the 17th, we continued our march due east till nine o'clock, when we altered our course to the north and had to scramble through great quantities of *mataky* roots or trumpeters, which proved that the ground began to be lower, and indeed at last it became very marshy—but luckily, though now in the wet season, we had as yet very little or no rain. This evening we encamped about four o'clock, Colonel Fourgeoud being ill with a cold fit of the ague.

I now turned into my hammock, reflecting on all the wonders and wonderful bustle of this world, while the silver moon glittering through the verdure of the trees added beauty to the quietness and solemnity of the scene. I fell most profoundly asleep, but not longer than till about midnight, when we were all awakened in Hell's darkness, and a heavy shower of rain, by the hallooing and shouting of the Rebel Negroes, who also discharged several musket shots, but not any at our camp, at which we were extremely astonished, but could not in the least understand the meaning. This disturbance continued till near daybreak, having expected every moment to be surrounded, when we unlashed our hammocks and proceeded on our march due north toward the place, where by conjecture, the hallooing noise had come from, while we were extremely fatigued for want of sleep, especially Colonel Fourgeoud, who could hardly support himself because of the ague. We had not marched two miles, I having the vanguard, when a Rebel Negro sprang up at my feet from under a shrub, where he had been concealed asleep, but who (while we were forbidden to fire upon stragglers, and without him firing at me) disappeared like a stag among the underwood. Of this I no sooner made report to the Old Hero than, swearing he was a spy (which I believe was true), he shook off his illness and redoubled his pace with vigor. With Colonel Seybourgh damning me for marching too fast, our pursuit was nonetheless to no purpose, at least this day, since about one o'clock we were led into a bog that we could hardly get out of, and were thus obliged to return back to our last night's lodgings, having lost two private men of the Society, who were missing.

Innumerable, indeed, are the many plagues and dangers one is hourly exposed to in the woods of this tropical climate. And while I only make mention of such few as must appear new to the reader, most of us were perpetually tormented with all those others that now I pass over in silence, as having been already described. Yet a recapitulation only of their names may not be amiss to refresh the memory of those who have a heart to sympathize with our sad sufferings. I have already mentioned the mosquitoes, *mompieras,* patat- and scrapat lice, chigoes, cockroaches, common ants, fire ants, horseflies, wild bees, and spiders. Besides the prickly heat, ringworm, dry gripes, putrid fevers, boils, *consaca,* bloody flux, thorns, briars, alligators, snakes, and jaguars, &c. But I have said nothing yet of the bush worms, large ants, locusts, centipedes, scorpions, bats, and flying lice, the *crassy-crassy,* yaws, lethargy, leprosy, and dropsy, besides a thousand other grievances that no less forever kept us company, and the description of which I must delay till the most suitable opportunity for inserting them into this narrative.

Such were the torments that a parcel of poor, emaciated, forlorn, and, I may say, half-starved creatures had to struggle with in a strange country, who were dying by dozens, and scores, without assistance, or pity, frequently with not so much as a friend to shut their eyelids, and always without a coffin or shell to receive their bones, being for the most part promiscuously thrown together into one pit, no better than I have seen a heap of carrion thrown to the dogs.

On the 19th, we again broke up and, after keeping a little to the south, marched east till ten o'clock, when we were overtaken and joined by a party of one hundred Rangers, with their conductor, a Mr. Vinsack, which made us now just three hundred. However little Colonel Fourgeoud affected to care for these black soldiers at other times, he seemed very far from displeased with their company at this time, when he knew he was fast approaching an enemy, whom certainly the Rangers knew better how to engage than Marines; and it will ever be my opinion that *one* of these free Negroes was preferable to half a dozen white men in the woods of Guiana, which seemed their natural element, while it was the bane of the Europeans. Colonel Fourgeoud now gave out orders to march in three columns, viz., his own regiment in the center, the Society troops on the right, and the Rangers or black soldiers on the left, all within hearing of each other, and to have a few *flankers* or riflemen dispersed without the whole. Thus arranged, we advanced forward till about midday, when we changed our course from east to northeast and again continued our march over a *biree-biree* swamp or quagmire, which are very common and dangerous in this country, being a deep, soft, miry marsh, only covered over with a thin crust of verdure, strong sufficient in most places to carry the weight of a man, and trembling if walked over it, like the head of a Devonshire creampot when a fly crawls over the surface. Yet should this crust give way, whoever breaks it is swallowed up in the chasm, where he must inevitably perish if not extricated by immediate help; thus it has happened that men have sunk into it over head and ears, who have never more been heard of. Quicksands are quite different from this, yet only by their gradual suction, whereas the effects of quagmires are instantaneous. To avoid these accidents, we crowded together as little as possible, which indeed occasioned a very long rear, yet we could not get over without several men sinking through it, as if the ice had broken under their feet, and some in my presence were up to their armpits but, happily, they were all extricated. In the afternoon we passed through two old fields, where formerly cassava seemed to have been planted, which indicated our certain approach to the Rebel settlement. And next falling in with Captain Meyland's old path (which we knew by the marks cut upon the trees), we were sure of it, but this evening it being too late to engage the enemy, we encamped a few miles from the swamp in which Captain Meyland with his party had been defeated.

Having had a very long march, and the men being much fatigued, Colonel Fourgeoud allowed both huts and fires, which indeed surprised me, being so near the Rebels, while at other times he prevented these comforts when he was sure to be a hundred miles from them. However, I availed myself of his bounty, and having got some pigeon peas from my sergeant, Fowler, which he had picked up in the old cassava grounds, and caught hold of one of the kettles, I invited him and a captain of the black corps called Hannibal to a share, who having conjointly with me thrown their salt beef and rusk biscuit into the mash, and stirred it round with a bayonet, we made a very excellent supper, but in a confounded dark, gloomy night with heavy rain.

Hannibal, observing that we should certainly see the enemy tomorrow, asked me if I knew in what manner Negro engaged against Negro, and having answered in the negative, he gave me the following relation.

Massera (said he), both parties are divided into small companies of eight or ten men and commanded by one captain, with a horn such as this (he showing me his). By that, they do everything I want, and either fight or run away, but if they go to fight, they separate immediately, lie down on the ground, and keep firing at the flash of each other's pans through the green. Each warrior is supported by two unarmed Negroes, the one to fill in his place if he is killed, and the other to carry away the dead body, and prevent it from falling into the hands of the adversary.[1]

From this discourse I perfectly understood his meaning, which I have since seen put in practice and which, for the clearer conception of the reader, I have now illustrated, with the following plan and where the whole engagement is seen at one view.

In this, the two columns *E* and *F* are supposed to be first engaged, where No. 1 in column *E* commences the attack by firing at random in the opposite bushes, and instantly retires by shifting his place to No. 1 in column *C,* where he reloads; while No. 2 in column *F* fires at the flash of his pan, and advances in the same manner, shifting his station to No. 2, to reload in column *D;* and at the flash of whose pan is fired by No. 3 in *E;* and again at his by No. 4 in *F;* &c., &c., this continuing in a seesaw manner, through both lines, till No. 8 has fired in *F,* when all have shifted their stations; and the same maneuver is continued with columns *C* and *D;* beginning again by the identical numbers 1, 2, 3, &c., at the top; and these lines having shifted their places, still the firing is repeated by the lines *A* and *B,* and thus ad infinitum, till by sounding the horn one of the parties gives way by flight, and the battle is over. I shall only add that when the forest is thick, in place of laying on their bellies, or kneeling, each Negro skulks at the back of a thick tree, which serves him as a bulwark, from which he fires at his adversary with more certainty[2] and less danger, like the Shawanese and Delaware Indians, according to Mr. Smith's tour through the United States of America, in that passage where Major Lewis was killed near the River Ohio.

Captain Hannibal mentioned to me also that Boni was supposed to be present in person among the adjoining Rebels, who was born in the forest among them, notwithstanding his being a Mulatto, but which was occasioned by his mother escaping to the woods from the ill treatment of her master, by whom she was pregnant. And having so often mentioned the different shades between black and white, I do in the same plate represent them to the reader at one view, where from the two above colors is produced the *Mulatto,* from that with black, the *Samboe,* and with white the *Quadroon,* &c. This sable warrior further made me acquainted with the names of several Rebel commanders, besides Boni, and against whom he had frequently battled for the Europeans, such as Quamy, who was the chief of a separate gang and had no connection with any others, Coro-

---

1. All the Negroes have a savage custom of mangling and tearing the bodies of their slain adversaries in a shocking manner, some even devouring part of them with their teeth like the Caribbee Indians, who are certainly cannibals.
2. Usually resting their pieces against the trunk or in the forked branches.

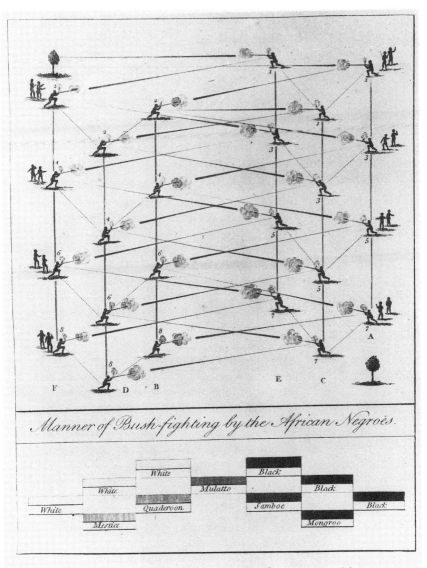

Manner of Bush-fighting by the African Negroes.

		White		Black
	White		Mulatto	Black
White		Quaderoon		Samboe	Black
	Mestice			Mongroo	

Gradation of Shades between Europe & Africa.

Plate 54

mantyn Codjo, Ariko, and Jolicoeur—the two last being celebrated captains, whose revenge was insatiable against the Christians, particularly
Jolicoeur, who had great reason indeed. He also mentioned the noted
Rebel Negro chief Baron, whom he believed was now serving under the
great Boni.

The names of the capital Rebel settlements, he said, were the following, viz., some already destroyed, some in view, and some of which only
the appellation was discovered, but all which I thought so very *sentimental*
that (as helping to elucidate our ideas of the Negro nation) I have thought
proper to give them a place in this narrative, together with their translations and meaning into English, viz.,

Boucou	It shall molder before it shall be taken.
Gado Saby	God alone knows it and no person else.
Cofaay	Come and try me, if you be men.
Tessee See	Take a tasting, if you have a liking.
Mele Me	Do disturb me, if you dare.
Boosy Cray	The woods lament.
Me Salasy	I shall be taken.
Kebree Me	Hide me, O ye surrounding verdure.

The others were:

Quamy Condre	From the name of the chief.
Pinnenburg	From the pines which formerly surrounded it.
Caro Condre	From the Indian corn or maize it produced.
Reisee Condre	From the quantity of rice it afforded.

Such were the names of the African warriors and their settlements. And
now in the hopes of a glorious victory, viz., to do good without commit-
ting cruelties, I shook hands with the black captain Hannibal, and fell
most profoundly asleep by fatigue (as I have said) in a dark gloomy night
with heavy rain, during which time I dreamt of nothing but blood and
gore, fire and smoke, &c.

On August 20th, we set out, still northeast towards the swamp, while
my melancholy evaporated with the rising sun, and which swamp we
entered about eight o'clock, when we soon found ourselves in the water
till above our middles, and expected (as Captain Meyland had met with)
a very warm reception on the opposite shore. However, having waded
through this marsh (which was above half a mile broad), the van rapidly
mounted the beach with cocked firelocks and screwed bayonets, the
whole body following close behind, without meeting with the smallest
opposition. But here was a spectacle almost sufficient to dampen the spirits of the most intrepid soldier, viz., the ground being strewn with the

skulls, bones, and ribs, still covered with part of the flesh and besmeared
with the blood of those unhappy men killed with Captain Meyland,
which that gentleman indeed had found means to bury, but which had
since been dug up by the Rebel Negroes, for the sake of their clothes, and
so they could mangle the bodies, by tearing them limb from limb like
savage brutes. Among these, the fate of Meyland's nephew, that promising young man, was peculiarly to be lamented, who came all the way
from the mountains of Switzerland in hopes of preferment, to be shot in
a marsh in Surinam, and whose bravery was equal to that of his uncle,
but whose intrepidity in voluntarily exposing himself had been too often
without any bounds. Such is the enthusiasm of ambition.

However, this being the second or third group of human bones we met
with during our peregrination, I frankly acknowledge they were no stimulant for me to engage with Negroes, while those relics seemed rather to
spur on the common soldiers with a view of taking revenge for the loss
of their massacred companions.

Having so often spoken of marching through a swamp, I think it will
not be amiss to illustrate the description by the annexed drawing, where
the first figure represents Colonel Fourgeoud, preceded by a Negro slave
as a guide, to give notice when the water is too deep, and followed by
some of his officers and private Marines, wading through the marsh in a
heavy shower of rain till above their middles, and carrying their ammunition and their accouterments above their heads as they can, to prevent
them from dragging through the swamp; while in the offing may be seen
how the slaves carry the burdens, and in what manner sometimes the
Rebel Negroes fire on the troops out of the palm trees &c., and which
situation of marching is certainly the most dangerous in Surinam, where
they may be attacked from under the surrounding bushes, without being
able to return the fire more than once, since in such a depth of water no
soldier can load his musket without wetting the lock, and who generally
is already too much animated by the heat of the action. But to proceed.

Being now come into a kind of a footpath made by the enemy, we had
only to follow it, which led us (after a little turning) in a due westerly
direction. At this time, Sergeant Fowler, who preceded the vanguard,
came to me declaring that the sight of the skulls &c., had made him terribly sick, and that he at this moment felt himself the greatest coward in
the party, being riveted to the ground without he could absolutely advance one single step, or knew what to do with himself to conceal it, and
I only having time to d——n him for a pitiful scoundrel, he lagged astern.
At ten o'clock we met a small party of the Rebels, each with a green
hamper on his back, who having fired at us, without we returned it, let
drop down their bundles and took to their heels, back towards their vil-

lage, and whom we since learned were transporting rice to another settlement for the subsistence of Boni's people, when they should be driven
from this called Gado Saby, which they daily expected ever since they
had been discovered by Captain Meyland. The green hampers (which
were most curiously plaited with the manicole leaves, and which they call
warimbos) our men cut open with their sabers, from which actually burst
forth the most beautiful, cleaned rice that ever I saw, which was scattered
and trampled underfoot, we having no opportunity to carry it along. A
little after this, we saw an empty shade where an outguard had been kept
to give intelligence of the approach of an enemy, but which deserted their
post.

We now vigorously redoubled our pace till about twelve o'clock, when
two more musket shots were fired by an advance guard of the enemy, as
a signal to Boni of our approach, and a little again after which we came
to a fine field with rice, Indian corn, &c., viz., Major Medlar and myself
with the vanguard, and a party of the Rangers. We here made a halt for
the two colonels, and to let the long rear close up, some of whom were
at least two miles behind us. However, in about half an hour we all got
together, and we once more proceeded by cutting through a small defile
of wood, into which we no sooner had entered, than (ding, dang) the
firing at last commenced from every side, the Rebels retiring and we advancing, till finally we arrived in the most beautiful, oblong, square field
with rice in full ripeness that ever I saw in my life, and in which appeared
to our view the Rebel town at a distance, in the form of an amphitheater
sheltered by the foliage of a few ranks of lofty trees which they had left
standing, the whole presenting a truly romantic and enchanting *coup
d'oeil* to the unconcerned spectator.

In this field, the firing now lasted like one continuous peal of thunder
for nearly forty minutes, during which time the Rangers acted with wonderful skill and gallantry, while the white soldiers were too much animated, the one firing over the other at random, yet a few of which I saw
with the greatest deliberation imitate the blacks, and among whom was
now the daunted Fowler, who being roused by the popping in the beginning of the onset, had rushed to the front and fully reestablished his tarnished character, by fighting the enemy at my side like a brave fellow, till
the muzzle of his gun was split by a shot from the Rebels, which prevented him from recharging. I myself received a ball between the shirt
and the skin, and my lieutenant, Mr. Cabanes, had the sling of his fusee
shot away, while several were wounded, some mortally. But I saw not a
single man drop dead at my feet, to my great astonishment, and for
which I will presently account.

The stratagem of the enemy of surrounding and interspersing the field

March thro' a swamp or Marsh, in Terra-firma.

Plate 55

with the large trunks and the roots of fallen trees made our advancing very different and dangerous, and at the back of which fortifications they lay lurking and firing upon us, without themselves could be materially hurt, and over numbers of which timbers we had to scramble before we could come to the town. However, we kept advancing, and while I thought this excellent generalship in them, their superstitious simplicity surprised me much, of which I'll only relate one instance. A poor fellow, trusting in his amulet or charm, by which he thought himself invulnerable, advanced frequently on one of these trees, till very near us, and having discharged his piece, walked off the way he came, to reload with the greatest confidence and deliberation, till at last one of my men (an intrepid Walloon named Valet) broke the bone of his thigh with a ball, and down he came, now crawling for shelter under the same tree which had supported him. But the soldier went up to him instantly, and placing the muzzle of his musket in his mouth, blew out his brains, in which manner several of his countrymen were knocked down. Even at this moment, my sensibility got so much the better of my duty, and my pity for these poor, miserable, ill-treated people was such that I was rather induced to fire with eyes shut, like Gil Blas when he was among the robbers, than to take a proper aim, of which I had frequent opportunities.

In short, being now about to enter the town, a Rebel captain wearing a tarnished gold-laced hat, and carrying a wisp of flaming straw in his hand, seeing their ruin inevitable, frustrated the storm in our presence by setting the town on fire, which by the dryness of the houses instantly occasioned one general conflagration, when the popping from the wood immediately ceased; and which masterly maneuver not only prevented that carnage to which the common soldier is too prone in the heat of victory, but gave them the opportunity of retreating with their wives and children, and carrying off their best lumber. While our pursuit, and even our falling on any of the spoils, was at once also frustrated by the ascending flames and the unfathomable marsh which we soon found to surround them. Upon the whole, to draw this picture would be a fruitless attempt. Thus I shall only say that the incessant noise of the firing, mixed with a confused roaring, hallooing, damning, and singing, the shrill sound of the Negro horns, the crackling of the burning houses, the dead and wounded all weltering in blood, the cloud of dust in which we were involved, and flames and smoke ascending were such a scene of beautiful horror (if I may use the expression) as would not be unworthy of the pencil of Hogarth—and which I have faintly tried to represent in the frontispiece, where I may be seen, after the heat of the action, dejectedly looking on the body of an unfortunate Rebel Negro stretched at my feet.

I have just said the battle was ended. And now made their appearance the two chiefs: Fourgeoud, having lagged astern to drink a basin of his *tisane,* being seized with a violent griping in his bowels from the time the firing began, which he called *un choc* or *coup de main,* and Colonel Sey-bourgh, having been employed in beating up the rear with his cane, and thus preventing them to hang an a——e. At this time, after congratulating each other with this glorious victory (though not a prisoner was taken), we washed off the dust, sweat, and blood, and refreshed ourselves with a dram and a bit of bread—the fatigues of the day, which was so scorch-ingly hot, having nearly exhausted us. We then went to inspect the smok-ing ruins of the town (while the dead were buried, and the wounded were dressed by the surgeons), which we soon discovered to have consisted in nearly one hundred houses, or huts, some two stories high.

Here, among the glowing ashes, were now picked up a few trifles that were saved from the flames, such as a silver spoon and fork with the mark of B-W,[3] some knives, earthen pots, &c., among which one with rice and palm-tree worms came to my share, which (having wanted no fire to dress the contents, and I wanting no appetite) I emptied in five minutes and seldom have made a better meal, though some were afraid it had been left behind with a view to poison us, which however proved to be with-out foundation. For the plate, which I determined to carry off as a trophy, I well rewarded the men who picked it up, and have made use of it ever since. But here we also found something of a different nature, viz., three skulls upon stakes, which were part of the relics of our own people for-merly killed. What surprised us was to find two Negro heads, which had the appearance to be fresh cut off, and which we since heard had been executed during the night of the 17th, when we heard the shouting and the firing.

Having buried them in one pit, we now returned to sling our ham-mocks, under those fine and lofty trees which I have before mentioned, where, I am sorry to relate, we shockingly saw the Rangers employed in playing at bowls with those heads they had chopped off from their ene-mies, and who related that on reconnoitering the surrounding skirts of the wood, they had found much scattered blood, of which the bodies had been carried away by the other Rebels. To stop or reprimand them from the above inhuman diversion was to no purpose, of which they seemed as fond as bloodhounds of carrion, telling us it was Negro fashion. And which festival they crowned, after mangling and kicking the heads, by cutting off their lips, cheeks, ears, and noses; they even took out the jaw bones, which they next barbecued or smoke-dried, together with the

---

3. Formerly pillaged from the estate Bruinswijk in Cottica.

right hands, to carry home to their wives and relations as trophies of their victory. That the above custom generally prevails among barbarous nations is a well-known fact, proceeding from a motive of insatiable revenge, and is no small proof that Man, the boasted Lord of the Creation, is in his natural state nearer connected to the brute than civilization (which, in other words, only is polity) shall be ever able to contradict. Indeed, in this one instance, Colonel Fourgeoud might have prevented their proceeding by his authority, but which in my opinion he sensibly avoided, observing that as he could not do it by persuasion, it would be breaking their native spirit to do it by his power. So much for barbarous customs.

It was now about three o'clock P.M., and we as I said were busied slinging our hammocks, when we were suddenly surprised by an attack from the enemy, but who after exchanging a few shots, were soon repulsed. This unexpected visit, however, put us upon our guard during the whole night, by allowing no fires to be lighted and doubling the sentinels all around the camp. Thus situated, I being excessively fatigued (besides several others), I ventured into my hammock, where I soon fell asleep; but not for longer than the space of an hour, when my faithful black boy Quacoo awakened me in pitch darkness crying, *"Massera, Massera. Boosee Negro, Boosee Negro,"* and hearing at the same time a brisk firing, while the balls rustled through the branches about me, I imagined no other than that the enemy was in the middle of our camp. In this surprise, and not perfectly awakened, I started up with my fusee cocked, and (not knowing where I ran) overset Quacoo, and next fell myself over two or three bodies that lay on the ground, and which I took to be shot. But one of which, damning me for a son of a bitch, told me *if I moved I was a dead man,* since Colonel Fourgeoud, with all his troops lying flat on their bellies, had issued orders no more to fire, the men having spent most of their ammunition the preceding day. I took his advice and soon discovered him to be one of our grenadiers, called Thompson.

In this situation we continued to lie prostrate on our arms till next morning when the sun rose, and during which time a most abusive dialogue ensued between the Rebels and the Rangers, both parties cursing and menacing each other at a terrible rate, the first reproaching the others as being poltroons, and betrayers of their countrymen, whom they challenged the next day to single combat, swearing they only wanted to wash their hands in the blood of such scoundrels who had been the capital hands in destroying their fine settlement, while the Rangers damned the Rebels for a parcel of pitiful skulking rascals, whom they would fight one to two in the open field if they dared to show their ugly faces, and that they had deserted their masters being too lazy to do their work, while they (the Rangers) would stand by the Europeans till they died. After which they insulted each other by a kind of war whoop, then sang victory songs, and sounded their horns in defiance; after which once more the popping began. And thus *ad perpetuum* the whole night till break of day, the music of their manly voices &c. resounding amid the echoing solitude and surrounding woods with redoubled force; and which being already dark and gloomy added much to an awful scene of pleasing dreadfulness; while according to me the *tout ensemble* could not but inspire the brave with thoughts of fortitude and heroism and stamp the trembling coward for what he is.

At last poor Fourgeoud entered into the conversation, by the help of myself and Sergeant Fowler, who spoke the language, as his interpreters, but which created more mirth than I before heard in the Colony. He promised them life, liberty, meat, drink, and all they wanted, but they replied with a loud laugh that they wanted nothing from him who seemed a half-starved Frenchman, already run away from his own country, and that if he would venture to give them a visit in person, he should not be hurt and might depend on not returning with an empty belly. They called to us that we were more to be pitied than themselves, who were only a parcel of white slaves, hired to be shot at, and starved for fourpence a day, and that they scorned to expend much of their powder upon such scarecrows, who had not been the aggressors by driving them into the forest and were only obeying the commands of their masters; but if the planters and overseers dared to enter the woods themselves, not a soul of such scoundrels should ever return, no more than the Rangers, some of whom might depend on being massacred that very day or the next, and they concluded by swearing that Boni should soon be the Governor of all the Colony. After this they tinkled their billhooks, fired a volley, gave three cheers which were answered by the Rangers, and all dispersed with the rising sun, to our great satisfaction, being heartily tired of such company.

Whatever small our loss, our fatigues were such that only the hardships suffered since by the British troops at Gibraltar could be compared to them, where also (notwithstanding the contest lasted such a length of time) the loss of men by the enemy's fire was but very inconsiderable. However, the mystery of our escape (which in Gibraltar was owing to fortification) was this morning unraveled by the surgeons who, dressing the wounded, extracted in place of lead bullets only pebbles, coat buttons, and silver coins, which could do us little harm, penetrating scarcely more than skin deep, while even gold could do themselves as little good in a wild forest, where they had nothing to buy for it. We also observed that several of the poor Rebel Negroes who had been shot had their pieces supplied only with the shard of a spa-water can in place of a flint, which could not so well answer the effect &c. And this must account for their little execution on the bodies of their cruel besiegers, who nevertheless were pretty well peppered with small scars, and contusions. Inconceivable are the many shifts which these people make in the woods.

Inventas aut qui vitam excoluere per artes;
Who by invented arts have life improved.

And where in a state of tranquillity they seemed, as they had said to us, to want for nothing, being plump and fat, at least such we found those that had been shot. For instance game and fish they catch in great abundance by artificial traps and springs, which they preserve by barbecuing, while with rice, cassava, yams, plantains, and so on, their fields are ever overstocked. Salt they make with the ashes of the palm trees, like the Gentoos in the East Indies, or use red pepper. We even discovered, concealed near the trunk of an old tree, a case-bottle with excellent butter, which—the Rangers told me—they made by melting and clarifying the fat of the palm-tree worms, and which fully supplied the above ingredient, while I absolutely found it more delicious. The pistachio or *pinda* nuts they also convert into butter, by their oily substance, and frequently use them in their broths. The palm-tree wine they are never in want of, which they make by cutting deep incisions of a foot square in the fallen trunk, where the juice being gathered, it soon ferments by the heat of the sun, when it is not only a cool and agreeable beverage but strong sufficient to intoxicate. And soap they have from the dwarf aloes. To build their houses, the manicole or *pina* tree answers the purpose; their pots they fabricate with clay found near their dwellings, while the gourd or the calabash tree gives them cups &c. The silk-grass plant and *maureecee* tree provide them in hammocks, and even a kind of cap grows naturally upon the palm trees, as well as brooms. The various kinds of *nebees* supply the want of ropes; fuel for fire they have for the cutting, while a wood called *bee-bee* serves for tinder to light it, by rubbing two pieces on each other, and which by its elasticity makes excellent corks. Neither do they want candles, being well provided with fat and oil, while the bees also afford them wax and a great deal of excellent honey. As for clothes, they scorn to wear them, preferring to go naked in a climate where the mildness of the weather protects them from that cursed incumbrance. The Rebel Negroes might breed hogs, fowls, &c., for their supply, and keep dogs for hunting and watching them, but this they decline from the apprehension of being discovered by their noise—even the crowing of a cock being heard in the forest at a considerable distance. After this digression, I shall return once more to my journal.

Colonel Fourgeoud now made it his next business to destroy the surrounding harvest, and this morning, I was ordered to begin the devastation with eighty Marines and twenty Rangers by cutting all the rice &c. that (as I have said) was plentifully growing in the two above fields, which I did. And during this time, I discovered a third field, south of the first, which I also demolished and made report of to Fourgeoud, to his great satisfaction.

In the afternoon was detached Captain Hamel, with fifty Marines and thirty Rangers, to reconnoiter behind the village and find out, if possible, how the Rebels alone found means to pass to and fro through an unfathomable marsh, while we could not pursue them. This gentleman discovered a kind of floating bridge made of *maureecee* trees, so fastened that but one man could pass abreast, on which were then seated a few Rebel Negroes to defend the communication, and who instantly fired on the party, but were repulsed by the Rangers, who brought down one of them but who was carried away by his companions.

It being now too late, on the morning of the 22nd our commander ordered a detachment to cross the bridge on discovery at all hazards. Of this party, I led the van, when we took the pass without opposition, and having all marched, or rather scrambled, over this defile of floating trees, we found ourselves in a very large field of cassava and yams, in which were about thirty houses but all forsaken, being the remains of the old settlement called Cofaay. In this field, we separated into three divisions to reconnoiter, viz., one marching north, one northwest, and the other west, when the mystery again was unraveled of why the Rebels had kept shouting, singing, and firing round us the whole night of 20th, viz., not only to cover the retreat of their friends by cutting off the pass, but by their unremitting noise preventing us from hearing them, who were the whole night employed—men, women, and children—in preparing hampers or *warimbos* with the finest rice, yams, cassava, &c., for their subsistence during their escape, and of which they had only left us the chaff and dregs for our contemplation, to our great and inconceivable astonishment. This most certainly was such a piece of generalship in a savage people, whom we affect to despise, as would have done honor to a European prince, and even Frederick the Great himself needed not to have been ashamed of it, with which remark I beg leave to end this long chapter.

CHAPTER 21st

Spirited conduct of the Rangers and Rebels—A skirmish—
Fine scene of brotherly affection—The troops return to
Barbacoeba—Plan of the field of action &c.—A slave killed
by the oroccoco snake

Colonel Fourgeoud, thus seeing himself fooled by a naked Negro, was ramping mad and swore he would pursue Boni to the world's end, but his ammunition and provisions were expended for the present, and even if they had not been, it would have been the most Don Quixote scene that could be invented to think now of overtaking them. However, the Hero persevered in this impracticable project, which he began by dispatching Captain Bolts with one hundred men and thirty Rangers, besides a number of slaves, to fetch a quantity of shot and a week's provisions from Barbacoeba. He also gave out orders to subsist on half allowance, which he bid the poor men supply by picking rice and preparing it the best way they could for their subsistence, which was also the lot of most of the officers, and of which number I was one. It was no bad scene to see ten or twenty of us, beating the rice with heavy wooden pestles, like so many apothecaries, in a species of mortar, cut all along the trunk of a leveled purple-heart tree for that purpose, viz., by the Rebels, before they had expected to be honored by our visit. This exercise was nevertheless very painful, and verified the sentence pronounced on the descendants of Adam, that they should eat bread by the sweat of their brow, which trickled down my forehead, in particular, like a deluge, yet which profusion of fluid we were at liberty plentifully to supply by water, but nothing else, this being at present the only beverage in the camp.

Among other vegetables, we had the good fortune to find here a great quantity of wild purslane, which only differs from the common in growing nearer the ground, the leaves being less, and more of a blackish-green color. This vegetable grows wild in the woods of Guiana, and may be either eaten as a salad or stewed, without reserve, being not only a cooling, agreeable food, but reckoned an excellent antidote against the scurvy.

We saw here also a great quantity of gourd, or calabash trees, which are very useful to the Negroes and natives of the country. This tree grows to the height of a common apple tree, with large, thick, pointed leaves. The gourds it produces are of different forms and dimensions, some being oval, some conical, and some round, growing often to ten or twelve inches in diameter. The shell is thin, hard, and very smooth, being covered over with a shining green skin or epidermis, which becomes brown when the gourd is dry and fit for use. The heart or pulp is a pithy or spongy substance, which is easily extricated by the help of a knife. Various are the uses to which these gourds are employed, such as bottles, powder horns, cups, basins, dishes, &c., while I myself seldom traveled without one, which served me by the way of a plate in the forest, and which the Negroes generally adorn by carving on the outer skin all sorts of fantastical figures, filling up the vacancies with chalk dust, when some of them are very pretty.

The Rangers, having been out to reconnoiter, returned this afternoon with the news that they had discovered still another field of rice to the northeast, which they had destroyed, and this pleased Colonel Fourgeoud very well, but when I in the dusk of the evening now observed to him that I saw several armed Negroes approach at a distance, he turned pale, exclaiming, "I am undone," and ordered the whole camp to turn out immediately for their defense. In a few seconds, these Negroes were sufficiently near, however, to discern that several among them were carried on poles in hammocks, when Fourgeoud again called out, "We still are totally ruined; this is no enemy but Captain Bolts, beaten back with all his party." And so it was, which unlucky gentleman (having delivered the wounded to the surgeons) made his report that, having entered the cursed swamp where Captain Meyland was defeated, he was attacked by the enemy on the opposite side, who had made a dreadful havoc among his Rangers, without hurting at this time one single European. Among these was a valiant fellow called Captain Valentine, who, while sounding his horn to animate his companions, it was not only shot away, with his pouch also, but himself dreadfully wounded in five different parts of his body. This man was met by his brother, named Captain Avantage, who seeing him mortally wounded, a scene of such real fraternal affection ensued as one seldom meets with in a civilized country. Kneeling at his side, he sucked out the blood and gore from his bloated breast, and cherished him by the manly promise that he should fight his foes until he himself was killed and should meet him again.

In short, Colonel Fourgeoud now saw that the Rebels had kept their promise of massacring the Rangers (some of which first, Captain Bolts had declared, openly fired from the tops of the palm trees on his men, after which sliding down with agility, they disappeared), while the latter were forming for revenge on their haughty adversaries and could hardly be restrained from an immediate pursuit.

Thus our Mighty Hero, now perceiving his mad scheme of following the enemy frustrated, and even in danger of total destruction, being cut off from every supply, while he had neither ammunition nor provisions left in his camp, and little else but sick and wounded to defend it, began seriously to consider a safe retreat, to which he was urged besides by the incessant murmuring of the troops in general, who were not only starved but harassed to death by daily fatigues and nightly watches.

Thus on August 24th, having detached one hundred and forty men, commanded by two field officers, to destroy the old settlement and field called Cofaay, and of which party I again had the honor to be one, the camp broke up in the afternoon immediately after our returning, during which last trip we had picked up out of the marsh some utensils, such as tea kettles, iron pots, &c., which the Rebels had formerly pillaged from the estates and had now thrown in the water to conceal them from us, with a view to returning and fishing them up when we should have left Gado Saby.

If during this last expedition we neither made captives nor booty, we nevertheless did the Colony a material piece of service by rooting out this concealed nest of their enemies, who being once discovered and driven away from their capital settlements (as I have remarked already) never more think of returning to live near the same spot. Indeed I may say more, and almost pronounce this last victory as decisive. I say almost, since except for demolishing a few plantations for immediate subsistence, and from a spirit of revenge, the Rebels were by this discovery struck with such a panic that from the present period not only their depredations were less, but they soon after retired so inaccessibly deep into the forest that they could neither do any material damage nor be joined by deserters.

But now I must relate an act at least of impolicy in Fourgeoud, which in the opinion of many deserves a worse epithet, viz., this evening on our way home, when we entered the noted marsh, he snatched up one of the empty bread-boxes which, having stuffed with a hammock, he carried before him crying *"Sauve qui peut."* At this moment, a Walloon named

Mattow stepped up to him and replied, "*Mon Colonel,* but few can, and I hope fewer will follow your example. Drop your shield, and don't intimidate your soldiers. One brave fellow creates others. Thus follow thy Mattow and fear for nothing," saying which he instantly threw open his bosom and, charging his bayonet, was the first man that mounted the opposite beach with intrepidity, when the rest soon followed. Meeting no opposition, we a little after encamped where we had passed the night before the action, and for the above act of heroism this private Marine was since promoted to be a sergeant. While I should think myself deficient in not paying the Walloon soldiers the compliment in general of being a parcel of very gallant fellows.

On the morning of the 25th, we again set out early and now having a beaten path before us, we reached our general place of rendezvous, Barbacoeba, on the afternoon of the following day, but in such a shocking situation that had the Rebel Negroes seen us they must not only have claimed the victory on their side, but absolutely have pitied us in the bargain. Almost the whole of the detachment were knocked up, the others starved, while every soul of the slaves were employed in carrying the sick and wounded, many mortally, in their hammocks on long poles, while they could hardly support themselves, which was the end of taking Gado Saby.

In the hopes it will not be disagreeable to the reader, and to show the masterly maneuvers of our sable foes to more advantage, I here present him with a plan of this extraordinary settlement, together with our different stages after leaving our encampment on the borders of the River Cottica, viz.,

Nos. 1, 2, and 3 are supposed to be the general rendezvous at Barbacoeba and the two succeeding days' marches.

No. 4. The spot where we heard the firing and shouting of the Rebel Negroes on the night of the 17th.

No. 5. The latitude where the troops were joined by the Rangers.

No. 6. The last night's encampment before the engagement.

No. 7. The beach on the opposite side of the marsh, where Captain Meyland with his troops had been defeated.

No. 8. The advanced post of the Rebels where the first shot was fired at the troops.

No. 9. The field with rice and Indian corn, entered without opposition.

No. 10. The pass or defile in which the firing commenced.

No. 11. The beautiful field with rice in which the action continued forty minutes.

No. 12. The town of Gado Saby, in flames at a distance.

No. 13. The spot from where the Rebels fired on the camp and held the conversation with them on the night between the 20th and 21st.

No. 14. The ground of the old settlement, Cofaay, with the floating bridge that covered the retreat of the Rebels.

No. 15. The different fields with cassava, yams, plantains, &c., that were discovered and demolished since.

No. 16. The field of rice destroyed by myself on the 21st.

No. 17. A field demolished by the Rangers on the 23rd.

No. 18. The swamp or marsh surrounding the settlement.

No. 19. The quagmire or *biree-biree* adjoining it, and

No. 20. The forest.

Having before mentioned how we erected our huts, I will here also add a small plan of the manner of arranging them during our encampment in the woods of Guiana, which was generally in the form of a triangle, as being the most secure way of defense in case of being surprised, but this was only when the situation of the ground would permit it, which was wide distant from being always the consequence. In this plan,

No. 1. Is the hut of Colonel Fourgeoud or the commanding officer in the center with a sentinel.

No. 2. The huts of all the other officers, in a small triangle surrounding the Commander in Chief.

No. 3. The angles of the outer triangle, being the huts of the privates in three divisions, viz., the main body, the van, and the rear guard, with sentinels at proper distances to cover the front.

No. 4. Powder chests, provisions, medicines, &c., &c., with a sentinel.

No. 5. The fires in the rear of each division to dress the victuals, and round which the Negro slaves are lodged on the ground.

No. 6. A coppice of manicole trees to erect the huts &c.

No. 7. A rivulet or creek to provide the troops with water, and

No. 8. The surrounding forest.

I shall now once more return to my narrative, by observing for the honor of Colonel Fourgeoud's *perspicacity,* that in place of Barbacoeba being in a state of sending him provisions at Gado Saby as he had wished, it could hardly afford daily bread to his emaciated troops that came to it, who having for so many days lived on rice, cassava, yams, Indian corn, &c., were soon after attacked by the flux. For while the above nourishment will keep the Indians and Negroes as strong as horses, the Europeans cannot long subsist upon it without animal food, and which was so scarce that even the Jew soldiers of the Society troops ate salt pork when they could catch it. For my own part, I was still among the few that were healthy, which was a miracle, having indeed fared very hard for want of my private provisions which, as I have mentioned, I had left at the neighboring estate Mocha. However, expecting now to go and fetch them in person, I was in good spirits also; but I was disappointed, Colonel Fourgeoud declaring he could not spare me a moment while I was well. Thus, I waited patiently for some opportunity to send for them, during which time I existed (sharing with my black boy) on the pitiful allowance of a private soldier, some mountain cabbage and palm-tree worms excepted, and a few *warapa* fish, and during which time Colonel Seybourgh treated all the captains with a roasted sheep, excepting me alone, at the same time hinting some reports not to my credit, relating to the time when I left Maagdenburg, which last insolence exasperated me so much that I swore that he, his sheep, and his reflection might go be d——nd together, concluding that in a little it would be ten to one but I would have a piece even of his tongue, and instantly wrote for a certification from the surgeon of the regiment.

This sarcasm extremely pleased most of the officers, whose hatred for him was as strong as their regard for me, and who generously offered to supply me with some wine, and share of their provisions, of which I however declined partaking, while themselves who enjoyed less health stood very much in need of them. Yet so famished was I at this time, that I vow to God I could almost have wished myself in an English kennel, where I might feed plentifully with my brother hounds on a piece of carrion, while indeed the Irish beef that was left among us was little better, from which when a worm deserted, I caught him back not to diminish the quantity. As for the miserable slaves, they were now so starved that, having killed a *quata* monkey (the Lord knows how), they broiled it with the skin, hair, guts and all, which they devoured with their teeth before it was half dressed, like a parcel of cannibals, offering me a limb, which however, hungry as I was, I thought proper to refuse. Upon the whole, had I not at this time been possessed of sterling health and spirits, I must have sunk under the load of oppression.

And on the 1st of September, the bloody flux raging in the camp to a high degree, he sent off all the sick officers and privates, without exception, not to be recovered in the grand hospital at Paramaribo, but to linger and die in the rivers, where they were to relieve others to undergo the same misery, viz., his own sick to Maagdenburg in Commewina, and those of the Society to Vredenburg in Cottica. So severe was Colonel Fourgeoud to the officers that even those who were past recovery could not have a servant of the troops to attend them, whatever price they offered, some of whom I have seen extended between two trees, while the filth for want of assistance was dripping through their hammocks. Of

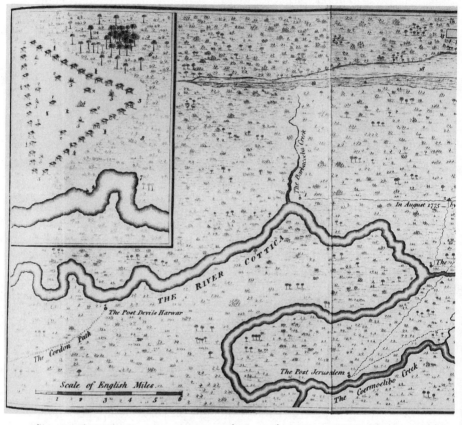

_ *Plan of the* **Principal FIELD of ACTION** *between the Rivers COTTICA and MARAWINA;*

Plate 56

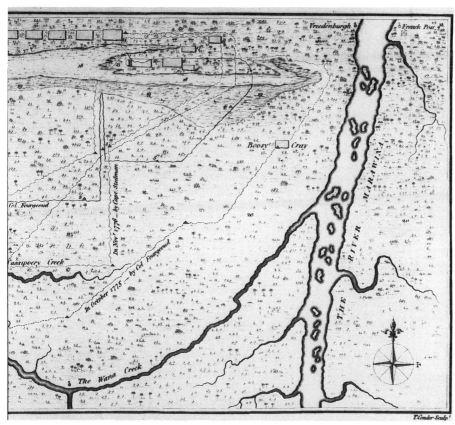

with a Sketch of the manner of Encamping in the WOODS of SURINAM.

this number was Ensign Strows, yet whom he nevertheless, in this dreadful situation, ordered to be transported to Devil's Harwar.

At last Colonel Fourgeoud himself was seized with the flux, when his beloved *tisane* could little more avail, yet he soon recovered by the plentiful use of claret and spices, which his companion Seybourgh made use of as a preservative against the loss of his health, but which by swallowing in overplentiful doses rather promoted the loss of the little he had remaining of his reason.

In such a situation, and in such a despicable encampment, the Old Gentleman had nevertheless the vanity to expect a deputation from the court at Paramaribo, with congratulations on his victory, in consequence of which he had built an excellent shade, and sent for a few sheep and hogs to entertain them. But the deputies never arriving, he cut their throats for the poor soldiers, to whom for the first time in his life he distributed one pound each.

Indeed, their number was at present very small, which was, however, recruited the day following by a hundred men from Maagdenburg in Commewina, and by nearly as many from the Society post Vredenburg in Cottica, who brought the account that Mr. Strows was dead at Devil's Harwar, besides a great number of privates who had assisted at the taking of Gado Saby and who had expired while they were being transported from Barbacoeba. The intelligence now also arrived that the defeated Rebels had crossed the River Cottica below Patamacca, intent on mischief and marching westward. In consequence of which a captain and fifty men were immediately detached by water to reconnoiter the banks near the Pinnenburg Creek, who returned the eighth and confirmed the unhappy intelligence. However, our indefatigable chief again determined to pursue them, but had no slaves to carry the ammunition and provisions, since they had been sent home to their masters' estates nothing but skin and bone. I shall relate what happened the two days following, till the arrival of the fresh ones, viz.:

On the ninth were sold to the best bidder and on credit the goods of the deceased Ensign Strows, for which the poor soldiers, regardless of any price and only wishing to come at some clothes and refreshments to keep soul and body together, actually paid at the rate of seven hundred per cent.

On the 12th, the good Mrs. Godefrooy again sent up a flat-bottomed barge with a fat ox, oranges, plantains, &c., for the private soldiers; the ox was accordingly knocked in the head and the vegetables distributed among them. The same evening some little provisions also arrived for me from Joanna, with a few bottles of wine, though part was stolen and part was damaged on the way, which nevertheless made me extremely happy.

When we talk of provisions in the woods, we only mean such as rum, sugar, lime juice, coffee, tea, Boston biscuit, and cheese, and sometimes a bacon-ham or a keg of sausages, since not much else can be carried through the forest by a single Negro slave, we being allowed no more. Indeed, shirts, stockings, and shoes are generally necessary, but of the two last articles I never made any use, being accustomed, as I have said before, to walk barefooted, which I had now practiced for above two years, with considerable benefit to my limbs, when compared to the ulcerated and rotten shanks of my companions. The fresh supply of our Negro slaves now being arrived, the necessary preparations were made to pursue the Rebels the very next day, directing our first course toward the spot formerly called Jerusalem, of which I have made mention in 1773, when I commanded the fatal cruise in upper Cottica.

September 13th. At last being prepared to leave Barbacoeba, the provisions &c. were sent before us by water to Jerusalem, escorted by the sick officers and private men, while several others already unfit for duty went to recover in the rivers, and three of the last-come slaves deserted to return to their masters. Indeed, so very scarce were men at present, Fourgeoud's whole army being a second time mostly knocked up, that till further orders not any of the sick gentleman were allowed a servant to attend them, while the poor slaves were obliged to do double drudgery and were persecuted in the most barbarous manner, by beating them, starving them, and fatiguing them to death. For instance, this morning I saw the free Negro Gousary knock down a poor black man for not taking up his load, and Fourgeoud knock him down a second time for doing it too soon, while the wretch not knowing what to do, called out for mercy in the name of Jesus Christus and was actually knocked down a third time by an enthusiast, for daring to use a name to which he had not the smallest pretensions. I have before remarked that the above Gousary, with his companion Akara, had been Rebel captains in the colony Berbice where, before they surrendered, they had committed the most diabolical murders. These were the men whom Fourgeoud now employed to manage the slaves, and with whom they had no more compassion than if they had been beating on tanned leather.

In short, the camp broke up, and bidding farewell to Barbacoeba, we entered the woods keeping course southeast, and passed the night on the opposite beach of the Cassipera Creek. During this day's march, a large drove of *warree hogs* or wild boars broke through our line, several of whom were cut down by the men with their sabers, and stabbed by their bayonets, but none shot, firing at game being forbidden by the Commander in Chief. These were cut in pieces and divided among the whole, to whom they proved a very seasonable dainty.

On September 14th, we marched southwest till about noon and arrived at Jerusalem, where the van had got an hour before us, being all thoroughly soaked by the heavy rains, and one or two men with ruptures in the groin by falling over roots and large stones. Here, to my great astonishment, we again found the identical Mr. Vinsack with a hundred fresh Rangers, who having heard of the Rebels passing upper Cottica, had been prevailed upon to resume his office, and now once more offered his service to Colonel Fourgeoud, who was happy to accept it.

Just as we entered the above camp, which was much overgrown with long grass, one of the slaves unfortunately was bitten in the foot by a small serpent called here the *oroccoco* snake, from its color resembling the bird of that name (to wit, the owl). In less than a minute, the man's leg began to swell, while he was seized with the most excruciating pains, and soon after got convulsions. At this time, one of his companions having killed the snake, made the patient drink its gall mixed with half a glass of spirits, which I gave him, and he seemed (perhaps from imagination) to bear his misfortune with more temper. However, not for long, when the fits rather increasing than not, he was instantly sent to his master's plantation where he died.

September 16th. Having rested here one day, Colonel Fourgeoud detached two strong parties to reconnoiter, viz., Lieutenant Colonel Des Borgnes with one hundred men to the Wana Creek in upper Coermotibo, and Colonel Seybourgh with an equal number to the creek Pinnenburg in upper Cottica, which last returned just before midnight with two canoes he had found hauled ashore on the opposite side, and not far below the mouth of the Claas Creek. This immediately confirmed that the Rebels had gone westward intent on mischief, having brought the empty canoes down the Claas Creek from the Rice Country, to send them back loaded with booty from the estates they had in view to pillage.

In consequence of this news, the proper preparations were immediately made to pursue them with vigor, and the fruits of which expedition I intend to make the subject of the following chapter.

CHAPTER 22nd

*Alarm in the Perica River—A detachment marches to its
relief—Ambuscade—Wonderful effect of the biting of a bat—
Scene in a quagmire*

On September 19th, Colonel Seybourgh marched with one hundred Marines and forty Rangers, who did me the honor to pitch on me for one of his party, and who was upon the whole so civil and so polite, in opposition to what he had been lately, that I knew not at all how to account for it. In short, having crossed the Coermotibo Creek, we kept course southwest by south till we came near the River Cottica, where we encamped.

September 20th, we followed along the banks of the River Cottica till near the Claas Creek, which I formerly swam across with my saber in my teeth, and slung our hammocks early, while I was detached with a few Rangers to lay an ambuscade in the mouth till it was dark. Here, however, I discovered nothing at all, except that the Rangers were possessed of the same superstition as the Rebels with regard to their amulets or *obias* making them invulnerable. They told me that, just as the latter got them from their priests, so they bought them from their Graman Quacy, a celebrated and cunning old Negro whom I will in proper place circumstantially describe. "D——n you, fool," said I. "How, then, do any of you or them come to be shot?" When I was answered, "Because like you, *Massera,* they had no faith in the amulet or *obia*." This piece of policy in Mr. Quacy, however, had the virtue of making all his free countrymen brave fellows, whose undaunted valor had so often surprised me, besides it was no small accumulation to his own wealth, which for a black man in Surinam was not a trifle.

On September 21st, an express arriving by water from Colonel Fourgeoud that the alarm guns[1] had been fired in the River Perica, we instantly crossed to the opposite or west shore of the River Cottica. There, the Rangers, with a party of Marines, were again ordered to lie concealed in ambuscade, in hopes of cutting off the Rebels or their retreat, when they should return to cross Cottica with the booty. In the afternoon, a Rebel Negro was seen with a green hamper, who, alarmed by the smell of tobacco (some of the Rangers smoking), stopped short of his own accord. He was instantly fired at by me and a Ranger, and the *warimbo* or hamper dropped, but he himself escaped. This bundle we found stuffed with a dozen of the finest table linens, a cocked gold-lace hat, and a couple of superb India chintz petticoats, which I gave all to my black companions, the two last articles excepted, reserving them as a present for Joanna. The free Negroes or Rangers, now rushing forward like hounds to meet the enemy, I asked liberty to follow them, and calling for volunteers, a great number presented themselves, which, however, Colonel Seybourgh reduced to four only, with which he sent me off. And having scrambled through thorns and briars (woven together like a net) which tore one of my legs in a terrible manner, I overtook them. Shortly after which we discovered thirteen fresh huts where the Rebels, by conjecture, had slept but a few nights before. In consequence of this, I now dispatched a Ranger back to Colonel Seybourgh to give him the intelligence and ask permission for the Rangers and myself to march forwards to Perica without delay, but the answer was for us instantly to rejoin him without omission. We now returned to the camp, the Rangers in particular very discontented, and making wonderful remarks, where we found a reinforcement just arrived from Jerusalem of sixty men, black and white, with positive orders for us to break up and march early the next morning for Perica River. During this whole night a strong party again lay in ambush.

At six o'clock next morning all was ready, but some unaccountable dilly-dally taking place, it was very late before we left the camp, during which time we were informed that a canoe had been seen crossing the river with one single Negro in it, who was no doubt the poor fellow on whom we had fired the day before.

I cannot here forbear relating a singular circumstance respecting myself, viz., that on waking about four o'clock in my hammock, I was extremely alarmed at finding myself (like a cold fowl in jelly) weltering in congealed blood and without feeling any pain whatever. In short, the

---

1. By this are meant minute-guns which are fired on those estates which are in danger and, which being regularly answered by the neighboring plantations, soon alarm the whole river, and bring assistance.

mystery was that I had been bitten by the *vampier* or *specter of Guiana,* also called the *flying dog* of New Spain, which is none other than a monstrous large bat that sucks the blood from men and cattle when they are asleep, sometimes till they die. And as the manner in which they proceed is truly wonderful, I will give an account of it. Knowing by instinct that the person they intend to attack is in a very sound slumber, they pitch generally near the feet where, while they keep fanning (with their enormous wings to keep them cool) they bite a small piece out of the tip of the great toe, which orifice is so very small that the head of a pin could not be received into it, and is consequently not painful, yet through which opening they keep on sucking blood till they degorge it. They then begin again and thus continue sucking and degorging till they are scarce able to fly and the sufferer sometimes sleeps from time into eternity. Cattle they generally bite in the ears, but always in such places where the blood flows spontaneously, perhaps in an artery, but for this I must leave the faculty to account. Having now got the wound filled with tobacco ashes, as the best cure, and washed the gore from myself and also from my hammock, I observed several small heaps of congealed blood upon the ground, all around the place where I had lain, the surgeon judging by conjecture I had lost at least twelve or fourteen ounces during the night.

I have said already that it was very late before we left the camp, by some unaccountable dilly-dally. However, we started at last (I having the vanguard) with the Rangers, and the poor Marines loaded, N.B. with nine days' provisions on their backs. In this condition we had not proceeded long when one of the Rangers sounded his horn and they spread out (I among them) and fell down flat on the ground, with firelocks cocked and ready to engage, but which proving to be a false alarm caused by a stag rushing through the foliage, we all soon rose and rejoined. Having marched plumpety-plump the whole day through the water and mud, at three P.M. we encamped on a high ridge where not a drop of it was to be met with, till we had dug a hole for the same purpose, when it was so thick that we were obliged to drink it through a cloth. Here I was again accosted by the lieutenant colonel, who invited me to some supper in his hut and treated me, upon the whole, with very uncommon civility.

On September 23rd, we again marched course west and northwest, while it rained very hard and we entered in a quagmire that lasted three hours. To me who had the rear today, it was peculiarly distressing, the Negro slaves with their burdens sinking under the surface every moment, while the loaded Marines had enough to do to mind themselves, and I was too weak by the late loss of blood &c. to give them any assistance. Coming near the beach, I perceived several dead Negroes scattered on the ground, with their heads and right hands chopped off, while the bodies were fresh, which made me conclude they must have been Rebels very lately killed in some engagement by the troops and Rangers stationed in the Perica River, while had we been allowed to pursue on the 21st, when we were ordered back, the enemy must have been between two fires, in which case few could have escaped, and all the plundered spoil must have been retaken, just as would have happened two years before when I was stationed at Devil's Harwar. Had I been at such times provided with men and ammunition to pursue, I might have done the Colony a material piece of service, and which two capital blunders I am sorry to relate—but adherence to truth and impartiality obliges me to it. Let these remarks not brand me with the name of cruel, since no one could have a greater feeling at seeing such manly youths stretched dead among the shading foliage as now I saw, and finer bodies than two of them in particular were never beheld in any country.

Such is the fate of war which, however dreadful through all its different stages, is no less a necessary evil, and which can no more by man than by the other links of the creation be avoided. *En fin,* during my making the above remarks, my poor loaded slaves remained still entangled and struggling in the quagmire, while the commanding officer with all the other troops (having got on a dry ridge), were fairly out of sight, and out of hearing, by which separation the rear guard with all the provisions &c., and in such a situation particularly, not only ran the hazard of losing all the baggage but of being cut to pieces in the bargain. Having not a single European that had strength remaining, I now gave over the command to my lieutenant, and rushed forward myself through the wood till I overtook the party, when reporting the situation of the rear guard to Colonel Seybourgh, I begged he would slacken his pace till they were able to extricate themselves and come up from the marsh, without which I could not be accountable for the consequence. To this, the reply was that he would make camp when he met with good water, and I returned instantly to the rear. Having now struggled till it was pitch dark, in a most distressed and dangerous situation, the last man was finally dragged out of the mud, and we proceeded on till we entered the camp.

On the morning of the 27th, we now once more finally broke up, and arrived in the forenoon at the estate Soribo in the River Perica, to defend the plantations, but which was already completed, as I supposed it would be, before we made our appearance, having been six days cruising upon a march which, by going straightforward, might have been performed in three.

On the 28th, Colonel Seybourgh with the other officers went to dine and carouse at the other post, called Belair, where the whole was invited, and which party returned in the evening with two live sheep which I

alone never tasted, and the Perica news, viz., that on the 20th, the estates
Schoonauwen and Altona had been pillaged by the Rebels whom we had
routed at Gado Saby, and who had also paid a visit to the plantation Poel-
wyk, but been beaten back by the slaves; that the Rangers stationed at an
estate called 's-Haagenbosch had pursued them on the 21st, overtaken
them on the 23rd, killed several, and brought back most of the booty;
also that on that very day, another party of the Rebels had made an attempt to seize the powder magazine at 's-Haagenbosch while the Rangers
were in pursuit of their associates (which was extremely cunning), but
had been repulsed by the manly behavior of a few armed slaves, one of
whom (belonging to the estate Timotibo) took an armed Rebel by himself and next discovered their camp at the back of his master's plantation,
for which he was handsomely rewarded; and from all which I and a few
other gentlemen made up the conclusion that, if Seybourgh's party on the
16th had marched forward in place of retiring (which, however, were
then his orders), the above whole mischief that happened since at Perica
might have been prevented and the retaliation of the Rebels frustrated,
that the fellow we fired at on the 21st was certainly one of the plunderers
on the 20th,[2] and that the bodies found dead on the 23rd had been shot
that very same day.

2. If this loaded Negro could walk from Perica to Cottica in two days, query: Why could
not Mr. Seybourgh have marched it in three? (N.B. six was the actual number.)

CHAPTER 23rd

Second march to Gado Saby—Account of a living skeleton—
Enchanting landscapes—Devastation—The Commander in
Chief falls sick and leaves the camp—Some Rebels taken—
Misery

On October 9th, Colonel Fourgeoud returned from the Wana Creek, having sent down the half of his party sick in barges, who the day following (they being greatly augmented by the invalids of Jerusalem) were all transported to receive the *coup de grace* in the hospital at Devil's Harwar. Meanwhile, all the Rangers took their leave and marched with their conductor, Mr. Vinsack, to the Perica River. Fourgeoud's news was that, having found during his cruise a hundred empty houses, and seen a few straggling Rebels but taken none, he also found a scalp fixed to the branch of a tree, which we conjectured to be the remains of the unfortunate Schmidt who was lost, and which is here very uncommon as no *tomahawk* is ever to be seen in all this country.

Three days after this came up Quacoo (who was recovered) and the news that Captain Stoelman with some Rangers had espied a fresh nest of Rebels (by a large smoke in the forest appearing at a distance) but had not yet attacked them; that Captain Friderici with a party of sable volunteers was ranging the Lee Shore below Paramaribo; that the two men we had lost on the 18th of August had miraculously found their way to the post at the Marawina River; and that no less than twelve fine Negro slaves had just deserted from the estate the Gold-Mine to join the Rebels. This last so animated Colonel Fourgeoud that this indefatigable man (being determined to persevere to the last drop) again entered the woods early on the morning of the 15th, although he and his little army were now reduced to next to nothing, and having but the evening before buried one of his own countrymen, a volunteer called Matthew. But death was so common to us on this expedition that after losing our dearest friend or relation, the first question generally asked was "Has he left any rum, brandy, or tobacco?" *"Pauvre Laurant,"* said I to his shriveled *valet de chambre* (for being still healthy, I was again selected to be one of this party), "the brave Fourgeoud is like fire. He is to the Colony an excellent servant, but I think to both you and me a d——nd bad master." The man shrugged up his shoulders, replied *"Oui, foutre,"* with a heavy sigh, and entertained me with a pinch of snuff.

We set out exactly northeast, when just a little before starting seven Negro slaves again ran away to their masters, and about an hour after, my box with all my bottles was dashed to pieces by falling from the head of another, to such a rate were these wretches disgusted and fatigued. This evening we encamped, unknown to us, near the Cassipera Creek. Thus having no water, we dug a pit for it as we had done before, and no more huts were allowed to be built till further orders, which indeed was now of little consequence, the dry season being fairly set in. The day following, we again marched northeast when we arrived where Fourgeoud had discovered the hundred houses, and which was no other than a temporary settlement erected by the Rebels as a shelter or asylum on their expected retreat, before they were dislodged by us at Gado Saby, and to which they had given the name of Boosy Cray, the Woods Lament. On this spot we encamped and took particular notice of Boni's house, which was built like a watering machine, elevated from the ground, and with two doors, that he might the better see around him and prevent a surprise, also to keep him more healthy, he having in some action received a dangerous wound in the groin, which we knew since by a prisoner. Near Boni's house were the private baths, here being no river, where his women washed themselves morning and evening.

On October 18th, having again marched the same course for a few hours, we fell in with a beaten path which (though in a roundabout way) seemed to be a communication between Gado Saby and Boosy Cray, and having followed this, which now led us due west for a few hours, we found a miserable Rebel Negro, just alive and no more, covered over with manicole branches. He was nothing but skin and bone, and had one eye nearly knocked out of the socket. I put my bottle to his mouth and he swallowed a few drops of rum and water when he said with a low voice *"Dank ye, me massera,"* but could say nothing more. Fourgeoud ordered him to be carried with us in a hammock, and we encamped near a *biree-biree* or quagmire.

Innumerable indeed are the various fine trees that are daily met with in this country, and where they may be had for the cutting. Yet when one considers the distance some grow from the rivers, the great labor in felling and working them, the number of slaves required to drag them through the forest, where no horses can be employed, the many dangers, and loss of time, &c., the enormous price for best timber in Guiana will be easily accounted for.

I am well persuaded that while some of my readers wish me in Greenland for these digressions, others wish me at the Devil for dwelling at all on the expeditions &c., but I have read the fable of the man, the boy, and the ass, and while I am well convinced that I cannot please all the world, I will at least, by those varieties, have a chance to gratify a few of every denomination without exception. This is my plan and, assuredly, a better one than to be tied down to the whims of one particular set of people. Thus I will ever (gentle critics) proceed in my own way.

Most enchanting were some parts of the forest which we passed during this march, to which the dry season much contributed, and where simple nature greatly outshone and overpassed the most strenuous endeavors of art, such as open green savannas interspersed with meandering brooks of limpid water, the borders adorned with rural flowers, while here and there small clumps of elegant shrubs, or a single beautiful tree, scorned to be left growing designedly to enrich the scene, the whole surrounded by a vast wood of lofty palmettos, waving their sea-green foliage above the variegated copses of never-fading verdure, blossom, and fruit, as if to invite the panting wanderer under its cooling shades, till in the cooler hours he may return to enjoy the bracing pleasures of the crystal flood, and contemplate nature's beauties undisturbed! One universal silence reigned all around. How often now did I think on Joanna, and wish with herself alone to swim through life in these Elysian Fields, while as oftentimes I thought on the primitive bliss enjoyed by our first parents in the Garden of Eden.

October 19th, we fell in with our own old path, which we followed, leading directly to the fields of Gado Saby, where quantities of rice &c. appeared again in full bloom, and (which we having cut down and burnt) the poor Rebel Negro was ordered (neither seeming to die or recover) to be buried alive, and so he was. However, not covered up with earth but, by my care, with green boughs, after which we slung our hammocks being almost choked with smoke.

On the 20th, we marched to visit Cofaay, when I observing the unhappy captive Negro still alive, after removing the branches, he was by my intercession once more transported with us, while the slaves being discontented with such a load, took every opportunity in my absence to torture him by bouncing him against stones and roots as they went along, and dragging him through mud and water, &c. Here different patrols went out to reconnoiter, while the rest encamped in the western part of Cofaay, who, besides several carcasses (being the relics of our late engagement) also discovered no less than four beautiful fields in one chain, still due west from Cofaay and stocked with cassava, yams, plantains, maize, pistachio nuts, and pigeon peas, all which, the morning following, were again cut down and destroyed by fire. After this, returning to our last night's camp, we found it in flames, and in consequence slung our hammocks east in the skirts of the woods. Now recollecting that the poor Rebel black was left all alone, I ran back by myself to the burning camp to afford him some assistance, but where having sought him in vain for a considerable time, through a thick cloud of smoke, I was glad to save myself from being lost or made a captive by returning before it was dark to my companions, who only laughed at me and blamed me much for my temerity. Thus was this miserable object consumed by the flames, who but the day before had escaped from being buried before he was dead.

Having now completed the devastation, we marched back to Jerusalem, where we arrived perfectly exhausted on the 24th; the Old Gentleman was at last so ill himself with a frenzy fever that he was confined to his hammock and not expected to live through the night, which indeed was the sincere wish, however wicked, of all the camp.

But still he persisted in commanding, and the following morning showed his authority by ordering a private Marine to run the gauntlet, viz., to be flogged through the ranks with leather slings till within an inch of his life, for having dared to cough (he being bad with a cold) within his hearing, and by bastonading another who was barefooted for asking shoes. A captain was also dismissed from the service and confined in Fort Zeelandia for having married without asking his consent, &c., &c., &c.

In short, sickness and death again raged through the camp, and everything was in the greatest confusion. On the 1st of November, twenty-five Negro slaves again ran away, and on the 3rd came the news that no less than fifty armed Rebels were seen swimming across the River Cottica, about a musket shot above Barbacoeba. In consequence, Seybourgh was sent out on a patrol with the few remaining healthy men, who were almost ready to attack their own officers for hunger and distress, smoking paper and chewing leaves and leather to supply the want of tobacco.[1] As

---

1. All soldiers, sailors, and Negroes are perfectly miserable without this ingredient, which, they say, keeps up their spirits, and which some almost prefer to bread.

for myself, few people at this time could be more wretched, having hitherto received neither my provisions nor clothes from Mocha. Thus was I almost naked as well as starved, with a running ulcer in my left foot, since the ambuscade in Perica; and not a friend who could give me any assistance. While to make my misery complete, my remaining blood was, during the two following nights, sucked away by the vampire bat or specter, till I fainted in my hammock, and was almost sorry to recover, particularly when being informed by a letter that Joanna and her boy were dying with a putrid fever at Paramaribo.

On November 12th, at last, arrived one of my boxes from the estate Mocha with Sergeant Fowler, which fellow (independent of my situation) made me laugh aloud when producing now a letter from his mother in Europe, written in rhyme and copied from an old almanac without either sense or meaning, yet it made him happy. My box did me the same, though three-fourths of my things were rotted and devoured by the cockroaches &c. This evening also Colonel Seybourgh's party returned, having seen nothing, and two days after this Colonel Fourgeoud was so dangerously ill that at last he determined, the next day following, to relinquish his command and go to town for his recovery.

On November 15th, went down sick to Paramaribo Colonel Fourgeoud (and a whole bargeful of others to Devil's Harwar in the hospital), who having sacrificed all his troops, had at last fallen himself a victim to his unbounded ambition and avarice, for he and they might have toiled much less, and lived much better, had this poor man but chosen it, while equally as much service for the Colony might have been performed. In short, even had he possessed all the military virtues of Caesar or Alexander, they must have been despicable so long as he lacked the feelings of a man, and these no one stood in need of in more superlative degree (perhaps Nero or Seybourgh excepted) than did the identical Colonel Louis Henry Fourgeoud.

The command of the remaining scarecrows now devolved on the good lieutenant colonel who, strange to tell, that very evening inherited the distemper with the supremacy, for no sooner was the barge with the Old Hero rowed out of sight, than this gentleman was attacked in the same manner with a frenzy fever, which indeed now was very common among all ranks, broiling at Jerusalem under a burning sun (for it was now in the dry season), when we ought to have been in the woods, but for which excursions, as I have said before, the heavy rains were most unhappily preferred.

On December 3rd returned, after fourteen days' absence, Major Medlar's party with a captive Rebel woman and her boy, about eight years old, taken in a small field with bitter cassava; the poor woman was pregnant and under very great alarms, but tenderly treated by Medlar, who was always a humane, well-thinking gentleman. But most unluckily, he had lost two of his best men, one Schoelar, a corporal, and the other called Philip van de Bos, a private Marine, who (having meant to refresh themselves with a few roots of the above cassava) were both inadvertently poisoned and died during the night with excruciating pains and convulsions. The antidote is said to be cayenne pepper and spirits, neither of which were at that time to be had.

The woman confirmed that Boni was wounded, besides the names of Gado Saby and Boosy Cray; she said the poor Negro we had found was called Isaac and that he had been left for dead; and that one Captain Ariko had a new settlement near the sea called Fissy Hollo. Nothing could equal, she assured us, the discipline that Boni kept up among the Rebels, who was absolutely despotic, and had executed two of his people but three days before we took Gado Saby, only on suspicion of having hinted a few words in favor of the Europeans.[2] She said none of his people were trusted with arms except such as had first served him some years as slaves, and had given him unquestionable proofs of their bravery and fidelity, and which were but few in number compared to the others who were his vassals, and bound to do (without murmuring) just exactly as he thought proper, but that he was still more beloved than he was feared, on account of his inflexible justice, and great courage.

The following day the poor woman and her boy were sent to Paramaribo with Ensign Cabanes, who had seized them, and had nearly taken a young girl about fifteen but who, through her great agility and being stark naked, slipped through his hands. It being proved at the Court that the above woman had been forcibly carried off by the Rebels (though many years before), the poor thing was pardoned, and joyfully returned to her master's plantation. It was very remarkable that when the boy saw the first cow or horse, he nearly fell into convulsions with terror, nor could he bear to be approached by any white person, he never having seen one before, and whom in his language he called *yorica,* signifying the Devil.

On the 11th, came the news that a number of armed Rebels were just seen opposite to Devil's Harwar, who proved since to be on their retreat from the River Commewina, where on the 5th they had burnt the dwelling house of the estate Killenstyn Nova, with Mr. Slighter, the overseer,

---

2. During the night of the 17th of August, when we heard the frequent firing and hallooing, and which were the two heads we found on the 20th placed upon stakes.

in it, ransacked the whole plantation, killed and carried off thirty-three Negro women, and chopped off the limb of a Mulatto child with a saber in revenge to its father, and that the Rangers from Perica were in the woods for their pursuit. The same day arrived Captain Friderici, who was now entered from the Society troops into Fourgeoud's regiment, and who confirmed to us the above Rape of the Sabines &c. Meanwhile, finally (after starving four months), I received all my things from Mocha, three parts rotted and devoured by the cockroaches, and the rest of which I distributed among the sick Marines. Also the cheering account that my little family were past danger and recovering at Paramaribo, which so much raised my spirits that the following morning I reported myself fit for duty, which, Heaven knows, I was not, but to which I was also much induced for want of air and exercise in my confinement. This evening, a boat full of Caribbee Indians rowed up Coermotibo for the River Marawina, by the communication of the Wana Creek.

On December 20th, orders being arrived from Colonel Fourgeoud (who was much better) to break up our camp at Jerusalem and march to the Wana Creek, the sick were sent down in large barges to Devil's Harwar, which was chock full, and several of whom were at this time laboring under a disease something like the tympany, called here the *kook,* being a prodigious hardness and swelling in the belly, occasioned (it is said) by drinking bad water without any spirits, which was our daily and general beverage.

On the 22nd, at six o'clock in the morning, we all decamped from this spot, marching up along the banks of the Coermotibo Creek, through a perfect bog, in which an old slave sticking fast with his burden got his head terribly cut by a soldier, and was left where he was. Another Negro was knocked overboard from one of the baggage boats that kept us company and was drowned.

December 25th. Having now once more flounced through deep mud and heavy showers like amphibious animals, we encamped at another small brook called the Java Creek, three miles below Wana, and in such a trim that most assuredly we were more worth seeing than the lions in the Tower. Here now all rested, while I alone with a small party was selected the next day to go and reconnoiter the old camps at Wana Creek. In the evening we returned, having seen exactly nothing but mud and water, through which we had waded till up above our middles.

December 27th. So dreadfully ill were we now encamped (while at the Wana, it was totally impracticable) that all the newly arrived ammunition and provisions were obliged to be supported on wooden rafters, while we could never step out of our hammocks without being in water at least above our knees, in consequence of which a whole barge full of sick soldiers was again sent down the Coermotibo Creek, among whom the poor old Negro with his fractured skull, who had found means yesterday to rejoin us, even in his shocking condition, and which floating charnel house weighed anchor on the last day of the year, with which I shall beg leave to end this dreary chapter.

CHAPTER 24th

Two volunteer companies erected of free Mulattoes and free Negroes—Colonel Fourgeoud's regiment receives orders to sail for Europe—Countermanded—Sample of sable heroism

To what good star I was obliged this day, in the middle of all the above bustle, I know not. But true it is that the colonel, having sent for me, not only solicited my future friendship (and declaring he was sorry for all the ill he had ever done me, for which he principally blamed Gibhart, his adjutant and spy), but taking me by the hand as a proof of his real regard, permitted me from that moment to go to Paramaribo, or to where I pleased to refresh till further orders. This had such an effect on my side, that having converted every drop of my rum into grog, we sat down together with two more officers, and drowned all former animosity in eternal oblivion, till we could hardly see or stand, in which condition I took my leave that very evening of my new friend, and the camp at Java Creek.

January 2nd. Having slept during most of the passage, in the morning I breakfasted at Devil's Harwar, where the wretch Gibhart had just died, to my great satisfaction, and I arrived in the evening at the estate Beekvliet, for my Negroes had made extraordinary dispatch *fumming watra* all the time to encourage each other.[1]

On the 3rd, I arrived at the fortress Amsterdam, where I was entertained with an excellent fish dinner. And then for Paramaribo, where I arrived this evening at six o'clock and found Joanna with her boy perfectly recovered, after having both been blind &c. for above three weeks,

---

1. That is, one of the rowers beating the water with his oar at every stroke in such a manner that it sounds different from the rest, to which the others sing a chorus.

and with whom being invited to lodge at the house of my friend De Graav, I was perfectly happy.

The next day I dined with Colonel Fourgeoud, who now was as well as ever, and who gave me a very indifferent meal of salt provisions[2] but an uncommonly hearty welcome. He acquainted me that two new companies of free Mulattoes and two of free Negroes, all volunteers, had just been raised, that the Saramaka and Auka Negroes were deceitful rascals; that a few Rebels had been killed in Cassewinica Creek; that he was in hopes to root up Fissy Hollo; that Boni, with his people, were almost starving in the forest (notwithstanding their late depredations, which could not last much longer); and that he was fully determined, if he should lose his last man, to make this Rebel foe surrender, or else harass him till he and his gangs by hunger and distress should be obliged to quit the Colony, to all which I answered *Bravo*.

Thus, I kept on daily, visiting my friends, viz., Mrs. Godefrooy, the Demellys, the Gordons, and the Macneyls. I even spent a very agreeable day with the black Mrs. Sampson or Zubly, who was now a widow. And I was present at a Mulatto ball, who were all free, independent settlers, where the music, the lights, the country dances, the supper, and above all the dresses were so superb, and their behavior so decent and genteel, that the *tout ensemble* might serve as a model for decorum and etiquette to the more fair and polished inhabitants.

On the 20th, seeing a number of Indians and black people of both sexes swimming at the back of Fort Zeelandia, young Donald Macneyl and myself completed the group by stripping and getting in among them, and never did I see greater feats of activity in the water, the Negroes fighting a sham battle by plunging, or rather tumbling like porpoises, when they strike each other with their legs at a wonderful rate but never use their hands, and while the Indians, who were of the Arowaka nation, swam and dived like amphibious animals.

Being sufficiently refreshed, we sat down upon the beach near the twenty-one-gun battery, where I had the opportunity to examine the features and figure of one of their young females. She had a live parrot which she had stunned with a blunt arrow from her bow, and for which I gave her a double-bladed knife. So wonderfully expert are the Arowaka Indians at this exercise that they frequently bring down a macaw or even a pigeon in full flight.

On the 25th, I was ill with a fever and was bled in the foot, in which the orifice being struck too deep (for struck it was, as they bleed the

---

2. This he absolutely held as the best regimen for health, notwithstanding he had brought several cooks from Europe.

horses), I again became lame, during which time Colonel Seybourgh, who was at last also sick, arrived from the Java Creek to recover.

Now Colonel Fourgeoud, while he was just ready to renew his operations (having already sent a small detachment to the Jews-Savanna for intelligence), received letters from The Hague, with orders to break up the expedition immediately, and with his few remaining troops to sail for Holland without delay. In consequence, the transport ships were put in commission on the 27th, and all the officers and privates received their clearance, which made them very happy, while all at Paramaribo were alive except myself. Alas, alas, poor Joanna.

However, on February 14th, ill as I was (with a bad foot, a sore arm, the prickly heat, and all my teeth loose with the scurvy), I found means to scramble out with a thousand florins in my pocket, which having divided between Fourgeoud and Mrs. Godefrooy, for the redemption of the black boy Quacoo and my Mulatto, I returned home without a shilling in my pocket. Yet by this small sum of five hundred florins, though not adequate to the eighteen hundred which I owed that lady, she was induced generously to renew her persuasions of carrying Joanna and the boy with me to Holland. This Joanna as nobly as firmly refused, declaring that independent of all other considerations, she could never think of sacrificing one benefactor to the interest of another, and that her own happiness or even mine—which was dearer to her than life—should never have any weight, till the debt of her liberty should be paid by me or by her own industry to the last farthing, and which she did not despair to see one day completed. She added that our separation should only be for a time, and that the greatest proof I could ever show her of my real esteem was now to undergo this little trial of fortune, like a man, without so much as heaving a sigh in her presence, which last she spoke with a smile, next embraced her infant, then turned suddenly about and wept bitterly.

At this moment, I was called to Mr. De Lamarre's, who had just died, and by which Joanna's sister was also become a widow, but left a slave with two beautiful children in the bargain. In short, I determined to weather one or two dreadful years in her absence and began to prepare for the voyage.

February 15th. I have said that we were ordered to leave the Colony, and that all was alive, myself alone excepted, but now by letters from Holland our dereliction was again countermanded for six months longer, and everyone was damped, while I again suddenly was revived, determined to live on bread and salt till Joanna's redemption should be fully accomplished. But what grieved me to the heart was, alas, the other news from Europe, viz., that the Scots Brigade had been asked to come to Britain by his Britannic Majesty, without I could possibly be one of the

Indian Female of the Arrowauka Nation.

Benedetti Sculp.

Plate 61

number, while on the other hand an American company was put into my offer, but which I refused without hesitation and with contempt.

Not yet being recovered, I now stayed some time longer at Paramaribo, where (at the house of a Mr. Rynsdorp) I saw a Portuguese Jew teaching his children the Christian religion, while the pious mother of the charity house nefariously kept flogging the poor slaves daily because they were, she said, unbelievers. To one black woman, in particular, she wantonly gave four hundred lashes, who bore them without a complaint, while the men she always stripped *perfectly* naked, that not a *single* part of their body might escape her attention. To what is religion come at last?

On the 21st, Mr. Rynsdorp, the son-in-law of Mrs. Godefrooy, now took me with his sailing barge for a change of air to Nut en Schadelyk, one of his own coffee estates, where I saw a white man who had lately lost both his eyes in one night by the bats or specters, and next day sailing up the Commewina River, he accompanied me to the delightful cacao plantation, Alkmaar, the property of the above lady, where the Negro slaves are treated like children by the mistress, whom they all look up to as their common parent. Here were no groans to be heard, no fetters to be met with, or no marks of severity to be seen, but all was harmony and content.

At this time, the celebrated free Negro Quacy, who was the prophet, priest, and king of the Rangers, &c., went to Holland on a visit to the Prince of Orange, with letters of recommendation from Fourgeoud, whose praises he was to resound and to complain about the Governor not treating him with due respect. This now being the period of the sessions, another Negro's leg was cut off for skulking from a task to which he was unable, while two more were condemned to be hanged for running away altogether. The heroic behavior of one of these men before the Court deserves particularly to be quoted; he begged only to be heard for a few moments, which being granted, he proceeded thus.

> I was born in Africa where, defending my prince during an engagement, I was made a captive, and sold for a slave on the coast by my own country-men. One of your countrymen, who is now to be my judge, then became my purchaser, in whose service I was treated so cruelly by his overseer that I deserted, and joined the Rebels in the woods. Here, again, I was con-demned to be a slave to Boni, their chief, who treated me with twice the severity I had experienced from the Europeans, till I was once more forced to elope, determined to shun mankind forever, and inoffensively to end my days by myself in an unbounded forest. Two years had I persevered in this manner, quite alone, undergoing the greatest hardships and anxiety of mind, mostly for my dear family who are perhaps starving on my account in my own country. I say, two miserable years had just elapsed, when I was

discovered by the Rangers, taken, and brought before this tribunal, who are now acquainted with the truth of my wretched life, and from whom the only favor I have to ask is that I may be *executed* next Saturday or so soon as it possibly will be convenient.

This speech was uttered with the utmost moderation by one of the finest-looking Negroes that was perhaps ever seen, and to which his former master, whom as he observed was now one of the judges, made the following laconic reply. "Rascal, that is not what we want to know, but the *torture* this moment shall make you confess crimes as black as yourself, as well as those of your hateful accomplices." To which the Negro, who now swelled in every vein with rage and ineffable contempt, said "*Massera,* the very jaguars have trembled for these hands," holding them up, "and dare you think to threaten me with your wretched instrument? No, I despise the greatest tortures you can now invent, as much as I do the pitiful wretch who is going to inflict them," saying which he threw himself down on the rack, where amid the most excruciating tortures, he remained with a smile and without they were able to make him utter a syllable, nor did he ever speak again till he ended his unhappy days at the gallows.

Having dined on March 8th with Colonel Fourgeoud, where we celebrated the Prince of Orange's anniversary (and while Mr. Rynsdorp gave a treat to all the soldiers), he acquainted me that the Rangers were alone encamped at the Wana Creek; that the pestilential spot Devil's Harwar was entirely forsaken at last; and that the two lately raised companies of sable volunteers had taken a few prisoners and killed others on the Wanica-Path behind Paramaribo.

I was at this time a good deal better, but still not quite recovered. He who had formerly treated me so severely now even insisted on my staying some time longer at Paramaribo, nay, gave me an offer to return to Europe, which I absolutely refused. In short, about the middle of the month, I was as well as ever I was in all my life, when with Fourgeoud I daily went a-visiting the ladies, but at some of whose company no man could help being disgusted, so languid were their looks, and so unrestrained their conversation, that a Mrs. N— even asked me *sans cere-monie* to supply the place of her husband, while she might as well have asked me to drink a tumbler of salts for a relish. However on the 17th, at least my eyes were better feasted, when going to dine with Colonel Texier of the Society troops, I first took a walk in the orange grove and the Governor's gardens. Here, peeping through among the foliage, I soon spied two most elegant female figures indeed, the one a fine young Samboe, the other a blooming Quadroon, which last was so very fair-complexioned that she might have passed for a native of Greece, while the roses that glowed in her cheeks were equal to those that blew in the shrubberies.[3] They were both as they came to the world, walking hand in hand and conversing with smiles on a flowery bank that adorned the side of a crystal brook, into which they plunged the moment they heard me rustling among the verdure. I could not help being riveted to the place for some time. And true it is, again and again, that where the whole shapes are exposed to view, the features attract the smallest attention, while it is equally as true that the human figure of either sex, whether white, black, copper-colored, or olive, when naked particularly among the green or verdure, exhibits a very beautiful creature, to which the most splendid apparel cannot give any additional elegance.

However, though these were but slaves, I discreetly retired, by which I escaped, perhaps, Actaeon's fate inflicted by Diana, and leaving them to enjoy their innocent and healthful amusement of bathing, I spent the remaining hour before dinner among the shading fruit trees, flowery bowers, and meandering gravel walks.

On the 22nd, captains Van Geurike and Friderici, with Sergeant Fowler, all were sent on an embassy to the Auka and Saramaka Free Negroes, if possible to implore their assistance against the Rebels, which they always continued to promise, but never yet performed, while Colonel Fourgeoud gave them presents. Having saved a poor black woman from two hundred lashes, by replacing a dozen pieces of china which she had broken by accident, while another was killed this day by a Frenchman (who then cut his own throat from remorse, his companion director hanging himself), and having visited the poor Negro who had lately lost his limb, I packed up my boxes to set out the very next morning on my sixth campaign and a second time to take command of the Hope in the Commewina River, just before which arrived at my lodgings six Negro slaves loaded with presents of every kind that was valuable in the Colony, from my friends.

---

3. It is to be remarked that though Europeans look pale under the torrid zone, the native inhabitants have often a freshness peculiarly engaging, particularly Mulattoes and Quadroons.

CHAPTER 25th

Singular method of detecting a thief—Rencounter between the Rangers and Rebels—Amazonian feat in a female Negro slave—The regiment receives a second order to return to Europe

Adieu then, once more, Paramaribo, and my dear Joanna, who had by this time made great proficiency in her learning &c., and farewell my sweet little Johnny, who for the present absorbed all her attention.

On the 29th, late in the evening, we made the Gold-Mine, where seeing a Negro boy and a girl suspended from a high beam with a rope tied to their hands, which were behind them (thus in the most agonizing tortures, and with their shoulders half out of joint), I without the smallest ceremony cut them down, swearing to demolish the overseer for inflicting this new mode of torture, unless he promised to forgive them, which he miraculously did.

On the day following, we arrived at the Hope, where I immediately took command of the whole river. An hour before our landing at this place, I had discovered a little theft by means of a very singular experiment which I must relate, viz., finding all my sugar gone along with most of my rum, I told the Negroes, six in number, that this was not ship-shape Bristol-fashion, and that I was determined to find out the plunderer by making a *parrot's feather* grow on the tip of his nose. After which, pronouncing a few incoherent words and making two or three circles with my saber on the tilt, I crept under it and shut both the half doors after me. Here I continued my ejaculations again, peeping through the crevices at the rowers with great attention, and without their knowledge, when I soon observed one of them (as regularly as he tugged at his oar) bring up one of his hands to his nose. I stepped up to him, crying, "I see the parrot's feather. Thou art the thief, thou rascal," to which the poor, superstitious fellow instantly answered *"Jaw, me massera,"* when being seconded by the rest, and kneeling for mercy to the *sorcerer,* he was pardoned with all his accomplices, who (for their confession) got a dinner of salt beef and a gourd full of groats in the bargain.

April 1st. Being now once more the Prince of Commewina, I built a high palace on twelve stakes, in imitation of Boni's, the prince of the Rebels, in Boosy Cray, and which aerial habitation was very necessary, the whole post being inundated by others' neglect, and become a complete mirepool, while my former cottage was long since demolished. I here also found the greatest misery among the Marines, who were almost naked, having sold even their very shoes, for fresh provisions.

On the 28th, I paid a visit to the Honorable Thomas Palmer at his estate Fairfield, which gentleman was late king's counsellor at Massachusetts Bay, where I saw both the planter and his Negro slaves happy and contented under his careful administration. Indeed, few estates in the West Indies could, perhaps, brag of greater prosperity, either in productions or population, while the courtesy and hospitality of the proprietor to strangers was conspicuous throughout the Colony.

Returning from this plantation to the Hope, I was now acquainted by Colonel Fourgeoud, in a letter, that Mr. Vinsack with his Rangers had taken eleven Rebels, besides killing several others, yet that another party of Rangers had been attacked by the Rebels, a few of whom had unluckily been shot dead in their hammocks while asleep. During these skirmishes, one remarkable presence of mind was exhibited by a Rebel Negro, viz., a Ranger having leveled his firelock was just going to shoot him, when the Rebel called out holding up his hand, "What, Sir, do you mean to kill one of your own party?" which the other believing to be true replied, "God forbid," and dropping the muzzle of his piece, instantly received a ball through the body from his adversary who, being safe, disappeared like lightning. One of the captive Negroes related that, the evening before they were taken, a Rebel (formerly deserted from Faukenberg) was sabered to pieces, as had been the other two before we took the town of Gado Saby.

On May 6th, it blew a hurricane so violent, accompanied by thunder and lightning, that most houses on the Hope were unroofed, and trees uprooted, yet my aerial habitation had the good fortune to remain standing, in which with pleasure, on the 8th, I introduced both my dear Joanna and her boy, who were come once more to live with me. Thus, I bid fair to be again as happy as I had been in 1774—the more so, since my family, my sheep, and my poultry were twice the number, to which if added that I had begun to plant a beautiful garden, I might with some degree of justice claim the name, if not that of a planter, at least that of a little farmer.

In short, on the 9th we were all invited by Mr. De Graav to dine at his beautiful plantation Knoppemonbo, where this good man had foretold to me before my boy was born that he and his mother one day should be free.

May 13th. I went on a short visit to my French acquaintance, Monsieur Cachelieu, at his plantation Egmond. Here I found, among other company, a planter named d'Onis who was an Italian and had but one arm. So violent was this unhappy man's disposition that he lately ordered to be flogged a Negro woman who was advanced eight months in her pregnancy, till (it was said) her very intestines appeared through her body, and all this for having broken a crystal tumbler. One of his male slaves trying to evade his severity another time was shot dead during his elopement, and not a slave belonged to his estate who was not cut and carved by the lash of his whip from the neck to the heels.

On the 26th, I saw a most surprising performance of activity, strength, and courage in a young Negro female (called Clardina) at the Hope, where a wild stag having strayed from the rest, at the moment it came galloping over the footpath, she seized it in full speed by the hind leg, and not being able to stop it, allowed herself to be dragged several yards till she was terribly wounded, before she would let go her grip. Show me such a woman on the whole European continent.

The Hope had now again truly become a charming habitation, being perfectly dry, even in spring floods, and washed by pleasing canals that let in the fresh water on every side, while the surrounding hedges were neatly cut, enclosing gardens that afforded fruit and vegetables of every species. Also the houses, bridges, &c. were repaired, and finally the strictest adherence to cleanliness among the men recommended, by which precautions not one sick person out of fifty was found on the 28th, where sloth, stink, disease, and mortality had so lately before swayed their destructive sceptre, and in which both the land- and sea-scurvy, besides the venereal disease, had no small share; the above scorbutic complaint differing in the one covering the whole body with blotches, and the other affecting the teeth and gums. As for myself, I now enjoyed the greatest flow of health and spirits, while most of my old shipmates were dead or returned to Europe, nay, not a single officer was at this time in rank above me, except such as had formerly been inured to the West India climate.

My very soldiers and Negroes were completely happy, among whom the most perfect harmony consisted, while I frequently indulged them with a merry evening and a graybeard of rum. One night, in the middle of this festivity, I secretly ordered the sentinel to fire his piece, and make a false alarm, as if the enemy was on the estate; when I had the satisfaction to see them seize their arms, and rush out with the greatest order and intrepidity, which experiment I was induced to put in practice as it was reported that the Rebels intended to pay a visit to the River Commewina. However, this joy and festivity lasted not long, because of the setting in of the dry season, when mortality once more began to rage, ten or twelve men dying daily at the Java Creek and Maagdenburg, while those under my command at the Hope diminished hourly.

On June 4th, with the spring flood, my dams broke through, which put the whole post under water and created such a confusion that to drink the king's health was quite out of our memory. Meanwhile the overseer, a Mr. Blenderman, refused me every assistance, and so hot a quarrel at last ensued that he was fain to make his escape from the plantation. I have frequently mentioned the insolence of those brutes, but I must complete their character by saying that most of them are the scum of the earth, and having been brought up in Germany, or elsewhere, under the cane of some corporal, now distribute their sauce and barbarities with double interest where they dare. "Well," said one of these rascals ironically to an old free Negro, "don't you believe that the monkeys are a parcel of damned Christians that have been thus transformed for showing so much leniency to such as you?" "No, Sir (replied the black man). We think not that the monkeys are damned Christians, but I and all of us believe that many Christians are a parcel of damned monkeys." Nor did ever any repartee give me greater satisfaction. Of the administrators, I shall say nothing nor of the appraisers of estates, having I think already mentioned that the first get ten percent of all the produce, and the second get riches for the purchasers and themselves, by selling under value what is entrusted to their care.

On June 7th, I being informed that a Mr. Morym, the administrator of the Hope, was on the opposite shore, in a piece of newly cultivated ground, with the impertinent Blenderman, I rowed over to them armed with a bludgeon, and asked for immediate satisfaction from the latter, that is to beg my pardon or take a broken head in his master's presence. He chose the first, and having promised to repair my dams, I broke my stick, which I threw at his feet, when a reconciliation was again reestablished.

June 23rd. A patrol arriving from Rietwyk in Perica brought the news that Colonel Fourgeoud's troops were just returned (from a cruise to the Marawina) at the Java Creek, and that between them and the Rangers several Rebel fields had been destroyed during this campaign, which sable allies for their faithful services were now complimented by the Society with new arms, and had been clothed for the first time in green livery. But the other news of more importance was that the ambassadors were returned the 15th instant from the Auka and Saramaka Negroes, having made a fruitless journey there, since neither of these gangs would lend the smallest assistance, in consequence of which Colonel Fourgeoud (being tired himself, and having perfectly exhausted his troops, while indeed most of the Rebel settlements were destroyed) at last determined to break up the whole expedition, and of which he previously acquainted the Prince of Orange.

Thus, on the following day, I received an order to leave the River Commewina on the 15th current, and with all the troops under my command to row down to Paramaribo, where the transport ships for our departure had been put in commission. I instantly read this order to all the men, to their great and unspeakable joy, and next began to make the preparations, yet my breast labored with heavy sighs.

O my dear Joanna, O my boy, who at this time became so very ill, the one with a fever, the other with convulsions, that no life in either was expected. On July 8th, my little family continued so ill that I thought it proper to send them to town under a physician, and on the 10th, I sent all my sheep and poultry to Faukenberg, one couple of fat yews excepted, which I killed and with which I entertained in two days twenty-four gentlemen of the river, having received white bread, fruit, and Spanish wine to help out the feast in a present from Mr. Gourlay, while the villainous overseer at the Hope, even refusing me the fuel to dress the victuals (which we then got out of the forest), was deservedly hunted out from among the company.

On the 13th, I ordered down the troops from Clarenbeek, where lately a hospital had (a second time) been erected, and who this evening anchored off the Hope. Next day, an officer of the Honorable Society arrived to relieve me, whose men from that moment began to do the duty— when I removed my flag from the Hope to the barges, and in the evening took my last farewell from Faukenberg and Joanna's relations who, crowding round me, expressed their sorrow at my departure, and invoked the protection of Heaven for my safe and prosperous voyage. On the 15th, we finally left the Hope and (at ten o'clock, having marched my troops on board) I fired my pistol at twelve, as a signal to weigh anchor, after which we immediately rowed down the River Commewina.

CHAPTER 26th

The troops on board—Again ordered to disembark—Great dejection—Mutiny—Insolent conduct of an Auka Negro captain—Near two hundred sick sent to Holland—General description of the African Negroes—Of unhappy and happy slaves

Having anchored last evening off the estate Berkshoven, where I spent the night ashore with my good friend Mr. Gourlay, we now continued to row down, when I took farewell from the Honorable Thomas Palmer.

The day following, I passed the evening with Captain Macneyl, and on July 18th my fleet arrived safe (in conjunction with the barges from Maagdenburg and Cottica) at anchor in the roads before Paramaribo, where three transport ships lay ready to receive us, on board of which (an hour after) I embarked the troops that had been under my command. I next stepped ashore myself where, having made my report to Colonel Fourgeoud, I had the pleasure to find Joanna with her boy perfectly recovered.

The next day I was again sent on board to make proper arrangements for the voyage, and on the 20th was entertained with no contemptible dinner by the Old Gentleman, Fourgeoud.

On the 21st, we once more received our clearance, N.B. in card money, by which we lost considerably, where I instantly went to Mrs. Godefrooy and again gave her all that was in my pocket, being no more than forty pounds. This excellent woman renewed her entreaties that I ought to carry Joanna and her boy with me to Holland, but to no purpose. Joanna was unmovable even up to heroism, no persuasion making the smallest impression on her till, she said, we should be able to redeem her by paying the last farthing that we owed. Thus situated, we both affected to bear our fate with resignation, while both were equally tormented with the agonies of death.

July 24th. Our men having been embarked since the 18th, the officers now joined them. Thus, the poor remains of this fine regiment were finally embarked to weigh anchor, and to proceed to Holland the next day, while all were jovial and happy, *one* only excepted who suffered excessively. And who this *one* was that reader who possesses sensibility can easily discern, without giving me the pain to enter on particulars. Adieu, then, Paramaribo, adieu my friends, and adieu thou who art dearer to me than my life itself.

July 25th. At the very moment of departure, a ship entered the River Surinam with orders for the regiment to reenter the woods again immediately, till they should be relieved by a fresh party sent from Holland for the purpose. The will of his Serene Highness the Prince of Orange was instantly read to the men from the quarter-deck of each vessel, together with his most sincere thanks for the manly and spirited conduct they had supported during so long a trial, and so many great and unprecedented hardships—which news, however, struck such a damp upon their spirits that in all my life I never saw people more distressed, I being, in my turn, the only happy person now, who had but just before been the most completely miserable. In the middle of this gloomy scene, the poor men were now ordered to give cheers, which those on board one of the vessels absolutely refused, but Colonel Seybourgh and, most unluckily, I were ordered to compel them to it. When he with a cane in one hand and a cocked pistol in the other, like a frantic, first began by beating, and next calling them upon the quarter-deck by threatening with bitter oaths instantly to blow out the brains of all those who should now disobey his orders.

If the troops were sorry, the colonists were extremely glad at this, our second debarkation in the town of Paramaribo, where indeed a petition signed by the principal inhabitants had but two days before been presented to Colonel Fourgeoud, through a Mr. Jacott, imploring our regiment, if it was at all possible, to stay some time longer, and give the finishing stroke to the Rebels, whom we had so gloriously persevered in routing and harassing, and this was certainly true. For though we had not made many captives, we had, in conjunction with the other troops and Rangers, demolished (perhaps) every settlement of any consequence that the Rebels possessed within the bounds of the Colony, and driven them to such a considerable distance that (a few of their detached parties excepted) both the depredations and deserting of slaves were incomparably less than at our first arrival, which was better than making with them a shameful peace, as had been made before with the Rebels of the Auka and Saramaka settlements, and which (without our coming to Guiana) would have again most probably been the consequence. As a sample of what these fellows are when independent, I must relate what happened between one of them and myself at Paramaribo, where the troops had leave to refresh before they were (once more) to reenter the forest.

On July 26th, the day after our debarkation, I was dining at Captain Macneyl's (who was now come to town from his estate) when a captain of the Auka Rebel Negroes (at present our allies) came in to ask money from his lady and was very importune, seeing which I desired her in English to "Give him a dram, and he would be gone," but which the fellow understanding, called me without to the door, and then lifting his silver-pommeled cane, asked me if that was my house, and what business I had to interfere. "I am (said he with a thundering voice) Captain Fortune Dago So, and if I had you in my country at Auka, I would make the earth drink up your blood, Sir." To which I replied (drawing my sword) that my name was *Stedman,* and if he spoke one syllable more, I would make the dogs run away with his guts, when he snapped his fingers and went off, leaving me in a very disagreeable state of mind, and cursing Fourgeoud for ever showing to those rascals so much indulgence. Returning from dinner in the evening to go home, I now again met the identical black bully, who instantly stepped up to me saying, "*Massera,* you are a very brave and gallant fellow. Won't you give some money to the Auka captain?" which I sternly refusing, for the present, he kissed my hand and showed his teeth in token of reconciliation, he said, and let me go, promising to send me a present of pistachio nuts which, by the by, never came, nor if they had should I have tasted them.

However, I must acknowledge that they are unfairly dealt with, the Society of Surinam not sending the yearly presents according to their shameful capitulation, and they disregarding Fourgeoud's flattery as a paltry trifle, without which perhaps they would be more true and faithful allies than they have been, at least since we came to this colony.

Although we now continued to stay in Surinam, I must observe that surely our future service could but little avail for its prosperity, our being so very few in number, and out of which number (small as it was) were on August 1st sent sick and incurable to Holland no less than nine officers and above one hundred and sixty private men; I myself was at this time very ill with an ague and was offered to be one of the party but refused to go, being determined to see out the expedition, which it was evident could last but a few months longer.

Everything being now settled in peace and quietness, I got so well on the 10th that I walked to Mrs. Godefrooy to acquaint her that I now wished to emancipate at least Johnny Stedman, and begged her to become bail before the court for the usual sum of three hundred pounds that he should never become a charge to the Colony of Surinam; but which she firmly declined, to my utter astonishment (as she ran no risk), till I was acquainted that she had refused the very same favor to her own son. What could I do? My boy was obliged still to remain in servitude till I could find bail for his free manumission, and while I had not the smallest cause to blame his excellent new proprietor.

When speaking about slavery, I think it will not be at all out of character to give a general account of this set of people who are so very little known in Europe. I have already mentioned the mode of their being purchased, imported, and sold, and thus shall now confine myself to their manners, both natural and as dependents, in which I flatter myself to bring some truths to light that have hitherto been buried in obscurity, at least to the generality of mankind.

In the first place, as to the complexion of a Negro or his being black, this is (as I have said before) entirely owing to the burning climate in which he lives, which is still more heated by the sandy deserts over which the trade winds pass before they come to him, since the Indians of America, existing under the same degree of latitude, but who get this wind refreshed by the Atlantic Ocean, are copper-colored, and the inhabitants of Abyssinia &c., who receive it cooled by the Arabian and Indian seas, are entirely olive. Thus, north of the great River Senegal, the complexion changes from black to brown among the Moors, as it does towards the south among the Kafirs and Hottentots. And I am of opinion that the woolly texture of the hair is the derived effect, proceeding from the very same cause. The epidermis or cuticle of the Negroes I have seen dissected more than once; this is very clear and transparent, but between which and the real skin lies a thin follicle which is perfectly black, and, when removed by very severe scalding or flagellation, it exposes a complexion not inferior to that of the European.

On the estate Vossenburg in Surinam were even born two *white Negroes,* whose parents were yet both black as others; the one was a female sent to Paris in 1734 and the other a boy born in March 1738. But these were monsters, such as one that was lately exhibited in England, whose skin was not a natural white but resembling chalk, nay, even their hair on every part was the same, while their eyes were a perfect blood-color[1] and with which they saw very little in the sunshine; neither were they fit for any kind of labor, while their mental faculties corresponded with the incapacity of their bodies.

With regard to the shape of the African Negroes, it is from head to foot absolutely different from the European mold, though not in any de-

---

1. This is well-known also to be the case with many animals, such as rabbits and mice, that are perfectly white but have their eyes perfectly red.

gree inferior, in my opinion, when prejudice is laid aside. Their features, indeed, with high cheekbones, flat noses, and thick lips, appear to us deformities but among themselves are esteemed perhaps quite the reverse. But even with us, their black eyes and white teeth are deemed ornamental, and one certain advantage in a black complexion is that all those languid, pale, sickly-looking countenances so common in Europe are never exhibited among them, nor are the wrinkles and ravages of age nearly so conspicuous, though I must acknowledge that when a Negro is very ill, his black changes to a disagreeable sallow olive.

As for great strength and activity, their shape is assuredly preferable to ours, being generally sturdy, and muscular near the trunk, and slender towards the extremities; for instance, they have mostly a remarkably fine chest but are small about the hips, while their buttocks are round and prominent. Their necks are thicker than ours, and their genitals conspicuously larger. A Negro is very stout about the thighs, so are his arms above the elbow, but both his legs and wrists are very slender, in which description much of the Herculean make of Mr. Broughton, the late famous boxer, may be traced. And as for the deformity of their limbs, this is entirely accidental, owing to the manner in which they are carried as infants on the mother's back, with their tender legs tied close round each side of her waist; this mode of nursing alone creates the unnatural bend with which they are not born. Nor are their children ever taught to walk, but left to creep among the sand and verdure where they please, till gradually they acquire strength, and inclination to erect themselves, which they do very soon. But by this method, the position of their feet is much neglected, yet by which means (and daily bathing) they acquire that native strength and agility for which, according to me, they are so very remarkable, while it derides the dispute so often resumed, and proves that man was surely born to walk upon two legs. Another cause of this bend in their limbs is that during the two whole years that they suck, after the mother has made them drink a large quantity of water, she shakes them twice a day by every limb with so much violence that all the infant's joints crack, and after which, by a leg or arm, they are tossed into the river to be outwardly scrubbed. But this deformity is fully compensated by the health and vigor which is annexed to such an education, and from which benefit, their female race not being exempt, makes them a generation not inferior to the men, in size alone excepted, while some of them in point of running, swimming, climbing, and dancing, if not in wrestling, are even their superiors.[2] Nor are these hardy daughters of the torrid zone

---

2. That to breed an Amazonian race of females depends on education has been proven, after many disputes, by the soundest philosophers.

less remarkable for propagation, I knowing a female servant at Mr. De Graav's house, called Lesperanza, who bore actually nine children in the course of three years, first four, next two, and then three, which they bring to the world without pain, like the Indian women, resuming their domestic employment even the same day. Their infants are as fair as any Europeans the first week; from which they are only distinguished by the boys having the parts of generation partly black, after which their whole body gradually becomes the same color.

Their women also come early to the age of maturity, but in this it may be said as with the fruit of this climate, soon ripe, soon decayed, yet those people live a considerable time, I having seen one or two that were past a hundred years and, in the *London Chronicle* for October 5th, 1780, is even made mention of a Negress called Louisa Truxo, who was then living at Tucomea in South America at the surprising age of 175 years. In what tables of longevity is to be found such a European? While this venerable person probably had spent most of her youth in hard labor as other slaves, which though a Negro can bear it in a tropical climate better than a European, this is both unnatural on the coast of Guinea, and in Guiana, where without toil, the necessities of life are spontaneously produced and vegetation flourishes forever. One singular remark I have made on the constitution of the Negroes, is that while they can bear the heat, they can also bear moderate cold better, at least, than I could do, for I have seen them sleep in the dewy moonshine, nay, in the wet grass, perfectly naked without any hurt, while I was glad (especially in the early mornings) to have a fire under my hammock. And in regard to hunger and thirst, and even pain in sickness, &c., no people can be more patient. This short sample sufficiently ought to show that the African Negroes, though by some stupid Europeans treated as brutes,[3] are made of no inferior clay but in every one particular are our equals.

I have formerly mentioned the names of above a dozen Negro tribes, all of which know each other from the different marks and incisions made on their bodies. For instance, the *Coromantyn* Negroes (who are the most esteemed) cut three or four long slashes on each of their cheeks, as I have represented in the face of the armed free Negro or Ranger (see Plate 7), and the *Loango* Negroes (who are reckoned the worst) distinguish themselves by puckering, or marking the skin of their arms, thighs, &c. with square, elevated figures like large dice (see Plate 68); these also sharply point the foreteeth, which makes them look frightening, like those of a shark, while all the males are circumcised in the manner of the Jews. But

---

3. By Linnaeus the whole human race, the whole human race together, is classed among the monkeys.

the most remarkable thing is that the females of the *Papa* nation actually have the same excrescence on the pudenda which is said to be conspicuous in the female Hottentots at the Cape of Good Hope.

Among the strange productions of nature deserves highly to be noticed a kind of people who are known by the name of *Accorees* or *Twofingers,* who live among the Saramaka Negroes in the very upper parts of the river of that name. This heterogeneous tribe are so much deformed on hands and feet that while some have but three or four fingers and toes on each, the greatest number have absolutely but two fingers and two toes on each hand and foot, which are hideous to look at, resembling the claws of a lobster, or rather limbs that have been cured after mutilation by fire, or some other accident. This deformity in one person would be nothing very uncommon, but that a whole community should be inflicted with this singularity is a phenomenon that I think cannot be accounted for, without it perhaps be owing to their mingled blood. For they are neither Negroes nor Indians, yet partake of both without the smallest resemblance to Samboes. In short (however strange), such people there assuredly are, and two of which were shown to me at Paramaribo, but at too great a distance to make the proper ocular observations. While as a further proof of their existence, an engraved copper plate with one of their figures was presented by the Society of Surinam to the Society of Arts and Sciences at Haarlem in Holland. Nay, I was even assured that some men with the rudiments of a tail existed in Guiana, before ever I read Lord Munbodo's *Antient Metaphysics,* but which, however, wanted confirmation to insert here as a truth. When I acquainted His Lordship with the above *ludus naturae,* the Accoorees, he seemed highly delighted with the subject, which he did not discredit, yet testifying his surprise that it should be a whole community.[4] I shall now quit this subject, to prevent my being suspected of dealing in the marvelous, and continue with what will seem better to quadrate with nature.

With the languages of the African Negroes I am very little acquainted. However, as a specimen, I will repeat just a few words for that called *Coromantyn,* for which I must credit my boy Quacoo, who belongs to that nation. For instance,

"Go to the river and fetch me some water."
Co fa ansyo na baramon bra.

"My wife, I am hungry."
Me yeree, nacomeda mee.

---

4. Query: Why should it appear more surprising to see a race of these people than a race of men with one leg, one eye, dog's heads, and long tails?

But as for that spoken by the black people in Surinam, I pretend to be perfectly well-acquainted with it, being a composition of Dutch, French, Spanish, Portuguese, and mostly English, which last they liked best and have retained since the English nation were possessors of the Colony. This mixed speech (in which I have even seen a printed grammar) ends mostly with a vowel, like the Italian, and is so sweet and sonorous that even among the genteelest European companies, nothing else is spoken in Surinam. It is also extremely expressive and sentimental, such as, "good eating," *sweety muffo;* "gunpowder," *mansanny;* "I will love you with all my heart so long as I live," *Mee saloby you langa alla mee hatty so langa mee leeby;* "a pleasing tale," *ananasy tory;* "live long, so long till your hair becomes as white as cotton," *leebee langa tay, tay, ta-y, you weeree weree tan witty likee catoo;* "small," *pekeen;* "very small," *peekeeneenee;* "farewell, goodby, I am dying and going to my God," *Adiosso, crobooy, mee de go dede me de go na mee gado.* In this sample may be perceived many corrupt English words which, however, begin to wear out near the capital town, but are retained near the distant plantations. At the estate Goed Accoord, I have heard an old Negro woman say, *"We lobee fo lebee togeddere,"* by which she meant, "We love to live together." At Paramaribo, to express the same, they tell you, *"We do looko for tanna macandera."* But what is extremely surprising is that some of their expressions are perfectly as those at Liege in Germany, viz., *looco,* "to see," *me cotto,* "my petticoat," &c., while *camisa* and *yam,* which in the Gypsy language denotes "a shirt" and "food" or "victuals," is the same in the Negro dialect of Surinam.

Their vocal music is like that of some birds, melodious but without time; in other respects it is not unlike that of some clerks reading to the congregation, one person pronouncing a sentence extempore, which he next hums or whistles, when all the others repeat the same in chorus; another sentence is then spoken and the chorus is renewed a second time, and so ad perpetuum. As a specimen of it I will try to put the following notes to music, supposing a soldier going off to battle is taking leave of his mistress.

one bus adiosi - o daso adiosso me dego me loby fo fighty me man o

na inny da boosy amimba o daso adiosso me dego—

Such is their vocal music, while that of their dancing and instrumental music (which is perfectly to time) I will speak of in the future, having already hinted at that of the Loango Negroes.

However, that these people are not divested of a good ear, and even of a poetical genius, has been frequently discovered when they had the advantage of education, witness among others a black girl called Phillis Wheatley, who was a slave at Boston in New England; she even learned the Latin language and wrote thirty-eight elegant pieces of poetry on different subjects, which were published in 1773. While who has not heard of that wonderful Negro, Ignatius Sancho, whose very sublime letters and sound philosophy would even add luster to the brightest European genius of the age.[5] And with regard to memory and calculation, I shall only produce Thomas Fuller, a Negro slave, the property of a Mrs. Cox in Maryland, North America, who was living so late as the year 1788. And to gratify the reader verbally I shall copy one of his anecdotes as related to a gentleman at Manchester in a letter by Doctor Rush of Philadelphia. Being once asked by a respectable company of the above town (who were traveling through Maryland and had heard of his amazing powers) how many seconds a man of seventy years and some odd months, weeks, and days had lived, he told the complete number in a minute and a half. The gentleman who had put the question (taking up his pen and calculating the same sum by means of figures) then told the Negro he was mistaken, as the number he had declared was certainly too great. "Top, *Massera* (said the slave), you have forgot the leap years," and having included the seconds they contained, their sums were exactly found to be the same. This same man multiplied nine figures by nine from memory before another company. Now, that such amazing mental faculties should be possessed by an African black who could neither read nor write must appear astonishing, yet such they were without the smallest manner of doubt.[6]

To what I have said I shall now add that all Negroes believe firmly in a God whose goodness they trust more than many whining Christians, nor have they any fear of death, confident they will see some of their friends and relations again in another world, but not that if they die abroad they will rise in their own country (as good Mr. Clarkson, Miss Merian, and many others erroneously were taught to believe). That no Negro ever breaks an oath I have already in the beginning of this work clearly demonstrated, to the shame and infamy of those Europeans who break it daily, and treat with contempt this race of people more religious than

---

5. His letters &c. are printed in two volumes by Dilly at London, price: six shillings in boards.

6. See the supplement to the *Town and Country Magazine* for 1788. Negroes, however, in general keep no time, calculating even their age by the growth of a tree.

themselves. Neither does a Negro ever eat or drink without offering a libation.

They also bring their offerings to the wild cotton tree which they adore with high reverence.[7]

> This proceeds (said an old black man to me) from the following judicious cause. Having no churches on the coast of Guinea, and this tree being the largest and most beautiful growing there, our people assemble often under its branches to keep free from the heavy showers of rain and scorching sunshine, when they are going to be instructed. Do not you Christians pay the same homage to your Bibles &c.? We well know that our tree is but a wooden log covered with leaves of green, nor is your book assuredly any more than a piece of lumber composed of leaves of paper.

The *gadoman* or priest delivers his lectures under this tree, for which the vulgar Negroes have so much veneration that they will not cut it down upon any consideration whatever. Indeed, nothing can be more superstitious than the common class of these people, while they are still more kept in darkness by their pretended *looco-men* or prophets, who find their interest in their blindness, by selling them *obias,* or amulets, as I have already mentioned, with other charms, not unlike those hypocrites who even sell absolution for a comfortable living. Nor are a kind of *Sibyls* wanting among them, who deal in oracles; these sage matrons dancing and whirling round in the middle of an audience, till they absolutely froth at the mouth and drop down in the middle of them. Whatever she says to be done during this fit of madness is sacredly performed by the surrounding multitude, which makes these meetings exceedingly dangerous among the slaves, who are often told to murder their masters or desert to the woods, and on which account the excessiveness of this piece of fanaticism is forbidden in the Colony of Surinam, on pain of the most rigorous punishment. Yet it is often put in execution in private places and is very common among the Auka and Saramaka Negroes, where captains Friderici and Van Geurike told me they saw it performed. This is here called *winty play,* or the dance of the mermaid, and takes its origin from time immemorial, the classic authors making frequent mention of this unaccountable practice.

---

7. This tree, which the Negroes call *cot-tan teeree,* grows to a considerable height and thickness. It is very straight and covered with a strong, gray, prickly bark; the boughs spread to a considerable circumference, with small digitated leaves. The cotton (which it produces triennially) is not very white and, being neither very plentiful, is little sought after. Upon the whole, this tree bears some resemblance to the British oak, yet it surpasses both in elegance and magnitude the largest in that island.

But what is still more strange is that these unaccountable women, by their voice, know how to charm the *ammodytes* or *papa* serpents down from the trees.[8] This is an absolute fact, nor is the above snake ever killed or hurt by the Negroes, who on the contrary adore it as their friend and guardian, and are even happy to see it enter their huts. Nay, when the above sibyls have called or conjured down the ammodytes serpent from the tree, it is even common to see the reptile twine and wreathe about their arms, neck, and breast, as if the creature took delight in hearing her vocal music, while the woman strokes and caresses it with her hand.

Thus I have described some strange peculiarities which, however absurd, are not so much so as those of the vulgar Europeans believing in the apparition of ghosts, and the incantations of witches, some of which poor creatures (or at least supposed to be so) were inhumanly burnt among us so late as the middle of the last century.

One more glaring instance of superstition among the Negroes I must relate, and I will have done with this subject, which is, that every family is distinctly prohibited, from father to son, to eat of one particular kind of animal food. This may be either fowl, fish, or quadruped, but whatever it is, no Negro will touch this, while I have seen some good Roman Catholics eat roast beef in Lent, and a religious Jew devouring a slice of a fat flitch of bacon.

However ridiculous some of the above rites of devotion among the African blacks, they are certainly necessary to keep the rabble in subjection, and their *gadomen* or priests know this as well as do our clergymen in England. And in one thing these illiterate mortals have assuredly the advantage of the modern Europeans, viz., that whatever they believe they believe it firmly, which is more than the generality of the former can boast of. And as for the good works of the Negroes, or indeed of the Indians, being better or worse, I will not pretend to determine, but this I know, that their faith is never staggered, on which delicate point they thus are never troubled with the qualms of a guilty conscience. Upon the whole, I think them a happy people and who possess so much friendship among each other, that they need not to be told to love their brethren as themselves, since the poorest Negro among them, having but an egg scorns to eat it alone, but were twelve others present and every one of them a stranger, he would cut or break it into as many shares.[9] While

---

8. This creature is from three to five feet long and perfectly harmless; it has not the smallest apprehension to be hurt, even by man, while the indescribable brilliance of its colors are perhaps another inducement for the adoration of the Negroes.

9. This proves that the word Negroish is very ill-applied when meant to describe greediness or self-interest.

should one single dram of rum be divided among such a number, still is this not done, as I have said, without first spilling a few drops on the ground as an oblation to the gods. Come here now, thou hypocrite, and take an example from thy sable brother: but alas, I am afraid it is too true, "that no more than the Ethiopian can change his skin or the leopard his spots, no more is it in thy power to do good who art accustomed to do evil." Thus keep thy canting Moravians at home,[10] and try not to lead a people from the paths of innocence into a mystery which is too frequently abused, and is too intricate, as well as too sacred, even for thyself well to understand it. A name (which too often only cloaked with godliness) has been for ages dyed in scarlet and reeking with the warm streams of human blood, nay, at which three-quarters of the world still shudders and hears pronounced with contempt and abhorrence.

What racks and tortures have not been invented by the gold-thirsty enthusiast, particularly on the American Indians, and poor Negroes transported from the coast of Africa, their native home, who only struggle to relieve their lost liberty.

> What good man can reflect the tear-stained eye,
> When blood attests even slaves for freedom die?
> On cruel gibbets high disclosed they rest,
> And scarce one groan escapes one bloated breast.
> Here sable Caesars[11] feel the Christian rod:
> There Afric Platos, tortured, hope a god:
> While jetty Brutus for his country sighs,
> And sooty Cato with his freedom dies!

But by what I have advanced, let it however not be understood that I am an enemy to Christianity—as I have said before, God forbid—nor an enemy to any religious sect whatever, but most undoubtedly the greatest friend to those whose actions I know best to correspond with their morals.

Let us now proceed to take a cursory view of the natural character of the African Negroes. This I will first represent under its blackest colors, contrary to the rules of painters, and next introduce those fair shades to which I know they are entitled.

In the first place, no people have greater thirst for revenging an injury,

---

10. Moravian preachers have been sent over (and I am persuaded, with their best intentions) to convert the Indians and Saramaka Negroes, but hitherto without the smallest good effect.

11. The above names are generally given to imported Negro slaves, with such as Nero, Pluto, Charon, Cerberus, Procersmina, Medusa, &c., given in exchange for Quacoo, Quacy, Quamy, Quamina, Quasiba, and Adjuba, which latter assuredly have not a less agreeable sound.

even biting their very lice with their teeth, because they first bit them. Indeed, I never yet saw a Negro forgive another person who had willfully offended him, and for which the only apology I can make is the strength of their passion, they being equally grateful on the other hand, and next the old Grecian adage which says that

> A generous friendship no cold medium knows,
> but with one love, with one resentment glows.

However, their abominable cruelties, as those of all barbarous nations, are truly shocking, witness the colony Berbice, where during the late revolt they made no scruple to cut up alive their European mistresses who were with child in the presence of their husbands, besides many other horrors too dreadful to relate. And in the art of poisoning not even the Accawau Indians are more expert, which some of these wretches carry under their nails, and by only dipping the thumb in a tumbler of water, which they carry as a beverage to the objects of their hatred, infuses a slow but no less certain death.[12] Nay, whole estates as well as private families have become the victims of their wrath and experienced their fatality, putting to death even scores of their own friends and relations, with the double view of depriving their proprietors of their best possessions and at once delivering those Negro slaves whom they love best from under the lash of their tyranny.

These unhappy monsters are distinguished by the name of *wissy men,* perhaps derived from wise-, or knowing-men, and by their subtle genius sometimes carry their destruction to a most dreadful length before they are detected. The other vices of this nation consist in their being thieves by nature, generally stealing what they can come at with impunity, and in regard to intemperance in drinking they are without any bounds, I have seen even a Negro-wench empty a china bowl with two bottles of claret at one draught, which I myself had given her to make the experiment.

I ought not to forget that the *Gango* Negroes are reckoned anthropophagi or cannibals, just as are the Caribbee Indians, that is, from an unsatiated retaliation on their enemies. Among this class of Rebels, after the taking of Boucou, some pots were found on the fire with human flesh in them, such as hands, feet, &c., which one of the officers had the curiosity to taste, declaring it was not inferior to other meat.

I shall now only observe that black and heinous as are the above

---

12. This is an absolute fact of which I only would be convinced after the most scrupulous information and ocular demonstrations.

crimes, they are the natural effects of revenge and avarice alone. But how many crimes are known among us that are unnatural? Over the one and the other, let me quickly spread a sable veil, and dispel this gloomy cloud by the sunshine of their virtues.

Their genius has been already conspicuously observed, so has their gratitude, which they will even carry to such a length that they would die for those who have showed them any particular favor, while nothing but the faithfulness of a dog can equal that fidelity and attachment they have for those masters who use them well, which shows that their affection is as strong as is their hatred. The Negroes are naturally good-tempered, particularly the *Coromantyn* and those of *Nago,* while of the passion of love they are not unsusceptible, witness the jealousy of their wives, to whom their resentment for incontinency is absolutely implacable, but as for what they did before they bear that title, it gives them no uneasiness. And such is the delicacy of these people that I don't remember ever (among the many thousands that I did live with) to have seen one offer a kiss in public to a woman, while the maternal tenderness of the mothers is such for their children that (during the two years while they are at the breast) none cohabit with their husbands, thus it seldom happens to see one of them pregnant again, which they deem both unnatural and preju-dicial to the sucking infant, the case of Lesperanza being no exception, whose babies died almost so soon as they came into the world.

As for the exemplary cleanliness of the Negro nation, it is peculiarly remarkable, they being at least three times a day overhead in the water, and in which the *Congo* tribe are still distinguished from the rest, being the very next thing to amphibious animals.

The Negroes are spirited, brave, and patient in adversity, while their undaunted fortitude in going to death through every torture approaches even to heroism; no Negro ever sighs or complains, though he is expiring in the middle of surrounding flames. Indeed, on no occasion whatever can I remember to have seen an African shed a tear; yet to beg for mercy they never fail when they are ordered to be flogged. While if they are punished without deserving it (in their own opinion), immediate suicide is too often the fatal consequence, especially among the *Coromantyn* Ne-groes, who frequently, even during the act of castigation, throw back their head and by doubling the tongue have got a method of swallowing it down, by which it swells, when they choke themselves upon the spot and drop down dead in the presence of their masters. Yet when they are sensible of having deserved correction, no people can be more humble or go through their unhappy fate with so much resignation. Others have got a practice of eating common earth, by which the stomach, being prevented from ordinary digestion, causes them to dispatch themselves without any immediate pain, yet by which they linger perhaps for a whole twelve months in the most wretched condition.

The swallowing of the tongue, which always takes place during the very moment of discipline, has of late been prevented in Surinam by the humane method of clapping a fire brand or burning stick to the victim's face, which serves for the double purpose of singeing his lips and suffocation; and by which means he is divested (for the present) from putting into execution his fatal determination.

Against the ground eaters, who are very common, the severest punishments are decreed by the laws, but without much effect, they being but seldom detected in the commission of this act of desperation.

Having thus far described the mental and bodily faculties of the African Negroes in a natural condition, we will now doubly view them in a state of bondage, first under all the oppressions that they are exposed to under a rod of barbarous tyranny, and next as protected by the mild hand of justice and humanity. While the one picture (I am almost afraid) will occasion such a shudder that any further perusal of this work will be dropped and laid aside, but I pledge my word that the other will make full and ample compensation, and in which state of servitude I will finish delineating the striking peculiarities of the Negro character, which I have thus far brought to a conclusion.

That there have been slaves from the earliest times (witness Philemon and Onesimus) needs no comment. Indeed, we are all dependents in a less or more degree, but how to treat those whom fate has subjected to our commands? That is the question. And how they are treated in the Colony of Surinam shall presently be seen.

The reader may remember that I have introduced them in the ninth chapter as landing from the coast of Guinea in a lamentable state of skin and bone. I have there said that under the care of other old Negro slaves, they soon become very fat and sleek, and learn the language of the Colony, when they are next sent to work in the fields, to which at first they cheerfully submit, but I have known newly imported Negroes, to my surprise, who absolutely refused to do any work at all, either by good or by bad words, promises or threats, nay, even rewards, or blows, till the wonder ceased, by being informed by the others that these unhappy people had been princes, or people of the first rank and condition, in their own country, who by some misfortune in war &c., had come to this infamous state, but whose pride and heroic sentiments preferred even instant death to vile servitude, and upon which occasions the rest of the slaves have dropped down upon their knees, imploring the masters to allow themselves to do the work required, which generally being granted, the same homage and respect is shown to the captive prince that he was accustomed to in his own country. I remember having had a charming-looking new Negro called William to attend me, whose wrists and ankles being galled by the tying of a rope, I enquired for the cause.

> My father (said he) was a king, and treacherously murdered by the sons of a neighboring prince. I, to revenge his death, went daily out a-hunting with some men, in hopes to retaliate on the assassins, but I was surprised, taken, tied, and sold to your European countrymen on the coast of Guinea, which was deemed a greater punishment than killing me at once.

The history of Quacoo, my black boy, was still more strange.

> My parents (said he) lived by hunting and fishing, from whom I was stolen with two little brothers when we were all very young and playing in the sand. Being carried (alone) some miles in a bag, I became the slave of a king on the coast of Guinea, with many hundred more, who, when our master died, had all their heads chopped off to be buried along with him, myself alone excepted, with other children of my age, who being bestowed as presents to the different captains of his army, my new master again sold me to the captain of a Dutch ship for some powder and a musket.

How hard must this not be already, to be dragged over a turbulent sea to a strange country, never more to repatriate, let them be used as well as even it is possible.

In short, no sooner do these wretches begin to flag in their work than whips, cow skin, bamboo canes, ropes, fetters, and chains are introduced, till they are ready to sink under toil and oppression, nor with some masters can their tasks ever be fulfilled, making them fag on day and night, even Sundays not excepted. Nay, I recollect a strong young Negro called Marquis, who having a wife he loved and two fine children, generally finished his task (which was to delve five hundred feet according to the usual custom) before four o'clock in the afternoon, that he might thus have some time to cultivate his little garden, and fish or fowl for his family; hard, hard, did Marquis labor to earn this additional pittance. This humane master, however, apprised of his industry, for his encouragement now told him that if he could delve five hundred feet by four o'clock, he could assuredly finish six hundred before sunset, to which, from that day, the unfortunate man was absolutely condemned for ever after. Add to this that in Surinam they are next to being kept perfectly naked, while their chief food consists in little more than a bunch of plantains, indeed, about twice a year they receive a scanty allowance of salt fish, with a few leaves of tobacco, which goes by the name of *sweety-muffo*. Still more provoking is that if a Negro and his wife have never so great an attachment to each other, the woman, if handsome, must yield to the loathsome embraces of a rascally manager, or see her husband cut to pieces by the whip for daring to think of preventing it, which truly drives them to distraction. By these and many other complicated evils, several either kill themselves, run away to the woods, or become spiritless and languish under various diseases (the effects of the above bad usage), such as the *lota,* which is a white scorbutic spot that externally covers the body, the *crassy-crassy,* or itch from top to bottom, the *yaws,* which is a most disagreeable disorder by which the patient is covered all over with yellow ulcers, and is a most disgusting spectacle. This disease most Negroes have once in their life, yet only once; some people have compared it to the French pox, while it is so infectious that if a fly that has been feeding on one of the above martyrs (who are generally covered with them) picks on an open scratch of any healthy person, he is almost sure to be inflicted with the cursed malady, which continues for several months together. The general cure in Surinam is to put them under a salivation, to which may be added a spare diet and uninterrupted exercise to promote perspiration, when the poor devils absolutely look like decayed and corrupted carcasses. Still more dreadful than this is the *boassy* or *leprosy,* which is incurable forever. This consists of a swelling of the face, limbs, &c., while the whole body is covered over with scales and ulcers, the breath stinks, the hair falls out, and the fingers and toes, becoming putrid, drop off joint after joint, till they expire, which is often not under the course of many years. The lepers are naturally lascivious, and apt to convey the disease to whoever comes within their reach, on which account (at the plantations) they are separated from every other society.

Another disorder called the *clabba yaws* or *tubboes,* which I had nearly forgot, is very troublesome and often lasts a very long time. This consists of painful sores about the feet, and mostly under the soles, which (being between the skin and the flesh) must generally be cured by being burnt with a red hot iron, or cut up with a lancet, when the warm juice of roasted limes with success is squeezed into the wound.

The African Negroes are also subject to worms of many species, both subcutaneous and internal, owing to wading in stagnant waters and to the crudity of their diet, &c. Among the former is one called the *Guinea-* or *lint-worm,* which exists between the skin and the flesh, and is sometimes two yards in length, while it is not thicker than the second string of a bass viol, shining and as white as silver; this insect occasions very dangerous and painful swellings in those places where it coils itself, which is most usually about the legs; the method of cure is to seize the head, when it appears above the skin, and gently to extract the worm by winding it about a stick, which operation cannot be done too carefully, for should it break (which often happens) not only the loss of the limb but the loss of life itself is frequently the fatal consequence. Some are infested with six or eight of those worms at one time.

Besides the above dreadful worms and calamities, the Negroes are subject to every other complaint peculiar to the Europeans, who are not free in Guiana from the loathsome and dangerous distempers I have just described in the African blacks.

After what I have said, it is little wonder to see some estates crowded with miserable objects who are mostly left by the overseer under the care of the *dressy Negro,* and whose skill consists in giving a dose of physic or spreading a plaster only. As for the numbers whose bodies are raw from neck to heel by constant whipping, these are left to cure themselves or continue to do their work without a skin, if they think proper. I shall now regularly continue the links of this black chain.

By the above complicated oppressions from nature, and a drunken rascal of a manager, it must follow that numerous slaves become unfit to do any work, some being too weak, others skulking from it from fear, and others becoming old before their time, but for all these desperate evils, this despotic *basha* nevertheless finds a cure, which is no other than to kill them outright, which loss devolves (not on him but) on his master, to whom, to be sure, he is proud to show none but such slaves as are hardy and able to do the work, telling him at the same time, that the others died by the venereal disease, and for which the villain's word alone is sufficient, as Negroes are not tolerated to give evidence in any case whatever.

Dictio testimonii non est servo homini.

Yet should, by some unforseen accident, a European chance to prove the murder, the delinquent pays (as I have said) about fifty pounds only as a fine, besides the price of the slave if his master requires it, and for which price of blood he may butcher on from January to December. And this he does assuredly, whenever his passion or bloody inclination leads him to it, having such frequent opportunities to evade the penalty, even when the magistrates are present, some of which stratagems I will now relate. For instance, I have known it to happen that such a brute, being tired of an old Negro, and only wishing to get rid of him, took him out a-fowling when, desiring him to discover the game, the first bird that started he shot the poor man dead upon the spot, which is called an *accident* without any further enquiry is made about it. Others have been killed in the following manner to get rid of them: a strong stake being fastened in the ground, the slave was chained to it in the middle of an open plain and under burning sunshine, where one gill of water, with one single plantain, was brought every day till he was starved to death. But this is not called dying with famine by his master who, declaring he had wanted neither meat or drink till he expired, is honorably acquitted.

Still another method of murdering with impunity has often been put in practice. This is to tie them stark naked to a tree in the forest, with arms and legs expanded, under pretense of stretching their limbs, but where they remain (being regularly fed) till they are absolutely stung to death by the gnats or mosquitoes, which is, to be sure, a most infernal punishment and a child of the most diabolical invention. Nay, kicking them overboard, with a weight chained to their heels by which they are inevitably drowned, is called accidental death, while even by the orders of a woman, Negro slaves have been privately burned to death, miserably chained in a surrounding pile of flaming faggots. As to the breaking out of their teeth for tasting the sugar cane cultivated by themselves, or slitting up their nose and cutting off their ears from private pique, these are looked upon as laughable trifles, not worth so much as to be mentioned or to come into consideration.

In short, to such a pitch of desperation has this unhappy race of men sometimes been driven, that from spite to end their days and to be relieved from bondage, they have even leaped into a cauldron of boiling sugar, thus at one blow depriving the tyrant of his crop and his servant.

The above sketches, together with those acts of barbarity I have so frequently related throughout this work, are assuredly sufficient to melt the heart of the most unfeeling with compassion. Nor is it to be wondered that armies of Rebels at every hazard assemble in the forest to seek revenge and liberty.

I shall now end the dreadful scenery by a general remark on the effect which this diabolical usage has on population.

In Surinam are supposed to be, at an average, about 75,000 Negro slaves, but out of which number, if we extract the children and the superannuated men and women, I am confident no more than 50,000 are ablebodied, and calculated to do any work, thus two out of three, which is a large allowance.

The Guinea ships that import slaves from Africa being from four to ten in number, and having on board each vessel a cargo of from 250 to 300 slaves, we will suppose the yearly importation to be about 2,500 to supply and complete the above 50,000, and then we will find the mortality to be just five percent, viz., more dead than born, notwithstanding each Negro has a wife or two if he chooses. By which it is proven that the complete number of Negro slaves, consisting of 50,000 healthy people, is exactly extinct once every twenty years, which is truly shocking to human nature, and more so when one reflects that this is but in one colony.

What must the mortality be throughout the whole American settlements? The calculation is 100,000 per annum; thus in twenty years, two millions of people are murdered to provide us with coffee and sugar.

> But hark! the Afric' genius clanks his chains,
> And damns the race that robs his native plains!

Now, O fie be to thee, wretch, who art the cause of the above complicated miseries, yet which (bad as they are) Heaven hath compassionately prevented from being universal, as I shall (by impartially reversing the picture) make appear, and not (like the reverend gentlemen Ramsay and Clarkson) only show the darkest shades through a glass, carefully preserving and concealing the most elegant touches from the public investigation. No. In a manly manner will I bring truth to light, and fairly expose the good as well as the bad to the eye of a candid world. That is to say, the good, when the Negro slaves are treated as they ought to be treated, which at some estates they are, and might be always if the cancer was once eradicated from the root where it lies, viz., from the laws which are deaf to the cry of the afflicted dependents, while the master is invested with that unbounded despotism which ever ends in a tyrannical usurpation. And shall I ever honor the result of a late process in London, where a Negro slave being supported (by the rod of justice and humanity) against his master, enjoyed that liberty to which, in a free country, he had a right by the laws of nature. Now to proceed.

In the first place, I will introduce a Negro family in that state of tranquil happiness to which they are all entitled when they are well-treated by their owners. They are supposed to be of the *Loango* nation by the marks on the man's body, while on his breast may also be seen the letters J.G.S., being the initials of my name, and supposed to be the cipher by which each master knows his property. He carries a basket with small fish on his head, and a net, while a large fish is in his hand, all caught by himself; and while his wife (who is pregnant) is employed in carrying different kinds of fruit, spinning a thread of cotton, and comfortably smoking her pipe of tobacco, still besides all which she has a boy on her back and another playing by her side.[13]

Under such a mild government, no Negro's work is more than a healthy exercise, which ends with the setting sun, viz., at six o'clock, when the rest of the time is his own, which he employs in hunting, and fishing, cultivating his little garden, or making baskets, fishnets, &c., for

---

13. For the above picture, I was offered fifty florins by Mr. A. Rynsdorp at Amsterdam.

Family of Negro Slaves from Loango.

Blake Sculp.^t

Plate 68

sale; with which money he buys a hog, sometimes a couple, or a quantity of fowls or ducks, all of which he fattens with the spontaneous growth of the soil, without they cost him either cash, or much trouble, and which in the end afford him considerable profit.

Thus pleasantly situated, he is exempt from every anxiety, and looks up to his master as the common protector of him and his family, whom he adores not from fear or flattery but from a conviction of his being the object of his care and attention. He breathes in a luxurious warm climate like his own, thus wants no clothes, besides which incumbrance and expense, he saves the time of dressing, undressing, washing, &c., and enjoys much more health and pleasure by going naked.[14]

His house he can build after his fancy, the forest affording him all that he wants to make it comfortable for the cutting. His bed is a hammock, or a mat called *papaya,* and his elbow his pillow. If he is wearied standing, he sits squat upon his hams, which he is taught by nature. His pots he makes himself, and his dishes or gourds grow in his garden. He never lives with a wife he does not love, exchanging her for another the moment he, or she, is tired, yet which more seldom happens here than in a European state of matrimony. Besides his master's allowance of plantains &c., which are two bunches a week, his female friend has the way to make him many savory dishes, such as: *braff,* being a hodge-podge of plantains and yams boiled with salt meat, barbecued fish, and cayenne pepper; *tom-tom* is a very good pudding, composed with the flour of Indian corn and boiled with flesh, fish, cayenne pepper, and the young pods of the *okra* or *althea* plant; *pepper-pot* is a dish of boiled fish and capsicum, eaten with roasted plantains; *gangotay* is made of dried-, and *afoofoo* of green plantains; *acanara* and *doquenoo* are composed of the flour of maize, the last eaten with molasses &c. His general drink is the limpid stream, sometimes sweetened and corrected with a dram of new rum. If he is indisposed, he is cured for nothing, yet but seldom troubles the faculty, being perfectly skilled in the knowledge of herbs or simples, besides which scarifying and puckering the skin are a constant practice, which serves for a bleeding; even the inconvenience of vermin he removes without a comb by pushing up all his hair in clay, which being dried on his pate and then washed with soap and water, makes him clean beyond every conception. Indeed, in regard to cleanliness, no people can surpass

---

14. How preferable this is to his modernized countrymen, who walk the streets of London with their hair combed and powdered in a tail, which makes them look like monkeys. The young women, however, in Surinam are mostly supplied with chintz petticoats, generally of ten breadths, gold ear-drops, garnet bracelets, &c., while a silk handkerchief tied round the head is very common.

some Negro slaves, particularly their teeth, which are forever kept as white as ivory, for which they use nothing more than a sprig of orange, which (being bitten to the consistency of a small brush) they are forever rubbing their gums with, nor is any Negro (male or female) ever seen without this little green tool, which besides has the virtue of sweetening the breath.

So much for the body, and in regard to the soul, he is seldom troubled with any qualms of conscience or fear of death, being firm and unshaken in what he was taught to believe. And when he is no more, his companions or relations carry him to some grove of orange trees, where he is interred with uncommon expense for those people, being put in a coffin of the best wood and workmanship, while the cries and lamentations of his surviving friends pierce the sky. The grave being filled up and green turf neatly spread over it, a couple of large gourds are put by the side of it, the one with water, the other with boiled fowls, pork, cassava, &c., as a libation, not from a superstition (as some d——nd idiots believe) that he will eat or drink it, but as a testimony of that regard which they have for his memory; while some even add the little furniture that he left behind, breaking it in pieces over the grave. This done, everyone takes his last farewell, speaking to him as if he lived, by testifying their sorrow at his departure, however that they hope to see him in a better place, where he now enjoys the pleasant company of his parents, dearest friends, and ancestors, when another dismal yell ends the ceremony, and all return home where (a fat hog being killed, with fowls, ducks, &c.) a general feast is given by his relations to all the other Negroes, which ends not till the following day. Now those who were his nearest connections, both male and female, cut their hair and shave the head round and, having tied a dark blue handkerchief, they wear this mourning for a whole year. After this, once more visiting the grave, offering a libation, and taking their final farewell, another hog &c., is killed, and the funeral rites are quite ended by a second feast, which finishes with a joyful dance and songs of praise in memory of their dear relation.

No people can more esteem or have a greater friendship for each other than the Negro slaves, who enjoy each other's company with an unbounded pleasure, during which they are not destitute of diversions such as *soesa*, which consists of dancing opposite to each other and clapping their hands on their sides to keep in time, when each with pleasure throws out one foot. If they meet across, the party wins one point, if sides, it is for the other, till one or the other has got twelve, sometimes twenty points, who gets the game. So very eager are they at this play, in which sometimes six or eight couples are engaged at once, that the violent exercise having killed some of the Negroes, it is forbidden by the magistrates at Paramaribo. *Awaree* is an innocent amusement, consisting in pitching with a large kind of marbles in defect of which they use the *awaree* nuts. The men also cudgel and wrestle, yet at this I think them inferior to either those of Cornwall or Devon.

But swimming is their favorite diversion, which they practice every day at least twice or thrice, promiscuously in groups of boys and girls, without distinction like the Indians. Both sexes show astonishing feats of courage, strength, and activity; nay, I have not only seen a Negro girl beat a hardy youth in swimming across the River Commewina (while I was one of the party), but on landing challenge him and beat him stark naked at a two-mile race, while every idea of shame on the one side and of insult on the other are totally unknown.

I shall now say something of their music and dancing. I have already mentioned that of the *Loango* tribe in particular, and thus will now describe that practiced by the other nations in general. First their instruments of sound (which are not a little ingenious) are all made by themselves, and consist of those represented in the annexed plate, where:

No. 1, which is called *qua-qua,* is a hard sounding-board elevated on one side like a boot jack, on which they beat or drum time with two pieces of iron, or two bones.

No. 2 is the *Kiemba toetoe,* or hollow reed, which is blown through the nostrils, like the nasal flute of Otaheytey; it has but two holes, one at each end, the first serving to sound it, the other to be touched by the finger.

No. 3 is the *Ansokko bania,* which is a hard board supported on both sides like a low seat, on which are placed small blocks of different sizes, which being struck with two small sticks like a dulcimer gives different sounds that are not at all disagreeable.

No. 4 is the *great Creole drum,* being a hollow tree open at one end and covered on the other with a sheepskin, on which they sit astride and so beat time with the palm of their hands, answering the effect of a bass viol to the *qua-qua* board.

No. 5 is the *great Loango drum,* being covered at both ends and serves the same purpose.

No. 6 is the *Papa drum,* beaten as the others.

No. 7 is the *small Loango drum,* beaten together with the great one.

No. 8 is the *small Creole drum* for the same use.

No. 9 is called *coeroema;* this is a wooden cup ingeniously made and covered also with a sheepskin; it is beaten with two small rods or drumsticks after the manner of the *qua-qua* board.

No. 10 is the *Loango bania,* which I thought exceedingly curious, being a dry board on which are laced, and kept close by a transverse bar, different sized elastic splinters of the palm tree, in such a manner that both ends are elevated by other transverse bars that are fixed under them, and the above apparatus is placed on

No. 11, which is a *large empty gourd* to promote the sound; the extremities of the splinters are snapped by the fingers, something in the manner of a pianoforte, and have the same effect.

No. 12 is called by the Negroes *saka-saka,* being a hollow gourd with a stick and handle fixed through it, and filled with small pebbles (not unlike the magic shell of the Indians); this they hold above their head and rattle it to measure while they dance.

No. 13 is a *conch* or sea shell, which (by the lungs) they sound for pleasure, or to cause an alarm &c., but is not related to their dancing.

No. 14 is called *benta,* being a branch bent like a bow, by means of a slip of dry reed, or *warimbo,* which when held to the teeth, the string is beaten with a short stick, and being shifted back and forwards sounds not unlike a jew's-harp.

No. 15 is the *Creole-bania;* this is like a mandolin or guitar, being made of a gourd covered with a sheepskin, to which is fixed a very long neck or handle; this instrument has but four strings, three long and one short, which is thick and serves for a bass; it is played by the fingers, and has a very agreeable sound, more so when accompanied with a song.

No. 16 is the *trumpet* of war, to command advancing, retreating, &c., and is called the *too-too.*

No. 17 is a *horn* used to replace the other, or on the plantations to call the slaves to work.

No. 18 is the *Loango too-too* or flute, which they blow (as the Europeans do) after the common way; it has but four holes for the fingers, yet independent of which they make it produce a variety of sounds.

Such are the musical instruments of our African brethren, to which they dance with more spirit than we do to the best band in Europe.

To what I have said I will only add that they always use full, or half measure, but never triple time, in their dancing music, which not unlike a baker's bunt (when he separates the flour from the bran) sounds *tuckety-tuck* and *tuckety-tuck,* ad perpetuum.

To this noise, however, they dance with uncommon pleasure, and sometimes foot it away with great art and dexterity.

But to proceed with my description of a happy slave. Every Saturday evening, he shuts up the week with an entertainment of this kind, and at

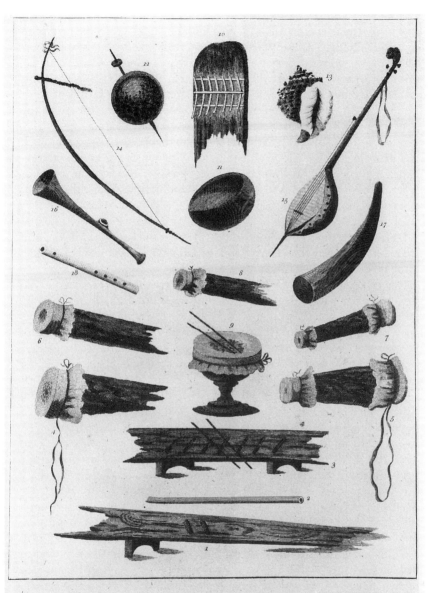

Musical Instruments of the African Negroes.

Plate 69

least once a quarter is indulged with a grand ball, to which the neighboring slaves are invited, and where the master often contributes to the happiness by his presence, or at least by sending a present of a few jugs of kill-devil or new rum. At these grand balls, the slaves are remarkably neat, the women appearing in their best chintz petticoats, and many of the men in fine Holland trousers, and so indefatigable are they at this diversion, that I have known the drums to continue beating without intermission from sunset on Saturday night till that celestial orb again made its appearance on the Monday morning following, being mostly accompanied by cheering, hallooing, and clapping of hands. The Negroes dance always in couples, the men figuring and footing, while the women turn round like a top, and their petticoats expand like a circle, which they call *waey cotto*.

During this, the bystanding youths fill about the liquor, while the girls encourage the performers and wipe the lather from the brows and sides of the unwearied musicians.

It is indeed, upon the whole, astonishing to see with what good nature, and even with a degree of good manners,[15] these dancing societies are kept up, of which I still repeat they are so very fond that I have known a newly imported Negro (for want of a partner) to figure and foot it for near the space of two hours to his shadow against the wall.

All that I have now said above in regard to their being happy is still but a trifle when compared to that felicity of living till they die with their parents and nearest relations, while their children are forever near them, and provided for, to the end of their lives. Nay, some have the satisfaction to see their offspring about them to the third or fourth generation.

How wide different is not this from the generality of Europeans, who spend (under the name of Liberty) a wretched existence, enveloped in a turbulent sea of care and anxiety, while their descendants are even happy if by being wafted to all the different corners of the earth, and being torn to all eternity from their presence, they can only get bread, though steeped in bitterness and the sweat of their forehead. Good God, what are our soldiers and sailors? Are they not dependent under the very severest laws? Do they not sell their liberty for a precarious subsistence, and to serve as marks to be shot at? Away detestable prejudice, which cannot see its own chains on account of their gilding; and hail, thou happy people, who under the name of slavery enjoy often the purest bliss, which is to say, in other words, that the African Negro slaves who have the good

---

15. The Negroes generally salute each other by shaking hands, when they meet the tops of the middle fingers, snap them three times, and make a bow, saying, *How dee matee,* "How are you, friend?"

fortune to be under a master who is really a man enjoy that state of felicity that is superior to most, and even inferior to none.[16] This, to be sure, is too seldom the consequence at present, Heaven knows it, but such may be the general case in time to come, when good sense and humanity shall have dictated such laws for the government of the African Negro slaves, as shall be proved to be for the permanent good of both the ruler and the subject. And that such laws can exist I will give a hint of, as I have promised, before I leave these pages.

Attesting that I was acquainted with a free Negro woman (at Deventer in Holland) who since voluntarily gave up her liberty, and again preferred to be a slave in Surinam (in which state I also knew her), I will take my final farewell of the African Negroes, and put an end to this very long and tedious chapter by the old and judicious remark that all sublunary happiness consists in imagination only, when health of body and peace of mind are not interrupted by oppression.

---

16. Such is the confidence some planters have in their slaves that they even trust their infants to a Negro wet-nurse, who to be sure treats them generally with the greatest tenderness and affection.

CHAPTER 27th

*The rape of the Sabines—Shocking execution and African
fortitude—The spanso bocko, a punishment*

On August 12th, news came to Paramaribo that though the Rebels had
desisted of late from cruelties and insurrections, they had still ventured a
second Rape of the Sabines by taking away all the women at the estate
Berg en Dal on the Blauwe Berg, called also Mount Parnassus, in the
higher parts of the River Surinam—notwithstanding a military post was
stationed at the above place. In consequence, a party of the Rangers was
instantly detached thither to assist in pursuing them &c., and about the
same time, the long-projected Cordon, or path of circumvolution around
the Colony, was also begun to be cut by seven hundred Negro slaves,
which path was henceforth to be manned with military pickets at proper
distances to defend the estates against any further insurrections from
without, and prevent desertion to the enemy from within.

The above Mount Parnassus is situated on the west side of the River
Surinam, distant from Paramaribo (if one includes the windings of the
river) above one hundred miles. It being a pleasant situation, I present the
reader with a view of it in the plate annexed, as also of the village called
the Jews-Savanna which is distant from town (in ligna recta, as I have
said) something more than forty but by water above sixty miles. Here,
the Jews have a beautiful synagogue and keep their solemn feasts and fes-
tivals. Here, they also have their capital, schools, and seminaries, while
at this village reside some very respectable Jewish families, these people
possessing particular rights and privileges in this colony, with which they
were endowed by King Charles the Second, when this settlement was

English, and which I never yet knew Jews to possess in any other part of the world whatsoever.

From Paramaribo, or indeed from the fortress New Amsterdam, the River Surinam (like the Cottica and Commewina) is beautifully lined with sugar and coffee plantations, as are also several creeks or small rivers that communicate with it, such as the Paulus, Para, Coropina, and Pararac creeks, &c., but above Mount Parnassus not a single estate (that may be so called) is to be found, neither is the river any longer navigable, not even for small craft, on account of the prodigious rocks and cascades, or waterfalls, with which it is obstructed, winding through between excessively high mountains and an impenetrable forest, which form an enchantingly romantic *coup d'oeil* indeed, but debar the possessors of the Colony from making such discoveries as might perhaps reward their labor with very considerable riches. But to proceed.

If (as I have just mentioned) cruelties by the Rebels had become less common in the rivers, barbarities still continued in a shocking degree in the metropolis, where my ears were deafened with the clang of the whip and the shrieks of the Negroes. Particularly, I saw with horror from my window a Missy Spaan, who lived next door to Mr. De Graav, order a young black woman to be flogged across *the breasts,* and nowhere else, till she was cut to pieces. Infernal b——ch, could I have disciplined thee at this moment, what would have been thy portion? I now got in a whiskey and rode out to dissipate myself, when the first thing I saw was a Negro girl called Europa fall naked from a garret window, onto a heap of broken bottles; this was indeed an accident but mangled her (though not dead) in such a condition that I cannot describe it. Damning my unlucky fate, I turned the horses and drove to the beach, as the only place to avoid every scene of cruelty, but here I had the mortification to see two Philadelphia sailors, while fighting on the forecastle of their vessel, both fall over their ship's bow and be drowned, while on board another American brig I discovered a little tar, defending himself from the cross-trees with a hatchet against a sergeant and four armed men for a considerable time, having threatened to shoot him out of the rigging, he at last surrendered and, being brought ashore, was dragged to Fort Zeelandia in company with two more, by a file of musketeers, where for having been drunk on duty, they received a *fire-cant* each, at the captain's request, that is being bastonaded or beaten on the shoulders by two corporals with bamboo sticks, till their backs were swollen like a cushion; however arbitrary this mode of correction, the captain fully explained the necessity of it, the private American sailors being of a turbulent spirit indeed when in liquor, while if sober they may be fairly classed among the best seamen in the world.

View of the Settlement called the Jew's Savannah.

View of the Blue Bergh called Mount Parnassus.

Plate 70

Early on the morning of the 16th, while musing on all the different dangers and chastisements that the lower class of people are subjected to, I heard a crowd pass under my window. Curiosity made me start up, dress in a hurry, and follow them, when I discovered three Negroes in chains, surrounded by a guard, going to be executed in the savanna. Their undaunted look, however averse I may be to cruelties, fascinated my attention and determined me to see the result, which was viz., that the sentence being read (in Low Dutch which they did not understand), one was condemned to have his head chopped off with an axe for having shot a slave who had come to steal plantains on the estate of his mistress, while his accomplice was flogged below the gallows. The truth was, however, that this had been done by the mistress's absolute command, but who being detected and preferring the loss of the Negro to the penalty of five hundred florins, allowed the poor man to be sacrificed; he laid down his head on the block with uncommon deliberation and even stretched out his neck, when with one blow it was severed from his body.

The third Negro, whose name was Neptune, was no slave, but his own master, and a carpenter by trade. He was young and handsome, but having killed the overseer of the estate Altona in the Para Creek in consequence of some dispute, he justly lost his life with his liberty. However, the particulars are worth relating, which briefly were that he, having stolen a sheep to entertain some favorite women, the overseer had determined to see him hanged, to prevent which he shot him dead among the sugar canes. This man being sentenced to be *broken alive upon the rack,* without the benefit of the *coup de grace,* or mercy stroke, laid himself down deliberately on his back upon a strong cross, on which with arms and legs expanded he was fastened by ropes. The executioner (also a black), having now with a hatchet chopped off his left hand, next took up a heavy iron crow or bar, with which blow after blow he broke to shivers every bone in his body, till the splinters, blood, and marrow flew about the field. But the prisoner never uttered a groan or a sigh. The ropes now being unlashed, I imagined him dead, and felt happy till the magistrates, moving to depart, he writhed from the cross till he fell in the grass, and damned them all for a pack of barbarous rascals. At the same time, removing his right hand by the help of his teeth, he rested his head on part of the timber and asked the bystanders for a pipe of tobacco, which was infamously answered by kicking and spitting on him, till I, with some Americans, thought proper to prevent it.

He then begged that his head might be chopped off, but to no purpose. At last, seeing no end to his misery, he declared that though he had deserved death, he had not expected to die so many deaths. "However, you Christians (said he) have missed your aim, and I now care not were I to lie here alive a month longer," after which he sang two extempore songs, with a clear voice taking leave of his living friends, and acquainting his deceased relations that in a little more time he should be with them to enjoy their company forever. This done, he entered into conversation with two gentlemen concerning his trial, relating every one particular with uncommon tranquillity, but said he abruptly, "By the sun it must be eight o'clock, and by any longer discourse I should be sorry to be the cause of your losing your breakfast." Then turning his eyes to a Jew whose name was De Vries, "Apropos, Sir (said he), won't you please pay me the five shillings you owe me?" "For what to do?" "To buy meat and drink to be sure. Don't you perceive that I am to be kept alive?"—which (seeing the Jew look like a fool) he accompanied with a loud and hearty laugh. Next observing the soldier who stood sentinel over him biting occasionally on a piece of dry bread, he asked him how it came that he, a *white man,* should have no meat to eat along with it. "Because I am not so rich," said the soldier. "Then I will make you a present. First pick my hand that was chopped off clean to the bones, Sir. Next begin to myself, till you be glutted, and you'll have both bread and meat which best becomes you." And which piece of humor was followed by a second laugh, and thus he continued when I left him, which was about three hours after the execution. But to dwell more on this subject my heart

—Disdains
Lo! tortures, racks, whips, famine, gibbets, chains
Rise on my mind, appall my tear-stained eye,
Attract my rage, and draw a soul-felt sigh,
I blush, I shudder, at the bloody theme.

In the adjoining plate, see the above dreadful chastisement.

Now, how in the name of Heaven human nature can go through so much torture, with so much fortitude, is truly astonishing, without it be a mixture of rage, contempt, pride, and hopes of going to a better place or at least to be relieved from this, and worse than which I verily believe some Africans know no other Hell. Nay, even so late as 1789, on October 30 and 31 (at Demerara), thirty-two wretches were executed, sixteen of whom in the above shocking manner, without so much as a single complaint was heard among them, and which days of martyr are absolutely a feast to many planters.

I should be rather inclined to think that Britain is the standard of humanity, by being the first nation (whether politically or not) that attempted the abolition of the slave trade.

I must now once more return to the savanna, where one of the strang-

The Execution of Breaking on the Rack.

Plate 71

est circumstances took place that ever befell me in my life, the effects of which might have been not a little prejudicial to a weak mind, had I not chanced immediately to find out the cause from whence they proceeded.

Being desirous to know if the unhappy executed Negro was still existing, about three in the afternoon I walked by myself to the spot of his sufferings, where, while I was ruminating on his miserable fate, the first thing I saw was his head at some distance, placed on a stake, nodding to me backwards and forwards, as if he had really been alive. I instantly stopped short, and seeing no person in the savanna, nor a breath of wind sufficient to move a leaf or a feather, I acknowledge that my resolution of advancing further had almost failed me till, reflecting that I must be mad indeed not to approach this head and find out the wonderful phenomenon if possible, I stepped forward and instantly discovered the natural cause by a vulture's perching upon the gallows, as if he meant to dispute with me for this feast of carrion, which bird, having already picked out one of the eyes, had apparently fled at my first approach, and by kicking the skull with its talons as it took its sudden flight, occasioned the motion already described. I shall now only add that after living nearly six hours, the poor wretch had been knocked in the head by the commiserating sentinel, the marks of whose musket were perfectly visible by a tremendous fracture in the skull.

August 24th. It now being the birthday of the Prince of Orange, the whole corps were entertained with salt beef, salt pork, barley, pudding, and hard peas. And this day (poor Joanna being inflexible in her resolution) I ratified the agreement with the good Mrs. Godefrooy, in presence of her mother and other relations, whereby the above lady bound herself never to part with her, to myself alone excepted, until she died, and in which case not only her liberty, but a spot of ground for cultivation, besides a neat house built upon it &c., should be her portion forever to dispose of as she pleased. She then returned my remaining bond of nine hundred florins, and gave Joanna a present of a purse with gold containing nearly twenty ducats, besides a couple of elegant pieces of East India chintz, advising me at the same time to make a request to the Court for little Johnny's immediate manumission, which she observed was a necessary form, whether I should be able to get the bail usually required or not, and without which formality, even if I had the bail ready to appear, nothing should be done to his advantage. Both of us having thanked this heavenly woman, I went to sup with his Excellency the Governor, transported with joy, to whom giving in my request in full form, he coolly put it in his pocket with one hand, while he gave me a hearty squeeze with the other, and shaking his head, told me frankly that he would lay it before the Court, but at the same time was perfectly convinced my boy must die a slave, without I could find the necessary bail, which (he was at the time well persuaded) very few people would wish to appear for.

Thus had I, after spending so much time and labor, besides the expense of above a hundred guineas already paid, still the heartfelt mortification to see this dear little fellow, of whom I was both the father and the master, exposed to perhaps eternal servitude. As for Joanna, she was now perfectly safe. But alas! Poor Johnny. Who feels not for this infant? While, assuredly, I alone was the only cause of all these complicated evils that threatened his early youth, and as such, with justice, I take the whole blame upon myself. However, one consolation still presented itself, viz., that the famous Negro Graman Quacy formerly mentioned, who was just returned from Holland, brought the news that, partly by his interest, a law was there enacted by which all slaves were to be free six months after their landing at the Texel, which indeed on application of their masters might be stretched to twelve, but not a single day longer on any account whatsoever.

By this, being persuaded I should one day joyfully fetch both him and his mother over the Atlantic, my heart was relieved from the weight of a millstone.

Who the above Graman Quacy was, I will more sufficiently explain before I take farewell from the reader. Suffice it to say for the present that the Prince of Orange, besides paying his out and homeward passage, and giving him several presents, such as a large gold medal &c., sent him back to Surinam dressed in a suit of blue and scarlet, trimmed with broad gold lace, while on his hat he wears a white feather, and looks, upon the whole, not unlike one of the Dutch generals, which made this king of the Negroes very proud and even saucy.

On the 25th, the Governor of the Colony gave a large feast to several of his friends at his indigo plantation, which was situated but a few miles at the back of his palace, where I had the honor to be invited as one of the party, and the pleasure to inspect the process of making indigo.

Dinner being over at the Governor's indigo plantation, I now departed with His Excellency's coach to the waterside, where a tent-barge and eight oars lay in waiting to row me down to the estate Catwyk in Rio Commewina, where I was invited by Mr. Goetzee, a sea officer, who was the proprietor of this beautiful country seat. Here no amusements of any kind were wanting, such as carriages, saddle horses, sailboats, billiard tables, &c. But what embittered the pleasure was the inhuman disposition of Mr. Goetzee's lady, who flogged her Negro slaves for every little trifle. For instance, one of her foot-boys, called Jacky, lately not having rinsed the glasses according to her mind, she ordered him to be whipped the next morning, but the lad gave her the slip, for having taken farewell from the other Negroes of the estate, he went upstairs, laid himself down upon his master's own bed where, placing the muzzle of a fowling piece in his mouth, by the help of his toe, he drew the trigger and blew out his existence. A couple of stout Negroes were instantly sent up to see what was the matter, who (finding the bed bespattered with blood and brains) threw the body out the window for the dogs, while the master and mistress were so very much alarmed that they have not got the better of it to this day.[1] Nor would any one lie in the same apartment, till I chose it by preference, being assuredly the most pleasant room and the best bed in the house. What added much to the alarm of the family was the circumstance of a favorite child lying fast asleep in the same apartment where the catastrophe happened, till such time as they were informed it had not received the smallest damage.

September 7th. I had not been fourteen days on this plantation when a female Mulatto slave called Yettee, for having jocosely said that her mistress had some debt as well as herself, was stripped stark naked, and in a very indecent as well as inhuman manner flogged by two stout Negroes before the dwelling-house door (while both her feet were locked to an iron bolt) till hardly any skin was left upon her thighs &c.

Five days after this only, I had the good fortune to get her relieved from the iron bolt that was across her shins, but a Mrs. van Eys, alleging she had affronted her only by her looks, prevailed on Mrs. Goetzee to renew the execution the same week, when she was so cruelly beaten that I expected, upon my soul, she could never more recover.

Tired with this barbarity, on September 16th, I left the estate Catwyk, determined no more to return to it, but still accompanying Mr. Goetzee to visit some of his other plantations in Cottica and Perica. On one of these, called the Alia, a newborn female child was presented me by way of compliment to give it a name, which I called Charlotte, but the next morning during breakfast seven Negroes were again tied up and flogged here, some with a cowskin,[2] which is very terrible. From here, also, I made my retreat to the estate 's-Gravenhage, and there meeting a Mulatto youth in chains, whose name was Douglas, I recollected with horror his unhappy father who had been obliged to leave him a slave and now was dead. In short, being heartily tired with my jaunt, I was glad to make haste back to Paramaribo.

September 29th. Here the news was that Fourgeoud's *valet de chambre*

---

1. The above unhappy people were since poisoned by their slaves, though more than six years later.
2. The name given to the dried penis of a bull.

had given up the ghost, who was reported to have actually been buried before he was yet quite dead. Such was at last the end of *pauvre, pauvre, Monsieur Laurant.* Also that (having been drunk in an alehouse) no less than thirteen of our poor men had severely run the gauntlet and as many were terribly bastonaded, the greatest number of whom since died in the Colony, a poor recompense for the many dangers and hardships they had sustained in helping to protect it. Also a Quadroon youth and a Dutch sailor were found murdered on the beach. Going now to take a walk on this plain or esplanade, I was called in by Mr. Stolkers, who next conducting me three stories high,

> from this window (said he) leaped one of my boys lately, to escape a gentle flogging. However, being only fainted, we soon brought him to life again by a hearty scouring on the ribs. Thus he did not escape. After which, for having risked himself (that is to say his master's property) and frightened my wife, she ordered him to be sent to Fort Zeelandia, where he received a most confounded *spanso bocko.*

The punishment called a *spanso bocko* is extremely severe, and executed in the following manner: the prisoner's hands being lashed together, he is lain down on the ground, when both his knees are thrust through between his arms, and separated from them by a strong stick as he lies on his side, the end of which being placed in the earth or held perpendicular, so that he can no more move than if he was dead. In this locked position, he is beaten on one breech by a strong Negro with a handful of knotty tamarind branches, till the very flesh is cut away; he is then turned over on the other side, where the same dreadful flagellation is inflicted, till not a bit of skin is left, and the spot of execution is dyed over with his blood, and after which the raw, lacerated wound is washed with lemon juice and gunpowder, to prevent a mortification, when he is sent home to recover as he can.

The above punishment is sometimes repeated at every street in the town of Paramaribo, which is a severity absolutely beyond conception. However, it is never thus inflicted without a condemnation from the Court, though a single *spanso bocko* may be ordered by any proprietor, either at home or by sending the victim to the fortress, with a line to the public executioner to whom is paid some trifle in money for taking the trouble. Neither age nor sex are a protection from this inhuman castigation.

I next was addressed by a Monsieur Rochetaux, whose Coromantyn cook, having spoiled his *ragout,* had just cut his own throat to prevent a whipping; Mr. Charles Rynsdorp's Negro lately did the same, &c., &c.

Now, is it to be wondered that the Negro slaves rise up in rebellion against their masters, and commit the enormities I have so frequently mentioned? Assuredly it is not.

Not recollecting if I have ever described in what manner they generally attack the estates, this naturally leads me to it. Having lain during the night lurking in the adjoining bushes that surround the estate, they always appear and do instant execution about the break of day, when it is most difficult to repulse them. At this moment, massacring the Europeans, they plunder the dwelling house, which they next set on fire, and then carry off the Negro women, who they load with the spoils, and treat very rudely should they make opposition.

I have said that on the 24th of August I gave in a hopeless request to the Governor for my boy's emancipation, and on the 8th instant I saw (with joy and surprise) an advertisement posted up containing, "that if any one could give in a lawful objection why John Stedman, a Quadroon infant, the son of Captain Stedman, should not be gifted with the blessing of freedom &c., such person or persons to appear before January 1st, 1777."

I no sooner read it than I ran with the good news to my friend, the Honorable Thomas Palmer, whom I not only had the mortification to find ill, but who assured me that the above was no more than a form put in practice on supposition of my producing the bail required, which undoubtedly they expected from my so boldly giving in my request to the Governor of the Colony. I now thought the blood would have sprung from my nose with astonishment and, without being able to utter one syllable, retired to the company of sweet Joanna, who bid me never to despair, that Johnny certainly one day should be free. She never failed to give me some consolation.

CHAPTER 28th

The troops again reenter the woods—The Rebels fly for protection to Cayenne—Third march to Gado Saby—A second reenforcement of troops arrive from Holland—Shipwreck of the transport ship Paramaribo—March to Rio Marawina—Dismal picture of distress and mortality—The Colony restored

On November 10th, everything being ready, I now once more left the metropolis, and in company with several other gentleman set out in a tent-barge for the encampment at the Cassipera Creek. This day, the whole colony was full of smoke, the woods having taken fire near the seaside by some unknown accident.

On our passage we met Colonel Texier, who came from the post at the Marawina with a detachment, and assured us that since the blow we gave the Rebels at Gado Saby, they were mostly fled to the other side of the above great river, where they got refuge among the French, who were settled in Cayenne. He had, however, taken a woman, and a Lieutenant Keen took two men and killed two more, while the two new sable volunteer companies had supported the honor of their colors (which they had received with so much ceremony from the Governor) by occasionally bringing in a few captives from the Lee Shore behind Paramaribo, in which they were assisted by the Indians, who had voluntarily fought and defeated the enemy there more than once. Thus, everything bid fair to see our expedition draw to an end, and the Colony soon reestablished to its former grandeur and tranquillity.

Now being ordered to march on discovery to Gado Saby &c., I set out on the 20th with two subaltern officers, three sergeants, seven corporals, and fifty men, besides a surgeon and the noted free Negro Gousary, and a box with eight hundred ball-cartridges (which when afterwards I examined proved to be no more than four hundred and eighty). In short, having lost Gousary for the space of four hours, we encamped near the banks of the same creek, not having advanced above six miles due west from its mouth. I acknowledge that after the long and many distresses I had already undergone during this cursed expedition, I was tired of it from the bottom of my soul.

November 21st, we marched seven or eight miles straight north, without finding a drop of water the whole day, this being in the heart of the dry season, which was this year extremely scorching, and the poor, loaded men being scarcely able to get forwards at all.

November 22nd. Having now changed my course to the northeast, and passed the quagmire, about noon we marched dry through the late fatal marsh, an hour after which, again keeping due west, we fell in with a large field of yams &c. which I demolished; then continuing forward, I encamped in the old settlement Cofaay, almost choked for want of water, not having met, as yesterday, with a single drop of water from the moment we set out. However, here the Negro slaves found means to procure us some to keep us from starving, though it was stagnated and stinking like a dirty kennel, which we drank through our shirt sleeves.

The next day I marched east from Cofaay to try for some fresh account of the Rebels by a path of communication, cultivated fields, and so forth; but we fell in with nothing, some delightful views and a large herd of *warree hogs* excepted, which by gnashing their teeth and stamping the ground before we saw them, we had actually mistaken for the enemy, and in consequence fresh primed and prepared for an engagement. About noon we returned to Gado Saby, where sitting down to rest from our fatigue, an old and tall Rebel Negro appeared suddenly in the middle of us, with a long white beard, a white cotton sheet tied about his shoulders, and a broken cutlass under his arm; seeing this venerable apparition I instantly started up and desired him to approach, swearing that no one under my command should dare to hurt him, but that he should get everything for his relief that I could afford. He answered *"No, no, Massera,"* with the greatest deliberation, and shaking his head in an instant disappeared like a shot, while two of my men (contrary to my orders) fired after him at the distance of perhaps six paces only, yet both missed their object, to my satisfaction—he being a poor, forsaken creature that had been left behind by the rest, gleaning his precarious subsistence from the ravaged fields we had formerly destroyed. What makes the Negroes so difficult to hit with a ball is that they never run straight forwards from it, but *see saw* or *zig zag* like the forked lightning in the elements. To complete my orders, I now once more ransacked Cofaay with its adjoining plains, though with a sore heart, on account of the poor, old, lonely, Rebel Negro, in which having cut down several cotton and plantain trees, okra or althea, pigeon peas, maize, pineapples, and some rice (all which had again spontaneously sprung up since our last devastation), I could not help leaving him a few rusk biscuits and a piece of salt beef, as also a bottle of kill-devil in return, after which we once more encamped in the fields of Cofaay.

Having so often mentioned rice, I think I will here say something of its growth, which is high about four feet, with furrowed stalks, and not unlike wheat; but they are knotted by intervals, and stronger. The leaves are like those of reeds, but not so dry. The seeds are produced somewhat like barley and placed on each side of the branches alternately.

Without this grain, our poor Marines must formerly have been starved, viz., in August 1775, when for all allowance they got per day, one rusk biscuit and three spikes of maize or Indian corn for five men, rice supplying, as I have said, the rest of their allowance.

November 24th. Having now fully completed my commission, I marched back with my detachment for the Cassipera Creek, shaping my course through the ruined field of Gado Saby, which was at present choked up to a perfect wilderness. From here we kept first to the southwest, and then due south, after which we slung our hammocks near a former encampment. It is to be observed that at this time all the marshes were next to being dry, on account of the hottest season I ever remember, while the fetid smell occasioned by the myriads of dead *warapa* fish that had been deserted by the water stank worse than Billingsgate, being sufficient to poison the Devil himself. Out among these putrid, finny tribes, our Marines and Negro slaves nevertheless selected the best, which they fried in the evening, and caused to serve them for a delicate morsel.

The morning following, we again marched southwest by west, and slung our hammocks not above four miles from the Cassipera Creek, and on the 26th (keeping south-southwest) we arrived in our camp much fatigued and emaciated (myself with a swollen face or the *erysipelas*), where I gave in my journal to Lieutenant Colonel Des Borgnes. I believe, upon my honor, that had we been ordered to remain twenty years on this expedition with a possibility of saving our lives, the different diseases, plagues, and torments would still have accumulated to which there was no end.

A command of fifty men was next sent out to reconnoiter Jerusalem &c. And finally on the 6th of December arrived in the River Surinam from Holland the long-expected relief, consisting of three hundred and fifty men, after a voyage of nine weeks and three days, of which they spent a fortnight at Plymouth in England. By these came now the unfortunate account that Captain Jocham Meyer (who had on board a considerable sum of money for our troops) was taken by the Moors and carried with his crew to Morocco, where they were condemned to be slaves to the emperor.[1] Also that the ship Paramaribo (Captain Spruyt), being one of the vessels that carried over the sick in the beginning of August, was wrecked in the Channel on the rocks of Ushant and entirely lost.

December 12th. Having now for more than a month been lodged in a paltry hut, beaten by the wind and rain (which set in unexpectedly) and being informed that (independent of the arrived relief) we were to stay still some months longer in the woods, which broke many hearts, I set about building for myself a comfortable house, which was finished without either nail or hammer in less than six days, though it had two rooms, a piazza with rails, and a small kitchen, besides a species of garden, in which I sowed in pepper-cresses the sweet names *Joanna* and *John,* while my next-door neighbor was my friend Captain Bolts, who made shift to keep a goat, and we lived extremely comfortably. Others kept hens, but not a cock was to be seen, for they, having first barbarously had all their tongues cut out to prevent their crowing to no purpose, had been since condemned to lose their heads. What was most remarkable in my own habitation was its entry, which was not by the door nor yet by the window, but by the roof only, where I crept in and out, having absolutely no other door. By this means, I was effectively protected from those frequent visitors who used to make too free with my eggs and bacon, besides interrupting me while I was drawing, writing, reading, &c.

The troops of the Society of Surinam who had been encamped at the Wana Creek (perceiving the rainy season thus prematurely setting in) wisely broke up and on the 26th, passing us, rowed down the River Cottica on their way to the plantations in the Perica Creek. But as for us, we were condemned to linger at Cassipera Creek, while Fourgeoud still kept at Paramaribo, as snug as a bug in a rug. With the above officers, we received intelligence that a few more Rebels had been taken at the Marawina, while we ourselves daily continued to send out patrols to right and left.

At last on the 29th, six barges came to anchor before our encampment, with part of the fresh troops that were arrived from Holland for our relief, which I could not help eyeing with compassion, and not without cause, many of them being already attacked with the scurvy and other diseases. We sent for bricks and built them an oven to bake fresh bread &c., and did all that we could to comfort them, but to little purpose, it being determined by Fourgeoud they should no more return to Paramaribo, where Heaven knows but few of them have since made their appearance, as shall soon be seen. I in particular (having received a supply of

---

1. The above captain and his crew have since been set at liberty.

wine from town) gave a hearty welcome to all the officers to cheer their spirits.

On January 3rd, six more barges arrived with troops from Paramaribo (having lost a man who fell overboard and turned another out of the ranks who was discovered to be branded on the back for being a thief), which completed the number of three hundred and fifty last arrived from Holland, to be murdered by a combination of misery and an unhealthy climate. Being informed that among these there was one Captain Small who (having exchanged with poor Ensign Macdonald who went over sick) came from the Scots Brigade, I instantly sculled down the river in a canoe to meet him and offer him any assistance, the more so as he was my friend and acquaintance. I had no sooner got on board his barge, when I found him suspended in a hammock with a burning fever, then not knowing me, on account of my dress, which was no better than that of the most ragged sailor, he asked me what I wanted, but when he reconnoitered his poor friend Stedman, changed from a good-looking, sprightly young fellow to a miserable, debilitated, tattered scarecrow, he gripped me by the hand without uttering a word, and burst out in such a flood of tears as much increased his illness, and showed the goodness of his heart to me, more than anything he could have uttered on the subject.

So early as the 12th, one hundred and fifty of these newly arrived people were now already ordered to march, when the strange Fourgeoud, to augment their hardships, made each carry (besides heavy accouterments and hammocks) a stuffed knapsack on his back, and of which party my friend Small was one, who being as corpulent as Sir John Falstaff, and I having accoutered him in the above manner, I vow to God, the poor lad could hardly walk at all, till—declaring to Fourgeoud that I must roll him along like a hogshead—he got leave to be debarrassed of part of his appendages. Everything being ready, the loaded detachment now made face to the right and set out with Fourgeoud to the River Marawina.

Indeed (while I must acknowledge that this chief was become to myself as civil as I could desire) equity requires of me to say that, to all others, he remained just as great a tyrant as ever I had known him.

So strict was the discipline at present in our camp that whoever made the smallest noise was severely punished. Nay, even sentinels were ordered to challenge rounds and patrols by no other sound than whistling, which was answered in the same manner. And on the 18th, when one of these was ordered to be flogged for his misbehavior, I found means (Fourgeoud not yet being returned) to get him pardoned, after he was already stripped. The following day, however, I showed that I could punish when things went too far, for seeing a large piece of boiled pork (about two pounds weight) flying past me like a bolt shot, and finding it was thrown by one Marine to another, while they were having a quarrel, I instantly ordered them to pick it up and (having cut it in two halves) stood over them till they swallowed every bit of it in my presence, sand and all, without either bread, drink, or anything else, which they since declared to me was such a punishment as surpassed my conception, and they should remember it the longest day they lived.

January 23rd. Now arrived for me from town a well timed supply of wine and fresh provisions, and the same day Colonel Fourgeoud with his detachment from the Marawina, while poor Small was melted down by appearance at least a dozen pounds. During this trip, our Commander had again discovered and destroyed fifty-nine houses, besides three fields of provisions which absolutely gave the finishing stroke to the Rebel Negroes, since having no more supply on this side of the water, they finally went to settle in the French colony of Cayenne. But his men had suffered prodigiously, especially those newly arrived, who were carried in hammocks by scores, while nearly thirty were left sick at the Marawina. At this time in the camp hospital were more than one hundred dangerously ill, while the above poor men died daily by half dozens, nothing being heard but sighs, complaints, and the dismal shrieking of the strix or Guiana owl, which forever kept them company during the night. The *amor patriae,* the *spleen,* and *cramp* so common in Surinam having also infected those that did the duty, it may be said there was not a happy person among them all.

In short, here appeared one covered with *bloody boils* from top to bottom, there another led along by two of his comrades in a *deep lethargy,* who in spite of pinching and pricking him, slept into eternity, and there a third, swollen like a hogshead by the *dropsy,* imploring the surgeon in vain to tap off the water, but being answered that it was too late, got leave to choke, or burst, the best way he could. In the hospital, some were seen clasping their hands and praying aloud to God to be relieved, while others lay at their side in a frenzy fever, tearing their hair, blaspheming their maker, and cursing the day that they first drew breath, &c. In short, all was dreadful beyond description.

On the 26th, mortality still gained ground while, by some accident, the camp also caught on fire, but was luckily extinguished without material bad consequence by the activity of the Negro slaves. And this same day (O strange to tell) without I asked it, Colonel Fourgeoud gave me the offer of a furlough to accompany him in person to Paramaribo, which I most greedily accepted.

Thus, farewell, thou cursed forest where I escaped so many deaths and underwent such misery as nothing can be compared to but the ten plagues of Egypt alone.

Having now made my friend Captain Small a compliment of my house and my fresh provisions, having supped on a dish of my fried cabbage- or *groe-groe* worms that were just come to perfection, and nearly got my throat cut by my other friend Captain Bolts for depriving him of this delicacy, and having entertained them both and some others (whom I never saw again) with a hearty glass of claret, I took my last farewell of them and on the morning of the 27th, at half past twelve o'clock, I rowed down the River Cottica with an elegant barge and eight oars, in company with two more officers and my chief, Colonel Fourgeoud, who now declared to us that having ransacked the forest in every direction, and driven the Rebels over the Marawina, he was now determined no more to return to the woods but in a few weeks to draw the long and painful expedition to a final conclusion, at which indeed nature shrunk and even Heaven itself must be offended.

Now, Reader, it remains for you to say that I have not led you about the bush, but through it, and without contradiction with indefatigable perseverance, the more so when it is to be considered that in the middle of the above hurry and distress, under which so many have sunk, I have often been deprived of pen, ink, and paper to make proper annotations, and which last defect I have even more than once supplied by writing with a pencil on my *cartridges,* or on a *bleached bone.* Had this not been the unavoidable case, many more, and perhaps more consequential, would have been the remarks I would now lay before thee, which one need never be at a loss to make in a country so replete with speculation, and where the different species of the animal and vegetable world are never to be enumerated.

Having the following day got the opportunity of a boat, I now pursued my voyage down the Cottica River to Paramaribo, where in a flow of spirits and perfect health (however strange) I arrived that very same evening, which was the end of my seventh and *last* campaign.

CHAPTER 29th

*Some account of a remarkable Negro—The troops prepare for
Europe—Description of a coffee plantation—Plan of reform
for the increase of population, and universal happiness—One
more sample of hellish barbarity, and example of humanity—
The regiment embarks*

January 28th. Being now once more arrived in town, and wishing to be
no longer troublesome to anybody, I hired a very neat small house of my
own at the waterside, in which we lived nearly as happily as we had done
at the Hope, but without the smallest marks of the emancipation of sweet
Johnny Stedman, which I had not a little flattered myself to have seen
accomplished towards the New Year. What could I do?

Having been further waited on by a number of planters, appraisers,
and administrators (among whom were, most assuredly, some very
pretty gentlemen), with felicitations on our victory over the Rebels, the
next who paid me a visit was none other than the celebrated Graman
Quacy, who came to show me his coat, gold medal, &c., which he had
got in a present from the Prince of Orange.

This being one of the most extraordinary black men in Surinam, or
perhaps in the world, I cannot proceed without giving some further account of him, the more so, as he has made his appearance once or twice
already throughout this history.

In the first place, by his insinuating temper and industry, this Negro
not only obtained his freedom from a state of slavery time out of mind,
but by his wonderful artifice and ingenuity has found the means of ac-
quiring a very competent subsistence. For instance, having got the name
of a *looco-man,* or sorcerer, among the vulgar slaves, no crime of any consequence is committed at the plantations but Graman Quacy (which signifies Greatman Quacy) is sent for to discover the perpetrator, and which
he so very seldom misses, because of their faith in his conjurations, and

his looking them steadily in the face, that he has not only often prevented further mischief to their masters, but come home with very capital rewards to himself. The corps of Rangers and all fighting free Negroes are next under his command, to whom by selling his *obias,* or amulets, to make them invulnerable (they, under the power of this superstition, fearing no danger and fighting like bulldogs), he not only has done a deal of good to the Colony but filled his pockets with no inconsiderable profits also, while his person is adored and respected like a god, and the above trash costs him nothing, being neither more nor less than a composition of small pebbles, eggshells, cut hair, fishbones, &c., the whole sewn up together in small packets which are tied on a string of cotton around some part of their body. But besides these and many other artful contrivances, he had the good fortune to find out the valuable root known under the name of *Quacy Bitter,* of which this man was absolutely the first discoverer in 1730, and which, notwithstanding its being less in repute in England than formerly, is highly esteemed in many other parts of the world for its efficacy in strengthening the stomach, restoring the appetite, &c. In 1761 it was made known to Linnaeus by Mr. Dahlberg, formerly mentioned, which Swedish virtuoso has since written a treatise upon it, and by which Quacy might have even amassed riches, were he not in other respects an indolent dissipating blockhead, whereby which he at last fell into a complication of loathsome disorders of which the leprosy is one, and which is, as I have said already, incurable forever.

Nevertheless his age (though he could not exactly ascertain it) must have been very great, since he used often to repeat that he acted as drummer, and beat the alarm on his master's estate when the French commodore Jacques Cassard put the Colony under contribution, which was in the year 1712.

Having taken a portrait of this extraordinary man, with his gray head of hair, and dressed in his blue and scarlet with gold lace, I here take the liberty in the annexed plate to represent him to the curious reader.

This very same week we again saw the efficacy of Graman Quacy's *obias* or amulets, a captain of the Rangers named Hannibal bringing in the barbecued hands of two straggling Rebel Negroes which he had shot himself, and one of which hands was that of the noted Rebel Cupido, formerly taken in 1774 but who since escaped from Fourgeoud in the forest, chains and all.

I now went out in my turn to visit some friends, among others Mr. Andrew Rynsdorp, who showed me the loop and button of his hat, which being diamonds, had cost him about two hundred guineas—such is the luxury of Surinam. Being entered on that article, I cannot help also mentioning the above Mr. Dahlberg, which gentleman when I waited on

The celebrated Graman Quacy.

Plate 76

him (besides a gold snuffbox surrounded in brilliants, value six hundred pounds sterling) made me remark two silver bits set in gold and surrounded with diamonds, with the inscription,

Soli Deo Gloria, Fortuna Boeticum, &c.

Having signified my surprise at this last adoration of two sixpences, he declared to me that they were all the money he had in the world when he came to Surinam from his own country, Sweden. "Did you work?" said I. "No. "Did you beg? "No." "You didn't steal, Sir?" "No. But, *entre nous*, I whined and acted the hypocrite, which is sometimes necessary and preferable to the other three." To which I answered, "Sir, your confession is confirmed by the usage to your Negro slave Baron after having promised his manumission in Amsterdam." One sample more of the extravagance and folly of the Surinamers and I have done: two of them quarreling about a most elegant carriage that was imported from Holland, a lawsuit ensued immediately to determine who was to have it, during which time the coach was left uncovered in the middle of the street till it lately fell to rubbish.

On February 10th, most of our officers being arrived from the camp at Paramaribo, Colonel Fourgeoud entertained us with a feast, as he pleased to called it (an old stable lantern with broken panes of glass hanging over our heads, which I expected a thousand times would have dropped into the soup). Here, he acquainted us that he had at last put a final end to the expedition having, notwithstanding so little bloodshed, accomplished his aim in rooting out the Rebels by destroying twenty-one towns or villages and demolishing more than two hundred fields of vegetable productions of every kind, and whom (he had gotten confirmed intelligence) were now to a man fled over the River Marawina, where they and their friends were settled and protected by the French colony of Cayenne—who not only gave them shelter, but French-like, supplied them with everything they wanted. Thus, *Fines coronant opus,* with which good news we all gave him joy, and drank further prosperity in a bumper to the Colony of Surinam, of which the future safety now alone depended on the new Cordon, or path of circumvolution, defended by the troops of the Society and the corps of black soldiers or Rangers. In Dr. Fermyn's works, Colonel Fourgeoud and his troops are twice mentioned as the saviors of the Colony, a compliment to which both he and they are with truth entitled, and what cannot but reflect to his honor is that in the middle of his hurry, and the severity to his own troops, his humanity never would permit him deliberately to put a captive Rebel Negro to death, nor even—if he could avoid it—deliver them into the hands of justice, well knowing that while it was his duty to extirpate them, nothing but the most barbarous usage and tyranny had driven these poor people to this last extremity of skulking in the forests.

Being now invited once more by Captain Macneyl to spend a few days on his coffee estate Sporksgift (from which I was prevented), I will however not quit the Colony without among the rest describing the process relating to a coffee estate. The buildings on a coffee plantation are, first, the dwelling house, which being pleasantly situated not far from the banks of the river, is thereby for the pleasure and convenience of the proprietor; adjoined to this are the outhouses for the overseer, bookkeeper, &c., the kitchen, the storehouse, and small offices. The other necessary buildings are a carpenter's lodge, a dock or boathouse, and two capital coffee lodges, the one to bruise the pulp from the berries, the other to dry them, &c. The rest consist of the Negro houses, the stables, the hospital, the watchhouse, and a few others, which altogether appear like a small village, while often the coffee lodges alone cost more than five thousand pounds sterling.

Being extremely desirous to please those friends who have advised me to accomplish this work, I still present them with a plan in the adjoining plate, where all the buildings, fields, paths, gardens, floodgates, and canals are marked, and explained by the necessary references, and which plan is contrived at the same time for elegance, convenience, and safety from the enemy's devastations—elegant, as being perfectly regular without any omissions or additions; convenient, as having everything at hand, viz., within the planter's own inspection, without either the noise or nuisance, at some estates unavoidable; and safe, being surrounded by a broad canal which by floodgates lets in the water fresh from the river, besides a drawbridge which, during the night, cuts off all outward communication.

I will now proceed to the planting ground, which is divided into large square pieces, supplied sometimes with two thousand beautiful coffee trees each, growing at eight or ten feet distance from each other. These trees, which begin to bear when about three years old, are in their prime at six, and continue to produce fruit till thirty, the manner of supplying them being from good nurseries, which on no coffee estates are ever wanting. Having already mentioned that they afford two crops every year, which generally are home before midsummer and Christmas, and at which times of harvest it is not unpleasing to see the Negroes picking the crimson coffee berries among the polished green, when all ages and sexes are employed to fulfill their task with ardor, and when the youths, who having first filled their baskets, wantonly run naked and play, shining like ebony among the luxurious foliage.

I will now conduct them before the overseer's presence, where all the

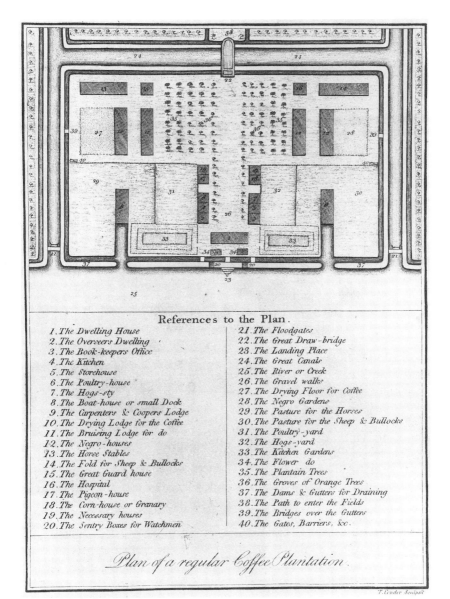

References to the Plan.

1. The Dwelling House
2. The Overseers Dwelling
3. The Book-keepers Office
4. The Kitchen
5. The Storehouse
6. The Poultry-house
7. The Hogs-sty
8. The Boat-house or small Dock
9. The Carpenters & Coopers Lodge
10. The Drying Lodge for the Coffee
11. The Bruising Lodge for do
12. The Negro-houses
13. The Horse Stables
14. The Fold for Sheep & Bullocks
15. The Great Guard house
16. The Hospital
17. The Pigeon-house
18. The Corn-house or Granary
19. The Necessary houses
20. The Sentry Boxes for Watchmen
21. The Floodgates
22. The Great Draw-bridge
23. The Landing Place
24. The Great Canals
25. The River or Creek
26. The Gravel walks
27. The Drying Floor for Coffee
28. The Negro Gardens
29. The Pasture for the Horses
30. The Pasture for the Sheep & Bullocks
31. The Poultry-yard
32. The Hogs-yard
33. The Kitchen Gardens
34. The Flower do
35. The Plantain Trees
36. The Groves of Orange Trees
37. The Dams & Gutters for Draining
38. The Path to enter the Fields
39. The Bridges over the Gutters
40. The Gates, Barriers, &c.

Plan of a regular Coffee Plantation.

T. Conder Sculpsit

Plate 78

baskets being inspected (and while the whips are unlashing), the flogging begins regularly every evening, without the smallest leniency on all those who have, either from idleness or incapacity, neglected to do their duty. After this ceremony, the coffee berries are carried home to the bruising lodge, and the Negro slaves return home to their houses.

The berries being bruised in a mill (for the same purpose, in the above lodge) to separate the kernel from the husk or pulp, they are next steeped a night in water to cleanse them, and then spread on the drying floor, which is in the open air and made of flags or flat stones, after which they are spread on garrets made for the purpose to let them evaporate and dry internally, and during which time they must be moved every day with timber shovels. This done, they are once more dried in large coolers or drawers that run on rollers out from the windows.[1] Then they still are put into timber mortars which are cut all along in a couple of very large trees, and beaten (by candlelight) with heavy wooden pestles like the rice at Gado Saby to divest them of a thin coat or pellicle that unites the two kernels in the pulp.[2] Being next separated from the chaff through a bunt-mill, once more thoroughly dried on the coolers, and picked (viz., the whole beans from the bruised, which are consumed in the Colony), they are finally put in barrels about three or four hundredweight each for transportation.

I will now only further observe that in Surinam some coffee plantations make above 150,000 pounds weight per annum, and that (as I have already mentioned) in the year before our arrival, viz., 1772, no less was transported *to Amsterdam alone* than 12,267,134 pounds of this ingredient, the prices of which have fluctuated from threepence halfpenny to eighteen pence; but which, calculated at the average price of eightpence halfpenny, produces a yearly income of no less than 400,000 pounds sterling, which is no despicable revenue, besides what goes to Rotterdam and Zeeland, and shows that the cultivating of coffee is highly worth the attention of the Surinam planters.

I will next try to fulfill my promise (however vain and ostentatious I may be deemed for my labor) and point out those means by which not only Surinam, but all the West India colonies, will accumulate wealth to themselves, and permanent happiness to the slaves that are under them, without having recourse to the coast of Guinea to supply their number, which will be fully and forever completed by the means of population alone. To accomplish this arduous undertaking, I will begin by showing how and in what manner the Negro slaves are divided and treated by the

---

1. To prevent them from being overtaken by showers of rain &c.
2. At this exercise the Negroes wonderfully keep time and always sing a chorus.

laws in this settlement only, without entering into the division or government of them in other colonies, yet by which those that are guilty may
take the hint. And then I will finish by pointing out how, in my opinion,
they ought to be divided and treated according to the laws not only of
humanity, but of common sense, when a thousand to one but my plan, if
ever executed, will have a salutary effect and a general felicity will be
accomplished.

I have before observed that in Surinam are supposed to be at an average
about 75,000 Negro slaves of all denominations, which allowing them
(for the sake of calculation) to be 80,000, are here divided in the following
extraordinary manner, viz., the plantations being about eight hundred in
number which (though some have but 24 Negroes, and others 400) we
will suppose to possess 100 slaves each, which completes exactly the
above number of 80,000 people. These are employed in this settlement
nearly as follows:

Employments	on one estate	on 800 estates
foot-boys or male servants to attend about the house	4	3,200
maids or female servants to wash, sew, iron, &c.	4	3,200
cook for the planter and the overseer, &c.	1	800
fowler or huntsman to provide game for the table	1	800
fishing Negro to provide fish for ditto	1	800
gardeners to provide the table and flower garden	1	800
to attend the bullocks and horses on the estate	1	800
to attend the sheep on the estate	1	800
to attend the hogs on the estate	1	800
to attend the poultry that is on the estate	1	800
carpenter Negroes to build houses, boats, &c.	6	4,800
cooper Negroes to make and repair the hogsheads	2	1,600
masons to build and repair the brick foundations &c.	1	800
at Paramaribo, some to trades, others for show or doing nothing	15	12,000
a Negro surgeon to attend the sick Negroes	1	800
sick and incurable that are in the hospital	10	8,000
a nurse for the Negro children that cannot be with their parents	1	800
children under age that can do no work of any kind	16	12,800
superannuated Negroes worn out by slavery	7	5,600

to work in the field, no more than 25 miserable wretches	25	20,000
Total, or complete number of slaves in the Colony	100	80,000

From this it appears that but 20,000 (viz., one-fourth of the complete number) are condemned to do all the labor of the fields, on whom alone, it may be said, falls the dreadful lot of untimely mortality that I have formerly mentioned. Whereas, if all the 50,000 able-bodied Negro slaves that are in the Colony of Surinam did equal drudgery, it evidently must follow that the above mortality, which is now five percent, would then increase to at least the number of twelve out of every hundred and completely extirpate the whole in little more than eight years' time.

Having thus at an average demonstrated how they are divided, I will briefly observe that while full 30,000 live better than the common people in England, and near 30,000 are incapacitated to do any work at all, the remaining 20,000 may be truly classed (that is in general) among the most miserable wretches that the earth can produce, who are worked, starved, insulted, and flogged to death, without being so much as allowed to complain for redress, without being heard at all, or ever righted; thus they are dead alive, since cut off from the most common privileges of human society.

I will now proceed by candidly asking the world if the above is not an infamous misapplication, not only of wealth, but of human flesh, which by a proper division and management might so much accumulate the one and facilitate the other. Then be it said that by abandoning pride and luxury, only in a moderate degree, at least 20,000 Negroes could be added to those now laboring in the fields, which would at the same time keep the above superfluous number of idlers employed and, by helping the others in the necessary occupation, greatly prevent that shocking mortality to which they are at present exposed by ill usage, and which reflects eternal shame and infamy on those who have it in their power to prevent it, and do not.

The other shocking causes of mortality and of depopulation are next the manner of government, to which I will now point out the grand ways of reform, by first beginning at the fountainhead, viz., the legislature. That sovereign power which alone is invested with the authority of making laws and breaking them ought in the first place to make it a sacred rule never to allow either the Governor or the magistrates of a colony to be the proprietors of more slaves than only those required to attend on their persons; and for this fundamental reason, that whatever laws and regulations such people may enact for the prosperity of the settlement and the good of the slaves, and from whatever good designs or motives, they will never see them enforced and supported longer than such time as they begin to clash with their own private interest. For even more than once, to my knowledge, it has happened that such lawmakers have been the first that broke them for the paltry benefit of causing their Negroes to work on a Sunday or, following the bent of their unbounded passions, by which sordid example from the magistrate the contagion soon must spread among the individuals, and next fall on the poor ill-treated slaves till it at last redounds back with doubled force against the blind and guilty forehead from which it originally sprang, and had its blasting birth.

No. Let the Governor and principal magistrates be chosen in Europe; let them be gentlemen of fortune and education, and above all, men of liberal ideas, men that are firm and proof to the tempting allurements of cursed gold, and whose passions are bridled by sentiment and manly feelings. Let these men be handsomely rewarded from that nation whom they so materially serve, and the colony which they so conspicuously protect, but let their salaries be stipulated, without depending on the blood and sweat of the miserable Africans. Then let such men enact impartial laws by which the Negro slaves are to work no more than their fair task, by which they are not to be racked, tormented, wantonly murdered, and infamously robbed of all that is dear next to their life, viz., their wives and daughters, &c.—laws by which they are to be properly fed, and attended when sick or indisposed, and above all, laws that will permit them to get a hearing, permit them to complain, and enable them to prove, by witness, the grievances to which they allude, and that will right them by a judge and impartial jury even partly composed of their own sable countrymen; by a judge and jury that will give eye for eye and tooth for tooth, that will not only protect the innocent and punish the guilty, but even reward virtue and merit in a slave. In those days nations will feel the benefit of their colonies, then planters will grow rich, and overseers grow honest. In those days, slavery will only consist in the name, when the subjects will with pleasure fulfill their limited task. Then and not till then will population increase sufficiently for the necessary work, and the cursed coast of Guinea trade be totally abolished, that now assuredly is carried on with barbarity and unbounded usurpation. Then the master will with pleasure look on his sable subjects as on his children, and the principal source of his happiness; while the Negroes will bless the day that their ancestors first set foot on American ground.

As for the Moravian missionaries that are settled among them to promote their faith &c., I have no objections, providing their morals go hand in hand with their precepts, but without which they ought (as a pack of canting hypocritical rascals deserve) to be stripped naked, then tarred and feathered by the Negroes, and flogged out of the colony. I will now proceed with my narrative which draws fast towards a conclusion.

On February 16th, being invited to dine with his Excellency the Governor, I now laid before him my collection of drawings and remarks on the Colony of Surinam, which I had the satisfaction to see him honor with the highest approbation. I then returned him my sincere thanks, not only for the material assistance he afforded me in completing this work, but for the unlimited marks of friendship and distinction with which he had treated me from first to last during the time that I resided in Guiana.

Availing myself of his protestations in wishing to be of further service to me, I ventured two days after to give him the following very uncommon request to lay before the Court, which with a smile on my private account (however strange) he promised to perform:

> I undersubscribed do pledge my word and my honor (being all that I possess for the present in this world) as bail, that if my last ardent request for the emancipation of my dear boy John Stedman be granted, the said boy will never to the end of his life become a charge to the Colony of Surinam.
> —was signed J.G.S.—

Having now done the utmost that lay in my power, I awaited the result with anxiety, but without the smallest appearance of success. Thus with a broken heart I was obliged at last to give him (sweet fellow) over for lost, or take him with me to Europe, which must have been plunging a dagger into his mother's bosom.

March 1st. A sergeant now arriving from the Cassipera Creek (where the last-come troops were fast dying away) brought the almost incredible account that the man I mentioned to be lost in the woods on February 10th was actually returned, after having been missing exactly twenty-six days, nine of which he subsisted on a few pounds of rusk biscuit and seventeen on nothing at all but water. He added that he had entirely lost his voice and was reduced to a perfect skeleton; however that by the care shown him by the officers, he promised to live.

I have even omitted truths which (on account of their strange singularity) must in the eyes of the vulgar and illiterate seem to border on the marvelous, yet while Almighty God knows that in the forest of South America are to be met with the very strangest occurrences, without being obliged to have recourse to exaggerations. For instance, who shall believe that nearly a whole detachment of eighty Marines, marching one day through a thick wood, all imagined they were stepping, one by one, over an enormous tree that obstructed their way (as is very common in Guiana) till finally it began to move and proved to be no other than a full-grown serpent of the *aboma* species, measuring, by Colonel Fourgeoud's computation, between thirty and forty feet in length, yet such is a truth as sacred as the truth of my existence. The above animal was neither killed nor hunted, the colonel ordering the remaining party to march round it in forming a half circle, in order that themselves at the same time might escape every danger.

On March 11th, I was almost struck dead with astonishment at seeing Miss Jettee (one of the daughters of the deceased Mr. De Lamarre), a lovely Mulatto girl aged fourteen, who had been christened in 1775 and educated like a young lady—I say, at seeing her dragged into court in chains with her mother and a few more of her relations, surrounded by a military guard. Having suddenly inquired for the cause, and almost attempted a rescue, she called out to me herself, crying most bitterly, that she was going to be tried by Mr. Schouten, her mother's master, for refusing to do the work of a common Negro slave, neither which she had ever expected, or to which indeed she had at all been brought up. The result, however, proved (O, shame to be mentioned) that according to the laws of the country, she was not only obliged to submit but (at his insisting) condemned for disobedience to be privately flogged, together with her poor mother and all her relations who had dared to support her. Nevertheless (by the humanity and to the immortal honor of his Excellency the present Governor, Mr. Wighers, who was at that time the fiscal or town clerk), the sentence was never put into execution, but forced was the unfortunate Miss Jettee De Lamarre notwithstanding, to stoop henceforth to the tyranny of her unmanly lord and master, pitied and lamented by all her acquaintances and every stranger that saw her. Such were the dreadful consequences of not having been timely emancipated, which made me tremble.

Let me now relate, strange to tell, what instantly followed, and what was of greater consequence to me than all that had happened hitherto in the Colony. This, Reader, was no less than a polite message from the Governor and the Court, acquainting me that (having taken my former services into consideration, together with my gallantry and humanity in offering my honor as bail to see my child timely made a free citizen of the world), they had presumed without further ceremony or expense to compliment me with a letter of his free emancipation from that day forever after, which was henceforth officially presented to me by the principal clerk of the town hall, to whom I gave five guineas. No man could be more suddenly transported from woe to happiness than I this day, while his mother shed tears for joy and gratitude, the more so as we had given over all hopes.

March 18th. The day of our departure now approaching from hour to hour, I about this time gave up my house, and at Mrs. Godefrooy's pressing invitation spent the few remaining moments in that which she had prepared for the reception of Joanna and her boy in her beautiful garden, charmingly situated under the shade of fine tamarinds and oranges, which she also neatly furnished with every accommodation that could be necessary, besides allowing her an old Negro woman and a girl to attend on them forever. Thus situated, how blessed should I have been to end with her the rest of my days, but fate ordained it otherwise.

In short, on the 22nd, I waited with Captain Small on Parson Snyderhaus, according to appointment, but who—to both our surprise—now peremptorily refused to christen the boy, saying that since I was going to Holland, I could not answer for his Christian education. We replied he was under two proper guardians. The blacksmith's son (for such he was) persisted, and we remonstrated but to no purpose; he was as deaf as his father's anvil, and I believe upon my soul quite as empty as his bellows, till finally tired out with his fanatical impertinence, I swore that I would sooner see him die a heathen than allow him to be christened by such a pitiful blockhead, while my friend Small could not help bestowing on him a hearty curse, and, slapping the door with a vengeance, we departed. Now coming to Joanna, who had him dancing on her lap, she asked us with a smile if we really thought herself the worse for the omission of the ceremony, to which we both replied, "No." "Then," continued she, "say no more on the subject and leave the rest to Providence," to which we agreed, at least for the present. And having cut out a lock of his hair to carry with me, we spent the evening very heartily over a bowl of punch.

In the evening I now went to take a short leave of my valuable acquaintances, such as Mrs. Godefrooy, Mr. and Mrs. Demelly, Mr. and Mrs. Lolkens, Mr. and Mrs. Gordon, Mr. Gourlay, Captain Macneyl, Doctor Kissam, &c., who had all (besides Mr. Kennedy and Mr. De Graav, who were gone to Holland) treated me with the most distinguished civility since I had been in the Colony. But my soul was too full of a friend that was still nearer to be impressed with that sensibility on separating from them, that it must have felt on another occasion. O my dearest Joanna; O my Johnny; consider for a moment the bitter circumstance of perhaps going to be torn from you both forever. But I must forsake you at least for a time, I must forsake you; my duty commands me, and I must obey.

Even now, while offering her still to accompany me, and while seconded by the inestimable Mrs. Godefrooy and all her friends, she was equally inflexible and her steady answer was as before, viz., that dreadful as appeared the fatal separation, which she forbode was for the last time never to meet again, yet she could not but prefer remaining in Surinam, first from a consciousness that with propriety she had not the disposal of herself, and secondly from pride, wishing in her present condition to be one of the first among her own class in America, rather than, as she was well convinced to be, the last in Europe, at least till such time as fortune should enable me to establish her above dependence. Not knowing in what respect most to adore this unhappy young woman (for that she was perfectly at this period) or indeed what to say at all, I determined calmly to resign myself to my trying destiny and exchanging a ringlet of her hair, prepared for the fatal moment of, by all appearance, an eternal adieu.

March 29th. The ships not being ready to go to sea till two days after, I now a little longer could keep her company, which seemed to cheer her. But alas, too dearly did we pay for the short reprieve, since finally I got an abrupt message that a second boat was waiting to carry me on board without delay. At that instant, O! Heavens, what were my feelings! Joanna's mother suddenly took the infant from my arms, while the all-worthy Mrs. Danforth supported her trembling self. At the same time, her brothers and sisters hung around me, crying and invoking Heaven for my health and for my safety, but she, the unfortunate Joanna, holding me by the hand, and who looked a thousand times more dejected than Sterne's Maria, spoke not one word. I perceived she was perfectly distracted; I was the same. The hour was come. I finally pressed them both to my bosom. The power of accent now forsook me, my heart invoked the protection of Providence to befriend them. I gave them my last embrace with my blessing. Here the beauteous Joanna, now but nineteen years of age, shut her tear-bedewed eyes; the color of her lips became the color of death, she bowed her head and motionless sank into her chair.

The scene was now too distressing to bear any longer. I roused my remaining fortitude, and leaving them surrounded by every care and attention, walked accompanied by my friends to the waterside. The boat delaying a few moments, I at this time still stepped up to poor Fourgeoud, gripping whose veteran hand, I could not, for my soul, but forgive him every injury he had ever done me. He was affected; this was a debt he owed me. I wished him every good and finally departed.

CHAPTER 30th

*The ships weigh anchor and put to sea—Review of the
troops—End of the expedition—Conclusion*

Everything being at last perfectly adjusted for our departure, both vessels
weighed anchor on the morning of April 1st, when with a fresh breeze at
east we put to sea, course northwest, taking our final leave of Surinam
and all Guiana.

Having still dispatched a letter to Messrs. Gordon and Gourlay, the
guardians of my late delight, I now fell into such a fit of despondency as
nothing could equal, and of which it was universally thought I should
hardly get the better. Motionless and speechless did I look over the ship's
stern, heaving sigh after sigh, till the land quite disappeared out of my
languid sight, after which—

But why should I torment the reader longer with what I could not help
feeling upon this occasion, both in mind and body? Suffice it to say that
in a few days, reason so far prevailed again as almost to make me ashamed
of my too great sensibility (not of my love) and that I gradually became
once more a man, like the rest of my shipmates, that is, I got the better
of my passion, but not of my affections, which, Heaven knows, never
more can forsake me while I live.

What could not but greatly contribute in restoring my tranquillity was
the happy reflection that (if I had in some measure hurt myself) I had at
least done material good to a few others by relieving three deserving
people from a state of bondage. Nor had I entered one farthing into debt
notwithstanding, while my constitution was perfectly sound, and my
character unspotted with the smallest blemish, favors of fortune that too
many of my friends could not boast of, several of whom had left slaves

behind them too nearly connected, while others were ruined both in their body and mind past all recovery. For instance, no less than four of the handsomest young officers in the corps went to Europe with incurable ruptures, while others lost the use of all their limbs and some their memory, nay, one or two were entirely deprived of their mental faculties, and continued in a state of insanity forever. In short, out of a number of near twelve hundred able-bodied men, now not one hundred did return to their friends at home, among whom perhaps not twenty were to be found in perfect health, all the others (a very few of the remaining relief excepted), being repatriated, sick, discharged, past all remedy, lost, killed, and murdered by the climate; while no less than ten or twelve were drowned and snapped away by the alligators. Among the dead were, including the surgeons, between twenty and thirty officers, three of which number were colonels and one a major, which were the fruits of this long and disagreeable expedition in the marshes and woods of Surinam.

One or two remarks I must still make before I leave this subject, which first are that among the officers and private men who had formerly been in the West Indies, none died at all; while among the whole number of nearly twelve hundred together, I can only recollect one single Marine who escaped from sickness. And next that of the few belonging to the corps that now were on their voyage for the Texel, I myself was the only officer who had sailed out with the regiment in 1772, those gentlemen excepted alone who now belonged to the staff or headquarters.

Thus ended perhaps one of the most extraordinary expeditions that was ever undertaken by European troops, and to which only the exploits of the American buccaneers can have a very distant resemblance. Be that as it may, having saved my life, it has afforded me in the end not only much instruction but a pleasing entertainment also, to recollect the very great hardships I have so luckily gone through and the many hazards I have so happily escaped. It has taught me in place of idle modes and fashions to know more about men and manners, and enables me now to look on those gifts of Providence with great thankfulness, which I formerly deemed insufficient for the meanest of my father's domestics. Thus it has accumulated on me a store of riches, if it is true that riches consist in contentment. And what gives me above all a peculiar satisfaction is that, by having so constantly employed my spare moments in drawing and writing, I have it now in my power to lay before my friends the history of a country so little explored and hitherto so very little known, particularly to the English nation, a nation which ever delights in new and useful discoveries.

July 29th. Having now once more exchanged my blue coat for a scarlet uniform, bought a very handsome English horse, and put my black boy

Quacoo in a brilliant livery, I entertained for the last evening my dearest shipmates with whom without exception at all I drank an everlasting friendship. Then, taking my final farewell from them all, the next morning I departed and set out to rejoin the old Scots Regiment, where I was since received with those true marks of unfeigned friendship as can only flow from the tenderest regard and warmest affection, while my heart felt no less glad to be again among them than they unanimously proved to be happy at my safe return.

Going now to take my last leave of Surinam, after all the horrors and cruelties with which I must have hurt both the eye and the heart of the feeling reader, I will close the scene with an emblematical picture of *Europe* supported by *Africa* and *America,* accompanied by an ardent wish that in the friendly manner they are represented, they may henceforth and to all eternity be the prop of each other. (I might have included Asia but this I omitted as having no connection with the present narrative.) We all only differ in color, but we are certainly created by the same hand and after the same mould. Thus, if it has not pleased Fortune to make us equal in authority, let us at least use that superiority with moderation, and not only proffer that happiness which we have to bestow on our superiors and equals, but with cheerfulness, to the very lowest of our dependents.

I must now draw this narrative to a final conclusion by once more mentioning the name of poor Joanna, and by acquainting the reader that, *Alas, Joanna is no more.*

From Mr. Gourlay in August did I receive the melancholy tidings, which pierced me to the very soul, that on the fatal fifth day of last November (a day ever-remarkable for treason in the annals of this island) this virtuous young creature had died by *poison,* administered by the hand of jealousy and envy, on account of her prosperity and the marks of distinction which her superior merit so justly attracted from the respectable part of mankind. While others insisted that her death was the consequence of a broken heart.[1]

Now her lovely boy was sent over the ocean to my longing arms, with a bill of nearly two hundred pounds, being his private property,[2] and whose faithful guardians both expired soon after the death of his well-deserving mother.

Not long had I been in this situation, when now a young lady, whom I thought nearest approached to her in every virtue, helped to support my

---

1. It is to be remarked and lamented that her younger brother, Henry, who had also obtained his manumission, expired in the same year and in the same languishing condition.

2. In a female Negro slave and three-score sheep had consisted the livestock of poor Joanna.

Europe supported by Africa & America

Plate 80

grief by becoming my other partner. She was of a very respectable family in Holland; I sought no other fortune, and with this amiable new companion and my boy, whom she tenderly loved, I peaceably retired to the fruitful country of Devon in England, where with my half-pay for all allowance, I make shift to make ends meet, and thank God for all his mercies—and where our two first English-born children, a beautiful boy and girl, we in gratitude to our bounteous Sovereign christened George William and Sophia Charlotte, after their majesties, the king and queen, praying unanimously for their lasting welfare and the uninterrupted prosperity of this happy nation.

And now farewell, my patient friends, who have been pleased to peruse this narrative of my sufferings with any degree of sensibility, particularly those whose sympathetic feelings have been roused by the distressing scenes they may have met with in reading, and whose good nature is ready to forgive the inaccuracies annexed to the pen and pencil of a soldier, debarred since his youth from a classical education. I say farewell, claiming no other merit whatever than in having spoken the simple truth, and without which may the pages annexed die with their author. But should this gift so rarely to be met with chance be found in my performance,

> Let one poor sprig of bays around my head
> Bloom while I live, and point me out when dead.

While, long, long may you live and be happy in this blessed island, accumulating wealth with honor and surrounded with victory, till the lowest subject among you shall have ascended to the highest pinnacle of unfading glory.

FINIS

EDITORS' NOTES

14. Negro insurrection in the colony of Berbice in 1763 . . . One of the largest slave revolts in the history of the Americas. Nearly the entire slave population rebelled and took control of the sugar colony of Berbice. The rebels' plans to establish an independent kingdom failed within the year, however, as much from internecine strife as from European pressures (Blair 1984). For Stedman's account of the insurrection, see 1790/1988, 76–77.

17. two black soldiers who were manumitted slaves . . . In 1772, the elite "Neeger Vrijcorps," or corps of Rangers, was formed, when the government purchased plantation slaves from their masters and promised them their freedom and other material benefits in return for fighting the Maroons. See Introduction, note 8.

19. But here Wowski pursued me again . . . Wowski, a "comic" female character—black, ill-mannered, slow-witted—in *Inkle and Yarico,* a very popular opera by George Colman the Younger produced in London in 1787. Later in his manuscript (1790/1988, 98), Stedman refers to the version of the Inkle and Yarico story published by Addison in the *Spectator* (no. 11). This very popular Noble Savage tale seems to have been first published in relatively full form in Richard Ligon's *A True & Exact History of the Island of Barbadoes* (1657, 54–55). See Sypher 1942, 122–37.

19. *in cuerpo* to battle with the gnats or mosquitoes . . . "In cuerpo" = in undress, naked.

22. the Governor, Mr. Nepveu . . . Jan Nepveu (1719–79). Although Stedman writes that Nepveu "was said to be a man of sense more than learning" (p. 55), Nepveu wrote a detailed and ethnographically important monograph in the form of commentaries on Herlein's 1718 description of Suriname ("Annotatiën," Sociëteit van Suriname 556, and Collectie Nepveu 19, Algemeen Rijksarchief, currently being prepared for publication by Silvia W. de Groot), as well as commentaries on Hartsinck 1770 (Collectie Nepveu 18, Algemeen Rijksarchief), and Stedman may have depended on Nepveu more than he admits for the ethnographic portions of the "Narrative."

26. Governor Mauricius . . . Johan Jacob Mauricius (1692–1768), governor of Suriname 1742–53. The complex story of his attempts to make peace with the Saramaka Maroons is discussed in detail, with supporting documents, in R. Price 1983b. Stedman's confused version of these events comes largely from Hartsinck 1770, 768–814.

26. the rebels on the island of Jamaica . . . In 1739, the Maroons of Jamaica signed treaties with the colonial authorities, ending temporarily seventy-five years of active guerrilla warfare.

28. By this accident the peace was immediately broken . . . Stedman's account of the peacebreaking, derived from Hartsinck, is false. The promised presents were never dispatched and the government "detachment" did not travel to Saramaka at the time agreed upon by the two parties. Both government and Saramaka versions of these events may be found in R. Price 1983a and 1983b.

28. runaway Negroes already settled . . . along the banks of the Djuka Creek . . . These were the Aukaner (Auka or Ndjuka) Maroons.

31. This same year, 1761, a peace was also a second time concluded . . . Stedman, loosely following Hartsinck 1770, has conflated several discrete incidents, badly confusing his account. Musinga's difficulties with the government, and with other Saramakas, occurred in 1766, and his separate peace was not established until 1769 (R. Price 1990).

32. a handsome quantity of arms and ammunition from the Colony . . . For the full lists of these tribute goods, see R. Price 1983b.

32. Both these tribes . . . [in all said to be] no less than fifteen or twenty thousand people . . . Stedman's combined population figures for the Ndjuka and Saramaka probably exaggerate reality by a factor of approximately two (R. Price 1990).

34. the barbarous Captain Coolingward . . . Clarkson's widely read *Essay* (1788, 98–99) describes this incident in detail: in September 1781, a captain (whose name is not mentioned), after suffering considerable loss of slaves from illness, threw 132 others overboard in order to cheat the vessel's underwriters. Clarkson calls this "a deed, unparalleled in the memory of man . . . and of so black and complicated a nature, that were it to be perpetuated to future generations . . . it could not possibly be believed" (ibid.).

35. who commands them in the forest by the different sounds of his horn . . . Both the black troops fighting for the colonists and the Maroons used signal horns in battle. For a photo of a Saramaka signal horn (*tutú*), see S. and R. Price 1980, 182.

35. a scarlet cap . . . Because of their caps, these soldiers were commonly called *redi musu* (Sranan for "red caps").

37. Another settlement of the Rebels . . . Maroon villages in this particularly inhospitable area, also known as "Devil's Marsh," date from at least the early eighteenth century and persisted for a century and a half (R. Price 1983a, 74–75).

37. Lieutenant Friderici . . . Juriaen François de Friderici (1751–1812). Later, governor of Suriname (1792–1802). See also page 38.

38. Baron . . . Recent archival research makes clear that though Baron was a military commander of some importance, he was never a real chief and that Boucou was ruled by Boni (Hoogbergen 1985, 80–85). The vivid story of Baron's mistreatment and escape from slavery, first published by Stedman, was repeated by later historians (see, for example, Wolbers 1861, 327; Debien and Felhoen Kraal 1955) but remains controversial. Oudschans-Dentz (1928/29) has cited a public announcement placed by Baron's former master, Dahlberg, in a 1775 issue of the *Wekelijksche Surinaamsche Courant* which denies that Baron ever left Suriname, was sold to a Jew, was deceived or mistreated, and so forth, and Oudschans-Dentz concludes that the story reported by Stedman is false. Other historians, however, suggest that Stedman's version has withstood the test of time (de Groot 1975, 33). The date of Baron's death, previously given as 1776 (ibid., 43), appears from recently published documents to have been instead 1774, during a battle in which his well-known comrade Jolicoeur may also have been killed (de Beet 1984, 21, 213; Hoogbergen 1984, 10; 1985, 85, 207). News of the death of these renowned Maroons was characteristically kept from the whites; in August 1775, Stedman remained unaware of their deaths (p. 208).

38. cutting off the ears, nose, and lips of one of them . . . Stedman refers here to a complex 1772 incident, described in more detail in recently published contemporary documents, in which a Ranger was captured by Baron's men and, at the behest of their gods, instead of being executed was whipped, had an ear cut off and his head shaved, and was then sent back to the whites with a defiant message (de Beet 1984, 135–36). The maiming and sending back of a traitor—a slave siding with the whites against the Maroons—is an important theme in Maroon historiography (see R. Price 1983a, 153–59).

42. the protector of Cery and her children . . . Jolicoeur . . . That Joanna, the supremely cultivated house slave, spent her childhood under the protection of Jolicoeur, who became a well-known guerrilla warrior, should not surprise. Ties of kinship, adoption, and friendship among Suriname's slave community were extensive. (Note, for example, how often Joanna's various relatives appear in the "Narrative.") Indeed, close relatives often found themselves separated, with one a slave and one a Maroon, and this fact had important implications for the success of ongoing Maroon intelligence operations.

47. Lavinia . . . "The lovely young Lavinia," poor but virtuous, in *The Seasons* ("Autumn") by the very popular poet James Thomson (see Stedman 1790/1988, xcv), has a tragic affair with her social superior Palemon, "the pride of swains . . . the generous, the rich."

47. For every Rebel prisoner a reward is paid . . . By 1685, the colonial government had already established bounties for the capture of maroons. At first, it was set at five guilders; two years later it was increased to three hundred pounds of sugar if the maroon had been expressly hunted down, and one hundred pounds otherwise; in 1698, it was increased to twenty-five to fifty guilders, depending on the specific circumstances of capture; and in 1717 bounties of fifteen hundred guilders each were earmarked for the discovery of two notorious Maroon villages, and six hundred guilders for any other village, plus a ten-guilder bonus per inhabitant (which was later expanded to the granting of freedom in addition to the usual bounty to any slave or maroon who disclosed the whereabouts of a Maroon village) (Hartsinck 1770, 2: 756–57). Stedman describes bounties during the 1770s on page 198.

50. Fortress Zeelandia . . . Fort Zeelandia has had a checkered history. During the twentieth century it has served as a prison, as the home of the Surinaams Museum, and currently as the headquarters of the Suriname military. See Fontaine 1972.

54. the Rebels, being apprised . . . by their spies . . . Maroon intelligence was well organized and efficient, consisting of slave informers, Maroons who allowed themselves to be recaptured only to escape again, and double agents (R. Price 1983a, 1983b).

56. a Jewess . . . Stedman's depiction of Jews as particularly cruel masters and mistresses perpetuated a longstanding Suriname stereotype. However, modern scholarship, based on archival research, suggests that there is no factual basis for such charges (Hoogbergen 1985, 37–38).

56. *vincere aut mori* . . . "victory or death."

61. to cut off the heads of the slain . . . Although Stedman interprets the Maroons' headcutting as trophy taking, the practice in fact involved a whole complex of ritual and belief relating both to self-protection against the avenging spirit of the deceased and to central West African–derived notions of manhood. The proper handling of a severed head was undoubtedly complex. The related hunting rites carried out by modern Maroons after killing a large animal (especially a tapir) have the same goal—to settle its spirit so it will not return to take vengeance. For further discussion, see R. Price 1983a, 145–46.

63. a fish which is here called *pery* . . . The pirhanha, *Serrasalmus rhombeus.*

63. Doctor Bancroft . . . Edward Bancroft (1744–1821), naturalist and chemist, who visited North and South America several times. He wrote *An essay of natural history of Guiana in South-America in several letters from a gentleman in the medical faculty* (London, 1749).

64. in what manner heavily loaded musketoons ought always to be fired . . . Until the middle of the twentieth century, most Saramaka Maroons fired their shotguns (used for hunting) in this same "under the hand" manner, rather than from the shoulder, because of the uncertainties of the force of the homemade charge.

66. the *ai* and the *unan* . . . There are indeed two species of sloths in Suriname: the three-fingered sloth, *Bradypus tridactylus* (pl. 16 [*bottom*]), and the two-fingered sloth, *Choloepus didactylus* (pl. 16 [*top*]).

66. a Jew soldier of the Society post . . . The Jewish population of mid-eighteenth-century Suriname, largely descended from Portuguese Jews who had arrived as already-experienced sugar planters via Brazil, was concentrated on the Suriname River plantations, with the settlement of Jews-Savanna (see pl. 70) their center. A separate Jewish militia was very active in pursuing escaped slaves during the first half of the eighteenth century, and Jewish soldiers played a special role in many of the massive anti-Maroon military operations of the middle of the century (R. Price 1983b).

66. a Negro woman and sucking child who had formerly been stolen by the Rebels and now had found means to make her escape . . . It was not uncommon for slave women who were taken by Maroons on raids to attempt to return to their plantations, almost always because of conjugal or kin ties there.

68. sharp pins stuck in the ground . . . The use of such devices was not limited to this village (R. Price 1979b, 6).

68. rice, yams, and cassava . . . Stedman sprinkles his text with information about Maroon crops and other foods. Together with the more detailed eighteenth-century missionary diaries and dictionary from Saramaka (R. Price 1990), his reports permit a rather full reconstruction of Maroon diet, the staples of which were (unirrigated or hillside) rice and manioc (cassava), combined with a variety of root crops, plantains, maize, peanuts, okra, capsicum, and many other cultigens. See also R. Price 1991b.

69. *"Ah, poty backera"* . . . "Ah, poor whitefolks."

70. letters to Holland with an account of his already begun exploits . . . Four-geoud's correspondence is now in the Algemeen Rijksarchief (Coll. Fagel), The Hague.

70. a couple of large black monkeys . . . There are eight species of monkeys in Suriname. Although JGS's reports of relevant local terminology seem confused, his descriptions and plates permit identification. His *keesee-keesees*, the two monkeys depicted in pl. 18 [*top*], are the brown capuchin, *Cebus apella apella.* His *monkee-monkees*, the two monkeys depicted in pl. 18 [*bottom*] (erroneously labeled there "kishee-kishee"), are the common squirrel monkey, *Saimiri sciureus sciureus.* His *quata* is the spider monkey, *Ateles paniscus,* depicted in pl. 42 [*bottom*]. His *saccawinkee* is the red-handed tamarin, *Saguinus midas,* depicted in pl. 42 [*top*].

76. The Negroes now cut him in slices in order to dress him and eat part of him . . . Neither the willful killing nor the eating of anacondas is conceivable by twentieth-century Maroons who, like contemporary coastal Afro-Surinamers, consider them vehicles of important deities, with the power to become avenging spirits. Among Saramaka Maroons, these beliefs were clearly present during Stedman's time (R. Price 1990). Perhaps Stedman's companions in this venture were slaves who hailed from African societies in which such snakes were not sacred. Stedman himself describes the ways boa constrictors were venerated (p. 264), as they still are today, but unlike Saramakas he does not view them and anacondas as vehicles for two closely related deities.

76. Mr. Parkinson's Museum . . . In 1795, Stedman presented "eighteen Surinam curiosities" to James Parkinson's Leverian Museum, which since the mid–1780s had been attracting crowds in London (1795). See also note to page 278.

76. It is called by Mr. Wesley . . . John Benjamin Wesley (1703–91), Methodist leader, wrote a natural history to which Stedman occasionally refers: *A Survey of the Wisdom of God in the Creation; or, A Compendium of Natural Philosophy* (Bristol, 1763).

80. I was now obliged to make slaves to soldiers . . . Stedman's fears were not idle. Throughout the early and mid–eighteenth century, it had been customary for slaves to constitute the numerical core of antimaroon military expeditions, but their role was almost always as unarmed bearers. Even so, the threat that these unarmed slaves posed keenly worried the white commanders and troops, as vividly evidenced in the documents in R. Price 1983b.

82. the Negro slaves being interspersed between the men to be guarded themselves . . . The fear of slaves on such military expeditions deserting to the enemy was realistic. The extensive documents in R. Price 1983b demonstrate that it was not unusual for 50 percent of the slaves on some of the larger eighteenth-century expeditions to desert, in spite of the extraordinary measures taken to surround them at night with armed guards.

85. ringworm . . . A mycosis that particularly plagued newly arrived Europeans in Suriname. A Moravian contemporary of Stedman in Suriname wrote,

> [In 1780] I was itching terribly all over. . . . There were little red rings, the size of sixpence coins, all over me. . . . I was itching all over, and day or night never had peace. . . . Even though I tried to tie my hands together at night so I would not scratch, I could never sleep for more than half an hour at a time. The only way I could find relief was by disrobing and throwing myself into the Suriname River, but I had to keep constantly moving so that I would not be attacked by the piranhas. (Cited in R. Price 1990, 199)

86. young Mr. Heneman . . . Stedman's friend, J. C. Heneman (1738–1806), became a military engineer and the most important cartographer of eighteenth-century Suriname. His two great maps of the colony, completed in 1784 and 1787, are at scales of 1:177,000 and 1:40,000, respectively (Bubberman et al. 1973, 65–66).

86. fine-looking birds called macaws . . . JGS's "blue and yellow macaw" is the blue-and-yellow macaw, *Ara ararauna*. His "Amazon macaw" is the scarlet macaw, *Ara macao*.

88. Mr. Clarkson's essays . . . Thomas Clarkson (1760–1846), a leading abolitionist who, with Wilberforce, was largely responsible for getting passed the 1807 act abolishing the British slave trade. The essays to which Stedman refers were *An Essay on the Slavery and Commerce of the Human Species, particularly the African* (1786), and *An Essay on the Impolicy of the African Slave Trade* (1788).

91. one hundred thousand people transported yearly . . . Modern estimates for the 1780s would place the annual number of Africans transported at closer to 60,000 (Curtin 1969, 266).

92. Botany Bay . . . Botany Bay (New South Wales) was visited in 1770 by Captain Cook, who proclaimed British sovereignty over the entire east coast of Australia. In 1788, the first British settlement, a penal colony, was established.

93. the twenty thousand Auka and Saramaka Free Negroes . . . For Auka (Ndjuka) and Saramaka population figures, see note to page 32.

93. Abbé Raynal . . . Abbé G.T.F. Raynal, author of the *Histoire philosophique et politique des établissements et du commerce des Européens dans les deux Indes,* 8 vols. (The Hague, 1774), translated as *A Philosophical and Political History of the Settlements and Trade of the Europeans in the East and West Indies.* For British readers this was "the best known . . . anti-slavery manifesto of the French Enlightenment. . . . Between 1776 and 1806 the work appeared in no less than fifteen English editions" (Anstey 1975, 123).

94. all captains are not Coolingwards . . . See note to page 34.

96. the Negroes are composed of different nations or castes . . . The interpretation of such lists, produced by many colonial writers, contains multiple pitfalls. A summary of information on the African provenience of peoples referred to by Stedman's labels would include: Abo—from what is now northwestern Cameroon; Bonia—uncertain; Blitay—possibly from Togo; Coromantyn—the Dutch shipped Fantis, Ashantis, and members of other interior Gold Coast peoples through their fort at Koromantin; Congo—various Bantu-speaking peoples were shipped under this label from the ports at the mouth of the Congo; Gango—Mandingo from what is now Southwestern Mali; Konare—uncertain; Kiemba—uncertain; Loango—from the great kingdom and port of that name near the mouth of the Congo, through which large numbers of slaves were shipped to Suriname; N'Zoko—uncertain, because both Bantu-speaking and interior Gold Coast peoples have similar names; Nago—the Ewe word for Nigerian Yorubas; Papa—from the area around Grand and Little Popo, in what is now Togo; Pombo—term derived from Mpumbu, the Kongo word for Malebo [Stanley] Pool on the Zaire [Congo] River, used in colonial accounts to refer to a large region in the interior of the Kongo; Wanway—an interior Gold Coast people. (N.B. In the 1796 edition [1:207] Bonia became Conia and Kiemba, Riemba, leaving unclear Stedman's own intentions.) For more detailed discussion of the African provenience of Suriname slaves, with references to a number of other colonial lists besides Stedman's, see R. Price 1976, 13–16. In general, Bantu-speaking slaves from Loango/Angola made up one-fourth to one-third of all imports to Suriname, with most of the remainder, during Stedman's day, coming from what is now Guinea, Sierra Leone, Liberia, Ivory Coast, and Ghana. The Slave Coast (modern Togo and Benin)—Suriname's major supplier until 1735—was providing few new slaves by the 1770s (ibid.).

96. the estate at present belonging to only two masters . . . By the 1770s, particularly after the Amsterdam stock market crisis of 1773, planter absenteeism reached an all-time high for Suriname, with large numbers of plantations being put into receivership.

98. hats, wigs, bottles, and glasses flew out his window . . . John Greenwood (1727–92), an American painter who spent nearly six years in Suriname, depicted a similar scene in his "Sea Captains Carousing in Surinam" (1758), now in the St. Louis Art Museum. (For a reproduction of this painting, see R. Price 1990, 102.)

101. "Kay, mi Massera. Da wan see cow" . . . "[Exclamation,] Master! That's a sea-cow."

102. one Boni, a relentless Mulatto . . . About 1765, the thirty-five-year-old Boni, together with his senior, Aluku, became joint leaders of the largest rebel group. Born in the forest, as Stedman notes, Boni had, according to different sources, either a white or an Indian father. Stedman is incorrect in asserting that Boni was not involved with Baron at Boucou; indeed, it was Boni, not Baron, who was chief of that fortress-village. It was sometime before Fourgeoud's conquest of "Rice Country," in 1773, that Baron and some fifty others left Boni's group. (For details, see Hoogbergen 1985, 78–85.)

103. the *nebees,* called by the French *lianes* . . . JGS uses this term quite generally for "lianas" or "vines," of which many species exist in Suriname (pp. 115, 117), as well as for the aerial roots of *Araceae* (p. 72).

103. The *manicole* tree . . . This is a palm, *Euterpe oleracea* Mart.

107. like Mohammed betwixt the two loadstones . . . After Islamist colleagues in Baltimore and elsewhere failed to elucidate this reference, we wrote a note saying that we were unable to identify its source. But while our critical edition was in production, we received a letter from Claude Lévi-Strauss, who had noticed the lacuna in our already published commentary on Stedman's "Poetical Epistle" (R. and S. Price 1985). The relevant portion (in translation) reads as follows:

> In seventeenth- and eighteenth-century Europe, a widespread legend held that Mohammed's coffin, made of iron, was under an arch of loadstones, which held it suspended in mid-air. . . . This was an ancient legend, applied only later to Mohammed. In his *Natural History* (book 34, end of chapter 14), Pliny attributed its origin to an Egyptian king. Authors from the beginning of the Christian era (Ausone, St. Augustine) also mentioned it. I believe that it was an Arabist from Oxford named Pockoke or Pokoke who, in the seventeenth century, made the connection with Mohammed's tomb. But there are a number of variations on the theme in the literature of antiquity. There is nothing surprising, then, that it was familiar to a man of the eighteenth century.

107. "*feegh Shinder-kneghte*" . . . This German curse permits multiple translations, from "cowardly knacker" to "rotten nigger driver."

110. Panting Corviser . . . This appears to be an allusion to a tale or fable concerning a shoemaker (corviser), but we have been unable to identify it.

110. one of whom, called Pass-up . . . See note to page 265.

113. grog . . . After "Old Grog," the nickname of Admiral Edward Vernon, who habitually wore a grogram cloak in foul weather and who, in 1740, issued the order that British sailors' rum ration would henceforth be diluted to prevent drunkenness. Grog referred to any unsweetened mixture of rum and water, but the usual mixture was a ratio of 1:2.

114. the rich man, when he begged water from Lazarus . . . Stedman alludes here to Luke 16.24, part of the parable of the rich man and Lazarus.

115. creeping on all fours like Nebuchadnezzar . . . Stedman alludes here to Daniel 4.33.

116. the Berbician Negro Gousary . . . See note to page 227.

117. the bloody flux . . . Probably acute bacillary dysentery.

117. *consaca* . . . The Sranan word for a mycosis, like athlete's foot, that is highly vulnerable to secondary bacterial infection in the tropics.

119. open sores and ulcers . . . Possibly filariasis with secondary infections, but an alternative possibility is "bush-yaws" (leishmaniasis).

121. *cosi va il mondo* . . . Italian, "that's the way the world goes."

123. to keep from starvation having been their only motive . . . The motives of "rebels" who turned themselves in to the whites were as difficult for the whites to judge as those of new maroons who turned up in the rebels' camps were for the rebels to judge. In the first case, given the destruction of crops and forced mobility of rebels in the Cottica area, starvation may indeed have been at play, but Maroon groups also frequently ran spies by having members of their groups "desert" back to the whites to gather intelligence and then escape again (R. Price 1983a). And slaves liberated by the Maroons sometimes chose, for family or other reasons, to escape back, on their own initiative, to slavery (see, for example, p. 66).

126. that [house] lately built by Governor Nepveu . . . Nepveu's house at Gravenstraat 6 was built in 1774 and named "Cura et Vigilantia." It is today owned by the government. For a description and illustrations, see Temminck Groll 1973, 125–30.

126. the Negro slaves excepted, who mostly lie on the ground . . . Saramakas still remember having to sleep on the ground on banana leaves, instead of in hammocks, as one of the most vivid humiliations of slavery (R. Price 1983a, 77).

130. a European man or maidservant being almost never to be met with . . . During the first decades of Suriname's colonial history, indentured Europeans labored alongside Indian and African slaves, but by the time of Stedman's visit to be white meant to be free and (aside from a scant one percent) to be black meant to be a slave.

130. The Negro slaves never receive paper money . . . The 1796 edition adds as prime reason that "as they cannot read they do not understand its value" (1:290).

131. a *caleebasee* (that is, a maid) . . . The fruit of the calabash tree (*Crescentia cujete*) plays a number of related symbolic roles regarding female sexuality and fertility in Suriname; the act of breaking or smashing a calabash may, for example, be part of rituals of divorce and childbirth.

132. they keep singing a loud chorus . . . This is a rare reference for Suriname of African women singing in chorus while performing labor; Stedman also describes (but in more detail) male slaves singing while rowing: see note to page 261.

132. Negro fishermen . . . Slave fishermen enjoyed special privileges throughout the Caribbean, in part because of their access to boats with which they could, if they desired, escape (R. Price 1966). Suriname fishing slaves are also mentioned in a 1749 document (R. Price 1983b, 81).

132. I have known slaves to buy slaves for their own use . . . The practice of slaves owning slaves, though not common, is mentioned several times by Stedman; at the time of her death, Joanna owned a female slave (p. 316). The practice of masters permitting their slaves to hire themselves out independently and remit a fixed sum to the master each week was common throughout the eighteenth-century Caribbean; men ranged from carpenters to blacksmiths, and women were often prostitutes (R. Price 1966).

134. Sir Hans Sloane . . . British physician (1660–1753) whose collection of books, manuscripts, plants, animals, and ethnographica formed the basis of the British Museum. Sloane visited Jamaica, Barbados, and other West Indian islands during the 1680s.

136. what Voltaire says in his *Candide* . . . For the relevant passage from *Candide*, see the opening paragraph of our Introduction.

137. *experientia docet* . . . "experience teaches."

143. geneva . . . Genever, Dutch gin.

144. ingenious wooden locks and keys . . . Wooden door locks, using mechanisms that were widespread in Africa, were reported as well by Hartsinck for eighteenth-century Suriname (1770, 17), and they continued to be manufactured by coastal Afro-Surinamers well into the twentieth century (van Panhuys 1925, 273). For examples made by Suriname Maroons, see S. and R. Price 1980, figs. 144–46.

149. "True to the Europeans" . . . Precious metal ornaments engraved with similar marks of planter gratitude are reported elsewhere for eighteenth-century Suriname: in 1730, Stedman's "celebrated Graman Quacy" (engraved by Blake in pl. 76) had been given "a golden breastplate on which was inscribed 'Quassie, faithful to the whites'" (van Sijpesteijn 1858, 92).

149. Jolicoeur . . . one of the fiercest Rebels in the forest . . . Joanna's uncle's account of Jolicoeur's revenge on Schultz, his former plantation manager, is complemented by that of two other eyewitnesses, one claiming that Jolicoeur killed the plantation's white overseer while Boni himself shot Schultz, the other that Jolicoeur brought Schultz to Boni who then shot him (Hoogbergen 1985, 84–85).

152. ill-treated a party of poor Indians . . . The relationship between Indians and Maroons in Suriname was variable and complex. During the early years of the colony, Indians and Africans toiled side by side as plantation slaves; in some cases, Indians facilitated Africans' escapes and harbored them in the forest; and settled groups of Maroons, likewise, assimilated some small groups of Indians. However, Indians were also prominent as guides on military expeditions against Maroons and were often particularly successful bounty hunters. In the neighboring Dutch colonies, during the Berbice rebellion of 1763, the frightened colonists were able to mobilize some two thousand Carib warriors to their cause. A rather extensive slave trade between the Caribs and the Dutch flourished between the mid-seventeenth and early nineteenth centuries (Whitehead 1987), and during the eighteenth century, Indians were regularly sold as slaves to planters in the Lesser Antilles, who used them both in domestic roles and to hunt and fish for their tables (R. Price 1976, 7–8; 1966, 1368).

152. at Paramaribo, an insurrection was discovered among the Negroes . . . A half-century later, the planters were not so fortunate. In 1832, three young slaves led an insurrection and succeeded in burning down much of the capital before being captured and brutally executed.

154. sent their heads barbecued to Paramaribo . . . In the 1796 edition, the barbecued heads became "right hands." The latter were, in fact, often used during the eighteenth century as tokens that a maroon had been killed, each right hand being worth a bounty (see p. 198). Stories about the taking of Chief Boni's head circulated widely in the colony over many years; modern versions and analyses may be found in de Groot 1980, Hoogbergen 1985, and Pakosie 1972.

155. the Auka Negroes (who were our allies by treaty) . . . The Auka, more commonly called Ndjuka, signed a treaty with the government in 1760. Something of their complex attitudes toward Boni's people during the 1770s can be gleaned from the documents in de Beet 1984 and Hoogbergen 1984, and from de Groot 1975 and Hoogbergen 1985.

156. the late Duke of Brunswick-Wolfenbuttel . . . Stedman had a special relationship with this commander. In 1784 he drew, engraved, and had published a portrait of him and, in 1785, sent him a flowery letter (in French) announcing the publication of the portrait and expressing his personal admiration. (The text is transcribed in Thompson 1962, 252–53, where a reproduction of the image faces p. 265.)

157. a medicine he called *tisane* . . . In French (Fourgeoud's native language), *tisane* refers to an infusion or decoction, usually of herbs.

159. *Loango-dancing* . . . Although rapid religious syncretisms among slaves of diverse African provenience were an earmark of colonial Suriname's first one hundred years (R. Price 1976), rituals and other performances associated with Loango, Papa, Nago, and other nations were still an important feature of late eighteenth-century plantation life. About 70 percent of plantation slaves were still African-born, with some 35 percent having arrived during the previous ten years (ibid.), so the occasional assertion of African ethnicity hardly seems surprising. In contrast, by Stedman's time similarly named performances among the Saramaka Maroons (e.g., "Luangu" or "Papa" rites and dances) clearly included people and ideas of quite varied African ancestry; there were hardly any African-born Saramakas still alive, and marriage was not in any sense endogamous by place of origin. Stedman's allusions to spirit possession are not intended to be limited to "Loangos"; it was and remains a central feature of Afro-Suriname religions in general. For a discussion of Luango dancing and rites among the modern descendants of Suriname slaves in the Para region, see Wooding 1981, 166–72.

160. European dancing as the height of insipidity . . . The 1796 edition adds here a lengthy footnote describing (in the words of one Emanuel Martinus) Spanish fandangos, which are so lascivious that the whole quotation—except for one word in Greek—is printed in Latin (1:365).

165. Caribbees . . . Piannacotaws . . . Stedman's "Caribbees" are the Caribs (Kalina or Galibi), most of whose descendants today live along the lower Marowijne in coastal Suriname, though during Stedman's time the great bulk of Caribs in the Guianas lived outside Suriname's borders, to the west. His "Accawaus" are the Akawaio, whose descendants live in the interior of Guyana. His "Worrows" are the Warau, whose descendants live in the delta of the Orinoco. His "Arrowouks" are the Arawaks, whose descendants live in coastal Suriname. His "Tawiras" might be the group sometimes called "Attoria" (Menezes 1977, 20); they might be the Taira who lived in the interior of what is now French Guiana, next to the Emerillon near the Brazilian border; but our own reading of Hartsinck (1770, 3), whence Stedman apparently got the term, suggests that Stedman might simply have misunderstood that writer, who was not naming a "tribe" but rather an Indian term allegedly meaning coastal, as opposed to inland, Indians. Finally, Stedman's "Piannacotaws" are the Pianakotos, a Carib group that lived far inland, from the upper

Corantijn toward the east, along the Suriname-Brazil border (Benjamins and Snelleman 1914–17, 175).

165. the most plausible causes why the Americans are a copper color . . . Environmental explanations of skin color were, by the time Stedman wrote, part of received wisdom, in spite of the several contradictions they encapsulated. They were accompanied by a widespread belief, deriving from Erasmus Darwin and Lamarck, that the effects of environmental influences were, at least to some degree, inherited (Jordan 1968, 13–20, 240–52, passim; see also Todd 1946).

165. Moravian preachers . . . The Moravians, who arrived in Suriname in 1735, were the first missionaries who actively proselytized among slaves, Indians, and Maroons (R. Price 1990). In 1757 they established an Indian mission on the Saramacca River; eight years later they began to work with the Saramaka Maroons; but the first slave was baptized by them in Paramaribo only in 1776, owing to widespread planter disapproval (see note to p. 177). Today the Moravian church (Evangelische Broedergemeente) is the largest Protestant denomination in Suriname.

167. the plantations were all laid in ashes by the Rebels in 1757 . . . Stedman refers here to the great Tempaty rebellion of that year, in which hundreds of slaves on several plantations successfully rebelled, with many joining the Ndjuka Maroons.

177. he could not yet be christened . . . Stedman here alludes to the fact that the major churches of the master class, the Dutch Reformed and the Lutheran, were generally opposed to the conversion of slaves. The Moravian and Roman Catholic churches, in contrast, were by Stedman's time beginning actively to seek converts among both slaves and Maroons. The large-scale conversion of Suriname slaves took place only during the second quarter of the nineteenth century (Van Lier 1949, chap. 6; Lamur 1985).

179. he proposed to me to paint his figure at large . . . The engraving modeled on Stedman's drawing is reproduced in our Introduction, fig. 2.

183. *Hodie tibi cras mihi* . . . "Today is yours, tomorrow mine."

187. Mr. Smith's tour through the United States . . . **Mr. Glen's act of barbarity** . . . John Ferdinand Dalziel Smyth (1745–1814), author of *A Tour in the United States of America,* 2 vols. (London, 1784), described how while visiting Virginia he and Mr. Glen went for a swim in the river: "whilst we were there, his wife and her sister, who were both young and handsome, came down to the water-side, and in a frolic hid our cloaths." The women soon disclosed the location of the clothes, and Smyth dressed. Glen, however, pursued his wife stark naked, brought her into the room where Smyth and the sister were, locked the door, and

> threw her down on the bed, and notwithstanding her utmost endeavors to Prevent him and disengage herself, committed an act that a mere savage would have been ashamed to have attempted in public.
>
> This he would afterwards boast of in all companies, in the presence of his wife and every other lady, as an excellent joke, and prodigious piece of humour. (1784, 1:133)

193. the Court of Policy and Criminal Justice . . . Van Lier (1971, 469–70) corrects some of the details of Stedman's description of the composition of the courts as well as that of the militia.

197. Without the consent of parents . . . **no respectable slaves are *individually* sold in Surinam** . . . Suriname indeed differed from most Caribbean slave societies in that, from the founding of the colony, it was standard policy not to break up slave families (mothers and children, husbands and wives) through sales. In general, slaves were sold not as individuals or family units but only as a large group, when the estate itself changed hands, and even this required special approval from the governor. Following the financial crisis on the Amsterdam stock exchange in 1773, with its attendant credit problems for Suriname planters, both absentee ownership and violations of these longstanding policies became more frequent, and it is possible that "respectable" (i.e., "house") slaves remained the main beneficiaries during this period. For discussion, see R. Price 1976, 19–20.

198. the Rangers . . . chop off the right hand of every Rebel Negro they kill . . . See note to page 47.

201. hair . . . plaited close to his head, by way of distinction from the Rangers . . . Male hairbraiding continued to be a special prerogative of Suriname Maroons, in contrast to coastal Afro-Surinamers, well into the twentieth century (see, for illustrations, S. and R. Price 1980, figs. 42, 43).

201. The rest are his *camisa* . . . This word continues to be used by Indians and Afro-Surinamers today to refer to loincloths or breechcloths, not (as in Spanish or Portuguese [or, as Stedman says, in "Gypsy language"—p. 261]) to shirts.

204. the dry-gripes . . . Apparently caused by drinking rum that had been contaminated by lead during the manufacturing process. For details on this ailment, which was widespread in the eighteenth-century West Indies, see Handler et al. 1986.

204. putrid fevers . . . Stedman uses this term to describe jaundice caused by yellow fever.

204. *crassy-crassy* . . . The Sranan word for scabies.

206. to carry away the dead body, and prevent it from falling into the hands of the adversary . . . This practice, as well as what Stedman describes as "mangling and tearing" the bodies of their slain adversaries, relates to rituals of power and protection (see note to p. 61).

206. the Caribbee Indians, who are certainly cannibals . . . The factual basis of Carib cannibalism remains the subject of much scholarly controversy. For two recent assessments, see Myers 1984 and Whitehead 1984.

206. Mr. Smith's tour . . . in that passage where Major Lewis was killed. . . In his *Tour* (see note to p. 187), Smyth describes the battle between twelve hundred white men and "the Shawnese, joined by the Delawares, and some other warriors of different nations, to the number of near nine hundred" (1784, 2:163). The "Major Lewis" whose death Smyth reports (2:167) was "Major Charles Lewis, a sensible, worthy, and enterprising man, and a brave gallant officer" (2:170).

212. like Gil Blas when he was among the robbers . . . In Alain-René Lesage's *Histoire de Gil Blas de Santillane* (Paris, 1715–35), the protagonist is forced by his robber-captors to participate in a gun battle during which he looks the other way while firing in order not to be held accountable, in the next world, for murder (bk. 1, chap. 9).

214. both parties cursing and menacing each other at a terrible rate . . . Pitched verbal battles, replete with insults and threats, were frequent in encounters between Maroons and black government troops, whenever they were in close proximity, especially at night. For a striking example from 1755, see R. Price 1983b, 116.

215. the hardships suffered since by the British troops at Gibraltar . . . The Great Siege of Gibraltar by Spanish (and French) troops (1779–83) inflicted terrible suffering on the defending forces.

219. gourd, or calabash trees . . . Maroons, Indians, and slaves used both calabashes (the fruit of *Crescentia cujete*), which grow on trees, and gourds *(Lagenaria siceraria)*, which grow on vines. For details, see S. Price 1982.

219. which the Negroes generally adorn by carving . . . In his description of calabashes and their decoration, Stedman draws directly on the words of Fermin (which he probably read in the 1770 Dutch translation, unavailable to us): "Il y a des Negres qui gravent sur la convexité de ce fruit, des compartiments & des grotesques à leur maniere, dont ils remplissent ensuite les hachures de craie; ce qui fait un fort joli effet" (1769, 1:194).

227. Gousary, with his companion Akara . . . Stedman offers some background on the "two desperados" Akara and Gousary in 1790/1988, 114. In fact, they were leaders of the Berbice rebellion under Coffy, who surrendered after Coffy's downfall and offered their services to the Europeans. As scouts and rebel-catchers, they were credited with bringing in some six hundred rebels in Berbice and were granted a full pardon. Fourgeoud, who was sent out from the Netherlands as commander of the state troops in Berbice after the rebellion, met Akara and Gousary there and, in 1765, they were brought to the Netherlands as part of a regular regiment. Fourgeoud was responsible for bringing them to Suriname (Blair 1984, 74–75).

228. a small serpent called here the *oroccoco* snake . . . This is the fer-de-lance, *Bothrops atrox*.

229. Graman Quacy, a celebrated and cunning old Negro . . . See note to page 300.

231. the *vampier* or *specter of Guiana* . . . The first part of JGS's description refers to the tropical American false vampire bat, *Vampyrum spectrum,* the largest New World bat. The true bloodsucking bat of Suriname, the South American vampire bat, *Desmodus rotundus* E. Geoffroy, is quite small and, as JGS indicates, usually bites humans on the big toe.

234. as no *tomahawk* is ever to be seen in all this country . . . In the 1796 edition, Stedman substitutes in a footnote, "as we were at peace with all the *Indians,* and scalping was never practised by the negroes" (2:160). Stedman's unsupported attribution of scalping to Suriname Indians may be the only such mention in the literature on the colony (Benjamins and Snelleman 1914–17, 105). For an excellent analysis of scalping (and accusations of same) among Indian and European adversaries elsewhere in the Americas, see Axtell and Sturtevant 1980.

235. Boni's house . . . Stedman later built himself a house modeled on this one and, in 1776, made a detailed pen-and-ink drawing of it (see 1790/1988, xc).

235. the private baths . . . where his women washed themselves morning and evening . . . Maroon women's ablutions still occur in the privacy of small enclosures behind their houses. These warm herbal baths, applied particularly to the genital area, are intended both to counter female pollution and to enhance sexuality. See S. Price 1984, 203.

236. the fable of the man, the boy, and the ass . . . One of Poggio's fables, concerning the difficulties of an old man who, with a boy, took an ass to market and, by trying to please every person he encountered along the way, ended up displeasing them all and losing his ass in the bargain.

238. a letter from his mother in Europe . . . For the text of this letter, see 1790/1988, 286 (cf. 1796, 2:170).

239. were both inadvertently poisoned and died . . . Manioc contains hydrocyanic, or prussic, acid, in variable concentrations, which must be expelled or transformed by cooking before it can be safely eaten.

239. none of his people were trusted with arms except such as had first served him some years as slaves . . . Though Boni's sense of discipline and the alleged length of the period during which he kept newcomers in servile roles were extreme among Suriname Maroons (see also pp. 246 and 250), new maroons were perceived as a serious security threat by all established groups. For discussion and examples of the realities behind these fears, see R. Price 1983a, and for comparative materials on other Afro-American Maroons, see R. Price 1979b, 16–18.

239. *yorica*, signifying the Devil . . . Though the Carib word *yoloka* refers to spirits, in both Sranan and the Maroon languages *yorka* or *yooka* refers only to "ghosts," the spirits of the dead.

240. chopped off the limb of a Mulatto child with a saber in revenge to its father . . . Maroons, like Suriname slaves, were deeply ambivalent about mulattoes, who were at once innocent victims of their parents' behavior (whether a white father's rape of a slave mother, or a mother's currying favor by sexual means), visible symbols of such master-slave violence or collusion, and often-"privileged" members of the slave hierarchy. Joanna represented one common type of mulatto adjustment to the sharply divided society; Boni, who was also a mulatto, represented the other extreme, and the details of his birth are often used to explain his especially violent hatred of whites. A particularly nuanced picture of Maroon ambivalence toward mulattoes in the eighteenth century may be read in "Paanza's Story" (R. Price 1983a, 129–34).

240. the tympany, called here the *kook* . . . Apparently a fermentative dyspepsia (van Lier 1971, 472).

240. the lions in the Tower . . . Ever since Henry I had moved the royal menagerie, including "lions, leopards, lynxes, porcupines, and several other uncommon beasts," to the (now-demolished) Lions Tower of the Tower of London, it had been considered one of London's prime "curiosities" (Pennant 1813, 2:22–24).

242. *fumming watra* . . . Sranan *fon* = "to beat."

243. black Mrs. Sampson or Zubly . . . Earlier in his manuscript, Stedman alludes to the scandal and discussion surrounding the 1767 marriage of Elizabeth Sampson, a wealthy free Negro woman, to a European named Zubly (or Zobre)—the first marriage of this kind in the colony (1790/1988, 79). See van Lier 1949, chap. 3.

243. a Mulatto ball . . . In late eighteenth-century Suriname, free blacks and mulattoes composed a much smaller proportion of the nonwhite population (approximately one percent) than in most New World plantation societies, but their balls and dance societies were a subject of considerable interest to whites. For example, "The free Negroes and coloreds as well as many slaves have among themselves dance societies. . . . They call such a group a *Doe,* and thus have the '*gold doe,*' the 'silver,' the 'amber,' the 'fashion,' and the 'love' *doe"* (F. A. Kuhn, 1824 letter, cited in R. and S. Price 1979, 134–35); see also Nassy's better-known discussion (1788, 2:38).

246. the celebrated free Negro Quacy . . . See note to page 300.

247. on the Wanica-Path behind Paramaribo . . . This area, like the Devil's Marsh a few miles to the north, provided hospitable ground for small villages of maroons. The Wanica-Path, leading to the Saramacca River, was also a frequent escape route for slaves fleeing the city.

248. an embassy to the Auka and Saramaka Free Negroes . . . These "embassies" are discussed in R. Price 1990. See also 1790/1988, 558.

250. a Rebel . . . was sabered to pieces . . . The 1796 edition specifies further that this execution of a maroon was ordered by Boni himself (2:223).

252. "many Christians are a parcel of damned monkeys" . . . Such "repartee," using monkeys as metaphors, continues today. For a fine exchange between an urban Afro-Surinamer and a modern Maroon, see R. Price 1983a, 12.

254. card money . . . Because of a shortage of silver coin, cardboard money resembling playing cards was introduced for local use in Suriname in 1761. See, for illustrations, Schiltkamp and de Smidt 1973, pls. 10–16.

255. a shameful peace . . . The idea that the 1760 and 1762 treaties with the Ndjuka and Saramaka, respectively, were "shameful" was commonplace among eighteenth-century colonial whites. One planter wrote in 1778 of the whites having "submitted to conditions so humiliating for us and so glorious for them" (cited in R. Price 1983b, 38). Stedman writes below of the whites' "shameful capitulation" (p. 256).

256. they [the Maroons] are unfairly dealt with . . . It seems significant that Stedman (and presumably his friend and informant on such subjects, Governor Nepveu) admitted in private that the government had reneged on its part of the treaties. During the 1770s, Saramakas consistently argued to Suriname officials that this was the case, but the officials just as consistently denied it in public.

257. two *white Negroes* . . . White "black" men or women—albinos—"aroused [eighteenth-century] interest which ranged all the way from scientific speculation to side-show curiosity" (Jordan 1968, 250). Jordan provides an excellent summary of the relevant mid-century scientific debates in France and England (ibid., 250–52). In Suriname, albinos continue to be relatively common and, among Maroons, are associated with water spirits (R. Price 1983b, 228).

258. Mr. Broughton, the late famous boxer . . . John Broughton (1705–89) was often called the father of British pugilism. Upon his retirement, he established various boxing arenas in London.

259. a Negress called Louisa Truxo . . . The *London Chronicle* for Tuesday, 3 October 1780, indeed describes the evidence, largely oral, that "demonstrates" Louisa Truxo's age to be "175 years."

259. names of above a dozen Negro tribes . . . See page 96 and our accompanying note. For a detailed discussion of body cicatrization among Suriname slaves and Maroons, see S. and R. Price 1980, 88–92.

259. By Linnaeus the whole human race . . . is classed among the monkeys . . . Carolus Linnaeus (1707–78) was the Swedish botanist and taxonomist whose *Systema Naturae* (1735) and *Species Plantarum* (1753) established the basis for the binomial system of nomenclature and the modern classification of plants and animals. See page 72 and Introduction, note 3.

260. *Accorees* or *Twofingers* . . . The "Twofingers" were a group of eight to ten tropical forest Indians with varying degrees of genetic deformity, who had come to live with the Saramaka about 1760. Suriname whites were absolutely fascinated by the Twofingers, who joined the lengthy lineage that included, among other exotic creatures of the European imagination in the Guianas, the Ewaipanoma (a race of headless people) and the Amazons. Details regarding the Twofingers, including contemporary illustrations, may be found in R. Price 1983a and 1983b. Stedman's "Accorees" refers to Akurio Indians, a small group of whom were also discovered, like the Twofingers, to be living with the Saramaka in 1763, when the first white person visited them in peacetime (ibid.).

260. Lord Munboddo's *Antient Metaphysics* . . . *Antient Metaphysics; or, the Science* *of universals* (1779–99), was written by James Burnet, Lord Monboddo (1714–99). Monboddo was a pioneer anthropologist and early evolutionist and would, naturally, have been intrigued by the Twofingers.

260. ludus naturae . . . "play of nature."

260. a few words for that called Coromantyn . . . The 1796 edition adds here that "they [Coromantyns] break off their words very short, in a kind of guttural manner, which I cannot easily describe" (2:257). For a Komanti word list from twentieth-century Maroons in Suriname, see Hurault 1983, 38–41.

261. that [language] spoken by the black people in Surinam . . . The history of Sranan, the creole language of Suriname slaves and still that country's lingua franca, is more complex than Stedman implies. For bibliographical and historical references, see Voorhoeve and Donicie 1963, R. Price 1976, and Smith 1987.

261. a printed grammar . . . Stedman is probably referring to C. L. Schumann's *Neger-Englisches Wörter-Buch* of 1781 (see Voorhoeve and Donicie 1963, 23).

261. sweety muffo [etc.] . . . Stedman's translations from Sranan to English tend to be at once over-literal (relying too heavily on cognates) and subjectively embellished.

261. the chorus is renewed a second time, and so ad perpetuum . . . The 1796 edition adds here, "This kind of singing is much practiced by the barge rowers or boat negroes on the water, especially during the night in a clear moonshine; it is to them peculiarly animating, and may, together with the sound of their oars, be heard at a considerable distance" (2:258). This type of call-and-response singing is, of course, characteristic of much Afro-American, and African, music.

261. one bus adiosio . . . The 1796 edition gives an interlinear translation of the song. The English reads, "One buss good-by o 'tis so good-by girl I must go I love for to fight like a man o Amimba I go to the woods o 'tis so good-by girl, I must go" (2:259).

262. Phillis Wheatley . . . Clarkson quotes three of Phillis Wheatley's poems and discusses her brief life (ca. 1753–84), as well as that of Ignatius Sancho, as an example of "African genius" (1788, 120–22).

262. Ignatius Sancho . . . Famous black actor who specialized in the roles of Othello and Oroonoko, friend of Hogarth and Sterne, painted by Gainesborough. Stedman may have been among the original subscribers to his book, *Letters of Ignatius Sancho, An African* (London, 1782, xlix).

262. Thomas Fuller, a Negro slave . . . Thomas Fuller, born in Africa ca. 1710 and the slave of Mrs. Elizabeth Cox near Alexandria, was interviewed in or about 1788 by two Pennsylvanians, who posed three questions: (1) how many seconds are there in a year and half? [47,304,000]; (2) how many seconds has a man lived who is seventy years, seventeen days, and twelve hours old? [2,210,500,800]; and (3) if a farmer has six sows, and each sow has six female pigs the first year, and they all increase in the same proportion to the end of eight years, how many sows will the farmer then have? [$7^8 \times 6 = 34,588,806$]. Fuller answered all three correctly. The most accessible source for Dr. Rush's letter is *American Museum* 5:62–63. Fuller's life and feats of mental calculation are discussed in Smith 1983, 178–80.

262. the supplement to the Town and Country Magazine for 1788 . . . We have been unable to locate Benjamin Rush's letter in this periodical. The only related essay in the Supplement (p. 623) is entitled "The Slave" and concerns courage and gratitude rather than intellectual prowess. See the previous note.

262. not that if they die abroad they will rise in their own country . . . The idea that death would bring diaspora Africans back to their "own country" was both widespread and sporadic. We believe that it is not a question of whether Merian, Clarkson, or Stedman was correct, but rather who the African or Afro-American informant happened to be. Many Africans in Suriname clearly did believe that, upon their death, they would fly back to the land of their birth; others believed they would, as Stedman suggests, pass into the land of the ancestors but never again cross the great ocean. The libations described by Stedman are intended as a way of sharing drink with the ancestors.

262. Miss Merian . . . Maria Sybilla Merian (1647–1717), naturalist and painter, lived in Suriname 1699–1701. Her famous book, *Metamorphosis Insectorum Surinamensium,* with vivid colored illustrations, was first published in 1705 at Amsterdam.

263. the wild cotton tree which they adore with high reverence . . . This is the silk-cotton tree, *Ceiba pentandra.*

263. winty play . . . Spirit possession was (and remains) a core feature of Afro-Suriname religious behavior. Today "Winti" has become the general name for coastal Afro-Suriname religion and has been described in detail by several authors (see, for example, Wooding 1981). For vivid descriptions by missionaries of eighteenth-century spirit possession dances among Maroons, see R. Price 1990.

264. to charm the ammodytes or papa serpents . . . Today, the *papa-gadu* cult remains a central part of the religion of both coastal Afro-Surinamers and Maroons. Boa constrictors, known as *papa, daguwe,* or *vodu* snakes, are the vehicles for gods; when such a snake is accidentally disturbed or killed, these gods may possess humans as avenging spirits. These snakes (like anacondas, which house related spirits) are sacred and protected.

264. every family is distinctly prohibited, from father to son, to eat . . . Among Afro-Surinamers, paternity is symbolically marked by the transmission from father to child at conception of a taboo, usually alimentary, the violation of which leads to a variety of sicknesses. In twentieth-century Suriname (M. and F. Herskovits 1936, 36–37), coastal people still call these *treef* or *trefu* (see also Stedman 1796, 2:264), deriving from the Hebrew *tereefa* (= prohibited food) of the large Suriname Jewish community, while Saramaka Maroons instead use the term *tata-tjína* ["father-taboo"], deriving from Bantu sources. In both cases, the belief seems related to prior African models such as the Ashanti *ntoro* complex (see Rattray 1923, 45–54; R. Price 1975, 52).

265. thy canting Moravians . . . See note to page 165.

265. The above names are generally given to imported Negro slaves . . . In fact, the naming system for eighteenth-century Suriname slaves was far more multifaceted, with a host of African names (often, during the late eighteenth century, Akan day names such as those Stedman cites) appearing in colonial documents alongside "classical" names such as Nero, Neptune, and Medusa and "fanciful" names such as Chocolate, September, or Pasop (Dutch for "Watch-out!"). The name of a plantation or owner was often added as a second name in the documents, for example, Kofi Charprendre or Kwaku van [= of] Sara de la Para. Whether such names were given by masters or slaves, and the differing but overlapping ways each group used them (as well as other kinds of personal names that were not recorded by whites), is a complex issue. For discussion, see R. and S. Price 1972 and R. Price 1983b.

266. other horrors too dreadful to relate . . . The 1796 edition adds here, as a footnote:

> It is a well-known fact, that a negro, having been ill-treated by the family in which he lived as a servant, one day took the following desperate revenge:—

The master and mistress being from home, he, having locked all the doors, at their return presented himself with their three fine children on the platform at the top of the house. When asked why he did not give admittance, he only answered by throwing an infant baby to the ground: they threatened—he tossed down the brother: they intreated, but to no purpose, the third sharing the same fate, who all lay dead at their parents' feet—then calling out to them that he was now fully revenged, leaped down himself, and dashed out his own brains amongst the amazed spectators.—Another stabbed the inoffensive husband to be revenged on the guilty wife; declaring, that to kill herself was only temporary, but to lose all that was dear to her must be eternal bitterness, while to himself it was the sweetest satisfaction. (2:266)

266. *wissy men* . . . These are sorcerers, often accused of being poisoners as well. The term is usually considered to have derived from English "witch." Among eighteenth-century Maroons, convicted sorcerers were burned at the stake; for several contemporary accounts and an illustration, see R. Price 1990.

266. *Gango* Negroes . . . Mandingos. On the realities and myths of cannibalism among Africans, see Evans-Pritchard 1965 and Arens 1979, 83–96.

267. particularly the *Coromantyn* and those of *Nago* . . . See note to page 96.

267. I don't remember ever . . . to have seen one offer a kiss in public to a woman . . . Stedman's observation fits with modern Maroon sensibilities on the subject. There is, however, one apparently contradictory piece of visual evidence: in Valkenburg's 1707 painting of a "play" on a Suriname River plantation, there is a couple clearly kissing in the foreground (R. Price 1983a, 109). We suspect that, in spite of the otherwise "realistic" style of this painting, the artist posed this particular couple in a conventional European posture.

267. the case of Lesperanza . . . See page 259. The lengthy postpartum sex taboo, usually associated with prolonged breast feeding, was a significant feature of child spacing in many parts of plantation America (see Higman 1984, 353–54), and it is still practiced (in truncated form) among Suriname Maroons.

267. eating common earth . . . Earth eating by slaves was a common but perplexing problem for masters throughout the Caribbean. Geophagy not only had a strong cultural focus, with West African antecedents, but it was related, unbeknownst to contemporary medical science, to intestinal helminthiasis (hookworm) as well as to malnutrition (particularly to calcium and iron deficiencies). Iron masks to prevent geophagy were common sights among Caribbean slave crews, yet the practice remained widespread, particularly for children and pregnant women. An excellent recent discussion may be found in Higman 1984, 294–98.

268. Philemon and Onesimus . . . St. Paul's Epistle to Philemon exhorts him to take back and forgive the runaway slave Onesimus.

269. the captive-prince . . . The number of references to captive princes and princesses in eighteenth-century writings on Suriname (and other Caribbean slave societies) attests to the importance of this literary theme. Aphra Behn's *Oroonoko* (1688), about mid-seventeenth-century Suriname, was the enormously popular prototype of the genre.

270. *lota* . . . Probably the superficial mycosis *pityriasis versicolor* (van Lier 1971, 476).

270. *yaws* . . . This description fits "bush-yaws," cutaneous leishmaniasis (van Lier 1971, 476).

270. to put them under a salivation . . . The descriptive phrase for a common eighteenth-century European treatment used for various ailments (most notably syphilis), whose goal was to produce an excessive flow of saliva by the administration of mercury. If this form of yaws were treponematous, it would of course be closely related to syphilis.

270. *clabba yaws* or *tubboes* . . . Probably treponematous yaws (van Lier 1971, 476).

270. the *Guinea-* or *lint-worm* . . . Van Lier (1971, 477) identifies this as *Filaria medinensis* or *Draculus persarum.*

271. *basha* . . . Usually written *basia, busha,* or *bastiaan.* Black overseer or slave driver on Suriname plantations.

271. *Dictio testimonii* . . . "The recitation of testimony is not as a slave for man."

272. 50,000 healthy people is exactly extinct once every twenty years . . . Some of the details of Stedman's demographic model are faulty, but his general picture of the costs in human lives of the Suriname slave system—one of the most extreme cases in the Americas—is generally correct. For detailed discussion of the historical demography of Suriname as a plantation colony, see R. Price 1976, 6–16.

273. Ramsay and Clarkson . . . James Ramsay (1733–89), who had lived as a missionary for nineteen years in St. Kitts, became a leading abolitionist in England, viewing slavery both "as an affront to humanity and as inhibiting missionary activity" (Anstey 1975, 248). Stedman would have known two of his pamphlets, *An Essay on the Treatment and Conversion of the African Slaves in the British Sugar Colonies* (1784) and *An Enquiry into the Effects of the Abolition of the Slave Trade* (1784). For Clarkson, see note to page 88.

273. no Negro's work is more than a healthy exercise . . . Note that even Stedman's *idealized* depiction of the slaves' work day in their master's fields, which he says allows generous time afterwards for hunting, fishing, cultivating a garden, making crafts for sale, and so forth, does not end until sunset.

275. *braff* . . . *tom-tom* . . . *gangotay* . . . All named items on Stedman's list of recipes appear also on the more extensive lists gathered contemporaneously among Saramaka Maroons by Schumann (1778), though ingredients often vary. For discussion of eighteenth-century slave and Maroon foods, see R. Price 1991b. The foods mentioned by Stedman continue to be prepared in the twentieth century by both coastal Afro-Surinamers and Maroons (see, for example, M. and F. Herskovits 1936, 15).

276. the funeral rites are quite ended by a second feast . . . The funeral rites scenario so briefly sketched by Stedman covers the most extensive rituals practiced by Suriname slaves and Maroons, which involved—over the course of about a year—a rich cultural complex of economic exchanges, large social gatherings and feasting, complex communications with the ancestors and gods, and a tremendous variety of specialized song/drum/dance performances.

276. *soesa* . . . An African-derived martial arts game/exercise/dance played by pairs of men and still known today, with affinities to Bahian *capoeira.*

277. *Awaree* . . . This board game of nearly worldwide distribution, brought to Suriname from Africa, is known among coastal Surinamers as *awari* and among Saramaka Maroons—who play it only at funerals—as *adjíbóto.* For discussion, see Herskovits 1929 and 1932.

277. *Otaheytee* . . . The usual eighteenth-century designation for Tahiti.

278. Such are the musical instruments of our African brethren . . . During the 1970s, we were fortunate to discover in the Rijksmuseum voor Volkenkunde, Leiden, a manuscript list demonstrating that thirty-nine of the forty-two objects described and depicted by Stedman (1790/1988, 318, and pp. 277–78 and in pls. 40 and 69) had at one time been accessioned by the museum. We were able to locate several, including the *great Creole drum,* the *Loango too-too,* and, most important, the *Creole-bania,* which represents the oldest Afro-American banjo still in existence anywhere. (See, for photographs and discussion, R. and S. Price 1979 and S. and R. Price 1980.) The complex route by which Stedman's Suriname collection reached the Rijksmuseum voor Volkenkunde, possibly via the Leverian Museum (see note to p. 76), is discussed in R. and S. Price 1979, 140.

280. The Negroes dance always in couples . . . For a fine depiction of a Suriname plantation dance in the slave quarters, see Valkenburg's 1707 painting reproduced in R. Price 1983a, 109.

280. living till they die with their parents and nearest relations . . . See note to page 197.

282. the long-projected Cordon, or path of circumvolution . . . See Introduction, note 11.

285. Neptune . . . sentenced to be *broken alive upon the rack* . . . Several literary specialists have suggested to us that Stedman's description of Neptune's death seems derivative from Aphra Behn's fictionalized account of the death of Oroonoko, set in Suriname a hundred years earlier:

> He [Oroonoko-Caesar] had learned to take Tobacco; and when he was as-sur'd he should die, he desir'd they would give him a Pipe in his Mouth, ready lighted; which they did: And the Executioner came, and first cut off his Members, and threw them into the Fire; after that, with an ill-favour'd Knife, they cut off his Ears and his Nose, and burn'd them; he still smoak'd on, as if nothing had touch'd him; then they hack'd off one of his Arms, and still he bore up, and held his Pipe; but at the cutting off the other Arm, his Head sunk, and his Pipe dropt, and he gave up the Ghost, without a Groan, or a Reproach. . . . They cut Caesar [Oroonoko] into Quarters, and sent them to several of the chief Plantations. (Behn 1722 [1688], 199–200)

Scholars familiar with the realities of eighteenth-century Suriname, however, will realize that the event Stedman describes as an eyewitness needed no literary precursor. From other contemporary sources, we know that such theatrical public executions—and the victim's stoic or defiant reactions—were relatively frequent during this period, and we see no reason to doubt the directness or veracity of Stedman's description. (See, for comparative examples, R. Price 1991a.)

286. which days of martyr are absolutely a feast to many planters . . . The 1796 edition here strengthens the chauvinistic tone of Stedman's following lines by substituting:

> Though I never recal to my remembrance, without the most painful sensation, this horrid scene ["The Execution of Breaking on the Rack"], which must revolt the feelings of all who have one spark of humanity, I cannot forbear exhibiting to the public the dreadful spectacle in the annexed drawing. If the reader, however, should be offended with this shocking exhibition, and my dwelling so long on this unpleasant subject, let it be some relief to his reflection, to consider this punishment not inflicted as a wanton and unprovoked act of cruelty, but as the extreme severity of the Surinam laws, on a desperate wretch, suffering as an example to others for complicated crimes; while at the same time it cannot but give me, and I hope many others, some consolation to reflect that the above barbarous mode of punishment was hitherto never put in practice in the British colonies. (2:297–98)

Stedman's several-page-long description of Neptune's suffering and death was quoted in full in Andrew Knapp and William Baldwin's *The Newgate Calendar,* 5 vols. (London, 1824), where it formed the centerpiece of their discussion of torture (1:136–43). "No longer deemed compatible with freedom . . . [execution by torture] was therefore abrogated in the year 1772. Yet . . . the inhuman practice still prevails in some of the English settlements abroad" (1:136).

290. a Mrs. van Eys, alleging she had affronted her only by her looks . . . Stedman's Suriname diary for this day explicitly attributes the punishment to Mrs. van Eys's own sexual frustrations: "Frow van Eys is in low Spirits for the absence of her d^r de g——v [apparently, her lover, the wealthy planter G.A.D. De Graav], it was that bich that gave poor brands [slave] mistres a Spance-bok [torture] at the Fort because he would not fuk herself, damn her" (*7 September 1776*).

291. The punishment called a *spanso bocko* . . . Governor Nepveu's description of the *Spaanse bok* (Spanish whip) reads:

> [T]he hands are tied together, the knees drawn up between them, and a stick inserted through the opening between the knees and the hands and fixed firmly in the ground, around which they then lie like a hoop and are struck on the buttocks with a guava or tamarind rod; one side having been struck until the skin is completely broken they are turned over to have the other side similarly injured; some use hoopsticks for this, although this is an extremely dangerous practice as it generally results in the slave's death, even though the chastisement is less than with the abovementioned rods. (Nepveu, cited in R. Price 1983b, 7–8)

Stedman's drawing of this punishment, planned as a plate in 1790, may have been omitted by the publisher as too gruesome. No known copy exists, and the plate was apparently never engraved.

293. the Indians, who had voluntarily fought and defeated the enemy there . . . The Lee Shore settlements are those referred to in the note to page 37. Arawak Indians had fought against such a community, alongside whites and slaves, as early as 1711 (R. Price 1983a, 75).

293. the noted free Negro Gousary . . . See note to page 227.

295. Having so often mentioned rice . . . Almost all rice grown by the Maroons was upland or dry (unirrigated) rice, grown like wheat, and it was often their staple food. For stories relating to the origins of rice among the Maroons, see R. Price 1983a, 129–34.

296. my own habitation . . . A sketch of this house was drawn by Stedman directly into his journal (see 1790/1988, xc). The unusual entrance is not visible in the sketch.

299. the end of my seventh and *last* campaign . . . The 1796 edition includes here:

> [at Paramaribo] I was most heartily welcomed by my many friends with the warmest congratulations on my still existing, after having escaped so many dangers, and been so long deprived of every comfort—torn by thorns, stung by insects—starved, tormented, emaciated, and wounded—often without clothes, health, rest, money, refreshments, medicines, or friends;—and after having lost so many of my brave companions, who lay buried in the dust.— Thus ended my seventh and *last* campaign in the forest of Guiana. (2:344)

300. the celebrated Graman Quacy . . . Other colonial sources, when combined with Stedman's descriptions, permit the following capsule biography of this extraordinary man. Kwasi was born in West Africa ca. 1690 and enslaved and transported to Suriname as a child. By 1730, he had discovered the medicinal properties of the tree that Linnaeus named in his honor *Quassia amara* (called in Suriname

"Quassiehout" or "Kwasi-bita"); and during the next six decades, amidst his many other activities, Kwasi served as the colony's leading *dresiman* (curer) and *lukuman* (diviner), with vast influence not only among blacks and Indians but also among European colonists. Kwasi's fame among Europeans was not, however, based solely on his medical talents; for more than forty years he was the colony's principal intermediary in dealing with maroons, serving first as a scout, then as a negotiator, and finally as spiritual and tactical adviser of the Rangers. Always the opportunist, Kwasi—who as early as 1730 had received from a member of the Council a golden breastplate on which was inscribed "Quassie, faithful to the whites"—became the slave of Governor Mauricius in 1744. His varied antimaroon activities during the next decade won him a letter of manumission, but personal freedom did not significantly alter his customary activities: he continued to conduct expeditions against maroons and to hunt them for a bounty, and he continued his varied medical practice.

In due course, Kwasi became a planter in his own right and, in 1776, as Stedman reports, in recognition of his many services to the colony the governor sent him all the way to The Hague, to be received by Willem V, Prince of Orange, who feted him with gifts. After his triumphant return to Suriname, Kwasi remained active on behalf of the colonists into his nineties, while he lived in a fine house in Paramaribo, given him for his use free of charge by the government. And it was during those final years that he became accustomed to receiving letters from abroad addressed to "The Most Honorable and Most Learned Gentleman, Master Phillipus of Quassie, Professor of Herbology in Suriname."

But the view of Kwasi given in the documents forms only half the available picture. Saramaka Maroons today preserve rich and powerful memories of this same man (whom they call Kwasímukámba), who came to live with them as a spy in the mid–1750s, escaped back to the whites, led a giant military expedition against them and, ultimately, had his right ear cut off by the Saramaka chief (see pl. 76). For details of this story, with both documentary and oral historical evidence, see R. Price 1979a and 1983a, 153–59.

303. Soli Deo Gloria . . . "Glory belongs to God alone, good fortune [to the] Baetici [inhabitants of an area of Spain corresponding to Andalusia and part of Granada]."

303. Fines coronant opus . . . "The end crowns the work."

303. Dr. Fermyn . . . Philippe Fermin, physician from Maastricht, served as a doctor in Suriname 1754–64. Stedman apparently met him during the 1780s (see 1790/ 1988, 114–15). His main works, written in French but translated into Dutch, German, and English, are Fermin 1769 and 1778. Stedman's admiration for Fermin's reportage (1790/1988, 591) was not shared by Governor Nepveu, who described his work as "so Superficial, inaccurate, and filled with contradictions that it is not even worth looking at" ("Annotatiën," unpublished document, Sociëteit van Suriname 566, Algemeen Rijksarchief).

306. the bruised [coffee beans] which are consumed in the Colony . . . This is an interesting example of a pattern that persists today throughout the Caribbean, the oldest continuously colonized region in the modern world system. Van Lier states that coffee was first planted in Suriname between 1711 and 1713 and first exported in 1721 (1971, 478). In the decades following 1750, coffee outweighed sugar as the colony's most valuable export (R. Price 1976, 17).

307. at an average about 75,000 Negro slaves . . . Stedman overestimates the slave population by about 50 percent and similarly exaggerates the number of plantations (van Lier 1971, 479). See also note to page 272.

312. to christen the boy . . . The 1796 edition adds to this page as a footnote:

I should not here omit to mention that in the colony of Surinam all emancipated slaves are under the following restrictions, *viz.*,

They are (if males) bound to help in defending the settlement against all home and foreign enemies.

No emancipated slave, male or female, can ever go to law at all against their former master or mistress.

And finally, if any emancipated slave, male or female, dies in the colony, and leaves behind any possessions whatever, in that case one quarter of the property also goes to his former owners, either male or female. (2:372–73)

313. more dejected than Sterne's Maria . . . The narrator of Laurence Sterne's *A Sentimental Journey* (1768), who had first been told Maria's sad tale by his "friend Mr. Shandy," seeks out "that disorder'd maid . . . [that] poor luckless maiden . . . [who is] crying . . . wandering somewhere about the road . . . the tears trickl[ing] down her cheeks" (Sterne 1941, 115–19).

315. out of a number of near twelve hundred able-bodied men . . . For discussion of the contradictory figures regarding the size of Fourgeoud's troops, see Introduction, page xxiv and note 12.

316. In a female Negro slave and three-score sheep had consisted the livestock of poor Joanna . . . See note to page 132.

REFERENCES CITED

Anonymous
1818   "William Thomson, LL.D." *Annual Biography and Obituary*, 2: 74–117.

Anstey, Roger
1975   *The Atlantic Slave Trade and British Abolition, 1760–1810*. London: Macmillan.

Arens, W.
1979   *The Man-eating Myth: Anthropology and Anthropophagy*. Oxford: Oxford University Press.

Axtell, James, and William C. Sturtevant
1980   "The Unkindest Cut, or Who Invented Scalping?" *William and Mary Quarterly* (3d ser.) 37: 451–72.

de Beet, Chris
1984   *De Eerste Boni-Oorlog, 1765–1778*. BSB 9. Utrecht: Centrum voor Caraibische Studies, Rijksuniversiteit Utrecht.

Behn, Aphra
1722   "The History of Oroonoko; or, the Royal Slave" [1688]. In *All the Histories and Novels Written by the Late Ingenious Mrs. Behn, Intire in Two Volumes*, 75–200. London: A. Bettesworth.

Benjamins, H. D., and Joh. F. Snelleman, eds.
1914–17   *Encyclopaedie van Nederlandsch West-Indië*. The Hague: Martinus Nijhoff.

Bentley, G. E., Jr.
1977   *Blake Books*. Oxford: Clarendon Press.
1980   "The Great Illustrated-Book Publishers of the 1790s and William

Blake." *Editing Illustrated Books,* edited by William Blissett, 57–96. New York: Garland.

Blair, Barbara L.
1984   "Wolfert Simon van Hoogenheim in the Berbice Slave Revolt of 1763–1764." *Bijdragen tot de Taal-, Land- en Volkenkunde* 140: 56–76.

Blake, William
1793   *America: A Prophecy.* London.

Bogan, James
1976   "Vampire Bats and Blake's Spectre." *Blake Newsletter* 37, 10 (1): 32–33.

Bubberman, F. C., A. H. Loor et al., and C. Koeman, ed.
1973   *Links with the Past: The History of Cartography in Suriname, 1500–1971.* Amsterdam: Theatrum Orbis Terrarum.

Buckley, Roger Norman
1979   *Slaves in Red Coats: The British West India Regiments, 1795–1815.* New Haven: Yale University Press.

Clarkson, Thomas
1788   *An Essay on the Slavery and Commerce of the Human Species, Particularly the African.* 2d ed. London: J. Phillipps [orig. 1786].

Corncob, Jonathan [pseud.]
1787   *Adventures of Jonathan Corncob, Loyal American Refugee.* London [1976 ed. Boston: Godine].

Counter, S. Allen, and David L. Evans
1981   *I Sought My Brother: An Afro-American Reunion.* Cambridge: MIT Press.

Craton, Michael
1975   "Jamaican Slavery." In *Race and Slavery in the Western Hemisphere: Quantitative Studies,* edited by Stanley L. Engerman and Eugene D. Genovese, 249–84. Princeton: Princeton University Press.

Curtin, Philip D.
1969   *The Atlantic Slave Trade: A Census.* Madison: University of Wisconsin Press.

Darnton, Robert
1984   "Working-Class Casanova." *New York Review of Books* 31 (11): 32–37.

Davis, David Brion
1966   *The Problem of Slavery in Western Culture.* Ithaca: Cornell University Press.
1975   *The Problem of Slavery in the Age of Revolution, 1770–1823.* Ithaca: Cornell University Press.

Davis, Michael
1977   *William Blake: A New Kind of Man.* London: Paul Elek.

Debien, Gabriel, and Johanna Felhoen Kraal
1955   "Esclaves et plantations de Surinam vus par Malouet, 1777." *De West-Indische Gids* 36: 53–60.

Edwards, Bryan
1794   *The History, Civil and Commercial, of the British Colonies in the West Indies.* 2d ed. London: J. Stockdale.

Erdman, David
1952   "Blake's Vision of Slavery." *Journal of the Warburg and Courtauld Institutes* 15: 242–52.
1969   *Blake: Prophet against Empire.* Princeton: Princeton University Press.

Essed, Hugo A. M.
1984   *De binnenlandse oorlog in Suriname, 1613–1793.* Paramaribo: Anton de Kom Universiteit van Suriname.

Essick, Robert N.
1973   "Blake and the Traditions of Reproductive Engraving." In *The Visionary Hand: Essays for the Study of William Blake's Art and Aesthetics,* edited by Robert N. Essick, 492–525. Los Angeles: Hennessey and Ingalls.
1980   *William Blake, Printmaker.* Princeton: Princeton University Press.

Evans-Pritchard, E. E.
1965   "Zande Cannibalism." In *The Position of Women in Primitive Societies and Other Essays in Social Anthropology,* 133–64. London: Faber & Faber.

Fermin, Philippe
1769   *Description générale, historique, géographique et physique de la colonie de Surinam.* Amsterdam: E. van Harrevelt.
1778   *Tableau historique et politique de l'état ancien et actuel de la colonie de Surinam, et des causes de sa décadence.* Maestricht: J. E. Dufour & Ph. Roux.

Fielding, Henry
1742   *The History of the Adventures of Joseph Andrews.* London: A. Millar.

Fontaine, Jos
1972   *Zeelandia: de geschiedenis van een fort.* Zutphen: De Walburg Pers.

Goveia, Elsa V.
1956   *A Study on the Historiography of the British West Indies to the End of the Nineteenth Century.* Mexico: Instituto Panamericano de Geografía e Historia.

de Groot, Silvia W.
1970   "Rebellie der Zwarte Jagers: de nasleep van de Bonni-Oorlogen, 1788–1809." *De Gids* 133: 291–304.
1975   "The Boni Maroon War, 1765–1793: Suriname and French Guiana." *Boletín de Estudios Latinoamericanos y del Caribe* 18: 30–48.
1980   "Boni's dood en Boni's hoofd: een proeve van orale geschiedenis." *De Gids* 143: 3–15.

Handler, Jerome S., Arthur C. Aufderheide, Robert S. Corruccini, Elizabeth M. Brandon, and Lorentz E. Wittmers, Jr.
1986   "Lead Contact and Poisoning in Barbados Slaves: Historical, Chemical, and Biological Evidence." *Social Science History* 10: 399–425.

Hartsinck, Jan Jacob
1770 *Beschrijving van Guiana of de Wilde Kust in Zuid-Amerika.* Amsterdam: Gerrit Tielenburg.

Herlein, J. D.
1718 *Beschryvinge van de Volk-plantinge Zuriname.* Leeuwarden: Meindert Injema.

Herskovits, Melville J.
1929 "Adjiboto, an African Game of the Bush-Negroes of Dutch Guiana." *Man* 29: 122–27.
1932 "Wari in the New World." *Journal of the Royal Anthropological Institute* 62: 23–38.

Herskovits, Melville J., and Frances S. Herskovits
1936 *Suriname Folk-lore.* New York: Columbia University Press.

Higman, B. W.
1984 *Slave Populations of the British Caribbean, 1807–1834.* Baltimore: Johns Hopkins University Press.

Hoogbergen, Wim S. M.
1984 *De Boni's in Frans-Guyana en de Tweede Boni-Oorlog, 1776–1793.* BSB 10. Utrecht: Centrum voor Caraibische Studies, Rijksuniversiteit Utrecht.
1985 *De Boni-Oorlogen, 1757–1860: marronage en guerrilla in Oost-Suriname.* BSB 11. Utrecht: Centrum voor Caraibische Studies, Rijksuniversiteit Utrecht.

Hurault, Jean
1983 "Eléments de vocabulaire de la langue Boni (Aluku Tongo)." *Amsterdam Creole Studies* 6: 1–41.

Jordan, Winthrop D.
1968 *White over Black: American Attitudes toward the Negro, 1550–1812.* Baltimore: Penguin Books.

Keynes, Geoffrey
1921 *A Bibliography of William Blake.* New York: Grolier Club of New York.
1969 "Introduction." In Charles Ryskamp, *William Blake, Engraver: A Descriptive Catalogue of an Exhibition,* 1–18. Princeton: Princeton University Press.
1971 *Blake Studies: Essays on His Life and Works.* 2d ed. London: Oxford University Press.

Lamur, Humphrey E.
1985 *De kersteningen van de slaven van de Surinaamse Plantage Vossenburg, 1847–1878.* Amsterdam: Antropologisch-Sociologisch Centrum.

Lewis, Gordon K.
1983 *Main Currents in Caribbean Thought: The Historical Evolution of Caribbean Society in Its Ideological Aspects, 1492–1900.* Baltimore: Johns Hopkins University Press.

van Lier, R.A.J.
1949   *Samenleving in een grensgebied: een sociaal-historische studie van Suriname.*
        The Hague: Martinus Nijhoff.
1971   *Narrative of a Five Years' Expedition against the Revolted Negroes in Suri-*
        nam . . . by Captain J. G. Stedman. Edited and introduced by R.A.J.
        van Lier. Barre, Mass.: Imprint Society.

Long, Edward
1774   *History of Jamaica.* London.

Menezes, Mary Noel
1977   *British Policy towards the Amerindians in British Guiana, 1803–1873.* Ox-
        ford: Oxford University Press.

Myers, Robert A.
1984   "Island Carib Cannibalism." *New West Indian Guide* 58: 147–84.

Nassy, David de Ishak Cohen et al.
1788   *Essai historique sur la colonie de Surinam . . . Le tout redigé sur des pieces*
        authentiques y jointes, & mis en ordre par les régens & représentans de ladite
        Nation Juive Portugaise. Paramaribo.

Oudschans-Dentz, Fred.
1928/29 "Het einde van de legende Dahlberg-Baron." *De West-Indische Gids* 10:
         165–67.

Pakosie, André R. M.
1972   *De dood van Boni.* Paramaribo.

van Panhuys, L. C.
1925   "Contribution à l'étude de la distribution de la serrure à chevilles."
        Journal de la Société des Américanistes (Paris) 17: 271–74.

Paulson, Ronald
1983   *Representations of Revolution (1789–1820).* New Haven: Yale University
        Press.

Pennant, Thomas
1813   *The History and Antiquities of London.* London: J. Coxhead.

Price, Richard
1966   "Caribbean Fishing and Fishermen: A Historical Sketch." *American*
        Anthropologist 68: 1363–83.
1975   *Saramaka Social Structure: Analysis of a Maroon Society in Surinam.* Rio
        Piedras: Institute of Caribbean Studies of the University of Puerto
        Rico.
1976   *The Guiana Maroons: A Historical and Bibliographical Introduction.* Balti-
        more: Johns Hopkins University Press.
1979a   "Kwasímukámba's Gambit." *Bijdragen tot de Taal-, Land- en Volken-*
        kunde 135: 151–69.
1979b   *Maroon Societies: Rebel Slave Communities in the Americas.* Edited and
        introduced by Richard Price. 2d ed., rev. Baltimore: Johns Hopkins
        University Press.

1983a   *First-Time: The Historical Vision of an Afro-American People.* Baltimore: Johns Hopkins University Press.
1983b   *To Slay the Hydra: Dutch Colonial Perspectives on the Saramaka Wars.* Ann Arbor: Karoma.
1990   *Alabi's World.* Baltimore: Johns Hopkins University Press.
1991a   "Dialogical Encounters in a Space of Death," in *In Word and Deed: Death and Creation in the New World,* edited by Gary H. Gossen and J. Klor de Alva. Austin: University of Texas Press.
1991b   "Subsistence on the Plantation Periphery: Crops, Cooking, and Labour among Eighteenth-Century Suriname Maroons." *Slavery & Abolition* 12: 107–27.

Price, Richard, and Sally Price
1972   "Saramaka Onomastics: An Afro-American Naming System." *Ethnology* 11: 341–67.
1979   "John Gabriel Stedman's Collection of Eighteenth-Century Artifacts from Suriname." *Nieuwe West-Indische Gids* 53: 121–40.
1985   "John Gabriel Stedman's 'Journal of a Voyage to the West Indies in Ye Year 1772. In a Poetical Epistle to a Friend.'" *New West Indian Guide* 59: 185–96.

Price, Sally
1982   "When Is a Calabash Not a Calabash?" *New West Indian Guide* 56: 69–82.
1984   *Co-wives and Calabashes.* Ann Arbor: University of Michigan Press.

Price, Sally, and Richard Price
1980   *Afro-American Arts of the Suriname Rain Forest.* Berkeley and Los Angeles: University of California Press.

Rattray, R. S.
1923   *Ashanti.* London: Oxford University Press.

Ray, Gordon N.
1976   *The Illustrator and the Book in England from 1790 to 1914.* New York: Pierpont Morgan Library; London: Oxford University Press.

Rigaud, Stephen F. D.
1984   "Facts and Recollections of the XVIIIth Century in a Memoir of John Francis Rigaud Esq., R.A." (Abridged and edited with an introduction and notes by William L. Pressly.) *Walpole Society* 15: 1–164.

Schiltkamp, J. A., and J. Th. de Smidt
1973   *Plakaten, ordonnantiën en andere wetten, uitgevaardigd in Suriname, 1667–1816.* Amsterdam: S. Emmering.

Schlegel, Klaus
1980   *Besselich am Mittelrhein.* Cologne: Verlag J. P. Bachem.

Schumann, C. L.
1778   "Saramaccanisch Deutsches Wörter-Buch." In *Die Sprache der Saramakkaneger in Surinam,* edited by Hugo Schuchardt, 46–116. Verhandelingen der Koninklijke Akademie van Wetenschappen te Amsterdam 14(6), 1914. Amsterdam: Johannes Müller.

van Sijpesteijn, C. A.
1858   *Mr. Jan Jacob Mauricius, Gouverneur-Generaal van Suriname van 1742–1751.* 's Gravenhage: De Gebroeders van Cleef.

Smith, Bernard
1960   *European Vision and the South Pacific, 1768–1850: A Study in the History of Art and Ideas.* Oxford: Clarendon Press.

Smith, Norval S. H.
1987   "The Genesis of the Creole Languages of Surinam." Ph.D. diss., University of Amsterdam.

Smith, Steven B.
1983   *The Great Mental Calculators.* New York: Columbia University Press.

Snell, F. J.
1904   *Early Associations of Archbishop Temple: A Record of Blundell's School and its Neighborhood.* New York: Thomas Whittaker.

Stafford, Barbara Maria
1984   *Voyage into Substance: Art, Science, Nature, and the Illustrated Travel Account, 1760–1840.* Cambridge: MIT Press.

Stephen, Leslie, and Sidney Lee
1967–68 *The Dictionary of National Biography.* Oxford: Oxford University Press.

Sterne, Laurence
1941   *A Sentimental Journey through France and Italy.* New York: Heritage Press [orig. 1768].

Sypher, Wylie
1942   *Guinea's Captive Kings: British Anti-Slavery Literature of the Eighteenth Century.* Chapel Hill: University of North Carolina Press.

Temminck Groll, C. L.
1973   *De architektuur van Suriname, 1667–1930.* Zutphen: De Walburg Pers.

Thompson, Stanbury
1962   *The Journal of John Gabriel Stedman, 1744–1797.* Edited by S. Thompson. London: Mitre Press.
1966   *John Gabriel Stedman: A Study of His Life and Times.* Stapleford, Notts.: Thompson.

Todd, Ruthven
1946   *Tracks in the Snow: Studies in English Science and Art.* London: Grey Walls Press.

Tyson, Gerald P.
1979   *Joseph Johnson: A Liberal Publisher.* Iowa City: University of Iowa Press.

Voorhoeve, Jan, and Antoon Donicie
1963   *Bibliographie du Négro-Anglais du Surinam.* The Hague: Martinus Nijhoff.

Whitehead, N. L.
1984   "Carib Cannibalism: The Historical Evidence." *Journal de la Société des Américanistes* (Paris) 70 (1): 69–88.
1986   "John Gabriel Stedman's Collection of Amerindian Artifacts." *New West Indian Guide* 60: 203–8.
1987   *The Carib Conquest, 1500–1800*. Leiden: Koninklijk Instituut voor Taal-, Land- en Volkenkunde.

Wolbers, J.
1861   *Geschiedenis van Suriname*. Amsterdam: H. de Hoogh.

Wooding, Charles J.
1981   *Evolving Culture: A Cross-Cultural Study of Suriname, West Africa, and the Caribbean*. Washington, D.C.: University Press of America.

DATE DUE